# The Meaning of Europe

# The Meaning of Europe

## Variety and Contention within and among Nations

**Edited by**
**Mikael af Malmborg and Bo Stråth**

*Oxford • New York*

First published in 2002 by
**Berg**
Editorial offices:
150 Cowley Road, Oxford, OX4 1JJ, UK
838 Broadway, Third Floor, New York, NY 10003–4812, USA

Berg is an imprint of Oxford International Publishers Ltd.


**Library of Congress Cataloging-in-Publication Data**
A catalog record for this book is available from the Library of Congress.


**British Library Cataloguing-in-Publication Data**
A catalogue record for this book is available from the British Library.


ISBN  1 85973 576 2 (Cloth)
       1 85973 581 9 (Paper)


Typeset by JS Typesetting, Wellingborough, Northants.
Printed in the United Kingdom by Biddles Ltd, Guildford and King's Lynn.

# Contents

# Contents

# Preface

This book aims to shed light on the role of the idea of Europe in nation-building processes. In this respect Europe is a contested concept within and among nations. It is a concept with multiple meanings. Therefore, the meanings of Europe in the title appear in the plural. The book is the product of research within the project 'The Cultural Construction of Community in Modernization Processes in Comparison', organized by the European University Institute and the Humboldt Universität zu Berlin, and financed between 1996 and 2000 by the Bank of Sweden Tercentenary Foundation. The framework of the research is also the European Forum 1999–2001 on 'Between Europe and the Nation State: The Reshaping of Interests, Identities, and Political Representation' (www.iue. it/RSC/EF), and the Robert Schuman Centre programme on 'European Identity', both organized under the auspices of the European University Institute in Florence. The Swedish Council for Research in Humanities and Social Sciences has also contributed generously to the realization of the book. Drafts of the chapters were discussed at a meeting with all the authors in May 2000 at Bivigliano, Florence. Paul Rouse has done exemplary editing work, binding the contributions together in a cohesive manner. We are most grateful.

Mikael af Malmborg and Bo Stråth
Stockholm and Florence, March 2001

## Post scriptum

Mikael af Malmborg died on 20 May 2001. During the editing Mikael fell sick. The disease gradually stripped him of his energies. Mobilizing his last efforts he managed with an admirable courage to finish his chapter on Italy. Together we wrote the Introduction under difficult conditions and completed the editing. Although not unexpected, the news of Mikael's death was a terrible shock and extremely painful. I realized that he fought a difficult battle, but he was so hopeful, so courageous and so full of spirit when we communicated. Mikael's youth and talent makes his death all the more cruel. In this very mournful situation, Mikael leaves behind a bright and impressive memory. It was a privilege to work so closely with him on this book. The last revision of the manuscript, which followed the observations and suggestions by an unknown reviewer at Berg Publishers, was my work. I want to thank the reviewer for his very valuable and constructive comments. Finally, I would like to thank James Kaye and Elizabeth Fordham for their great help in editing the revised Introduction.

Bo Stråth
Florence, September 2001

# Notes on Contributors

**Robert Frank** is a Professor at University of Paris I Panthéon-Sorbonne and his main field of research is the History of International Relations and of European Integration. His most recent publications are *La hantise du déclin: Le rang de la France en Europe, 1920–1960: finances, défense et identité nationale* (1994), *National Identity and Regional Cooperation: Experiences of European Integration and South Asian Perceptions* (with H.S. Chopra and J. Schröder, eds,1999) and 'Des guerres civiles européennes à l'unité de l'Europe', in Hélène Ahrweiler et Maurice Aymard (dir), *Les Européens* (2000).

**Miroslav Hroch** is professor in history at the Faculty of Humanities, Charles University, Prague. An expert in the comparative history of Modern Europe; in nation formation, national identity and the counter reformation; and in trade and politics, he has published such works as *In the National Interest: Demands and Goals of European National Movements: A Comparative Perspective* (2000) and *Social Preconditions of National Revival in Europe* (1985).

**Pablo Jáuregui** completed in 2001 his PhD thesis, entitled 'National Identity and the European Union: A Comparative Study of Britain and Spain', at the Department of Political and Social Sciences of the European University Institute in Florence. His main field of research is the study of national identities in the context of European integration. His previous publications include 'National Pride and the Meaning of "Europe": A Comparative Study of Britain and Spain', in D. Smith and S. Wright (eds), *Whose Europe? The Turn Towards Democracy* (1999).

**Klas-Göran Karlsson** is Professor of History at Lund University, Sweden. He has written extensively about Russian, Soviet and post-Soviet topics such as ethnic conflicts, migration and the history of historiography. Among his publications are *Historieundervisning i klassisk ram. En didaktisk studie av historieämnets målfrågor i den ryska och sovjetiska skolan 1900–1940* (History Teaching in a Classical Framework: The

Objectives of History Teaching in the Russian and Soviet School, 1900–1940) (1987), *Armenien – från berget Ararat till det bergiga Karabach* (Armenia – From Mount Ararat to the mountaineous Karabakh) (1990), *Europa och världen under 1900-talet* (Twentieth-Century Europe and the World) (1995), *Historia som vapen. Historiebruk och Sovjetunionens sönderfall 1985–1995* (History as a Weapon. The Uses of History and the Demise of the Soviet Union, 1985–1995) (1999).

**Piers Ludlow** is Lecturer in International History at the London School of Economics (LSE). His main field of research is post-1945 European integration history, including work on Britain's problematical role in this process. In particular he is now focusing on the development of the European Communities in the mid- to late-1960s. Among his publications in this field are *Dealing With Britain: The Six and the First UK Application to the EEC* (1997), 'Challenging French Leadership in Europe: Germany, Italy and the Netherlands and the outbreak of the Empty Chair Crisis, 1965–6', *Contemporary European History* (1999) and several other chapters and journal articles on relatively similar themes.

**Mikael af Malmborg**[†], PhD in history, was a researcher at the University of Lund, the European University Institute, Florence, and at St Anthony's College, Oxford. He was senior researcher at the Swedish Research Council and affiliated with the Swedish Institute of International Affairs and Södertörn University College, Stockholm. His main fields of research were the history of European integration, state- and nation-building processes in Europe and Swedish political history. His publications include *The Resilient Nation-State: Sweden and West European Integration, 1945–59* (1994), *Neutrality and State-Building in Sweden* (2001), and numerous articles on Swedish history and the history of European integration.

**Henrik Meinander** is director of the Finnish Institute in Stockholm. He has an MA and a PhD from the University of Helsinki, and an M.Litt. from University of Glasgow, and has been since 1997 *dozent* at both Helsinki University and Åbo Akademi. Appointed Professor of History at the University of Helskinki. Meinander has published three monographs, edited two anthologies and numerous articles in history of ideas, social history and sports history.

**Iver B. Neumann** is Research Professor at the Norwegian Institute of International Affairs. He is an international relationist specialising in

## Notes on Contributors

Russia, Europe and theory. His latest books in English are *Russia and the Idea of Europe* (1996), as co-editor with Ole Wæver, *The Future of International relations* (1997) and *Uses of the Other: 'The East' in European Identity Formation* (1999).

**Willfried Spohn** is Adjunct Professor of Sociology at the Free University of Berlin and is currently Jean Monnet-Marshall Professor at Columbia University and New York University in New York. His current historical-sociological research is on Europeanization, collective identities and the eastern enlargement of the European Union in a Western and Eastern European comparison. His recent books are *Can Europe Work? Germany and the Reconstruction of Postcommunist Societies* (with S. Hanson 1995) and *Modernisierung, Religion und kollektive Identitaet. Deutschland zwischen West- und Osteuropa* (forthcoming).

**Bo Stråth** is Professor of Contemporary History in the Department of History and Civilization/Robert Schuman Centre at the European University Institute, Florence. He has published widely on political and economic processes. His research focuses comparatively on modernization and democratization processes in Northern and Western Europe.

**Barbara Törnquist-Plewa** is Associate Professor and Senior Lecturer in East and Central European Studies at the Slavonic Department, University of Lund, Sweden, and deputy director at the Centre for European Studies, also at the University of Lund. Her main field of research is collective memory, myths and symbols and their role in the political mobilization of societies in Eastern Central Europe, as well as research on the processes of nation-building in East and Central Europe, especially Poland, Belarus, Ukraine, Slovakia, Czech Republic and Hungary. As well as editing several books and publishing numerous articles in the area, she has also written *The Wheel of Polish Fortune, Myths in Polish Collective Consciousness during the First Years of Solidarity* (1992) and *Språk och identitet i Vitryssland. En studie i den vitryska nationalismens historia* (Language and Identity in Belarus. A Study in the History of Nationalism in Belarus)(1997).

**Constantine Tsoukalas** is professor of sociology at Athens University. He is the author of many articles and books including *The Greek Tragedy* (1969), *A Voyage in Discourse and History* (1996), *From Peoplehood to Nationhood: Adventures in Meanings* (1999) and *War, Memory and Art* (2000).

**Gilbert Weiss,** an expert on Political Theory, European Studies, Discourse Analysis of communication/discourse processes in international organisations, is Vice-Director of the 'Research Center: Discourse, Politics, Identity at the Austrian Academy of Sciences'. His most recent publications are: G. Weiss, *Theorie, Relevanz und Wahrheit: Eine Rekonstruktion des Briefwechsels zwischen Eric Voegelin und Alfred Schutz, 1938–1959* (2000) and (with P. Muntigl and R. Wodak), *European Union Discourses on Un/employmen:. An interdisciplinary approach to employment policy-making and organizational change* (2000). He has also written numerous articles in this field.

# Abbreviations

| | |
|---|---|
| CAP | Common Agricultural Policy |
| CIA | Central Intelligence Agency |
| CIS | Commonwealth of Independent States |
| CSCE | Conference on Security and Cooperation in Europe |
| EC | European Commission |
| ECSC | European Coal and Steel Community |
| EDC | European Defence Community |
| EEC | European Economic Community |
| EFTA | European Free Trade Association |
| EMS | European Monetary System |
| EMU | Economic and Monetary Union |
| EP | European Parliament |
| ETA | Euzkadi ta Azkatasuna (Basque Homeland and Liberty) |
| EU | European Union |
| FPÖ | Freiheitliche Partei Österreichs (The Freedom Party) |
| GATT | General Agreement on Tariffs and Trade |
| GDR | German Democratic Republic |
| GNP | Gross National Product |
| KGB | Komitet Gosudarstvennoi Bezopasnosti (Committee of State Security) |
| KPN | Konfederacja Polski Niepodleglej (Confederation for Sovereign Poland) |
| LO | Landsorganisationen (Swedish Trade Union Conference) |
| NATO | North Atlantic Treaty Organization |
| OEEC | Organization for European Economic Cooperation |
| OSCE | Organization for Security and Cooperation in Europe |
| ÖVP | Österreichische Volkspartei (The Peoples Party) |
| PCI | Partito Comunista Italiano (Italian Communist Party) |
| PSOE | Partido Socialista Obrero Español (Spanish Socialist Workers' Party) |
| SPD | Sozial demokratische Partei Deutschlands (German Social & Democratic Party) |
| TPD | Towarzystwo Demokratyczne Polskie (Polish Democratic Society) |

## Abbreviations

| | |
|---|---|
| UCD | Unión de Centro Democrático (Union of the Democratic Centre) |
| UK | United Kingdom |
| UN | United Nations |
| US | United States |
| USSR | Union of Soviet Socialist Republics |

# Introduction: The National Meanings of Europe

*Mikael af Malmborg* and *Bo Stråth*

Europe is a contested concept that must appear in the plural. When the ancient Greeks talked about Ευρώπη, it is unclear from where and from what language they derived the term. One theory is that the origin is Semitic and that it meant the land in the sunset. From their position in the archipelago of the East Mediterranean, the land in the sunset was to the North as well as to the South of the sea basin. Since then the frontiers of Europe have shifted and there have been many and various discourses on the concept. Europe was not, and is not, an easily definable term with essential proportions, but has since Antiquity been discursively shaped through constant negotiation of whom to in- and exclude. The Greek view, where Europe bridged the Mediterranean, was transformed during the war against Islam into a divide *by* this sea, and Europe emerged gradually as synonymous with Christianity. Or, rather, Christianity substituted Europe as a concept for unification, with a stronger ideological and political connotation than the original Greek Ευρώπη. During the centuries that immediately followed 1095, the crusades strengthened the Mediterranean divide. The divide did not curtail commercial and other contacts, but accentuated the cultural distinction between a Christian Self and a Muslim Other.

These differences were further pronounced during the Ottoman expansion into the Balkans in the fifteenth and sixteenth centuries. The Turk peril was propagated through new printed media as the main threat to Christianity in the Habsburg Empire and, albeit less intensely, in France and in what today is called Italy. The Christian identification against the Ottoman rulers was more problematic in the Balkan peninsula inside the Ottoman Empire, as the Ottomans employed a tolerant regime with respect to religious politics. Moreover, the military and economic power struggle in the Levant, between the Habsburgs, France, Spain and the Italian city states, penetrated the Christian–Islamic/Ottoman divide and went in many respects beyond the religious dichotomy. Economic interaction and military conflicts between Ottoman rulers and European powers in the Mediterranean and in the Balkans were in principle not different from the corresponding interactions within Europe, although they were entangled with the discourse on the Turk peril. In constantly shifting constellations some European powers made pacts with the Ottoman rulers while others made war. In this way the constructed religious/ethnic borderline between Europe and the Turkish Other became a fluid European line of contention (Höfert 2001).

The substitution of Europe with Christianity as a concept for unification and concord was also undermined from within through religious warfare. When the connection between Christianity and unity was destroyed by the Thirty Years War, Europe took on new meaning in the emerging Enlightenment discourse and became a lodestar for unity. The term Europe came to fulfil the need for a more neutral designation of the common whole. As Denis Hay puts it: 'In the course of the seventeenth and the early eighteenth centuries Christendom slowly entered the limbo of archaic words and Europe emerged for its peoples as the unchallenged symbol of the largest human loyalty' (Hay 1968: 116). Norman Davies notes that in the early phase of the Enlightenment, 'it became an embarrassment for the divided community of nations to be reminded of their common Christian identity; and "Europe" filled the need for a designation with more neutral connotations' (Davies 1997: 7). To fill the void that was left by the Roman Catholic Church, the Enlightenment philosophers developed the idea of Europe as a community or a confederation that would guarantee concord and community. In 1751, Voltaire described Europe as '. . . a kind of great republic divided into several states, some monarchical, the others mixed . . . but all corresponding with one another. They all have the same religious foundation, even if divided into several confessions. They all have the same principle of public law and politics, unknown in other parts of the world' (Voltaire 1957 [1752]; cf Stråth 2000). For the Enlightenment philosophers Europe supplanted Christianity as the universal civilization project, and as a counter-image they formulated the notion of a despotic East.

The Enlightenment project as it was drafted by the *philosophes* in the eighteenth century first found broad support during the crisis of liberalism and the twentieth century of European civil wars, a tumultuous period in European history which brought a soul-searching of the same magnitude as had the wars of religion three hundred years earlier. The idea of a united Europe gained currency after the excessive invocations of 'the nation' in the First World War, both in a Central European form such as the Paneuropa movement founded by Richard Coudenhove-Kalergi in

1923 and, with a French and Western focus, in the proposal by Aristide Briand in 1929 for a United States of Europe within the framework of the League of Nations. These ideas reflected the self-contempt and humiliation felt by intellectuals and statesmen in the wake of the Great War, and were connected to the hopes of a lasting pacifist peace. As confidence in Europe gradually returned, however, the image of a declining West was soon transformed into a renaissance of the idea of European *grandezza*. The image of pacifist peace was transformed into the idea of an armed peace and there was tension between various inter-war projections of Europe. In the 1930s, the Nazis appropriated the idea of a unified Europe, while, for the resistance movement during the Second World War, the European idea took the form of a dream projected onto an uncertain future, a myth of exile. (Passerini 1998; Lipgens 1985). After the Second World War, as after the First, the dream of a pacifist Europe resurfaced only to be absorbed by the rhetoric of armed peace under the exigencies of the cold war. This was the palpable framework in which the European idea took concrete political form in the 1950s.

Thus there are many images of Europe in terms of content and form developed historically over centuries of contentious attempts to appropriate the interpretative power contained in the concept. The analysis of these processes should be both semasiological and onomasiological, investigating both various meanings of the concept of Europe and other terms employed to describe the same phenomenon.

So many meanings of Europe have emerged precisely because there has never been such a thing as 'Europe', in an essentialist sense, but only as imaginations. Europe has only existed as an invention of states, before the French Revolution of groups of states, and after the Revolution and the Napoleonic Wars by nation states.

With a focus on the two most recent centuries of European history, all of Europe seems united by one main dynamic: that of nation-state formation. The idea of modernity and the processes of democratization have been, and are to a large extent still, intimately linked with the nation state. The *longue durée* of European history is one of pluralism and contradictions. However, when we move up to the contemporary era this manifold heritage is overshadowed by the rather uniform ideal of one nation, one state; and during the last half of the twentieth century, the construction of a new European community or union was conceived in the light of these experiences: the image of Europe as a supranational unit is nothing other than the idea of Europe as a substitution for the nation state, as a bigger nation state transgressing the existing nation states. The imperial tradition in which European empires contained several nations in one state image would also finally be supplanted by the nation state idea. One can even argue that the story of the formation of the modern state *is* in great part the story of the formation of Europe, and vice versa. (Held 1995).

*A crucial question, to which academic research has so far paid little attention, is in this light how various meanings of Europe have been mobilized in the process of nation-state construction. Therefore, the aim of this book is to shed light on the role of the idea of Europe in nation-building processes.* The book addresses this main question through chapters on Greece, Italy, Spain, Britain, Sweden, Finland, Russia, the Baltic States, Poland, Czechia, Germany and France. The issue of Europe is addressed from its various national environments. The book undertakes an exploration of the meanings of 'Europe' in the construction of modern national communities. The term 'Europe' has been – and is – full of political content in each national setting. The conceptualization of Europe varies and is contested within – as much as among nations.

The book sheds light on the long-term shifts in the meanings of Europe – long-term being taken here to be the period since the Enlightenment. The focus is not on the idea of European unity per se, but on the wider meanings of Europe as a concept in various national settings. How have perceptions of Europe participated in national discourses? To what extent have Europe and the nation reinforced or contradicted one another? These and similar questions have a temporal dimension meaning that the answer changes over time depending on various contexts. Europe means variety. They have also a contentious bearing in the sense that the discourses on Europe are those of debate and conflict, where Europe was and is used as a mobilizing political instrument. In this role the meanings of Europe varied between utopia and dystopia. Europe is, in the view of this book, something that cannot be unambiguously defined but should be seen as a discourse and an ideological/political programme, that has been mobilized and invoked, in particular in the *Spannungsfeld* between Enlightenment ideas and religion. In this semantic field Europe takes on the proportions of an unattainable ideal of unity and community. It has been unattainable and utopian in the sense that the perfect situation of social unity is beyond human and social conditions. And, at the same time, the *belief* that the perfect society *is* achievable constitutes one crucial element of the idea of modernity. 'European' has been a powerful symbol in the quest for improvement ever since it took over the role of unifier from Christianity after the religious wars in the sixteenth and seventeenth centuries. This belief and the continuous striving for a better world has produced social energy and dynamics, but also resulted in the contradictions of modernity and of Enlightenment, as we have learnt from Zygmunt Bauman (Kaye and Stråth 2000). These processes are more than a history of ideas. They are political, and they can deliver institutional bench-marks for the social organization when utopia is appropriated and transformed into politics. It is precisely this process of appropriation, the implementation of the idea of Europe, and the connections between the various ideas of Europe and the nation, that are addressed throughout this book. The various chapters demonstrate the complexity and the contradictions in the concept of Europe by historicizing and situating it. At the same time they throw new light on national narratives. Through this demonstration of complexity and contradictions, possibilities are discerned and warnings are expressed for risks in the concept of Europe. This is what the book is about, not history per se, but as an instrument to interpret the present. The book wants to add to a cultural-historical understanding of Europe, of Europhile and Europhobe opinions. The focus is not on the European integration process but on European patterns of variety and contention in the views on Europe.

This focus is inspired by recent trends in academic theoretical debate, where concepts such as 'Europe' and 'culture' are increasingly seen as non-essential discursively shaped categories in a permanent flux where boundaries are constantly contested and negotiated. Chris Shore is one of the these exponents. However, while Shore, in his *Building Europe* (Shore 2000), focuses on how the nation is incorporated in images of Europe produced in the centre of Europe in Brussels, our focus is on how 'Europe' has been incorporated into images of the nation. We share with Shore the interest in the connections between the nation states and Europe. These connections are of a disparate nature: they reinforce one another, demarcating one another, overlapping, etc., but they are not synonymous. We also have the same view as Shore when we reject the idea of Europe as an expression of cultural unity founded upon a shared ancient civilization. Such thoughts only 'reify an outdated idea of cultures as fixed, unitary and bounded wholes that is both sociologically naive and politically dangerous' (Shore 2000: 58). Europe is not a fixed essence but labile and in a flux. European – and national – identities are always fluid and contextual, contested and contingent, and discursively shaped under various forms of inclusion and exclusion.

Our approach shares Gerard Delanty's theoretical view on culture (Delanty 1995 and 1999): the idea of culture as a unitary framework based on consensus, on core values, which are supposed to be embodied in European cultural identity, is wrong. The notion that social integration requires cultural cohesion in order to secure public commitment is wrong. From such erroneous views emerge meta-narratives where Europe transcends national societies and refers to a genuinely European cultural heritage. The image of a European cultural heritage becomes a discourse transcending the divisions of European history. European culture becomes a unified set of norms, interpreted as a homogeneous discourse, and takes on essentialistic, pre-established proportions (Delanty 1999: 226–7). As with Delanty, the view in this book is that Europeanization is cultural contention and pluralisation as opposed to cohesion. Europeanization is less a matter of social integration through cultural cohesion than one through institutional adaptation and cultural pluralization. In the long run, the viable model for a European identification is one that challenges the exclusivist kind of cultural identity. The adjectives 'European' and 'national' are not alternatives but are articulated in the recognition of multi-identification. The image of a European polity thrives in a framework of contention and plurality rather than one of cohesion. The struggle kneads together as a national election campaign does. This book tries to contribute to a critical theory of Europe that demonstrates that cultural and political diversity and heterogeneity lie beneath the dominant ideology (Delanty 1995: 7). The chapters of the book provide numerous historical examples which underpin such a theoretical approach.

We share the approach of the authors of *The Anthropology of Europe*, who emphasize the role played by the social sciences, including anthropology and history, in the emergence of various meanings of Europe. They underline the connection between scientific research agendas and shifting political conjunctures. The intensified European integration after the Second World War has gone hand in hand with a growing academic and political search for the roots of Europeanness in history, religion, science and culture. The meanings of Europe are a discourse of power on how to define and classify Europe, on the frontiers and limits of Europe, and on similarities and differences. The idea of Europe became, in historiography and sociology, a political idea and mobilizing metaphor at the end of the twentieth century, particularly in the wake of '1989'. In many versions the emphasis is on Europe as a distinctive cultural entity united by shared values, culture and identity. References are made to Europe's heritage of classical Greco-Roman civilization, Christianity, and then to ideas of Enlightenment, Science, Reason, Progress and Democracy as the core elements of this European legacy. There are subtexts of racial and cultural chauvinism, particularly when confronted with Islam. Europe acquires distinction and salience when pitted against the Other. When the differences within Europe are emphasized, this often occurs under the invocation of unity in diversity. Religious differences (Roman Catholic, Protestant, Orthodox Christianity) and linguistic differences (Romance, Germanic and Slavonic languages) are seen as correlated (Roman Catholic–Romance, Protestant–Germanic, Orthodox–Slavonic) and as underlying the major ethnic cleavages and conflicts, historically and contemporarily, in Europe (Goddard et al. 1994). In this book we too want to critically problematize and historicize such constructions of the meanings of Europe.

Europe as an entity is not a stable, sovereign, autonomous object but exists only in historical relations and fields of power. On this point we agree with John Borneman and Nick Fowler (Borneman and Fowler 1997). However, while they see the relationship of the European to this entity in a flux as a form of identification that works simultaneously as a strategy of self-representation and a device of power from a European centre, we focus instead on the construction of Europe before the EU in various national entourages. Since the 1950s, and increasingly since the 1970s, a political centre for value production ('Europeanization') has no doubt existed. Our point, however, is that there were earlier widely varying images of Europe in the nation states. An interesting question to investigate is how these earlier meanings of Europe have influenced and been influenced by the Europeanization drive towards European unity. When Borneman and Fowler, from their American viewpoint, argue that Europeanization has little to which it can appeal outside of future-oriented narratives of individualism and the market, and that if people become Europeans their identities no longer turn around categories of religion, folk, or national defence but around categories of exchange, difference, and value – all categories implicitly with the prefix of market – our question is: is it really so? We argue that Europe is closely tied to its historical connections with nation states, connections which future-orientated ideas of Europe as a market disconnected from its past cannot easily do away with.

Our view on the connections between the nation and Europe is thus more complex than in approaches where they are seen as alternatives or where the meanings of Europe are basically derived from only one European production centre. Writing in the time-typical post-Soviet and Maastricht mood of 1992, Mary Fulbrook discerns a possible future scenario where national identities are transformed into a new European identity (Fulbrook 1992: 10). Although she emphasizes the openness of historical processes, the national identities in the European case nevertheless seem to have one direction: from the nation to Europe. Our focus is not on the identity concept and on the transformation from one identity to another but on various and contested *meanings* of Europe and how these meanings have been elements of national self-projections. What this means for future developments in Europe is quite another question, but we do think that a simple dichotomy nation–Europe is as problematic as an identity concept with either a national or a European content where history would take us – or not take us – from the one form to the other. Moreover, in light of our view we also have a problem with the counter-position to Fulbrook taken by Alan Milward. The thrust of his argument is that Europe is not something normative, but the product of economic-ally derived national self-interests (Milward 1992). Our argument is that Europe is a constant and contested value flow.

Wintle et al. (1996) is a collection of articles which sets out to uncover cultural diversity and identity in Europe, what Europe means in the minds of Europeans and in terms of 'objective reality'. What are we to make of Europe? Has it an identity? Has it a culture? (Wintle 1996: 4). In many respects their analysis comes close to Milward's, although their focus is more on the issues of culture and identity than on Europe as a product of economic self-interests or as an instrument developed by national governments to produce popular allegiance. The questions in their context take the essential existence of Europe for granted and equip it with prop-erties. Our approach is rather the opposite, to problematize the concept of Europe and deny any essential proportions in it. Wintle et al. build up a problematic dichtotomy between reality and identity. Identity is, in their view, about image rather than realities and imageology is the study of interactions of projections of national and other identities. Identity is a category of perception rather than of reality. What a European cultural identity has been, is now, and will become in the future is not an objective reality but a set of aspirations and images. In their view Europe is real in an essentialist sense but a European identity is imaginary with the implicit understanding that images are not real. Therefore, a European cultural identity is not easy to locate and define. From the thirteenth century onward the only schemes for integration in Europe which have gained any foothold in political reality are those which have promoted the interests of the nation states, one of the contributors argues (Morgan 1996). Another contributor, Spiering, also locates the 'apparent unity of Europe' since the Second World War in the national interests of the member states rather than on the level of higher ideals. A causative projection of the nation into Europe is drafted. Thereby national identities emerge as at least partly naturally given: they are both nature and nurture, both nationally constructed, and therefore they provide an essential obstacle to a re-enforced European identity, as the Maastricht Treaty phrased it. To achieve a genuine EU-level identity analogous to national identities would require widespread violence as the founding of most nation states did. The alternative in the form of a gentle, well-meaning, benevolent pan-Europeanism is little more than naked idealism (implicitly as opposed to material reality). The nations, although partly constructed and imagined, emerge in this view as deeper, more real, and more essential entities than Europe, materially and psychologically founded as they are, whereas Europe remains an idealistic unit. Since war was a key factor that welded together the nations, the European Union will remain a *Zollverein* (Spiering:1996).

In demarcation to Wintle et al. 'Europe' is in this book not understood in essentialistic terms but basically as a discourse and an ideological programme not necessarily in opposition to the nation state or as an alternative to it, not only in the form of an unattainable ideal of unity but also as a carrier of certain values in national public life. In national political debates 'Europe' often enters as a dimension of national identity rather than a project of transnational unification. The universal pretensions are 'downloaded' and nationalized. Rather than 'How shall Europe be united?', the questions dwelt upon in public debate have been: 'How European is our nation?' 'How shall we relate ourselves to 'Europe'?' 'To what extent should we be European, something else or simply ourselves?' At the same time it is clear that there are feed-back effects in these processes. When European institutions and politics emerge, they transform the images of Europe. Since the 1950s, there has been, in this sense, a Europeanization of the nations, a Europeanization which during the cold war meant images of a West European community of destiny, but which since 1989 has become much more open. Open means that the images of Europe have lost orientation and confidence.

Europe and the nation states are in the view of this book seen as entanglements rather than exclusive alternatives. Meanings of the nations are inscribed in the meanings of Europe and meanings of Europe are inscribed in meanings of the nations. The intertwining means that various and contentious patterns of mutual support and reinforcement in some cases, and opposition and demarcation in others, emerge. This figure becomes even more complex when the regional level is considered. Since the 1970s, when the regional discourse gained power, the region has often been seen as an alternative to and a challenge for the nation states. This view has been reinforced by what has been interpreted as an operation bypassing the nation states when regional lobbyists in Brussels have tried to influence the allocation of EU resources through structural funds to poor regions. However, this cash-flow from Brussels to the regions also reinforces, rather than undermines, the nation states where the regions are situated. Therefore, the entanglement of EU and the member states also involves the regions. However, having said this, we want to emphasize that *our* aim in this volume is to go beyond the (West) European post-1945 integration and study the entanglements in a longer historical view where the historical meanings of Europe are investigated also in East European nations.

Rogers Brubaker suggests a new way of structuring the analysis of nations and nationalism, which is equally applicable to Europe and Europeanism. Instead of asking the classical question 'What is a nation?', he asks the more inductive question of how nation works as a practical category (Brubaker 1996: 16). Rather than asking 'What is Europe?' we should ask: How is Europeanness as a political and cultural form institut ionalized within and among states? How does 'Europe' work as a practical category, as a classificatory scheme, as a cognitive frame? What makes the use of that category within states more, or less, resonant or effective? What makes the Europe-evoking efforts of political entrepreneurs likely to succeed? What hinders them?

To understand how images of an emerging European order interact within existing collective identities in the EU today, we need to understand how the concept of 'Europe' has related to the nation-building project in a longer time perspective as well as how it has been transformed in the post-war European integration process. We take issue with views where nationalist ideology is simply replaced by a new ideology of 'Europeanism'. Such views are nothing but the introversion of the old imperial Europeanisation of the world through colonial expansion based on convictions of 'white man's burden' and a *'mission civilisatrice'*, introversion in the sense that the quest for civilization is turned inwards.

The book tries to grasp *la longue durée* of the relationship between nation and 'Europe', but the time-span is not the same for all cases and cannot be limited to an absolute chronology, such as the post-war era, the twentieth century, or the history since the French Revolution. 'Europe' has been a dimension of national identity construction long before the emergence of the EU, but its significance has differed widely. In some cases it has been perceived as an integral part of national identity, in others it represents a challenge or even a threat to the nation. Sometimes 'Europe' is at the core of the nation-building project; sometimes it competes with alternative Atlantic, Mediterranean, Slavic or Nordic macro-regional identities.

The tension between Europeanness and a 'true self' might be most accentuated on the periphery of Europe. The Slavophile versus the

Westernizing trends that run as a recurrent theme through Russian history offer an extreme example, but are by no means without their counterparts in other countries. Furthermore, the preferred definition of Europe also tends to vary with national viewpoint. Whether 'Europe' is defined as big or small, on cultural, geographical or political criteria, depends much on national vantage-point.

Furthermore, the images of Europe are not given once and for all but are transformed in confrontation with contemporary events. History must be understood as mental experience and will always stand in a relationship with the contemporary. Historical events should not be divorced from one another or from the present. Or, in the words of Benedetto Croce, every true history is therefore contemporary history.

The concept of 'European identity' was spread in the 1970s in the wake of the collapse of the dollar and the subsequent oil-price shock, at a time of general crisis for national economic governance. At the Copenhagen summit in December 1973 the leaders of the EC took the decision to introduce and promote a European identity (Passerini 1998: 4–5). The identity idea was based on the principle of the unity of the Nine, on their responsibility toward the rest of the world, and on the dynamic nature of the European construction. The 'responsibility toward the rest of the world' was expressed in a hierarchical way. First, it meant responsibility towards the other nations of Europe with whom friendly relations and cooperation already existed. Secondly, it meant responsibility toward the countries of the Mediterranean, Africa and the Middle East. Thirdly, it referred to relations with the USA, based on the restricted foundations of equality and the spirit of friendship. Next in the hierarchy was cooperation and constructive dialogue with Japan and Canada. Then came *détente* towards the Soviet Union and Eastern Europe. At the bottom of the list came China and Latin America and, finally, a reference was made to the importance of the struggle against underdevelopment in general. It need not be mentioned that Europe during the cold war was understood to be Western Europe where Eastern Europe belonged to the hostile Other. The astonishing fact that the Middle East was listed before the United States must be understood in the framework of the collapse of the dollar and the oil-price shock.

The launching of a European identity meant that such a phenomenon had not existed previously. Identity is a problematic and fuzzy concept. If taken literally, it means equality, sameness, the quality of being identical. It is a concept used to construct community and a feeling of cohesion, a concept to convey the impression that all individuals are equal in the imagined community (White 2000; Niethammer 2000). The utopian dream of a common identity was mobilized precisely in a moment when the cohesion of the European Community was conspicuous by its absence. 'Integration' was the concept of the 1950s and 1960s which was used in the cold war to conjure up images of European unity and for translating Europe into a political project. When integration failed as an instrument of mobilization, identity was promoted in its place.

When we explore how established national discourses are reconciled with an emerging European identification within the European Union, it is not the idea of European unity as such that we address, but rather the meanings of 'Europe' as a concept in various nations. How do perceptions of 'Europe' interact with the ideal discourse of the nation, to what extent do the two reinforce or contradict each other? The meanings of 'Europe' as they are registered in public statements by politicians, men of letters, publicists, university teachers, etc. are all expressions of political attitudes in a broad sense of the term. The aim of the book is neither, of course, to produce an exhaustive account of all the thinkers who could legitimately claim our attention, nor to grasp all the nuances and inconsistencies in the overall thought of the actors under examination. The ambition is to give an overview of the meanings of 'Europe' in texts of central importance to modern national self-understanding, to present a characteristic gamut of stances on Europe.

The Russian semiotician Yuri Lotman presents the conditions of the images of Europe in the form of a so-called semiospheric model:

> Imagine a museum hall where exhibits from different periods are on display, along with inscriptions in known and unknown languages, and instructions for decoding them; besides there are the explanations composed by the museum staff, plans for tours and rules for the behaviour of the visitors. Imagine also in this hall tour-leaders and the visitors and imagine all this as a single mechanism (which in a certain sense it is). This is an image of the semiosphere . . . all elements of the semiosphere are in dynamic, not static, correlations whose terms are constantly changing . . . What 'works' is not the most recent temporal section, but the whole packed history of cultural texts . . . In fact, everything contained in the actual memory of culture is directly or indirectly part of that culture's synchrony. (Lotman 1990: 126–7).[1]

---

1. In the same vein Yale Ferguson and Richard Mansbach object to the (neo-)realist view of the state as a generic and universalized organization. They characterize the world as a 'living museum' where earlier political forms and ideas are preserved behind the facade of a modern state system (Ferguson and Mansbach 1996: 282).

# Introduction

Established differences in national and macro-regional self-understanding influence attitudes towards European integration. Patterns of history are in no way deterministic, but Europhile versus Europhobe national discourses can predispose some nations to react mainly positively and others rather negatively towards the imposition of a European polity on the nation states. The 'Europeanization' of nation states is in part the outcome of deeply entrenched notions of the nation and of Europe, which does not, of course, exclude that the view on Europe – as well as on the nation – is also deeply contested within the various national settings. A parallel can be made to the argument of Robert Putnam on regional political reform in Italy that a successful democratization is the outcome of deeply entrenched civic traditions of social solidarity and involvement in community matters (Putnam 1993).

The emergence of a hegemonic great power or a new regional project poses a challenge to any nation state. At elite as well as popular levels a perceived genuineness, an established representation of the past, has to be reconciled with a new regional identity and culture. This process might run more or less smoothly, whether it is about incorporating democracy in an established national order, as in the late nineteenth and early twentieth centuries, or ideas of a European identity during the last few decades of the twentieth. It might 'activate' dimensions of the nation's history that support or contradict the established self-understanding.

The historical examples of the relationship between 'the nation' and 'Europe' in the following chapters will emphasize the role of religion (decline of religion, invocation of religious values, division between religions). The book's understanding of the connection between Europe and religion thus provides an alternative to the standard, rather uncritical, view of a specific European Christian heritage. Furthermore, particular attention is paid here to the 'periphery' of Europe, in the East and the North. In both of these respects we believe that we fill a gap in the existing debate.

In the conceptual history of Europe the interpretative power has in particular come from France, the sovereign actor *par préférence*. The France of the Enlightenment and the Revolution takes the lead and forces all of Europe to either follow the French lead or to develop its own form of emulation or reaction. The French view on Europe emerged in confrontation with those of the Roman Catholic Church and the Christian heritage. As Robert Frank shows in Chapter 13, from the French point of view the values of the French Revolution became European values. Europe thus became a self-reflection of France. A secularized and enlightened *mission civilisatrice* with a republican spirit succeeded an established Roman Catholic universalism. From the Christian mission the French civilization project inherited a quest for restless improvement of the human condition and a belief in progress. This quest was a transformation much more than a rejection of a Christian world-view. The salvation of the souls was replaced as a notion by that of History as a linear and progressive endeavour, and this in turn confronted the avant-garde with the critical choice between setting a shining national example, or actively spreading and propagating progress to other peoples. In its European version the Christian ideas of the selected people and the promised land is the idea of political and technological progress towards ever higher forms of social organization. This version took decisive impressions from the French Revolution and then from Karl Marx.

It must be emphasized, when we talk about *the* French, Austrian, Russian, etc. image or meaning of Europe, we do not ignore the fact that France, Austria and Russia are abstractions, which do not in themselves possess qualities, although the language of 'national interest' misleads thought in such a direction. With the French image we refer to one image with particularly great influence in the French debate, an image which contributed highly to the self-understanding of France as a nation, but it does not mean that this image was uncontested. In France, not the least, there was always a tension between different republican ideals as well as between them and a Roman Catholic counter-image. Without this counter-image the French images of Europe had not gained the power they did. Successful concepts and discourses need counter-concepts and -discourses to break through. Images and counter-images constitute and reinforce one another.[2]

The French image of Europe as secular and enlightened progress challenged every Catholic notion of Europe. Austria became through history a stronghold for such images. In the construction of the Turkish peril the Habsburg monarchs and their population saw themselves in the front line. They were the Christian bulwark against the expanding Islam under the Osmanic Empire. The victory over the Turks at Vienna in 1683 became in the self-reflection Austria's salvation of European Christian unity. Austria developed its traditional role of guardian of occidental Christianity into an alternative *Kulturmission* to the French civilization project. Under the impact of the intellectual and material mobilization against an experienced threat to the whole European culture, the Enlightenment discourse was framed not as liberation from the bottom-up but

---

2. For the term counter-concept, see Koselleck 2000: 36, 60, 66–7, 102–9, 143, 165, 211, 233, 298, 300, 363.

as concessions from above in terms of liberal political rights. The preconditions of the Habsburg Roman-German world image changed dramatically with the French Revolution and Napoleon when the universal revolution replaced universal Christianity. After 1789 *Europa* signified *l'Europe* – that is, French civilization as opposed to the tradition of the Holy Roman Empire. Gilbert Weiss demonstrates in Chapter 11 how two meanings of Europe and universalism, through bi-polarity, constituted one another in Austria. Europe and the Occident were key concepts, which indicated to which of the two lines of thought an argument belonged. The concept of Europe indicated an orientation towards the future and ideas of political progress. Occident, i.e. *Abendland*, 'the land of the evening', connoted the roots in the Christian, imperial past. Furthermore, Austria sought a middle way, between an East that was 'primitive' both in terms of occidental *Kulturmission* and European *Zivilisationsmission*, and the French *l'Europe*. Habsburg-Mitteleuropa positioned itself inbetween these two poles as a sort of 'middle-range enlightenment', or a 'middle-range Europe', a self-image that resurfaced under the sign of neutrality in the cold war.

The connection between Europe and progress emerged in a third version in Scandinavia, in this book represented by Sweden. It was a negative connection where Protestantism stood for progress and Europe for conservatism and Roman Catholicism. This image originally dated back to the Reformation and the Thirty Years War but gained a new political relevance in the 1930s in response to the Great Depression and the military threats represented by Hitler and Stalin. In the social-democratic transformation of the protestant values, Enlightenment was the basis for social progress. Revivalist movements in the nineteenth century claimed and gained a de-hierarchization of religion, where the individual had a personal responsibility for the images of the transcendental world, thereby circumventing the State Church clergy. The social democrats exploited this development politically. The pressure from the revivalist movements and their institutionalization in Free Churches provoked liberal-theological reforms of the Lutheran State Church. As religious practice was increasingly privatized the Church became a cultural institution under social democratic guidance in more general terms. The social democrats did not negate religion as the French Revolutionaries had done, nor did they defend it like Catholic Habsburg, but they transformed it through the separation between an emotional private sphere of religious belief and a cultural-political institutional State–Church sphere (for this distinction, see Hérvieu-Leger 2000). It is not difficult to conceive Nordic-style social democracy as a secularized form of Lutheran Protestantism. From this cultural Church sphere a political demarcation to the perceived Catholic (and conservative) Europe could be built. Swedish social democracy emerged as a prime mover of earthly progress, in a similar manner to that of French republicanism, although there seems to have been no direct contact between them. They shared a quest for earthly progress and in both cases the opposition against progress came from Catholicism. In France, however, it was Revolution and Europe against the Catholic Church. In Sweden, Europe connoted Catholicism and they were both perceived as a threat to the Swedish way of organizing society.

A Swedish image of 'Europe' as Catholic and conservative can already be discerned occasionally in the nineteenth century, but it only crystallized fully in the 1930s. Before the totalitarian era Europe could at times also be a concept of positive identification in the Swedish intellectual and political debate, to the Left as well as to the Right. This was particularly the case among the social democrats in the 1920s when they invested their hopes in internationalism, disarmament and European concord in the framework of the League of Nations. As the German national socialists appropriated the concept of Europe and gave it a new design, however, Swedish society demarcated itself against 'the Continent'. Although Swedes have only rarely explicitly renounced their European identitification the experiences in the 1930s and 1940s of totalitarianism and war in Europe and peace and economic progress at home became a formative experience with a long-lasting alienating impact on Swedish society.

The frustrations of being in Europe or demarcated from it is even more pronounced in Russian history, as Iver B. Neumann demonstrates in Chapter 8. However, the key concept in this story is Запад, the West, rather than Europe. The adherents of *zapad*, the Westernizers, from Peter I onward emphasized modernity in terms of economic and political improvement. They translated 'the West' as 'progress'. In the wake of the French Revolution liberal ideas of individual human rights were added to the agenda of modernization. The idea of a Western model to emulate was constantly challenged by the idea of a Slavic historical destiny demarcated from the West.

In some brief periods Europe has also appeared as a promise of a way out of the East–West tension that is a permanent and traumatic theme running through the entire history of Russia since its inclusion in the occidental state system in the seventeenth century. For a few years under Gorbachev, Europe seemed to be the key to a common home with the West in which Russia would ultimately be included as a normal partner. This common European home, however, never made it beyond the drawing board and, under President Vladimir Putin Russia instead resorted to a traditional strong-state-and-strong-leader ideal, defining Russia's identity by a binary code that juxtaposes Russia to the West and leaves little room for an inclusive European sphere. Needless to say this development was not only the result of an internal Russian debate but equally a reflection of changes in the Western and European image of Russia. The desire to become a civilized liberal capitalist *Rechtsstaat* comes from within, but the terms of the transition are partly set in interaction with Europe and the West. The Russians, Neumann concludes, are too caught up in their relationship with European culture and civilization to think entirely independently of it.

Greece represents a fourth case of connections between religion and nation-building by means of the concept of 'Europe'. The Greeks did not invent their own foundation myth, which was laid out by West European Enlightenment and Romanticist thinkers in their search for the roots of European civilization. The problem for the Greeks when they were confronted with the European discourse on ancient Greece was that the European foundation myth did not provide them with the links between classical antiquity and Greek modernity. One instrument with which this void could be filled was a 'racial' discourse, which emphasized distinction and excellence of Greeks when compared to the vast majority of Slavs on the Balkan peninsula. During the Greek war of independence of 1821–1827, a glorious heritage of struggle against oriental despotism was depicted, but this in the long run was a self-defeating approach. Constantine Tsoukalas demonstrates convincingly in Chapter 1 how problematic the ancient heritage was as a mobilizing element to say the least, since for most inhabitants the fiction lacked credibility. The only element of continuity came from the oriental Orthodox Church, officially recognized and sponsored by the Ottoman authorities ever since the fall of Constantinople in 1453 and therefore difficult to connect to a bulwark against oriental despotism. At this point the ambiguity in the construction of modern Greece commenced. Two opposite conceptualizations of 'real' Greece emerged. In one scenario there was the progressive, secular and rational Enlightenment project of revived ancient ideals. In the other, and conflicting, outline there was the religious conformity through an omnipotent Church rejecting all liberal ideals and opting for accommodation with the Ottoman Empire. The contention between these two views continued in the twentieth century, although under development of new internal contradictions in each narrative, when the liberal project in many respects was transformed into a socialist project under the impact of the Russian Revolution. The civil war after the Second World War fits well into this scenario of conflicting world-views.

In Latin Europe, nation and Europe have mostly been mutually supportive. This is especially so in Italy which in its self-imagination is characterized by a combination of being at the heart of the common European culture and being a laggard in terms of political and economic development in comparison to the centralized territorial states of Northern and Western Europe. From an Italian point of view, 'Europe' has had the dual appeal of working as a larger cultural self, and carrying strong connotations of modernity, democracy, prosperity and national stability. Nineteenth-century Italian Romanticism included a markedly idealized view of Europe, and the unification of Italy was seen as one part of a wider reordering of Europe, along the lines of republican, liberal and democratic ideals that were largely transalpine imports. The forging of a liberal Italian nation state after 1860 was therefore inherently combined with openness toward French republicanism, German idealism and British liberalism. Europeanization carried strong connotations of modernization, of catching up, of remedying the perceived anomalies of Italian society.

The Europeanism of the Risorgimento era, and the programmatic anti-Europeanism of the Fascist movement, made it natural for large parts of the resistance movement to take an active pro-European stance. The concept of Europe was instrumental to the construction of a new democratic national consensus, beginning with the non-socialist parties and gradually stretching to include socialists and Euro-communists.

Italy had historically, and still has, a strong cultural capital and weak state, and forms in this respect an antipode to Northern Protestant states such as Sweden whose history is characterized by a combination of being at the fringe of European culture and being a pioneer in terms of modern (welfare) state-building. The Swedish civilization mission is also the reverse of Italy's combination of national unification and radiation with and through Europe.

In Spain, Europe emerged as an instrument of demarcation against Franco. At the end of the 1970s the new democratic Spain was portrayed as a European Spain with value attributes such as being modern and pluralistic. Europe was a key instrument in the search for a new legitimate Spanish nationhood. Through entrance into the EC the new Spain could reinforce its democracy against the threats from fascism and nationalist separatism. In this reshaping of the Spanish nation with Europe, a civilization mission gradually emerged. The new democratic Spain was a global-minded, cosmopolitan and post-colonial bridge-builder between Europe and Latin America, and between Europe and the Arab world. The subtitle was that Spain would gain prestige by playing an honourable and worthwhile role in the international community. Europe as a symbol for modernity has an older origin in the pre-Franco Spain, however, as Pablo Jáuregui demonstrates in Chapter 3.

Outside the Gallo-German-Roman core the construction of Europe has often confronted nations with the choice of either being an outpost or opting out of Europe altogether. A number of examples in this book – Great Britain in the West and Finland, the Baltic States, Poland and Czechia in the East – illustrate this meaning of Europe, and also different ways of handling such a peripheral position.

In everyday English, the most striking feature is the synonymous use of 'Europe' and 'the Continent', that is, a geographical area which does not include the British Isles. 'Europe' is used as an alternative to 'Britain', not as a geographical area distinct from Africa, Asia or the Americas. In political terms, alluring alternatives to European cooperation have always emerged and there is in the British debate a powerful belief that the widest global cooperation is preferable to action at a regional level. In a contradictory way the British have often reacted with uncertainty, perplexity or hostility to ideas of European cooperation and integration and yet repeatedly they have found themselves deeply involved and entangled with nineteenth- and twentieth-century developments in Europe. The historical experiences of a world-wide colonial Empire promoted a kind of civilizing mission that was connected to specific European values such as the French one. In the imperial era soldiers dispatched from the United Kingdom were referred to as 'European' not 'British' or 'English'. Piers Ludlow emphasizes that there is a long tradition of suspicion toward continental politics which has often lead to the conclusion that Britain should lead Europe, or stay out. The British might be with them, but not of them. The British imperial mission mainly passed beyond Europe and has became increasingly Western and linked to the special relationship with the United States. 'Western' in this understanding often came close to 'Anglo-American', but there was also a British self-understanding of being a bridge-builder between Europe and the United States. Although France had a colonial heritage almost on a par with the British, the values and the mission emanating from the French Revolution were more European. Two competing civilization images emerged underpinning competition about positions of power and prestige. This competition peaked under de Gaulle and his language of Europe from the Atlantic to the Urals but excluding Britain and the United States.

It was only in the last few decades of the twentieth century that Europe became a symbol of modernity in British public debate, and then often in a purely instrumental manner. Paradoxically, this shift came at just about the time that the educational habits of the British upper class had ceased to be as linked to the classical European cultural heritage as they once had been, and at a time when modern popular culture came to play with Britishness versus Europeanness in a stereotypical manner.

Finland's national history has been characterized by a strong awareness of being either on the brink of Europe or on the margins of Russia or somewhere in between, as Henrik Meinander phrases it. Meinander traces two basic conceptions of Finland's national identity: the Fennoman that stresses the indigenous features of Finnish culture and sees Finland as a cooperative borderland between the West and Russia, and the liberal that is akin to the Russian *zapadniki* in the sense that it prescribes close integration with the Western and European cultures. For the Fennomans, Russia was in a cultural sense never outside Europe, but the feeling of standing at the edge of Europe was reinforced by the Russian Revolution, the Finnish civil war and the foundation of the Soviet Union, which effectively precluded any acknowledgements of the eastern layers of Finnish identity. The Finnish notion of Europe became increasingly polarized not least due to the experiences of Finland being left very much alone in the Second World War. Forced into a policy of friendly neutrality with the Soviet Union after the war Finland rediscovered its role as a mediator between East and West. The Finns began to admit that Russia, even in its Soviet manifestation, was a part of European civilization.

The accession to the EU in 1995 was supported by a feeling that the Finns had at last found an answer to two centuries of uncertainty and identity-searching. Finland had, as it were, ultimately found a synthesis of its two historical roles, to both be on the brink of Western Europe and serve as a bridge-builder toward a Europe that stretched to include Russia and Slavonic Europe. EU membership implies both an improvement of national security and an emotional homecoming.

'Europe' as an emotional homecoming is an even more striking theme by states formerly under Soviet occupation or domination, although this is a homecoming not yet fully accomplished. The European or Western component of Estonian, Latvian and Lithuanian national identity has always been easily defined as an antithesis to Russia or the East. Religion has placed the Estonians, Latvians and Lithuanians safely in a West European camp, but their ethno-linguistic features have also historically placed them somewhat apart. In the post-communist era 'Europe' and 'the West' have been the insignias of liberation, democracy and political and economic modernization. Many Balts have an inclination to define Europe in culture terms, as a superior cultural, political and moral objective. For many Balts 'Europe' and 'the West', perceived as cultural continuities, with absolute chronologies and a black-and-white coloration of the past, become sources of cultural strength. Nation-building and Europeanization in this respect are mutually reinforcing. In the post-Soviet context, Klas-Göran Karlsson concludes in Chapter 7, the Balts have taken 'Europe' to mean continuity, harmony, persistence, prosperity, stability and unity, in contrast to a chaotic and uncertain East.

The sense of being an outpost of Europe is an outstanding feature of Polish history too. While there is a streak of humble admiration and gratitude in the Finnish view of European civilization – in a classical poem the author Zacharias Topelius even depicted Finnish society by its very existence as 'a promissory note' to Western civilization – the Poles on the contrary have rather treated Europe as indebted to Poland for its civilization.

While the self-confident Polish elite before the eighteenth century elaborated a notion of being the eastern 'bulwark of Christianity' (*Antemurale Christianitatis*), the disintegration of the Polish state and its disappearance from the map of Europe and the spread of a secular idea of Europe conspired to endow Polish nation-building with an inferiority complex. Enlightenment concepts of civilization and progress threatened to degrade the former bulwark of Christian Europe to a part of the uncivilized East, as Barbara Törnquist-Plewa describes this process in Chapter 9. Poland ought to be Europeanized and 'Europe' in Polish discourse became a synonym of Modernity. Polish Slavophilism that emerged as an alternative to emulating Western Europe did not mean an escape from Europe like the Russian one, but an attempt to make the Slavic people play the role of a regenerative power in Europe. The same character was found in Polish Romantic messianism which contained a sharp criticism of Western European civilization but a criticism from within. The ideological creators of the Polish modern ethnic nationalism established firmly in the Polish soul the thesis of the Western, Latin character of Polish culture. The rebirth of Poland as a state in 1918 was treated by the Poles as a 'return to Europe'. The Poles perceiving themselves as belonging to Western civilization felt humiliated that they were controlled by an Eastern Soviet empire and thereby doomed to belong to the East. Therefore after the fall of the communist system in 1989 in Poland, one of the most widely used expressions was again 'the return to Europe'.

In the Czech case Europe emerged in the nineteenth century from the point of view of an endangered national existence, as a protective framework for Czech national ambitions against the German ruling nation in the Habsburg Empire. In Chapter 10, Miroslav Hroch depicts how a dominant theme of Czech nation-building became how 'small nations' could be integrated into the 'family' of the established European nations. Under conditions of the struggle for the Czech(oslovak) nation state during and after the First World War, the meaning emerged of a 'New Europe' that was in opposition to German nationalism and synonymous with 'Western' democracy. A myth was developed about the Czech lands as the 'heart' of Europe; after the Second World War, this transformed into an idea of Czechoslovakia as a bridge between (capitalist) Western and (socialist) Eastern Europe. This entailed a tension in the national discourse between the official political interpretation of the geographical meaning of Europe from the Atlantic to the Urals, and the cultural concept of Europe as an incorporation of Western values against Eastern and notably Soviet Russian backwardness.

In Germany, the institutional framework that would bring together the cultural nation and the political order remained contested, thus making the German question a common European concern. A clear notion of a German nation developed within the Holy Roman Empire, but a more clear-cut German nation-building project emerged only as a response to the challenge of the French Revolution and Napoleon's warfare. Europe's division between a Roman Catholic south and a Protestant north, and between a liberal and capitalist West and a conservative and agrarian East, between a notion of Christianity and a secularized Enlightenment identity went as a rift through the German nation. As Willfried Spohn notes in Chapter 12, the German nation state created in 1870–71 was neither small enough to avoid internal ethno-national conflict nor large enough to avoid irridentism outside its borders. Germany was unable to provide European leadership and German visions of Europe in the nineteenth century went in many contradictory directions.

After the First World War there seemed to be a fair chance to achieve a democratic German nation state, reconciled with its European neighbours, but this was impeded by both the lingering idea of a great German Reich and the limited will of other European leaders to be reconciled with Germany on the basis of European unity.

It was only after the Second World War that Germany achieved a congruence between the state and the nation and, under firm Western leadership, was integrated in a stable international framework – although it was a German nation divided into two states. In certain layers of society, identification with European culture also gained an important meaning as a remedy to traumatic collective memories and an alternative to the cultivation of German national culture.

With reunification the German question ultimately found a solution that was acceptable both to the vast majority of Germans and to their many neighbours. When Germany continues to define its interest largely in European terms, it is an identification with a somewhat transformed image of Europe – what Spohn calls a 'quasi-imperial orientation envisioning the EU as a renewed global player'. The post-war identity of West Germany was to a certain extent that of being an anti-power-state. Gradually, however, and especially since the end of the cold war, Germany has again become accustomed to power politics, not in *Alleingang* but neither without tensions within the European integration project. The alternative to a Europeanized Germany is no longer the threat of a Germanic Europe, but the weight of the reunited Germany nevertheless poses a challenge for the EU project in general and perhaps for France in particular.

These examples demonstrate how nation-building is often a matter of positioning the nation in a larger cultural-geographical context and whereby 'Europe' is used as a stereotype in the construction of both 'Us' and 'They', of self-identification and of distinction of 'the Other'. Such auto-stereotypes and xeno-stereotypes reinforce each other. The Greek case demonstrates that xeno-stereotypes are often incorporated in the auto-stereotypes. The examples demonstrate how 'Europe' has conveyed meanings of both 'one of us' and 'the other'. Such stereotypes are contested by other stereotypes and are therefore constantly renegotiated and adjusted to new points of departure (Stråth 2000). At the same time they exert inertia and make certain preferences and references more probable than others in the mobilization of populations and in the formulation and solution of problems.

The examples in this Introduction are just a sample of how the meanings of Europe vary over time and between nations. The ensuing chapters provide a fuller exploration of the meaning of 'Europe' in the construction of modern national identities. They analyse how national projects have been described in civilization mission terms, where 'Europe' has been one important element. Such meanings are often inscribed in a specific destiny based on the definition of and the identification with a particular historical heritage. Christianity has often been referred to as a specific heritage, one which distinguishes Europe from other civilizations. As will be demonstrated in the following chapters, however, there is not just *one* Christian heritage: various religious heritages – not only Christian, as the history of for example the Balkans demonstrates – have emerged in complex patterns of competition, support, overlapping, and exclusion, and images of Christian heritages have co-existed with atheist

Enlightenment ideas. Related to ideas of a specific destiny and of a civilization mission, also the religious element has been obvious in transformed 'secular' forms. This heterogeneous legacy has a direct bearing on the contemporary construction of Europe.

## References

Borneman, J. and Fowler, N. (1997), 'Europeanization' *Annual Review of Anthropology*, 26: 487–514.

Brubaker, R. (1996), *Nationalism Reframed: Nationhood and the National Question in the New Europe*, Cambridge: Cambridge University Press.

Davies, N. (1997), *Europe – A History*, London: Pimlico.

Delanty, G. (1995), *Inventing Europe: Idea, Identity, Reality*, London: MacMillan.

—— (1999), 'Social Integration and Europeanization', *Yearbook of European Studies* 12: 221–38.

Ferguson, Y.H. and Richard, W.M. (1996), 'Political Space and Westphalian States in a World of "Polities": Beyond Inside/Outside', *Global Governance*, 2(2): 261–87.

Fulbrook, M. (1992) (ed.), *National Histories and European History*, London: UCL Press.

Goddard, V.A., Llobera, J.R. and Shore, C. (eds) (1994), *The Anthropology of Europe: Identities and Boundaries in Conflict*, Oxford: Berg.

Hay, D. (1968), *Europe. The Emergence of an idea*, Edinburgh: Edinburgh University Press.

Held, D. (1995), *Democracy and Global Order*, Stanford: Stanford University Press.

Hervieu-Léger, Danièle (2000), *Religion as a Chain of Memory*, New Brunswick, NJ: Rutgers University Press.

Höfert, A. (2001), Wissen und Türkengafahr: Die Formierung eines ethnographischen Wissenskorpus über die Osmanen im Europa der Renaissance. PhD thesis, European University Institute, Florence.

Kaye, J. and Stråth, B. (2000), *Enlightenment and Genocide. Contradictions of Modernity*, Brussels: PIE-Peter Lang.

Koselleck, R. (2000), *Zeitgeschichten: Studien zur Historik,* Frankfurt/Main: Suhrkamp.

Lipgens, W. (1985) (ed.), *Documents on the History of European Integration. Vol 1. Continental Plans for European Union 1939–1945*, Berlin/New York: Walter de Gruyter.

Lotman, Y. (1990), *Universe of the Mind: a Semiotic Theory of Culture*, London: Tauris.

Milward, A. (1992), *The European Rescue of the Nation-State*, London: Routledge.

Morgan, P. (1996) '"A Vague and Puzzling Idealism . . ."' Plans for European Unity in the Era of the Modern State', in W. Michael (ed.), *Culture and Identity in Europe*, Aldershot: Avebury.

Niethammer, L. (2000), 'A European Identity?' in B. Stråth (ed.), *Europe and the Other and Europe as the Other*, Brussels: PIE-Peter Lang.

Passerini, L. (1998), 'Introduzione', in ibid. (ed.), *Identità culturale Europea: Idee, sentimenti, relazioni*, Florence: La Nuova Italia.

Putnam, R. (1993), *Making Democracy Work: Civic Traditions in Modern Italy*, Princeton: Princeton University Press.

Shore, C. (2000), *Building Europe. The Cultural Politics of European Integration*, London: Routledge.

Spiering, M. (1996), 'National Identity and European Unity', in M. Wintle (ed.), *Culture and Identity in Europe*, Aldershot: Avebury.

Stråth, B. (2000), 'Introduction: Europe as a Discourse', in B. Stråth (ed.), *Europe and the Other and Europe as the Other,* Brussels: PIE-Peter Lang.

Voltaire (1957 [1752]), *Le siècle de Louis XIV*, quoted by Denis Hay in *Europe: The Emergence of an Idea*, Edinburgh: Edinburgh University Press.

White, H. (2000), 'The Discourse of Europe and the Search for a European Identity' in B. Stråth (ed.), *Europe and the Other and Europe as the Other,* Brussels: PIE-Peter Lang.

Wintle, M. (1996), 'Introduction: Cultural Diversity and Identity in Europe', in Wintle M. (ed.), *Culture and Identity in Europe*, Aldershot: Avebury.

# The Irony of Symbolic Reciprocities – The Greek Meaning of 'Europe' as a Historical Inversion of the European Meaning of 'Greece'

*Constantine Tsoukalas*

## The Invention of Greekness

In full contrast with most national discourses, the discourses underlying modern Greek identities have been largely imported. Indeed, the main narrative foundations of the self-perceptions and images of Greeks were first laid out in Western Europe as components of a broader representation of the sources of European civilization. The most significant particularity of the ideal constructions embodied in modern Greek identity discourses thus resides in the fact that these images were not originally formed within the context of a national project seeking to pin down an exclusive historical past. They emerged and crystallized as side effects of a universal original myth concocted outside Greece and for reasons totally unrelated with the prospective nation. This indeed is the first paradox that sealed the future fate of modern Greek collective identities. Greeks are probably the only people in the world who did not have to invent or reinvent their own history and ancestral traditions on their own (Hobsbawm and Ranger 1993). Paraphrasing Adam Ferguson, one may say therefore that if, by definition, 'Greekness' must be the result of the Greeks' historical actions, it is certainly not the product of their deliberate historical design.

Though unintended in its consequences, this exceptional historical conjuncture proved to be both irreversible and ambivalent in its long-term effects. If the glorious idea of ancient Greece provided the founding myth of its modern counterpart, the meaning of the essential links between classical antiquity and Greek modernity remained undefined. The congenital ambiguity surrounding the new country's name is thus the result of an uncertain and dubious 'christening act'. It had certainly not occurred to those responsible for the resurrection of the ancient Greek 'nation' that its living offspring would inevitably seek a future of its own, a future now embedded in an unwarranted modernity. Indeed, in contrast to many new states such as Egypt, Syria and Israel that have reclaimed their ancient names without more ado, modern Greece provides the only historical example of a country including the word 'modern' in its current foreign denomination. Even today, to all intents and purposes references to Greek history *tout court* may sometimes refer uniquely to the venerated history of the ancients. Greek modernity is seen therefore as an uncomfortable discursive paradox, even as a contradiction in terms.

The reasons are obvious: as a direct ideographical side product of a consciously modernizing Europe in search of its classic origins, 'Greekness' referred to a semantic heritage that concerned the whole civilized world. The emergence and nomination of a Greek cultural modernity must refer therefore to a distinctive modern nation calling back to a historical foundation that could never appear as its exclusive and natural symbolical property. The country was thus to be named and perceived as both nominally identical and semantically distinguishable from its crystallized ancient image. The meanings and implications of the question whether or not temporal distance impaired cultural continuity were open to all interpretations. Even if Greeks themselves were sure of their own ancestry, those originally responsible for their resurrection remained sceptical as to the significance and legitimacy of the act of succession.

This, however, leads to a strikingly atypical representation of what ancestry may mean and be worth. Indeed, in contrast to most national historical narratives where the notion of continuity is given in advance, in the case of Greece, the object and narrative functions of continuity were not obvious. Uninterrupted linguistic and territorial continuities could truly be taken at face value. But language and geography can only provide the partial conceptual vehicles for a continuous narrative discourse focusing on historicized social totalities, usually circumscribed by political units (Ricoeur 1983: *passim* and 342f). In this sense, in order to build on the notion of a historical nation, the idea of a coherent and circumscribed cultural continuity should be arguable in empirically convincing terms. To the extent, however, that the continuing homogeneity of culture must remain an open question, it is always hard to pin down a definite object of historical continuity.

This is probably the main reason why racial discourses are often called upon to consolidate coveted national continuities. Greece was no exception, all the more so that from the very beginning, Modern Greek historians seem to have been affronted by an intellectual *malaise*. Truly, epistemological prudence rarely discourages inventors and perpetuators of national discourses from falling back on Herderian eschatological patterns. But statements pertaining to the continuity of universally-acclaimed ideas and values are more often than not invested in specific claims and appear as contested issues of ideological power. It is therefore natural that the 'eternal' Greeks should still be in trouble when called upon to circumscribe the continuity of their inimitable *Volksgeist* other than in racial terms. And it is also natural that the meanings of cultural continuity and discontinuity should be perceived as open discursive problems, destined to haunt the crystallization of Greek self-images from the very beginning. Clearly, the adopted name was not enough.

Thus, if the riddle of the continuous national civilization is still unsolved, this must ultimately be due to the strained spiritual relations between the obsessed godfathers and the adopted children. Indeed, both the cognitive and the normative ambiguities surrounding the continuity of Greek culture can be traced down to the congenitally-ambivalent position of 'Greekness' within the civilized European world. Imprisoned as they were in their universal semantic context, the notion and implications of an eternal idea of Greece impeded those who recognized themselves as its obvious legitimate heirs in shaping their own ancestral meanings in ways corresponding to their narrative needs. Accordingly, the main originality of modern Greek ideologists resides precisely in the fact that they were not free to imagine and construct their historicized national *Volksgeist* as merely specific in its inimitable singularity, but had also to cope with the implications of its acclaimed and unique universality. And there can be no doubt that a *Volksgeist* uncomfortably disguised in terms of a *Weltgeist* is not ideally suited to serve its specific nation-building purposes.

It is no accident therefore that, building on their linguistic, cultural and religious differences from their immediate neighbours, Greeks should still tend to think of their collective identity as being not only as empirically brotherless as a *factum*, but also as normatively singular as a *universalium*. Indeed, Greek territory is situated in the Balkan Peninsula, but Greeks are – and feel – totally unrelated to Slavs. They belong, of course, to the European West, but when speaking of 'Europeans' they almost invariably refer to the European Other to the exclusion of indigenous Greeks. And even when the now outdated notion of a Near East was still current, their religious confrontation with Muslims impeded the common use of any generic term including other peoples of the region.

It is undeniable therefore that the objective accidents of historical and linguistic geography strengthened the symbolic connotations of the unique cultural heritage. Like Finns, Hungarians and Basques, Greeks would have to develop their common destinies as culturally unique and self-sufficient. But unlike these peoples, Greeks were burdened by their unique claim to universality.

However, a small nation boasting of its eternal singularity is called upon to pay a high price, especially when this singularity can be seen as referring to a universal normative validity. Indeed, to the extent that wider hegemonic ambitions are objectively precluded – and this has certainly been the case for Greece, at least after the collapse of the Ottoman Empire which some overconfident Greeks had been hoping to conquer from within – it is hard to discursively combine the specific and the universal in convincing ways. A poor, weak and relatively backward country indulging in overarching cultural fantasies cannot help stepping into functional, symbolical and psychological pitfalls. It would seem therefore that the very awe brought about by the glory that was Greece turned out to be overwhelming for the youthful heirs grudgingly entrusted with a universally fetishistic legacy. The brilliant gift proved to be poisonous, or at least equivocal. Indeed, Jacques Derrida might have been thinking of Modern Greece when he asked: 'What is paranoia? Is it an economic circulation that neutralizes the gift through its reciprocation, or is it an exaggeration, a consummation and a destruction?' (Derrida 1991: 55). It is mainly of the effects of such a symbolic 'paranoia' that I shall speak.

## Tradition and Modernity: Name, History, Language and the Essence of 'Greekness'

As mentioned, the congenital ambivalence of modern Greek self-images can be traced down to the particularities surrounding their historical emergence. It should be added, however, that imported ideas of 'Greekness' did not relate only to ancient Greek civilization, but referred to the new idea of global civilization *tout court*. European idolization of classical antiquity emerged as a fundamental ingredient of the newly-defined essence of an inherently superior Western civilization. It was their own cultural self-images that Europeans were seeking to capture in their idealized historical looking-glass. Indeed, the notions of rationality, modernity, emancipation and progress emerged as necessary components of the conception of a universal and cumulative cultural evolution under the leadership of an inherently superior Europe. Ever since the eighteenth century, the cultural supremacy of the conquering Europeans was taken for granted. Within this context, 'Hellenolatry' provided the first systematic ideological construction founding the triumphantly Eurocentric Orientalist discourse (Said 1991). Unimpeachable cultural origins were thus called upon to legitimate power politics. As representatives of a universal civilization Europeans were systematically idealizing their own inimitable past.

However, the normative validity of a universal civilization in search of its own destiny could not be properly conceived without the elaboration of its negative discursive counterpart. Classical civilization and its privileged European offspring would have to be circumscribed and therefore supplemented by the construction of the Others, i.e. the non-European 'barbarians', obviously represented mainly by the East. Even if real frontiers between the two geo-cultural areas were clearly undefinable, it was obvious that from both a geographical and a cultural point of view modern Greece was situated somewhere along the imaginary dividing line between European civilization and Oriental barbarity.[1] To their detriment, their surprise and their eventual consternation, Greeks found themselves lying in a discursive purgatory. Ambiguities of classification were therefore inevitable. The descendants of the brilliant Hellenes would have to see themselves as eventually subsumable under both fundamental categories provided by the dominant taxonomic matrixes.

All the more so that this polarized conceptualization both of the world and of its historical background was promptly organized into a coherent and indivisible ideographical whole. No one could escape a strongly-worded normative pattern backed by all the discursive means economic and military power could provide. If most Europeans, even those situated outside the core of Western power, were led to take their overall Caucasian supremacy for granted, when exported out of the fields of their immediate ideological action, Eurocentric ideas had unforeseen and cumulative effects. For all peoples situated in the periphery, the strong normative distinction between civilization and barbarity, and later on between progress and backwardness, represented both an ideological challenge to be dealt with and an ominously devastating cultural and political threat. Invariably, Eurocentric discourses would be accepted, distorted or resisted, often all at the same time. Down to the present day, processes of modernization are universally painful and contradictory. And

---

1. Otherwise highly controversial, Bernal (1987) is invaluable in substantiating what he refers to as the ideological fabrication of ancient Greece in the eighteenth century.

even if, more often than not, the so-called antinomy between tradition and modernity is more mystifying than explanatory, it is usually in these terms that most violently-imported issues are considered and eventually solved. For most peoples suddenly brought into the world system, however, such normative dichotomies end up corresponding to clear-cut political or cultural dilemmas. But, in this respect also, Greece is a spectacular exception. Despite the fact that the country occupied a symbolically-privileged position in the imaginary hierarchy of civilization, it had emerged into independence as an underdeveloped, undernourished and undereducated country. Very naturally, therefore, Greeks found themselves entangled in an ambivalent love–hate relationship both with their historicized cultural vocations and duties, and with the distant model of their godfathers. For over a century, the ever-present image of Europe was a constant reminder of cultural patterns that could not possibly be emulated integrally. Hence the combination of inferiority feelings, wounded pride, puffed-up self-importance and uncritical admiration. Greeks were obliged to face a world dominated by a civilization originally nurtured by their forefathers, but since lost. Not simply were they called upon to accept the awkward superiority of an effective foreign cultural pattern, but also they thought of themselves as forefathers of a universal culture they could no longer understand, let alone follow. They were the original instigators of a progress they were entitled to, but of which they had been divested.

Furthermore, it should be underlined that Eurocentric considerations led to a new meaning of history as a continuous progress. Modernity was conceived as a necessary historical phase opening up the whole world toward emancipation through liberty, democracy, science and rationality. It was this universal normative dimension that armed the ideas of the Enlightenment with their unprecedented power and prestige. And this is precisely the reason why 'Hellenolatry' became so pivotal an element of European self-perceptions. The classical *polis* provided the much-needed ideological archetype for the civic, intellectual and artistic virtues of modernity. Thus, the projection of European cultural supremacy into the future paved the way toward the elaboration of discursive metaphors going back into the past. The idea of a common European civilization did not crystallize as a simple cultural option between alternative models coming out of the blue, but particularly aimed to present Europe as the product of a specifically European cultural vocation. The historicized essence of the spirit of Europe was seen therefore as reflecting an intrinsic continuity with an intellectual and cultural ancestry apt to anticipate a subsequently triumphal future. Accordingly, those who had already carried the sperms of universal progress were often depicted as a race having attained an early perfection. It is no accident that in both their intellectual and their physical characteristics, the ancients should be imagined as supermen. The German historian Ernst Curtius was more than explicit: Greeks not only featured an 'intrinsic harmony of bodies and limbs, mild and simple face lines, large eyes, straight noses and finely shaped mouths', but they were also 'very rarely fleshy or fat'. Their racial characteristics must therefore have been unique: indeed, 'if among other peoples beauty was the exception, among Greeks it was the rule' (Curtius 1865).

The implications were clear. Physical, intellectual and moral perfection can only be attributed to some kind of racial predilection or essential purity. Stemming as it did from an undefined North – a constant reminder of their European connection – Greek blood was generally acclaimed as unique and blessedly unmixed. European civilization could thus be conceived as the culmination of an inimitable autochthonous *Urkultur.* Accordingly, the ascent of the European West would be represented as the predestined process of maturation of a spirit that had developed throughout its long history uncontaminated from the influence of all 'inferior' peoples and races.[2] In this sense, 'Hellenolatry' provided a fundamental metonymic foundation for the coveted European allegory. Shelley's dictum 'We are all Greeks' is much more than a rhetorical exhortation. It reflects the urge to pin down the superior origins of a universal civilization destined to impose its liberating will upon the whole world. Indeed, in Karl Kraus's words, 'Origin is the aim': if Europe was to be seen as intrinsically superior to all non-Europeans, this was because it must have been so since the dawn of time. The splendour of the universal cradle of civilization provided the proof of the trans-historical supremacy of the races and cultures to which it gave birth.

The metonymic bias crystallized through 'Hellenolatry' set the ideological stage for the emergence of Modern Greece.[3] Even if reminiscences of ancient glory were not absent when the late Byzantine Empire was in decline, they did not become dominant until the end of the

2. Even today, the nineteenth-century German historian Jacob Philip Fallmerayer, author of many books (for example, Fallmerayer 1835), is often referred to as the nation's archenemy. He is guilty of having convincingly referred to the massive influx of Slavs into the Greek mainland in the early Middle Ages.

3. Following Kant and Jacobson, Tort (1989) aptly distinguishes 'metaphoric' classifications and biases founded on criteria of formal similarities from 'metonymic' ones resulting from notions of origin and alterity.

eighteenth century. Indeed, the idealized Western version of the inimitable Hellenic past was mainly brought to the forefront by the expanding commercial bourgeoisie that had been developing ever since the Ottoman Empire was led to open its economic relations with Europe. It should be kept in mind that in these pre-nationalist times the Greek language was already providing a sort of commercial *lingua franca* throughout the Balkan Peninsula. It is no accident therefore that when this early Greek-speaking bourgeoisie came in touch with European 'Hellenolatry' they were immediately convinced of their own collective vocation. Surrounded as they were by ancient ruins acting as inscrutable 'memory machines', in the sense of Gabriel García Márquez, they could only interpret their idealized origins as an indication of a new historic destiny offered them on a golden plate. As depositories of European *Urkultur,* they immediately believed themselves to be an elected people, if not by God, at least by universal History.

By the turn of the century, the messages were becoming clear. Rhigas Velestinlis, a radical freemason, instigated a multinational and multireligious liberation movement with a view to establishing a democratic Balkan federation on the basis of the progressive ideas of the Enlightenment. He failed and was eventually executed. But it was only the beginning. The Greek war of independence from 1821 to 1827 was also fought with increasing reference to the emancipating background of classical fighting against Oriental despotism. Very characteristically, for the first time, infants were being given ancient heroic names, in spite of the reaction of a Church which insisted they be named after established saints. Once awakened to the idea of progress, the eternal Greek spirit seemed to be destined not only to be liberated from the barbaric Ottoman yoke, but also to resurrect the principles of modernity, rationality and civilization across the entire backward Near East.

And, indeed, the myth seemed really to come true. Liberation from the Ottomans was eventually attained after long and bitter battles, but also stemmed from the gathering momentum of the romantic Philhellenic movement lobbying in favour of Greece all over Europe (see St Clair 1972). Ancient heroes called for emulation among their modern counterparts. Lord Byron's active participation in the war and his subsequent death during the siege of the small town of Messolonghi was a mere anticipation of the massive European military intervention that finally ensured the creation of the independent Modern Greek State in 1830. For once, the principles of the Holy Alliance seemed to cede to an enflamed European public opinion. This indeed is the first, and possibly the last, example of unanimous international recognition of the rights of a national liberation movement. The symbolic connotations were clear. The European powers were repaying their eternal debt to their glorified cultural ancestors.

Political independence set the scene for new and unforeseen developments. It was immediately clear both to romantic Europeans and to Greeks that the meanings and implications of cultural continuity between ancient and modern Greece were complex and self-defeating. Indeed, despite the strength of the founding myth, Greece remained an alien and incomprehensible fiction to most of the inhabitants of the area. The only palpable living tradition came from the Oriental Orthodox Church, officially recognized and sponsored by the Ottoman authorities ever since the fall of Constantinople to the Turkish Sultan in 1453. It should be kept in mind that for long centuries the survival of a uniform and written Greek language had been ensured by the extensive Greek-speaking ecclesiastical administration. After all, the New Testament was written in Greek. Indeed, it is only because of the power of the semi-autonomous Church that the distinctiveness of Christian populations had been reproduced. Going back to the Byzantine Empire, ecclesiastical mechanisms were thus paramount in preserving separate cultural identities.

It is precisely at this point, however, that the original ambiguity of the meaning of modern 'Greekness' set in. The main cultural problem faced by the emerging national society resided in the difficulty in combining two opposite conceptions of 'real' Greece. On the one hand, progressive, secular and rational interpretations of revived ancient ideals pushed society towards an unknown and alien modernity. On the other hand, the conservative religious conformity emanating from an omnipotent Church still jealous of its ecumenical privileges was suspicious of all forms of change. It is no accident that these two cultural patterns were immediately conceived in polarized and antagonistic terms. Even before the creation of the new nation state, all liberal ideas were rejected by an ecclesiastical establishment which generally opted for accommodation with the Turkish turban, if faced with the threat of having to deal with the power of the Papal tiara.

Inevitably, power and factional conflicts would make use of all possible forms of historical rationalizations. Ever since independence, the small and fragile Greek state was perceived as a threat to a privileged Patriarchate accustomed to living in functional, if insecure, symbiosis with the Sultanate. Predictably, political independence could only enhance the liberal and radical ideas stemming from Europe and eventually lead to a secularization of Greek society. In this sense, the battle between the spiritual and the mundane interpretations of emerging

'Greekness' reflected a deeper long-term antagonism over influence, prestige and power. The meaning of Greek national continuity and therefore the meaning of a resurrected Greece – and of its relation to the West – emerged as open issues even before the stabilization of the new political community.

This state of affairs had important ideological side effects. The narrative modes of the new national history were immediately open to challenge. Indeed, the universal symbolism of classical antiquity could not possibly be disregarded, but it was equally out of the question to look down upon the Orthodox Church. If statues and ruins were distant and mute, the largely illiterate peasant population continued to address the local clergy for advice, help, consolation and even material survival. It should indeed be kept in mind that the lack of any kind of feudal structures or landed gentry had rendered the influence of priests and monks even more pronounced than in the European West, where trad- itional social hierarchies and power dependencies had been internalized for centuries. Everyday cultural practices were thus largely identified with the Church, its rudimentary schools, its solidarity networks, its solemn rites and its feast days.

It was therefore obvious that ancient Greece could not be resurrected in its pure, ideal form. This, however, presented Greek historiography with a major problem. It would take almost a half-century to settle on a definitive narrative pattern combining both parts of the bi-cephalic tradition and thus ostensibly to bridge the enormous chronological and cultural gap between classical antiquity and the present. The inventive concoction of the term 'Helleno-Christianity', simultaneously leaning on classical memories and Byzantine traditions, provided an immediate rhetorical outlet to narrative dilemmas. But the problem was obviously much more complex. Agreement on the cognitive aspects of an eternal Greek history encompassing all its successive phases was finally reached and definitely sealed through the publication of an official history of the Greek nation by Constantine Paparhigopoulos in the 1860s. But a suitable narrative continuity could not solve the question of an accentuated normative discrepancy between the two terms of 'Helleno-Christianity'. The spiritual and cultural cleavages and tensions ran much deeper.

Once more, European narrative stereotypes were responsible for accentuating the problem. Indeed, as mentioned, the universal valoriz- ation of Western civilization was coterminous with the concomitant devalorization of non-European Others. But it should be noted that, ever since Edward Gibbon's *The Decline and Fall of the Roman Empire*, mainstream European historiography tended to relegate Byzantium and

Eastern Christianity to the limbo of Oriental barbarism. Even today, if the word 'Hellenic' pertains to pristine perfection, in all European languages the word 'Byzantine' generally connotes interminable and futile discussions, petty conspiracies and moral corruption. This imported ideological straitjacket proved literally to be suffocating for the new nation's self-image. Having been endowed with eternal glory, Greek ideologists were also obliged to handle the dirty end of the stick. The imported discursive themes could not be taken at face value. If 'Hellenolatry' was obviously to be adopted, Orientalist prejudices stood to be corrected.

But here again, a new system of discursive antinomies set in. Indeed, if Europeans must generally be 'right' in their cultural evaluations and hierarchizations, and specifically 'wrong' in their abhorrence of Byzantium, this could only be achieved by shifting the demarcation line between civilization and barbarity. Only thus would it be possible both to engage actively in the European contempt for culturally-inferior Muslims, Jews and even to a certain extent Slavs, and at the same time to safeguard the classical symbolical asset. Greeks were therefore pushed into elaborating their own national brand of Orientalism whereby they could continue capitalizing on their symbolic identification with the European West without abnegating their Byzantine ancestors who would have to be unilaterally promoted to a 'civilized' status.

However, subtle rationalizations are always full of discursive traps. It is no accident therefore that Greek Orientalism should develop into a confused and self-defeating mental exercise. Indeed, dominant Greek cultural and behavioural patterns were hardly distinguishable from the daily material and symbolic practices of the surrounding populations. The question of cultural demarcation from neighbours thus presented itself in contradictory terms. If in-built cultural differences and hierarchies were acceptable in terms of an axiomatic statement, the idea of a clear distinction of two worlds would collapse as soon as descriptive European categories were called upon in order to substantiate them. Conceptual patterns were entangled accordingly in an argumentative straitjacket. To the extent that Greeks thought themselves as having to fall into one of two preconceived and polarized mental categories, they would have to make impossible choices. The ensuing normative dilemmas and discursive contradictions were therefore predictable. To all intents and purposes Greeks could not easily adhere to the strict Eurocentric taxonomic bias to which they were subjected: they tended to think of themselves as Western in principle, but Eastern by vocation.

Consequently, it was more or less inevitable that self-perceptions should tend to move freely according to circumstances from a mutually exclusive 'either-or' taxonomic matrix to a composite notion of 'neither-nor' – or to accommodate 'both at the same time'. Greeks were thus led into falling precisely into the trap of interchanging positive and negative images of the Others, depending on their shifting and composite discursive preoccupations. Freely combining strict 'either-or' and flexible 'both at the same time' matrixes can only lead, however, to a series of insoluble 'double binds'. Hence, the paralysing riddle surrounding the narration of Greek origins and history. Changing contexts called for contradictory choices of identity discourses. The 'mirror stage' described by Jacques Lacan could not serve as a stabilizing identity mechanism once and for all (Gourgouris 1996: 10ff.).

It is natural therefore that all main debates about what Greeks are, and what they should be, can be traced back to this original discursive contradiction. For almost two centuries, issues have been revolving around the same congenital uneasiness in combining a modernity emanating from ancient classicism and a tradition embodied in actual everyday practices. The perception of the elemental course of time thus seems to be paradoxically inverted: the remote past was seen as more compatible with the oncoming future than the actual present. Precisely herein lies the profound originality of the dominant forms of Modern Greek *Kulturkampf*. Continuity was never seen as a simple and linear evolution. The intellectual and political scene has been marked therefore by this extraordinary discursive antinomy ever since independence. And it still is.

I shall briefly illustrate the point by referring to a number of striking episodes that mark this uninterrupted cultural struggle. Even before independence, the country's official name became the object of fiery debates. The alternative names of 'Hellenes', going back to antiquity, 'Romans' (*Romioi*) stemming from imperial times, but also referring to the Turkish denomination of Orthodox Christians as '*Rum*', and 'Greeks' (*Graikoi*), originally referring to early Christians in radical opposition to pagan 'Hellenes', obviously stood for antagonistic perceptions of 'Greekness'. However, the unbeatable symbolism of classical glory led the rationalist Westerners to win the first round. Greece was promptly named 'Hellas', thus sealing the uncertain fate of a people who, according to the 'national' historian, Constantine Paparhigopoulos, 'had not dared to preserve their ancestral name'. But it is noteworthy that despite their professed 'Hellenolatry' Europeans still use the term 'Greece'. This is only another example of the frequent ironic twists in the meanings of words.

However, unmitigated supporters of a future-oriented classical purism could not help losing the second round. As mentioned, the new nation's history emerged as an equally burning issue, particularly in respect to the normative interpretation of the Byzantine period within an uninterrupted historical narrative. Even though Byzantium was sometimes conceived of in terms roughly equivalent to those used in reference to the European dark ages, it was obviously impossible to refer to a long period of twelve centuries as a foreign, 'uncivilized' or 'un-Greek' historical interlude, as happened with the Roman period labelled 'Rome-ocracy', (from the second century BC to the third century AD) the period of Western domination under the crusader states known as 'Francocracy' (in the thirteenth and fourteenth centuries) or the Ottoman period (from the fifteenth to the nineteenth centuries) simply referred to as 'Turcocracy'. Byzantium was therefore symbolically rehabilitated and by 1860 had become an integral 'national' chapter within the unified and continuous historical periodization.

This finalized and generally accepted version of Greek history inevitably marked the consolidation of Greek collective identities. The country would inevitably think of itself in terms of what it *had been* all through its long historical course. But if recent Byzantium must be attributed the last word, classical revivalism could not possibly reign supreme. Like its 'Helleno-Christian' history, the country's character was accepted therefore as being congenitally hybrid in respect to its official status. The meaning of an eternal 'Greekness' is thus embedded in its unresolved discursive antinomies. Very characteristically, even today the secular Western Greek state is not totally separated from the official Eastern Orthodox Church, acknowledged as spiritually preponderant by successive Constitutions (Kitromilidis 1983: 51f.). Thus, by officially acclaiming the dominant faith of the country, constitutional charters engendered a number of legal anomalies: down to the present day, the Ministry of Education is also the Ministry of Cults, religious courses including catechism are represented in the curricula of all years of primary and secondary schools, parish priests are on the public payroll, religious blasphemy is a criminal offence, religious beliefs figure on identity cards, religious marriage is equivalent to civil marriage and incineration of the dead is prohibited. The Church has thus managed to cling to its spiritual and material privileges. Diachronic discursive ambiguities have been invested in synchronic institutional antinomies.

But this is not all. Later on, during the second half of the nineteenth century, it was the language question that occupied the centre of the political scene. This time, unmitigated archaeolatry ran hand in hand with religious traditionalism. However, the debate on the desirable degree of approximation to classical Attic norms reflected the same original ambiguity. If modernizers were unanimous in their urge to simplify a language that remained incomprehensible to the masses, all brands of traditionalists were adamant in their conservative stands. On this point the outcome was a draw, at least temporarily. But the intermediate solution agreed upon confirmed a structural diglossia that was not to be really solved until after the Second World War. This seemed to conclude the array of grand cultural issues. Greece seemed gradually to be becoming a 'normal' nation.

This did not prove to be the case, however. Even after the issues of name, history and language had been settled for better or worse, the effects of the congenital ambivalence did not die out. The cognitive and normative issues revolving around the nature and essence of 'Greekness' are still the objects of ardent debate. It is even possible that the final political solution of technical issues may have contributed to the exacerbation of the importance of questions that can afford to remain indefinitely indecisive in their ideological abstraction. Indeed, if a functioning modern State implies the existence of a name, an official language and a stable system of historical references, citizens can freely go on indulging in disagreements about essences and natures with impunity. The question of whether Greece is 'really' European, Eastern or an uneasy mixture of both can thus remain a central socio-political issue. There are few countries in the world so haunted by the spectre of compulsive collective queries.

## Post-war Perceptions of Europe

In view of the above, it is probably inevitable that Greek perceptions of Europe and of the emerging European order should develop on the basis of this highly-exceptional ideological background. The East–West dichotomy referring to Greek self-images pervaded the representations of European Otherness. Indeed, glorifying or menacing, the meaning of Europe and, more generally, of the West developed as a direct reflection of the blurred and contradictory image of Greece itself. It should be kept in mind that the discursive opposition between the archetypes of Hellenes and Romans (*Romioi*) is conceptualized as a confrontation between two mutually exclusive modes of existence, and as a conflict between two incompatible normative universes.[4] Symbols, values, behavioural patterns

---

4. Fermor elaborated a whole set of parallel characteristics, symbols, value and behaviour patterns that correspond to this archetypal opposition (Fermor: 1966). See also Herzfeld (1987).

and cultural features are promptly classified as referring either to an open-minded Western-oriented and progress-seeking rational cosmopolitanism, or as inspired by the indigenous and ultimately Oriental foundations of the cultural and religious core of the nation. Within this context, the quest for original 'third ways' was inevitable. But the elaborate sophisticated constructions insisting on the rich potentialities of an indefinable cultural synthesis between the two poles could not possibly solve the normative problems raised by the discursive cul-de-sac. Truly, contradictions often serve as sources of inspiration to poets. At the beginning of the twentieth century, Alexandria-born Constantine Kavaphy's ironic historical allegories played with the antinomies of the ambivalent Ptolemaic Hellenism split between classical Greek revivalism and early Christianity. Later on, Nobel prize winner George Sepheris experimented with the notion of 'Greekness' as a continuous process, where European modernism and native primitivism would constantly penetrate and enrich each other in a totally original symbiotic plenitude (Keeley 1982). Despite his surrealist inclinations, Odysseus Elytis, another Nobel laureate, heralded the eternal symbolic and material power of the inimitable Greek nature and language, resisting, transforming, and finally purifying and incorporating all external influences. Poetic exhortations, however, could not possibly penetrate the wide masses of a population exposed to polarized cultural discourses for many years. The archetypal self-images summed up by the opposition between Hellenes and *Romioi* was there to stay. Even today, the perceptions of Europe are shaped on the basis of this internal cultural pattern. Widespread modernist 'Euro-idolatry' is counterbalanced by pronounced reticence or even 'Europhobia'. The socio-psychological modes of conflict resolution through simultaneous identification and denial of the European Other still impregnate everyday discourses.

These discursive contradictions do not substantially correspond to clear-cut social divisions, nor have they given birth to distinct socio-psychological types. The opposition between the two discursive archetypes has mainly been – and still is – used in the ubiquitous process of rationalizing everyday individual strategies, options and behaviour, in sometimes totally contradictory ways. Conceptual couples such as rationality versus impulsiveness, discipline versus instinct, conformity versus liberty and spontaneity are represented as epitomizing two distinct visions of the world within fluctuating situations calling for rapid individual strategic adaptations. In this sense, if anything, this duality has resulted in a generalized versatility of behavioural patterns and ethical norms. Lying as they were between two archetypes, Greeks felt free to chose normative affiliations according to the whims of ever-changing circumstances. The European example was seen as both a model and a burden. Typically, the current word *koutofrangoi* (stupid Franks) serves to denote Western normative rigidity as opposed to Greek inventiveness and normative relativity.

This is hardly surprising in a country where individual survival and labour strategies have been exceptionally – and on the whole successfully – flexible and versatile. Indeed, until very recently, while Greece was distinguished by the highest percentage of self-employed persons in Europe, it also featured enormously high levels of multi-activity.[5] Agricultural work, public employment, petty entrepreneurial ventures, temporary emigration, and widespread underground activities (the last estimated to represent anything up to 40 per cent of GNP) were planned within families functioning as veritable quasi-firms. In this sense, an eclectic normative frame of reference can only have been eminently suitable.

Thus, cultural dichotomies persisted. And even though these dichotomies are of limited heuristic value, they still provide explanations for the acknowledged 'fields of meaning' and influence the representations of most political and ideological dilemmas which the country faced in the last few decades of the twentieth century. Successive versions of Europhilia and Europhobia have often come to the foreground as integral parts of the ongoing debate. The civil war between 1946 and 1949, the establishment and subsequent demise of the military dictatorship in 1967 and 1974, respectively, and the overall modernization process leading to the integration of Greece in the Common Market and the European Union were all marked by ambivalent representations of the essence of Greece. Thus, the question of the relations between Greece and Europe could not help being impregnated in smoky historical and ideological debates. Old and insoluble issues constantly re-emerge on an ever-changing social and political background.

At this point, some indications of post-war developments are called for. Undoubtedly, the most important single chapter of recent Greek history is the civil war and its tragic aftermath. In the late-1940s, communist insurgents and royalist nationalists fought each other to death, until the final victory of the latter led to the establishment of a repressive

---

5. As late as 1981, wage and salary earners in Greece did not represent more than two-thirds of the active non-peasant population. This is by far the lowest percentage among all European countries, where the rate of non-agricultural salarification was of the order of 80–95 per cent (OCED Labour Force Statistics). See also McGranachan et al. (1985: 216).

police state that dominated until the early 1960s. This is not the place to speak about the war itself, only of its discursive tones. On the one hand, within the communist Left, internationalist, anti-imperialist and anti-Western themes clearly dominated the scene. This was combined, however, with a pronounced 'Russophilia', with all its ultimately Oriental and Orthodox connotations. On the other hand, the nationalist camp was obviously characterized by strong traditionalist tenets, where the fatherland, the Church and the family were inevitably central. At the same time, however, nationalists could not help being vehemently pro-West, depending as they did on direct military and economic aid from Britain and the United States. Both sides were thus led to reproduce the discursive antinomies referred to (Tsoukalas 1980: 319f.). Though naturally leaning towards indigenous traditions, nationalist ideology was obliged to glorify the Western 'free world', while at the same time internationalist themes cohabited with the project of socialist emancipation of a Balkan East fiercely resisting the penetration of decadent Western culture. Both fronts found themselves entangled in the antinomies of their proper images. And this is probably one of the reasons why the fundamental imaginary dichotomy between East and West seems to have subsided in the 1940s and 1950s, at least in relative terms. The relentless political and ideological struggle between the Right and the Left was situated transversally in respect to deeper cultural cleavages. If both opponents referred to their own brand of authentic 'Greekness', the quintessential *Kulturkampf* did not play a significant role in the civil war. No side could afford to centre its discourse on cultural essences.

As passions eventually cooled, however, the old dilemmas came back to the forefront. But the situation had changed radically. The growing capitalist economy was by then distinctly separated both from the communist North and the underdeveloped Muslim East. Henceforth, there could be no further doubts concerning the country's political and cultural affiliations. Social and economic progress was envisaged as a function of the ideological and strategic umbrella of the United States, and Greece was by then definitely situated on the European side of the curtain separating East from West. This had already been the case, of course, in both the nineteenth and early twentieth centuries when modernizers like Venizelos had systematically promoted structural reforms. But the newly defined geopolitical and cultural separation from all other Balkan countries provided a decisive new factor inasmuch as the liberal-capitalist 'European destiny' of Greece presented itself in clearly 'Western' terms.

This was probably the turning point leading to the new perspectives opened up by the creation of the Common Market. Indeed, for the first time in its long history, Greece seemed able to disengage itself from its immediate geographical and cultural surroundings and to actively project the future within the broader framework of European developments. After having lived as a typically Balkan country among neighbours facing similar social and cultural problems (cf. Tsoukalas 1991: 1ff.), Greeks were becoming conscious of the long-term implications of their singular status. Paradoxically, the outcome of the civil war had contributed to a renewed glorification of 'brotherlessness'. The old imaginary cultural and ideological distinction between Greeks and nearby Slavic, Albanian and Muslim populations was enhanced. Potentially at least, Eurocentric Orientalist themes could once again be taken at face value: as the only 'free' and rapidly developing country in the area, Greece could plunge once more into its repressed fantasies. If the idea of Europe still functioned as the epitome of universal civilization, Greece had no reason to feel excluded in the long run. For the first time since independence, the country seemed to be following a path leading towards the 'final solution' of its congenital discursive contradictions.

These tendencies were further enhanced through the particular forms of social and economic development. Indeed, the main engines of growth in the 1950s and 1960s were shipping, tourism and remittances from Greek migrants abroad. In spite of its long-term structural shortcomings, this singular position of Greece in the international division of labour was not without positive consequences. Indeed, rapid horizontal and vertical mobility had been rapidly modifying the face of the country. Together with the economy, traditional, self-sufficient and autocentric behavioural patterns were being gradually eroded. The population of the metropolitan Athens area almost tripled, illiteracy practically disappeared and enrolment in third-level education soared. During the same period, social pressure was significantly relieved through massive emigration. Almost one-third of the country's active population, most of them of peasant origin, were absorbed in booming European economies, mainly in West Germany.

Emigration contributed not only to the relief of accumulated social tensions but also to the bridging of communication and cultural gaps with Western Europe. In a country where isolated peasant populations had been naturally bewildered and resentful of all forces, values and practices lying beyond their self-sufficient world, new prospects and possibilities were rapidly opening up. When most of the emigrants chose to be repatriated, they returned enriched not only with the money they had accumulated but also by the experience of a positive and familiar image of a developed Europe. Thus, first-hand awareness of the daily realities of the Western world penetrated wide strata of a population previously impervious to all foreign messages. The social effects of the booming shipping industry – it should be remembered that the Greek-owned fleet is the largest in the world – and of massive tourism, mainly catering to Europeans, ran in the same direction. It was becoming clear to all parties that further development was contingent upon continuing social and economic integration within a wider European area. The spectacularly increasing percentage of university-educated Greeks, most of them multilingual, was only the vanguard of the gradual cultural Westernization of the country.

Ironically, the European destiny of Greece was further consolidated, albeit indirectly, when in 1967 a military coup overturned the democratic government. Indeed, in contrast to the active role played by the CIA in the preparation of the coup and the subsequent support of the dictators by the American government, most European countries reacted vigorously. Greece was promptly expelled from the Council of Europe and many thousands of expatriate intellectuals, politicians and artists were offered shelter and jobs in most European capitals.

Thus, when the junta was overthrown and the new Prime Minster, Constantine Karamanlis, who had spent the seven junta years' self-imposed exile in Paris, officially sealed the 'European destiny' of the country, he was met with widespread acclaim. Despite the opposition of the Communist party – legalized after a quarter-century of underground activities – most Greeks felt both satisfied and proud when the country was finally accepted as a full-fledged member of the EEC on 1 January 1981. At last, Greece was an integral part of the developed – and by extension 'civilized' – West, not only on the symbolic but also on the institutional level.

This last statement, however, should be qualified. Until the late 1970s, the vigorous anti-imperialist stand of the orthodox aisle of the Communist party, which had split into Stalinist and Euro-communist factions, was seconded by the hardly less vociferous anti-EEC exhortations of the rising Socialist party under the leadership of Andreas Papandreou. And even if the latter's position shifted radically after he assumed power in 1981, it was the first time since the beginning of the century that the cultural demarcation between Europhilia and Europhobia seemed to correspond to a clear-cut political division between Right and Left. Though still invisible, the seeds of a new political front directly involving the political image of Europe had been planted.

The last twenty years of the twentieth century thus featured an explicit politicization of cultural discourses and antinomies. Indeed, the new conjuncture led to the resurrection of old themes in new forms. An important new element to be strongly underlined in this respect is that the persistence of the Greco-Turkish dispute enhanced the strong preoccupation with national security. If up to the century's end most threats of territorial integrity had been seen as emanating from the communist North, the main threat was by then seen as coming mainly from the East. The Turkish invasion of Cyprus in 1974 inaugurated a cold war that continues down to the present day to the effect that Greece is one of the very few European countries still suffering from an all-pervasive security syndrome. Military expenses continue to be the highest in Europe in relative terms. In this sense, the position of Greece in the European system led to a new ambivalence. Despite the fact that the protective political umbrella provided by the West is seen as strategically essential, the real or imaginary continuing threat from a NATO partner is naturally interpreted in the light of an unwillingness or incapacity of European allies and partners to offer protection and understanding. In view of this structural insecurity, the West is often represented as refusing to treat Greece as a rightful member of the 'civilized community' threatened by 'barbarians'. This is often interpreted in terms of a congenital 'European duplicity' or even as proof of the cultural complicity of an eternally anti-Orthodox West. Old fantasies are thus being continuously re-actualized to the effect that questions of identity and 'brotherlessness' give rise to explosive nationalist admixtures. Nationalist anxiety has provided the vehicle leading towards an exacerbation of cultural and religious fanaticism.

Furthermore, the rapid process of modernization pursued during the 1990s led to the exacerbation of internal social tensions. Indeed, for Greece to enter the EU as a solid partner, the country needed to conform to the social straitjacket imposed by the Maastricht treaty. Inevitably, the adoption of austere economic policies led to a significant growth in unemployment and to greater inequalities. Even more to the point, the gradual restriction of an enormous and unproductive public sector had deprived Greeks of their favourite socio-professional outlet. At the same time, underground economic activities seemed to be declining in relative terms while the extensive subsidies for agricultural production had reached their upper limit. Thus, even though the socialist governments in power for most of the 1990s resisted pressure to curtail the Welfare State, the new economic dynamism was not without its victims. The miracle of an economy featuring 'growth without development' seemed to have evaporated into thin air.

The political interpretation of this new development as a direct consequence of strong European pressure was almost inevitable. And there can be no doubt that this was the price to be paid for attempting a gradual normalization of Greek society on the basis of European blueprints. Indeed, the perspectives opened up by the versatile survival strategies that had been dominant since the end of the Second World War would gradually cease to be operational. It is no accident therefore that strong minorities should feel threatened by the coveted European destiny. Far from being a panacea, direct European competition and the new rules of an unknown game were dangerous and ominous. Clearly, for large strata that had reached relative financial well-being in the 1970s and 1980s, entering the pitiless globalized economy on their own terms would not be a piece of cake. It is no accident that while positive attitudes toward Europe were almost overwhelming until the late 1980s, registered negative voices grew steadily in the last years of the century.

It should finally be taken into consideration that at the end of the twentieth century massive immigration was rapidly modifying the traditionally ethnically homogeneous country. By then, foreigners, especially Albanians, represented over 10 per cent of the labour force, a fourfold increase in twenty years. Growing evidence of xenophobic and racist reaction was contributing to new forms of nationalist exhortations once more focused on an indigenous culture threatened in its trans-historical essential purity. And although the xenophobic discourse is not specifically anti-European, it serves to enhance all images of cultural self-sufficiency. Indeed, by their very nature, xenophobic tendencies are indivisible.

Thus, it seems as if the combination of increasing national insecurity, economic austerity and introspective xenophobia was impairing the political stability of the widespread pro-European consensus. This amounts to a tentative elaboration of a new anti-European political and cultural front combining components that stemmed from totally different intellectual and political origins. On the one hand, the extreme xenophobic and authoritarian Right calling for a closed cultural community, racial purity and 'law and order' was becoming more and more vociferous by the late 1990s. On the other hand, the radical anti-imperialist Left insisted at the same time on the need for a pronounced national isolation protecting the country from the nefarious effects of globalization. Finally, there are always some insignificant but strong-voiced minorities that call for more dynamic reaction against the Turkish threat. It is doubtful, however, whether the combination of these ingredients could have formed a coalition, were it not for the new role of the Church. Indeed, since his election in 1995, the charismatic Archbishop Christodoulos has been involved in redefining an unprecedented 'cultural front' on the basis of the country's threatened essences. After a transitory diminution of its prestige following open collaboration with the military junta – it is no accident that the colonels should have officially named their ludicrous regime 'Hellas of Christian Hellenes' – the Orthodox Church is once more trying to play a central political and cultural role.

## Conclusion

Thus, within this new context, the battle on trans-historic essences of 'Greekness' seems now to be more central to the political scene than at any other moment since the end of the civil war. The old debate between the antagonistic archetypes of Hellenes and *Romioi* is once more called upon to rationalize and substantiate the new emerging political fronts. Very characteristically, however, this is happening at the very moment when the European destiny of Greece seems to be irrevocably sealed. The Greek interpretation of the meaning of Europe thus seems to be undergoing considerable mutation when the access to the archetype of 'civilization' is nearer than ever before. Once more, it is the deep cultural ambivalence that seems to be coming to the forefront. In contrast to most other countries pondering the long-term effects of their European future, Greek Euroscepticism does not seem to be the product of divergent evaluations concerning the country's 'real' social, economic or diplomatic interests. And if, as things stand today, unmitigated anti-European feelings are limited to minorities, it is also true that these ideas do find occasional support among various strata of a population facing the unprecedented challenge of integration within a wider system.

One must conclude on an ironic mode. Essentialist and eventually even fundamentalist discourses seem to be rising at the very moment when the repressed dream of full integration in the European West is coming true. This only shows the persisting power of ancient discursive antinomies. As we have seen, the legacy of the glorified European meaning of ancient Greece could never be accepted at face value. And as we have also seen, the 'Helleno-Christian' synthesis did impede the crystallization of an antagonistic, if sometimes invigorating, modus vivendi between the two archetypal constructions. In this sense, probably more than the indigenous cultural element per se, it is mostly the long-established symbiotic synthesis between two nominally opposite conceptions that is threatened. The institutional realities within a united Europe will inevitably lead to new judicial and administrative regulations and norms that will not easily be circumvented with impunity. Like its name, its history and its language, Greece is now facing the necessity to normalize and standardize its political and behavioural culture. It is probably over the sacrifice of the country's essential ambivalence that most real or crocodilian tears are being shed. The most painful cultural and political choice is not the loss of a fixed tradition which is not threatened in itself, but the forced abandonment of anarchic and versatile behavioural, social and economic forms and practices. Truly, anti-materialist arguments are often invoked, modernizers being often looked down upon as vulgar Euro-gluttons to be sharply distinguished from a new unspecified brand of traditional idealists. But this is a deliberate misinterpretation of the individualistic, self-centred and normless behavioural patterns, which are really threatened by the impetus of the European normative conquest. Lamenting this irretrievable cultural loss, a prominent neo-Orthodox Greek intellectual recently spoke of a new *finis Graeciae*, thus reviving the lost ancient memories of the Roman conquest by the plunderer-general Mommius in AD 146. Literally, it is a process of belated mourning.

## References

Bernal, M. (1987), *Black Athena: The Afro-Asiatic Roots of Classical Civilization*, Vol. 1, New Brunswick, NJ: Rutgers University Press.

Curtius, E. (1865), *Greichische Geschichte*, Zweite Auflage, Band 1, Berlin: Weidmannsche Buchhandlung.

Derrida, J. (1991), *Donner du temps. La fausse monnaie*, Paris: Gallimard.

Fallmerayer, J.P. (1835), *Welchen Einfluss hatte die Beseizung Greichenlands durch die Slaven auf das Schicksal Athens und der Lanschaft Attika?*, Stuttgart und Turbigen.

Fermor, P.L. (1966), *Roumeli: Travels in Northern Greece*, London: Murray.

Gourgouris, S. (1996), *Dream Nation, Enlightenment, Colonization and the Institution of Modern Greece*, Stanford: Stanford University Press.

Herzfeld, M. (1987), *Anthropology in the Looking Glass*, Cambridge: Cambridge University Press, 1987.

Hobsbawn, E. and Ranger, T. (eds) (1993), *The Invention of Tradition*, Cambridge: Cambridge University Press.

Keeley, E. (1982), *Conversations with George Sepheris*, Athens: Agra.

Kitromilidis, P. (1983), 'The Enlightenment East and West: A Comparative Perspective on the Ideological Origins of the Balkan Political Traditions', *Canadian Review of Studies in Nationalism*, 10.

McGranachan, D., Pizzaro, E. and Richard, C. (1985), *Measurement and Analysis of Socio-economic Development: An Inquiry into International Indicators of Development and Quantitative Interrelations of Social and Economic Components of Development*, United Nations Research Institute for Social Development: Geneva.

Ricoeur, P. (1983), *Temps et récit: L'intrigue et le récit historique*, Paris: Seuil.

Said, E. (1991 [1978]), *Orientalism: Western Conceptions of the Orient*, Harmondsworth: Peguin [earlier edn Routledge & Kegan Paul].

St Clair, W. (1872), *That Greece might still be Free: The Philellenes and the War of Independence*, London: Oxford University Press.

Tort, P. (1989), *La raison classificatoire. Quinze études*, Paris: Aubier.

Tsoukalas, C. (1981), 'The Ideological Impact of the Civil War', in Iatrides, J. (ed.), *Greece in the 1940s: A Nation in Crisis*, Hanover and London: University Press of New England.

—— (1991), 'Enlightened Concepts in the Dark, Power and Freedom, Politics and Society', *Journal of Modern Greek Studies*, 9(1), pp. 1–22.

# –2–

# The Dual Appeal of 'Europe' in Italy
## *Mikael af Malmborg*

In the elections to the European Parliament in 1989 the Italians were asked if they were in favour of closer political unity within the European Community and if they wanted to give the European Parliament legislative powers. Of the 88 per cent who participated, 88 per cent gave an affirmative answer (*Britannica Book of the Year 1990*: 474). This is just one example that illustrates how the Italians have quite consistently maintained a positive attitude toward European unity. The economic and political integration of Europe has been a key to economic success and political stability, but Italy's Europeanness also has historical and cultural roots that stretch further back than the post-war integration process.

Italian nation-building has been characterized by an exceptional discrepancy between cultural and linguistic continuity and late political unification. As a *Kulturnation* Italy has a history that goes back to the Middle Ages and beyond. As a *Staatsnation* its history begins essentially in the 1860s with unification. The Italian meanings of 'Europe' must therefore be analysed in two different layers. In a cultural sense Italian society has long been recognized as a heartland of Western and European civilization. Modern European history, however, has had its gravitational centre to the north of the Alps, and Italy has been a laggard in terms of political and economic modernization.

Contemporary history appears very much as a fulfilment of universal ideals of perpetual peace and liberal democracy, at least in the Western part of the world. Yet, contemporary history cannot be understood solely as a linear progression, interrupted by occasional totalitarian backlashes. We still live in the wake of Romanticism, a general Western intellectual and literary movement that materialized in distinctly national forms and served to consolidate and 'nationalize' already existing territorial states or, as in Italy and Germany, to lay an intellectual and spiritual ground for unified and independent states.

The counter-forces generated by the Enlightenment continue to shape history, so that contemporary public opinion and decision-making must be seen as a blend of pure reason and romantic and organic ideals of society. The self-images, the historical and geographical memories and losses of memory that were established in the nineteenth-century processes of national consolidation, liberation or unification are by no means obsolete, although they are continuously being transformed. In real life the Enlightenment programme has always been blended with cultural, organic and particularist views of the Us and the Other. Romanticist national ideals and ideals of universal modernity are in continuous interaction.

## The Europeanism of Italy's *Risorgimento*

The unification of Italy was to a great extent the result of a traditional game of war and diplomacy, but the power-political achievements of Camillo di Cavour, Giuseppe Garibaldi and the Monarch, Victor-Emmanuel II, occurred against the backdrop of a qualitatively new vision of nationhood. The *Risorgimento* – reawakening – stemmed from an awareness that Italy was lagging behind and ought to catch up with Europe's enlightened and liberal order.

The unification and democratization of Italy implied a continuous compromise between a historical legacy of absolute monarchy, and ahistorical ideals of national and republican liberty. Although this was a fairly general feature of democratization processes in Europe, modern Italian history stands out as particularly marked by the contrasts between an inherited archaic reality and abstract visions of the future. Ideal types of 'nation', 'democracy' and 'Europe' are contrasted with an existing local reality (Galasso 1994: 16).

The high degree of identity between Italian culture and general European or Western civilization makes Italy an exception to the general nineteenth-century trend for each nation to search for its truly 'national' original myth to counter the avalanche of common Western or European culture. The Italians did not do that, and if they had done so the search would have been based on Virgil and other classics, written in Latin and thus not separable from the common European cultural heritage. In the construction of a modern Italian national identity there is no competing foundation myth to that of the classical Roman heritage. More 'Europe' can in this respect only reinforce Italy's own national identity. Conversely Italian culture has since long been recognized as a common European heritage, and this has given Italy a historical and cultural leading position in the construction of Europe.

The historian Federico Chabod underlines that 'nation' and 'Europe' should be seen as complementary concepts. The nineteenth century was an era of differentiation, but the framework of this process was a consciousness of a European whole. The main distinction in the Middle Ages had been between Christians and barbarians or pagans. In the days of Machiavelli, Europe began to be considered as an entity that was politically distinct from the rest of the world. Europe lived in freedom, Asia in tyranny. Europe was developed as opposed to the undeveloped world, dynamic in contrast to the idleness and apathy of other continents. The strongly nationalizing tendency of the nineteenth century, Chabod argues, was not the opposite of an enhanced European consciousness. The ideas of nation and Europe came hand in hand; they were intimately linked to each other. A European unity was only possible thanks to the diversity of the different historical developments of its component parts, the nations (Chabod 1961; 1974: 135–6).

Dante Visconti, similarly, emphasizes that the period of the *Risorgimento* was characterized by a massive secularization of the European idea. The debate on Europe was much livelier in the nineteenth century than it had been in the eighteenth century, but it was consistently discussed under the sign of the '*sentimento di nazionalità*' (Visconti 1948: 97–101; Bruyning 1994: 21).

Visconti's and Chabod's arguments are general but no doubt particularly apt for Italy. The idea that Europe constitutes a unity is widely diffused among Italian authors of the first half of the nineteenth century. In *Discorso sopra lo stato presente dei costumi dell'Italiani* (1824) the Romantic poet-philosopher Giacomo Leopardi argued that after the fall of French domination nationalistic prejudices were gone and there had emerged a stage of equality and cultural interaction between Europe's nations. In *Zibaldone* he wrote that 'its diverse societies . . . are so close to one another . . . that Europe forms one single family' (Puppo 1978: 192).

In a Romanticist manifesto, Giovanni Berchet's *Lettera semiseria di Giovanni Crisostomo*, there is the fundamental idea that all literatures should be recognized as equally valuable beyond and above any exclusive nationalism. Berchet writes that 'for me Homer, Shakespeare, Calderon, Camoes, Racine and Schiller are Italians as much as Dante, Ariosto and Alfieri. The Republic of letters is one and the same, and the poets are all compatriots therein' (*I manifesti romantici*; Puppo 1978: 186).

The author Giuseppe Montani turned against cultural and academic provincialism and called for a revitalized European humanistic culture of scholarly research and historiography. The free circulation of ideas through the active translation of foreign literature and new editions of classical texts would revitalize the enervated Italian literature and integrate it with the greater European culture. The aim was a universal literature that would be a manifestation of the historical process of unification of European civilization (Puppo 1978: 188).

The most prominent Europeanist was perhaps Giuseppe Mazzini (1805–1872). Mazzini saw the unification of Italy as a part of a spiritual renaissance for the whole of Europe. The nation was a moral and religious mission rather than a social and political programme, and Mazzini tried to promote this mission through popular movements, such as *Giovine Italia*, founded in 1832, and *Giovine Europa*, founded in exile in 1834. For Mazzini the nation was an element of a religion of humanity, and like all Italian democrats he saw Italy as a part of an ideal fatherland called Europe (Spadolini 1994: 8–9).

Mazzini took issue with those who confused national independence with intellectual isolation. He saw the history of European civilization as a continuing process of political, cultural and economic rapprochement of its various nations, reaching a decisive stage with the modern civic spirit of liberty. *D'una letteratura europea* begins with an epigraph attributed to Goethe: 'I catch a glimpse of the dawn of a European literature: no single people can call it theirs; everyone has contributed to its formation . . . There exists in Europe a concord of needs and desires, a common thought, a universal soul, which sets the nations on a path of conformity, a European tendency' (Mazzini 1933 [1829]; Puppo 1978: 189–90).

In his essay *On The Duties of Man* (1840) published in exile in London, Mazzini noted with satisfaction that 'at every page one talks of European federation, of European congress'. In stark contrast to the realities of Restoration Europe, Mazzini's concept of European unity was dynamic and progressive. In contrast to Romanticists such as Giovanni Berchet and Giuseppe Montani he envisaged a healthy competition for the prime position among the nations of Europe. Mazzini's fervent striving for national conformity, for an 'Italianization' of Italian society, bore the stamp of Christian eschatology, although he was anti-clerical and republican in his political actions. *Patria* and Europe were reconciled through the idea of mission. God had given each nation its own particular mission, and the harmonious totality of these missions would work for the common good, resulting one day in one *patria* for all humanity (Puppo 1978: 190).

In exile after 1834 Mazzini developed an idea of an 'Italian initiative', as opposed to the French primacy, ascribing to Italy a missionary guiding role into the new era of humankind. Italy ought to unite and gain independence not only as a duty given to her by Providence, but also to fulfil the mission of uniting Europe, as a third venture of universality under Italian leadership after those of ancient Rome and Roman Catholicism. This *Risorgimento* patriotism was guided by a religious spirit but it was also an expression of laic modernity, professing an idea of a new man who was able to liberate himself from every form of servitude and in an enlightened manner become the master of his own destiny (Gentile 1999: 16, 24).

A more explicitly Christian ideal of Italian nationality was elaborated by Vincenzo Gioberti. Gioberti merged the words of God with profane intellectual history in his own particular version of the myth of the moral and civic primacy of the Italians. In *Dal primato morale e civile degli Italiani* (1843), Gioberti presented an idea of how civil and political European unity, based on religious unity, would help overcome anarchy and war. The Pope was the natural arbiter of unity, peace and justice. The Vatican had given the first impulse to European civilization, and Italian history was identical with that of the papacy and the civilized Christian world. Italy, Gioberti claimed, was always, in civil and religious terms, the most cosmopolitan of nations. As the Catholic nation *par excellence* Italy was 'the creator, restorer and saviour of European civilization, destined to occupy the whole world and become universal'; it could rightfully call itself 'the mother nation of the human race'. As other nations had used Italy as an example in the past, they would continue to seek inspiration from Italy for their own *Risorgimenti*. Gioberti conceived of a unity of European literature and culture, but in contrast to Montani and Mazzini he saw it as a unity with Italy as its source and centre. In Gioberti's teleology Italy with Rome was the '*principio organico dell'unità europea*' (Gioberti 1843: 19, 76; Gentile 1999: 44–5; Puppo 1978: 191).

Following Croce's *History of the Nineteenth Century*, Dutch historian Lucas Bruyning divides Italian early nineteenth-century historiography into a neo-Guelf school (liberal-Catholic); a neo-Ghibelline school (liberal-laic); and a school of scientific, democratic historiography. These three schools had in common the conviction that there was a need for closer cooperation among the peoples of Europe, because a reordering of Europe would further the unification of Italy. The *Risorgimento* historiographers were deliberately *nazionalizzante*, whether they saw history as a path set by Providence that would carry a free Italy in a Christian Europe (as did the neo-Guelf Piemontese Cesare Balbo), sought national independence but refused to see papal Rome as the centre of Christian Europe (as the Sicilian Giuseppe La Farina), or treated history in a scientific, source-critical way (as the liberal Milanese positivist Carlo Cattaneo) (Bruyning 1995: 163–73, 216–17).

Scientific historians such as Cattaneo nurtured the most articulate and coherent vision of Europe. While the neo-Guelf notion of Europe was based on a rather traditional idea of balance of power, and the neo-Ghibellines were mainly concerned with the pervasive presence of the Church and were stuck in persistent anti-clericalism, Carlo Cattaneo elaborated a notion of 'Europe' as the 'natural consequence of a universal historical process that had advanced further in Europe than elsewhere'. He saw two tendencies at work in Europe: one unifying, of Asian origin, and one diversifying, which was inherently European. In exile in Switzerland after the abortive uprising of 1848, Cattaneo advocated a federal United States of Europe as a way of handling Europe's dual character of unity in variety and assuring peace and stability among its peoples (Bruyning 1994: 217; Tapparelli 1978: 444).

*Risorgimento* intellectuals elaborated both closed and open ideals of the nation. Italy, according to the former, should dwell on its own inherited greatness of the classical or Roman Catholic tradition rather than let itself be contaminated by foreign cultures. More dominant, however, was a vision of a European Italy, aware of the need to renew its civic life by closer contact with other nations (Fubini 1971: 20; Puppo 1978: 185). In terms of development and modernization, 'Europe' was often perceived as external to Italian identity, for instance in the *Rivista europea* (1841–), which saw its role as promoting awareness of foreign, and notably German, literature. Another similar review, *Crepuscolo*, drew on the Mazzinian notion of mission: every people represented an idea and had the mission to effectuate it, and knowledge of foreign literature was justified by a desire to expand the national literary arena. The Europeanizing agenda of *Crepuscolo* served the purpose of granting Italy a moral and intellectual framework, mediating connections with the outside world and placing it in the broad context of European culture (Puppo 1978: 193).

The thinking of Mazzini, Gioberti and others filtered down into various cultural and political movements, and the notions of mission and primacy developed into the most tenacious and seductive motifs of the Italian national myth. In various forms, and mixed with other ideologies and cultural movements, they recur all through the twentieth century (Gentile 1999: 46). Both Mazzini and Gioberti, however, regarded Italy's mission as civic and moral primacy. This implied no hatred towards other peoples and differed from imperialism in that it did not aim at political domination or injustice to foreigners.

The Europeanism of the Romanticists, Croce argued, was a result of their strong historical consciousness. They saw Europe 'as superior to the exigencies of the "spirit of the peoples" and the "nations", which they welcomed but considered to be just necessary and moments or antinomies fostering the unity of the Christian and European spirit' (Croce 1954 [1917]: 338). Bruyning points out that when *Risorgimento* thinkers referred to the unity of Europe they most often thought of *another* Europe than the existing one, for instance, Mazzini's notion of a Young Europe, as opposed to the 'Old' Europe of the *ancien régime*. The *Europeismo* of the Italian national debate before 1848 was an expression of an idealistic and progressive vision of history (Bruyning 1994: 21, 23).

## Complexes of Inferiority and Primacy

Parallel with an awareness of the noble heritage of the Italian peninsula, the Europeanism of the Italian Romanticism and *Risorgimento* was also much driven by a negative myth of the character of the Italians, of the scars imprinted on the mentality and habits of the Italians by centuries of servitude, backwardness and isolation from the currents of modern civilization. In his anatomy of the Italians Giacomo Leopardi regarded them as morally and intellectually inferior to other nations and lamented their cynical, buoyant, superficial and uncivil habits:

> Italy is, in moral terms, less endowed than perhaps any other European and civilized nation, because it lacks what has fostered and now confirms the progress of civilization, and has lost what the progress of civilization and the Enlightenment has destroyed. (Leopardi 1969 [1824]: 975; Gentile 1999: 38. Author's trans.)

This Italian self-image is also reflected in examples of usage of the term 'Europe' and its derivatives. The term *Europeismo* is registered for the first time in 1821, but only as a term in linguistics, of words or expressions that are common to several European languages, with either Greek or Latin roots or identical neologisms in several languages. Giacomo Leopardi wrote that *'si chiamino barbari i gallicismi, ma non (se così posso dire) gli europeismi, ché non fu mai barbaro quello che fu proprio di tutto il mondo civile, . . . come l'uso di queste voci che deriva dalla stessa civiltà e dalla stessa scienza d'Europa'* ('Gallicisms are called barbarous, but not (if I may say so) Europeanisms, which have never been barbarous since they are common to the whole civilized world, . . . such as the use of these terms that derive from the same civilization and science of Europe' (Author's transl.) (*Vocabolario Treccani*: 368).

A political usage was added in the early twentieth century. '*Europe-izzare*', and the reflexive '*Europeizzarsi*', appears for the first time in 1908, meaning 'to render conformable with European usage or taste, to give a European imprint to the civilization and habits of a country outside Europe' (*La Piccola Treccani*). Europeanization in this early sense signals a clear awareness of 'We' and 'They', of an 'Other' that possesses certain European features that the 'We' is exposed to or wants to acquire. It concerns territories and cultures outside Europe exposed to the political, economic and cultural penetration of the Europeans, but was also applied to Italian society itself.

Francesco De Sanctis, professor of literature and Italy's first Minister of Education, believed that he had found the cause of the defect in the 'Guicciardini man', the Renaissance Italian who was still alive in the national character and lived and acted in duplicity and simulation, cultivating solely his own *particulare*, for which he was ready to sacrifice fatherland, religion, liberty, honour, glory, in other words 'all that stimulates men to magnanimous action and makes a nation great' (De Sanctis 1957 [1869]: 21, 23; Gentile 1999: 42).

The Italian liberation movement was often seen as carrying a universal value. In 1911, on the occasion of the fiftieth anniversary of unification, *La Stampa* suggested that the heroes of the *Risorgimento* – Mazzini, Garibaldi and Cavour – should be seen as apostles, warriors and ministers of the principle for which the whole civilized world had longed, fought and suffered in the past century. 'With our revolution we have not only reconstituted the organism of one nation; we have augmented the beauty of the world, we have reconsecrated the nobility of life' ('Excelsior', in *La Stampa*, 20 April 1911; Gentile 1999: 43–4).

Such presumptuous claims to universality were the other side of what Emilio Gentile calls the 'burning inferiority complex' in relation to more developed countries that continued to be a driving force of Italian patriotism. As we have seen, this inferiority complex was balanced against a claim to primacy. All universal movements had emanated from the Italian peninsula: Roman civilization, Catholicism, Humanism and the Renaissance; the great cultural and intellectual movement that formed Modern Man. Through the *Risorgimento* the Italian genius had regained its role as 'the great mother of modern European civilization' (Gentile 1999: 44).

The men of the *Risorgimento* believed that the character of the Italians had to be remoulded. The call for a new moral and civic spirit of the people amounts to an entire genre and is still a persistent theme in the Italian national debate. For men like Cavour this was a duty entrusted to the liberal, monarchic State. For democrats and republicans such as

Mazzini it was an act of self-generation, a task for the Italian people itself. In any case it was a complicated task. Unlike older territorial states in Western and Northern Europe where a fairly solid state loyalty was in place before the era of democratization, Italy was democratized before the masses had been 'nationalized'. The Third Italy was born out of a marriage between monarchy and democratic ideals. The monarchic state could integrate Mazzini's 'religion of duty' and idea of a national civilizational mission by depriving them of their revolutionary and republican spirit, but regardless of whether it came from the top down or from the bottom up it was an immense task to simultaneously democratize society and forge a coherent nation state (cf. Lanaro 1992).

Within this national genre of self-examination 'Europeanization' has represented the remedy that can elevate the Italians to civic-mindedness and national solidarity. In spite of their internal disputes, both liberals and Marxists tend to treat Italy as a special case in relations to a supposedly normal West European development. In this respect the Italian history debate is reminiscent of the German *Sonderweg* discussion: just as German liberals were outmanoeuvred by Bismarck, Carbonari and Mazzini were marginalized by Cavour's Piemonte (Gramsci 1971: 118–19; Riall 1993: 52–3).

The Italian debate has often been built on ideal types of Italy and Europe. Mazzini elaborated manifestly ideal versions of the concepts of 'nation' and 'Europe' in his political programme. Croce analysed the main ideas of Italian history in the liberal era but failed to see the discrepancy between the history of political ideas and the history of social reality. Gramsci and his Marxist followers developed their own ideal types of European norm and Italian anomaly. Gramsci took it as a fact that where Mazzini's action party failed, the French Jacobins turned the bourgeoisie into the leading, hegemonic class and created the compact modern French nation. According to this view, the rise of fascism in the 1920s was the ultimate result of the 'passive revolution' of the *Risorgimento* that failed to integrate the masses. This schematic version of the French Revolution fits more with the self-image of French Jacobins than the lengthy and complex process of turning peasants into Frenchmen (Ginsborg 1979; Gramsci 1971: 79; Riall 1993: 52–4).

## Nation to Nationalism – Europeanism to Imperialism

The first half-century of Italy's existence as a nation state coincided with the generally rising tensions in Europe that culminated in war in 1914.

This challenged the Italians to revise their view of themselves and Europe. The Romanticist vision of harmony between Europe's Germanic and Latin cultures was replaced by a certain fear of the power of unified Germany and a more aggressive Italian nationalism. The myth of Rome gained in topicality. In culture and politics a tendency emerged to speak in defence of 'Latin civilization' against 'Germanic barbarism'. The cult of classical Romanness, which in the 1880s the poet Giosuè Carducci still combined with universal human ideals, in Gabrielle D'Annunzio assumed the character of an aggressive and exclusive nationalism. In *Canzone dei Dardanelli,* D'Annunzio inveighed against 'the old Europe avaricious and insane' (Puppo 1978: 195).

Toward the turn of the century enlightened and emancipatory nation-building was overshadowed by autarchy and imperialism, although the Italian conception of nation remained largely voluntarist, in contrast to naturalist and racist ideologies prevalent north of the Alps. The nation was still seen as a historical formation and not as a natural fact (Gentile 1999: 35–7). The *Risorgimento* perspective gave a particular ideological twist to Italian imperialism. In the Age of Empire the democratic Left was generally anti-nationalist and anti-imperialist, and Italy's own recent battle for national independence led the majority of the Italian political class to reject colonial expansion. On the other hand, with the *Risorgimento* fresh in mind, the myths of national independence and 'national' expansion in Africa were confused to the extent that the latter appeared as the logical or even ethical complement to the former (Bariè 1983: 154–5).

Italian nationalists developed their own peculiar justification in the form of the 'imperialism of the poor people'. The Italophile German sociologist, Roberto Michels, dismissed the nationality principle as a 'symptom of weakness'. Once a nation had gained independence, he argued, it naturally strove to transcend it. Providing a contrast to the power-political aspirations, strategic considerations, speculation and commercial calculations of English, German, Belgian and French imperialism, the Italians aimed only at providing bread, work and social dignity to the citizens of 'the great martyr of nations' (Michels 1914; Bariè 1983: 155–6; Gentile 1999: 105). Another theorist of Italian imperialism, Enrico Corradini, saw imperialism as a class struggle between nations, in which Italy, the poorest of Western nations, ought to fight for the 'proletariat' against the rich and bourgeois nations of Western Europe. This theme was also taken up in the official celebration of the invasion of Tripoli in 1911 (Bariè 1983: 156).

The national celebration in 1911 of the fiftieth anniversary of unification was surrounded by protests against 'the national lie'. Socialists, republicans and Catholics boycotted the celebration. The Florentine vanguard review *La Voce* published a theme issue on the southern question which began with an article with the symbolic title *Le due Italie*. The reality of this great Third Italy, wrote the anti-nationalist lawyer, Eduardo Cimbali, was that half a century after unification the nation was still painfully divided in two, 'one rich, healthy, cultivated, progressive and civil; and the other poor, segregated, malaria-infected, illiterate, retarded and barbaric: two Italies of which one is l'*Italia europea*, and the other l'*Italia africana*' (Cimbali 1912: 21–2; quoted in Gentile 1999: 65).

The ideal of nation and Europe was renounced in favour of a supposedly more authentic idea of state, empire and (belligerent) expansion. Modern times needed a new relationship between citizen and the state that left little room for the principles of individual liberty, parliamentary rule and, as Benito Mussolini pointed out, 'elitism' of the *Risorgimento*. Mussolini's conversion from socialism to fascism entailed a fusion between the myths of revolution and nation, and the aim of the fascist revolution was to forge a more homogeneous nation-state than that of the *Risorgimento* liberals. Two types of patriotism stood against each other. The progressive and democratic myth of nation turned away from great-power struggle and suggested Switzerland, Belgium, Holland, Norway and Sweden as models for the new Italy. These countries proved that a solid national creed was compatible with humanism, pacifism, democracy and liberty (Gentile 1999: 126).

Against organic and imperial nationalism the review *L'Unità*, founded in 1911 by the democratic socialist and federalist Gaetano Salvemini, defended a 'democratic nationalism' of Mazzinian inspiration. Against the myth of *La Grande Italia*, Salvemini in 1913 declared himself a citizen of '*la Piccola Italia*', 'of the Italy that is just liberating itself from centuries of intellectual and moral misery' (Gentile 1999: 84).

Similarly Benedetto Croce set himself the task of forming 'a modern Italian consciousness which is European and national'. Croce wanted to keep alive the individuality of the national consciousness while acknowledging the forces of modernization and internationalization. He saw the nation as a vital nucleus capable of eliminating some influences and absorbing others, and integration with Europe's intellectual and cultural life was a vital ingredient in this humanistic nationalism (Croce 1966: 39).

Croce was the main advocate of the old liberal European ideal, and kept alive the consciousness of a European spiritual and cultural unity in the totalitarian era – something that also amounted to a defence of reason, culture and science against politics. Croce's notion of Europe was an integral part of his 'religion of liberty', which in turn was closely connected to his view of Christianity. For Croce, liberalism was an unrenounceable ethical ideal, and to confess a Christian identity implied inscribing oneself in the Western cultural tradition of humanism, Enlightenment, Romanticism, liberalism, freedom, equality, and universal fraternity. Croce's discussion of political or legal structures was always subordinate to the moral problem of Europeanness.

As nationalist and imperialist ideals gained official status, Croce traced the thread of modern European history in the progressive development of the ideal of liberty that had sowed the seed of a new nationality in people's minds, a European nationality. He focused on the period from 1780 to 1830 as the classical, 'Hellenic' epoch of European culture and insisted that 'we all live in a common European culture' (Croce 1912; 1949: 282, 286). His *History of Europe in the Nineteenth Century* ends with an optimistic vision of a dawn of a new European consciousness, a new nationality, which would make the hearts of Europeans beat for their common fatherland in much the same way as a Neapolitan and a Piemontese had come together and united Italy (Croce 1932: 354).

This ideal of nation and Europe stands out as remarkably harmonious compared to most other national developments of the nineteenth century. It was also a far cry from the totalitarian reality of Italy and Europe in the 1930s. It was a remnant of an abandoned liberal idealism, but would also serve as a model – in a more materialist form – for the reconstruction of Italian democracy after 1945.

## The Fascist Turn Against Europe

The First World War appeared for many Italians as the twilight of the Mazzinian vision of a European family of nations. Others saw the war as a regenerating force, the glorious confirmation of Italy's greatness, a rite of passage to the status of great power. In this endeavour Italian nationalists drew heavily on their country's classical heritage, and combined it with an exaltation for modernity and industrial productivity. The precedent of the Roman legionaries endowed the Italian soldiers in the Libyan desert with a higher purpose, a *missione civilizzatrice*.

The decade from 1912 to 1922 was a time of struggle between nationalism and internationalism, and also between two opposed myths of nation. In 1912 the socialist party abandoned the reformist path, which might have led to a reconciliation of socialism and nation, and embarked upon a revolutionary path. More generally, ideals of national state and liberal democracy parted ways. For religious, ideological and social reasons large parts of the middle and working classes failed to see the existing state as their *patria*. For socialists, Catholics and republicans the state did not represent their 'true' Italy (Gentile 1999: 76, 79).

The new ambitious *italianismo* aimed not only at military conquest and colonial expansion, but at the creation and affirmation of an Italian modernity. At the origin of this *italianismo*, Gentile writes, 'was a conflict between the inferiority complex that the new generations felt vis-à-vis more advanced European nations, and their faith in the inherent virtues and greatness of the Italian nation'. Furthermore, this decade was decisive as a precursor of the civil war that would divide Italy from 1943 to 1945. The protagonists were much the same in the two periods, and both struggles were conceptualized by both sides in terms of a struggle between 'nation' and 'anti-nation' and, one might add, 'Europa' and 'anti-Europa' (Gentile 1999: 87, 98).

To this was added the Catholics' slow but fundamental adaptation to the national myth. The Vatican argued forcefully that a durable patriotism could never be achieved without reference to Catholicism. The Christian ethic could after all be combined with patriotism, and the Catholics gradually presented themselves as authentic representatives of the Italian nation. The nation, Father Agostino Gemelli argued, was not in fact an arbitrary product of Man's free will or given by nature, but was wanted by God and Providence (Gemelli 1918: 52–8; Gentile 1999: 130–1). Italy acquired its own Catholic myth of nation and ultimately caught up with the process that had long provided rulers elsewhere in Western Europe with a firm amalgam between Church and State.

Fascist intellectuals saw it as their task to remedy the excessively bourgeois, liberal and 'Europeanist' character of Italy's liberal era. The philosopher and politician Giovanni Gentile argued that the essence of the national revolution was 'redemption from that old Italy, proverbial among the European peoples for its incompetence, for its individualism, for its weak sense of state, for its tendency to close itself off in private egoism and the infinite abstraction of arts and intellectual speculation' (G. Gentile 1920: 71; E. Gentile 1999: 143). 'Anti-*Risorgimento*' was a concept that circulated in the fascist era, intended to signal a rejection of Italy's liberal modern revolution. Linked to this was an anti-Europe standpoint. During the harshest years of the fascist regime, a review appeared called *Antieuropa: rassegna mensile di azione e pensiero della giovinezza rivoluzionaria fascista*, published with official support by Asvero Gravelli. The review made great effort to imprint the contrast between the principles of the French Revolution and its *Risorgimento* off-shoot, and the new fascist order of submission, hierarchy and empire.

In their evaluation of the *Risorgimento*, however, the fascists were split into two camps. Giovanni Gentile's branch sought their inspiration in the historical Right and had Vincenzo Gioberti as their model. Another group led by Curzio Malaparte juxtaposed *l'Italia barbara* with *l'Italia civile* and wanted to reconstruct Europe as it had been before the *Risorgimento*. They turned against 'the European contamination', the Jacobin, revolutionary deviation. Some of them went as far as to try to rehabilitate Cardinal Ruffo and the supporters of the *Santa Fede* who had fought against Garibaldi (Spadolini 1994: 11).

*Antieuropa* insisted on the need to change the Italians physically, even through sterilization of those who suffered from serious mental illness (Lyttelton 1998: 226–7). The racial campaign of the fascists that started in 1938 was closely linked to an anti-bourgeois campaign that sought to eradicate the pacifist norms of the bourgeoisie, defined not as an economic class but as a political and moral category. The fascists were preoccupied with the low fertility of the middle classes, and believed they had found the reason for this 'demographic decadence' in 'bourgeois egoism', the excessively rational and calculating spirit of advanced bourgeois societies and the institution of celibacy. The fascist ambition to create a new man also included an ambition to transform people's spontaneous body language. The form of address 'Lei' was ridiculed as a remnant of courteous deference. Shaking hands was condemned as a symbol of nineteenth-century bourgeois society and replaced with a Roman salute. Traditional social deference was perceived as an obstacle to modern military and political discipline, based on a hierarchy of merits, equality and submission to the State. The racial policy aimed at improving the physical character of the Italians, and in fascist Italy there was room neither for the autonomous family nor for the hand-shaking, courteous European.

## Post-war National Consolidation – European Integration

In opposition to the fascist and Nazi *Neuordnung,* ideas of a new democratic Europe emerged in prison camps and exile. The Italian contribution to this emerging debate was often federalist – for instance, the *Manifesto per l'Europa libera e unita*, edited by Ernesto Rossi and Altiero Spinelli on Ventotene prison island in 1941. This and many other texts by communists, socialists, liberals and radicals testify to a vivid Italian interest in European federalism during and after the war.

The Italian early post-war debate was saturated with *Europeismo*. Italy's return to democracy was initially accompanied by an intellectual and emotional despair with nation statehood. The fall of the fascist regime spelled the end of monarchy and imperialism, and Italy's waning economic and political stability closed off the option of splendid sovereignty. The return of democracy, the fall of the monarchy, the reconstruction of Italian unity and the desire to unite Europe made the early post-war era look like a second *Risorgimento*.

After 1945 it was imperative to keep the *Risorgimento* idea of nation separate from the imperial or totalitarian ideals of nationalism, as historian Rosario Romeo and many others underlined, and on this sole point fascists and democrats could perhaps agree. Where the former's concept of nation had been totalitarian, imperialist and anti-European, the latter's was liberal, democratic and European. In the spirit of Mazzini the nation was seen as a concept of progress in European society, and for the post-war democratic generation it was a natural step from nation to European federation (Spadolini 1994: 10).

'Europe' became subject of an '-ism', signifying movement towards universalism and modernity. The term *Europeismo*, referring to the political, economic and cultural unification of Europe, had appeared already in 1917, and '*europeista' (uniformare alla cultura e al modo di vivere europei, l'acquisire tale cultura*) in 1933, but the terms only began to be used more often after 1945, both in relation to other European countries and in the context of Europe's relation to (former) colonies. Some examples of first uses illustrate this: '*diseuropeizzare*' (1948), '*europeizzazione*' (1952); '*eurocentrico*' (1963), '*eurocentrismo*' (1967), '*eurocomunismo*' (1975), '*eurocrate*' (1963), '*eurodeputato*' (1980) and '*eurolandia*' (1998).

*Europeismo* became an established term for European integration, a political and intellectual movement, defined in the encyclopaedias *Il Vocabolario Treccani* and *La Piccola Treccani* as 'the fundamental cultural and historical affinity that links the peoples of Europe, which tends to promote a progressive rapprochement between the European nation-states with the ultimate aim of constructing a spiritually and politically united Europe'. It has its roots in the cosmopolitan component of the French Revolution, often discussed in the course of the nineteenth century, but it was only after the Second World War that 'it lost its elitist character' and gave rise to political and juridical organizations and an economic and political integration process.

In the comprehensive *Enciclopedia del Novecento* (1977), there is a ten-page article on *Europeismo* by Altiero Spinelli, tracing the implementation of the idea of one nation, one state, *superiorem non recognoscens*, from the French Revolution to the Second World War – carrying the European peoples, in the prophetic words of the Austrian poet Grillparzer, *'von der Menschheit, durch die Nationalität, zur Bestialität'* (from Humankind, through Nationality, to Bestiality) – to the three main ideas of post-war planning: federalism, functionalism (the Mitrany and Monnet methods) and confederalism (exemplified with the policies of Churchill and de Gaulle).

The supplement (1998) comprises an equally comprehensive article on *Europeismo* by Antonio Giolitti and Sergio Romano, covering the most recent developments. The contents of these articles are not very different from those in any other national encyclopaedia. The difference is that *Europeismo* is presented as an '-ism'.

It should be emphasized that the post-war *Europeismo* did not elaborate just a single conception of Europe: different political, cultural or social groups in Italian society laid out their own preferred ideas. There were at least three distinct visions of Europe – a Catholic Europe, a workers' Europe, and a Western and lay Europe, of which the two former were dominant. The Western and lay Europe – dwelling on the traditions of the French Enlightenment and spirit of 1789, German nineteenth-century philosophy and British liberal democracy – was cultivated by a rather limited section of the educated upper and middle classes. In geographical terms France, Germany and Britain were always included, while Scandinavia and the Balkans were most often on the margins or outside all these three conceptualizations of Europe. To this should be added the tide of American technical, scientific and cultural influence that swept over Italy as everywhere else during the cold war. The main points of reference of the man in the street, Antonio Varsori suggests, were probably not Europe but a combination of local and regional traditions, and new myths and models that originated in the United States (Varsori 1993: 16–17, 23).

The post-war Christian democratic republic was devoted to European unity but also had a firm anchorage in the Atlantic security community. The construction of Europe was complemented with other frameworks, and archive-based studies show that the European integration policy of the Italian government was not as unconditional as the public rhetoric might suggest. The Pleven Plan for a European Defence Community in 1950 aroused no enthusiasm in Rome, and Prime Minister De Gasperi regarded NATO and the United States as the guarantors of Italian security. Even so, to do like the British and reject the European Defence Community plan was out of the question. In order to carry out such a policy,

Foreign Minister Carlo Sforza argued, a country would have to posses an economic and military great-power potential that Italy did not have. When De Gasperi devoted himself to a European Political Community beside the EDC, it was not as an expression of European idealism but as a *Flucht nach vorn*, which aimed at countering the negative consequences of a pure defence community (Magagnoli 1999: 77–8).

Italy sought a balance between Western European integration and cohesion of the Atlantic area, and was keen to assure active British and American participation. As European integration was a rather uncertain undertaking, Washington remained a much more important point of reference than Paris in security matters, and Italy furthermore wanted to bring Britain into the European Economic Community as a counterweight to Franco-German dominance. As Ambassador Roberto Ducci put it in 1963: 'Italy not being able to be independent by herself, and Europe being unable to proceed with real integration, then the more wealthy and more distant master is always the best one' (Nuti 1996: 115).

There was nevertheless a strong undercurrent of Europeanness in Italian post-war society. European projects enjoyed clear popular good-will in comparison to other international undertakings, such as the decision to join the Atlantic Pact in 1949. The decision was preceded by a debate in the Chamber of Deputies that lasted two nights and three days, during which Prime Minister Alcide De Gasperi and Foreign Minister Carlo Sforza had to fight against a large but patchy armada made up of pacifists, neutralists, Marxists, Catholics and advocates of '*Italia farà da sè*'. The entire concept of alliance gave uneasy associations: the pact with Nazi Germany was still fresh in people's minds. One of the most applauded speeches was the socialist leader Pietro Nenni's denunciation of the constraints of alliances, referring to the Steel Pact between Italy and Germany in 1939. De Gasperi and Sforza managed to convince the Christian democratic left, the liberals and the socialist right to accept the Atlantic Pact only when they argued that there Italy would rejoin the group of countries with which they intended to '*costruire l'Europa*' (Romano 1999). While alliance and Atlanticism were contentious concepts in the Italian context, a reference to Europe was resonant of national progress, liberalism and unity.

## Towards a Consensus of Nation and Europe

The absence of the Roman Catholics had been the weak spot of Italian unification, and it was really only after 1945 that the Church became a pillar of Italian political life. The defeat of 1943–45 forced the Church to reconsider its view of what would come after fascism. Pius XII originally advocated a sort of 'Spanish' solution with an authoritarian Catholic regime. With the victories of the Resistance and the democratic parties, however, the Church decided to support the Christian democrats, who were rapidly transformed into a mass party. The party leader De Gasperi argued in 1947 that the Catholic faith was the true cement of the nation. In the cold war the Catholics' loathing for communism prevailed over their traditional aversion towards liberal capitalist democracy. Under the pressure of the cold war the Church ultimately issued a discreet *expedit* after two centuries at loggerheads with modern Western society.

'Little Europe' might have been a community of predominantly Catholic states, but the post-war European integration project was not a particularly Catholic project. As we have seen, before 1945 'Europe' had appeared as an aspiration of lay and republican thinking rather than a Catholic idea in Italian nation-building. The idea of a United Europe had historically had a liberal, national and often anti-clerical content. Rather than a return ticket to *Respublica Christiana*, 'Europe' represented a break-up of the old order and the entry for Italy in to the club of modern, rationalized nation states.

In spite of being the leader of the Christian democrats, De Gasperi recognized that the presence of the Vatican as a state within the state was still a problem for Italy and one reason why the country needed a united Europe, in addition to the need to find jobs for the masses of unemployed labourers and to get outside support in the fight against domestic communism. Much as the papacy had been recognized as the main obstacle to Italy's unification ever since the days of Machiavelli, De Gasperi saw a need for a new European construction to assure the stability of the First Republic (Barzini 1968: 191–2).

It is true that when Italy contributed to the creation and consolidation of the EEC it was a country under firm Christian democratic rule, and some people within this little Europe were sceptical about integration precisely on this ground, much like the majority in Scandinavia or in Britain. The French socialist President, Vincent Auriol, in 1951 dismissed De Gasperi, Schuman and Adenauer as *'la triple alliance cléricale'*; they were *'trois tonsures sous la même calotte'* (Canavero and Durand 1999: 4).

If Catholicism promoted European integration it was in its capacity of a transnational confession, in contrast to nationally organized Protestant Churches. Individual Catholics were politically active but the Church as an organization was not engaged in the project of uniting Europe. The Popes sometimes spoke in favour of a united Europe, and the practical works of the Church contributed to reconciliation across national borders, but the Italian bishops were largely absent from the aspiring European unification movement in North and Central Italy. Canavero and Durand conclude that, even if never rejected, the idea of the European construction did not occupy a prime place in the values of a good Catholic, at least not until fairly recently (Canavero and Durand 1999: 5).

Furthermore, when the Italian communist party became increasingly Euro-communist, it accentuated the lay character of European integration. The Euro-communist movement rejected the subordination of all communist parties to the Soviet doctrine in one monolithic world communist movement, and defended the right of each party to base its policy on the traditions and needs of its own country. By increasingly recognizing its national identity and affiliation with the West European tradition, the PCI remained Italy's second-largest party. When it changed its name to Democratic Party of the Left in 1991 and ultimately seized power at national level, its main foreign contacts and sympathies had already long been with European socialist and labour parties, although it had never explicitly renounced its links with Moscow.

There had been several competing visions of Europe after the Second World War, but it was the Western and lay concept of Europe that won out in the long term. The post-war European integration process resulted neither in a Europe of the Church nor in a Europe of the proletariat, and Europe as a conservative revolution (an idea with some attraction as a way of countering the fascist reality in the inter-war years) was of marginal importance in Italian post-war debate. Italy's post-war history can best be described as a continuous consolidation of the Western and lay idea of nation and Europe. The historical achievement of the cold war era was that this project gradually came to enjoy the support of clerical and socialist forces as well. In the post-war construction of an Italian identity, 'Europe' did not represent a return to the old clerical order or the resurrection of the Holy Roman Empire, but connoted nation-building, the separation of religion from politics, modernization, secularization and democratization. What began as a counter-movement to the clerical and monarchical hierarchies of the *ancien régime* became in this way a project of consensus and national consolidation. It can be added, however, that in its geographical scope, its search for community and striving for progress towards an unattainable goal, the European integration project rests on centuries of Christian civilization. In this sense Italy's Europeanism is a form of secularized Catholicism, in much the same way as the Scandinavian social democratic welfare state is secularized Protestantism.

At pamphlet level the Italian European sometimes discussed Europe as an alternative to the nation state, and as in other countries with a totalitarian past the nation state has to some extent remained a dubious concept. On the real political agenda, however, there was never a choice between the nation and Europe. It was always an issue of national reconstruction and development within a suitable macro-regional framework.

If the European framework has been an instrument for the unification and consolidation of the Italian nation state, might Italy then turn away from 'Europe' when it is no longer instrumental to national needs? Several arguments can be made against such a pragmatic view in the Italian case. Regional separatism and disintegration destabilized Italian politics in the 1990s but were by the end of that decade not yet associated with a turn against Europe, as was often the case north of the Alps. In Italy, as elsewhere, the fall of communism became a motive for further integration rather than disintegration. The faction of the communist party that opposed the 'social-democratization' of the Left in the 1990s continues to be a significant force in Italian politics in the early 2000s, but is no longer the nucleus of a fundamentally different idea of Italy and Europe. To the traditional communist opposition has been added a type of post-Marxist, feminist and environmentalist opposition that sometimes takes a stand-point, as in the Maastricht debate, *Contro l'Europa* (Magli 1996). This kind of alternative is akin to similar movements in Britain, the United States and Scandinavia but in Italy is much less influential.

The inherent Europeanism of the Italian national tradition should on the other hand not be taken deterministically. Italy is located at the rim between two geopolitical zones and two civilizations: Europe and the Mediterranean. This geopolitical divide is reflected in the internal North–South divide that has marked Italy through the centuries, and has also left the country with a Mediterranean alternative to its European calling.

Let us make a counterfactual experiment. With a slightly different balance of power between Christian democrats and socialists and communists in 1947–48 we might have had a forceful Italian democratic socialism, not unlike the Swedish one, with a Palmiro Togliatti, or later an Enrico Berlinguer, who on the basis of Italy's geopolitical location between East and West could have developed an imaginative third-way ideology and an active neutrality policy. Such a policy could easily have been inserted into a narration of a special Italian tradition going back to Mazzini and Michels of Italy's calling as a shining example and a 'moral imperialist of the poor'. Such an Italy could have found plenty of room for itself as a neutral mediator between the cold war blocs in much the same way as Sweden did in the North or Austria in Central Europe.

Instead of a Christian democratic hegemony firmly anchored in Europe and the West, which in due course forced the Italian communists to distance themselves from Moscow and Europeanize themselves, such a neutralist and democratic socialist Italy could have claimed to be as much a true inheritor of a long, genuine Italian tradition as a sponsor of the Europeanism that is a salient feature today. Italy would then have been more like Austria or Sweden, facing the same kind of problems of mental adaptation after 1989, but the entire European project would of course have been a different one without Italy.

It is not a likely projection but a useful counterfactual exercise to remind us how little it might take to give a geopolitical framework that opens up for the cultural construction of a radically different national community.

## Conclusions: The Dual Appeal of Europe

As we have seen in this chapter, the positive meaning of 'Europe' is profoundly rooted in Italy's national tradition. The nineteenth-century liberal idea of the 'nation' was formulated as an integral part of the idea of Europe. The heritage of the *Risorgimento* prescribes a harmony between national and supranational unity. The *Risorgimento* was seen as a more general reordering of Europe along the lines of republican, liberal and democratic ideals that were largely transalpine imports. The forging of a liberal Italian nation state after 1860 was inherently combined with openness toward French republicanism, German idealism and British liberalism. Europeanization carried strong connotations of modernization, of catching up, of remedying the perceived anomalies of Italian society.

When thereafter the fascist movement explicitly renounced the kind of European liberalism that had prevailed in Italy after the *Risorgimento*, the Resistance movement became more inclined to identify itself as European. It was only in the imperialist and fascist eras that the concepts of nation and Europe were formulated in opposition to one another. This experience meant that the Italian understanding of Europe was drawn along unusually clear lines. Negative uses of 'Europe' are conspicuous by their absence outside early twentieth-century imperialism and fascism. In the reconstruction after 1945 Italy gained substantial political and economic rewards from the process of European integration. The concept of Europe was instrumental to the construction of a new democratic national consensus, beginning with the liberal middle ground and Christian democrats and gradually expanding to include socialists and

Euro-communists. 'Europe' stood as a promise of modernization, democracy and stability.

Italy's consistent devotion to Europe after 1945 has had a clear economic or political rationale, but if one treats this choice for 'Europe' as a mere response to political or economic problems one fails to explain the basic trust in Europe that is a salient feature of Italy's national tradition. From an Italian point of view, 'Europe' has the dual appeal of working as a larger cultural self and as an external political structure that guaranteed national stability, democracy, prosperity and modernity. In contrast to what is the case in the northern peripheries of the continent, the question of 'Europe' is present as a project of building a common future together with a circle of nations that share a common civilization and historical heritage, whether classical or Christian, with Rome as one essential epicentre. In the Italian tradition, nation and Europe have always been interwoven. Both the Enlightenment and the Romantic traditions are ingrained with positive attitudes towards 'Europe' that *preceded* the articulation of solutions to particular economic and political problems in the post-war era. This does not mean that the state elite is less prone than its counterparts elsewhere to formulate its policy priorities in terms of national interest, nor does it mean that Europe always comes first in Italian foreign policy. There have all the time been Atlantic, Mediterranean or other regional complements or alternatives to Europe. It does, however, help explain why the Italian electorate has a basic confidence in the European unification project that inclines it to accept efforts to integrate Italy into a European political edifice that political leaders in many other countries, especially in North-west Europe, need to formulate and justify in more explicit rational-interest terms. Italy's 'yes' to Europe comes from the heart as much as from the brain, just as much as the scepticism of many Danes, Swedes and British is a matter of feeling as well as thinking.

## Acknowledgement

The author wishes to thank Dr Ilaria Favretto, Milan, for valuable comments on a draft of this chapter.

## References

*Antieuropa: rassegna mensile di azione e pensiero della giovinezza rivoluzionaria fascista*, published by Asvero Gravelli.

Bariè, O. (1983), 'L'Europa e il Mediterraneo dall'unità d'Italia alla prima guerra mondiale', in *L'Unità d'Europa: il problema delle nazionalità*. Atti del XVIII convegno internazionale di studi italo-tedeschi, Merano: Istituto culturale italo-tedesco: 145–60.

Barzini, L. (1968), *The Italians*, London: Penguin.

Battaglia, S. (ed.) (1968), *Grande Dizionario della Lingua Italiana*, Turin: Unione Tipografico–Editrice Torinese.

Bruyning, L.F. (1994), *Europa in de Italiaanse geschiedschrijving van de eerste helft van de negentiende eeuw*, doctoral dissertation, Amsterdam University.

Calcaterra, C. (ed.) (1951), *I manifesti romantici, del 1816 e gli sctritti principali del conciliatore sul romanticismo*, Turin: Unione tipografico-editrice torinese.

Canavero, A. and Durand J.-D. (1999), 'Les phénomènes religieux et l'identification européenne', Paper presented at the conference Les identités européennes au XXe siècle – Diversités, convergences et solidarités, University of Paris I, Sorbonne, 30 September–2 October 1999.

Chabod F. (1961), *L'idea di nazione*, Bari: Laterza.

—— (1974), *Storia dell'idea d'Europa*, Bari: Laterza.

—— (1996) [1st Italian edn 1951], *Italian Foreign Policy: The Statecraft of the Founders*, Princeton: Princeton University Press.

Cimbali, E. (1912), *Esiste l'idea di patria e di patriottismo?*, Rome.

Croce, B. (1912), *De Sanctis e il pensiero tedesco*, Bari: Laterza.

—— (1954 [1917]), *Teoria e storia della storiografia*, Bari: Laterza.

—— (1932), *Storia d'Europa nel secolo decimonono*, Bari: Laterza.

—— (1949), *Una Famiglia di patrioti ed altri saggi storici e critici*, Bari: Laterza.

—— (1958), 'Cultura germanica in Italia nell'età del *Risorgimento*', in: *Uomini e cose della vecchia Italia*, Vol. II, Bari: Laterza.

—— (1966), *Memorie della mia vita*, Naples.

De Mauro, T. (ed.) (1999), *Grande Dizionario dell'Uso*, Turin: Unione Tipografico-Editrice Torinese (UTET).

De Sanctis, F. (1957), *Saggi critici*, ed. L. Russo, vol III, Bari: Laterza.

*Enciclopedia del Novecento* (1977), Rome: Istituto della Enciclopedia Italiana.

*Enciclopedia Italiana di Scienze, Lettere ed Arti*, Rome: Istituto della Enciclopedia Italiana. Fondata da Giovanni Treccani, 3rd suppl. 1949–1960, 4th suppl. 1961–1978.

Fubini, M. (1971), *Romanticismo italiano*, Bari: Laterza.

Galasso, G. (1994), *Italia - nazione difficile: Contribuito alla storia politica e culturale dell'Italia unita*, Florence: Felice Le Monnier.

Gemelli, A. (1918), *Principio di Nazionalità e amor di Patria nella dottrina cattolica*, Turin.

Gentile, E. (1999), *La Grande Italia: Acesa e declino del mito della nazione nel ventesimo secolo*, Milan: Mondadori.

Gentile, G. (1920), *Dopo la vittoria*, Florence.

Ginsborg, P. (1979), 'Gramsci and the era of bourgeois revolution in Italy', in J.A. Davis (ed.), *Gramsci and Italy's Passive Revolution*, London: Croom Helm.

Gioberti, V. (1920 [1843]), *Dal primato morale e civile degli Italiani*, vol I, Turin: Unione tipografico-editrice torinese.

Gramsci, A. (1971) [1st Italian edn 1947], *Selections from the Prison Notebooks of Antonio Gramsci*, Q. Hoare and G.N. Smith (eds and trans), London.

*Grande Dizionario Enciclopedico* (1987), Turin: Unione Tipografico – Editrice Torinese.

*Il Vocabolario Treccani* (2nd edn 1997), Rome: Istituto della Enciclopedia Italiana.

Lanaro, S. (1992), *Storia dell'Italia Repubblicana*, Venice: Marsilio.

*La Piccola Treccani* (1995), Rome: Istituto della Enciclopedia Italiana.

Leopardi, G. (1969 [1824]), *Discorso sopra lo stato presente dei costumi degl'italiani*, in W. Binni (ed.), *Tutte le opere*, vol. I., Florence: Sansoni.

Lipgens, W. (ed.) (1985), *Documents on the History of European Integration, Volume I: Continental Plans for European Union 1939–1945*, Berlin/New York: Walter de Gruyter.

—— (ed.) (1986), *Documents on the History of European Integration, Volume II. Plans for European Union in Great Britain and in Exile 1939–1945*, Berlin/New York: Walter de Gruyter.

Lipgens, W. and Loth, W. (eds) (1988), *Documents on the History of European Integration, Volume III, The Struggle for European Union by Political Parties and Pressure Groups in Western European Countries 1945–50*, Berlin/New York: Walter de Gruyter.

Lyttelton, A. (1998), 'La dittatura fascista', in: G. Sabbatucci and V. Vidotto (eds), *Storia d'Italia. 4. Guerre e fascismo 1914–1943*, Rome: Editori Laterza.

Magagnoli, R. (1999), *Italien und die Europäische Verteidigungsgemeinschaft. Zwischen europäischem Credo und nationaler Machtpolitik. Italien in Geschichte und Gegenwart*, Frankfurt et al.: Peter Lang Verlag.

Magli, I. (1996), *Contro l'Europa: tutto quello che non vi hanno detto di Maastricht*, Milan: Bompiani.

Mazzini, G. (1933 [1829]), *D'una letteratura europea.*

—— (1908 [1840]), *I doveri dell'uomo*, Milan: Società ed. Milanese.

Michels, R. (1914), *L'imperialismo italiano*, Milan.

Nuti, L. (1996), 'Italy, the British application and the January debacle', in R.T. Griffiths and S. Ward (eds), *Courting the Common Market: The First Attempt to Enlarge the European Community, 1961-1963*, London: Lothian Foundation Press.

Puppo Mario (1978), 'L'Idea di Europa dai Romantici a Croce', in *L'Unità d'Europa: aspetti e problemi nel mondo culturale tedesco dell'età contemporanea.* Atti del XV convegno internazionale di studi italo-tedeschi, Merano: Istituto culturale italo-tedesco: 185–97.

Riall, L. (1993), 'Elite Resistance to State Formation: the Case of Italy', in M. Fulbrook (ed.), *National Histories and European History*, London: UCL Press.

Romano, S. (1999), 'Patto Atlantico, compleanno di guerra', *Corriere della Sera*, 6 April.

Spadolini, G. (1994), 'Prolusione', in idem (ed.), *Nazione e nazionalità in Italia: Dall'alba del secolo ai nostri giorni*, Bari: Laterza, 3–14.

Tapparelli, E. (1978), 'L'unita d'Europa: aspetti storici e idealistici', in *L'Unità d'Europa: aspetti e problemi nel mondo culturale tedesco dell'età contemporanea.* Atti del XV convegno internazionale di studi italo-tedeschi, Merano: Istituto culturale italo-tedesco: 441–6.

Varsori, A. (1993), 'L'Europe de l'Italie dans les années de guerre froide', in R. Girault and G. Bossuat (eds), *Les Europe des Européens*, Paris: Publications de la Sorbonne.

Visconti, D. (1948), *La concezione unitaria dell'Europa nel Risorgimento italiano e nei suoi precedenti storici*, Milan: F. Vallardi.

# 3

# 'Europeanism' versus 'Africanism': 'Europe' as a Symbol of Modernity and Democratic Renewal in Spain

*Pablo Jáuregui*

'Regeneration is the desire; Europeanization is the means to satisfy it.'

José Ortega y Gasset

## Introduction: Entering 'Europe' with 'Honour and Satisfaction'

On 29 March 1985, the Prime Minister of Spain, Felipe González, made a special appearance on television to broadcast an important 'message to the nation'. A few hours earlier, his Minister of Foreign Affairs, Fernando Morán, had reached a definitive agreement in Brussels which would make possible Spain's adhesion to the European Economic Community at the beginning of the following year. The Spanish media had been intensively covering the final stretch of the negotiations during the previous weeks, and had therefore created an emotional climate of collective suspense and expectation throughout the country.[1] Since the death of Franco in 1975 and the first democratic elections of 1977, the goal of gaining accession into the EEC had been a top priority of every government. Indeed, the necessity of 'entering Europe' was an issue about which there was an overwhelming consensus among all the political parties represented in the Spanish Parliament. The negotiations with Brussels, however, ran into numerous difficulties, and dragged on for much longer than expected. This inevitably disappointed many Spaniards, who felt that after their successful *transición*, they now had every right to be wholeheartedly accepted into the European club of Western democracies.[2]

---

1. On the concept of 'emotional climates', see Barbalet 1998: 159–60.
2. On the negotiations with the EEC and Spanish aspiration to 'enter Europe', see Preston and Smyth 1984; Bassols 1995; Álvarez-Miranda 1996; and Torregrosa 1996.

After this long waiting period, however, Spain's European dream finally became a reality, and Prime Minister González marked the occasion with a passionate, patriotic address, in which he stated:

Today, with honour and satisfaction, I address all the citizens and peoples of Spain to transmit to them a message of hope in our future. Early this morning, a transcendental, irreversible step has been taken for our integration in the European Economic Community... For Spain, this is a deed of great significance. As a historic fact, it signifies the end of our age-old isolation. It signifies, as well, our participation in the common destiny of Western Europe. For democratic Spain, for the Spain which lives in freedom, it also signifies the culmination of a process of struggle of millions of Spaniards who have identified freedom and democracy with integration in Western Europe. For Spain as a social reality, as an economic reality, it undoubtedly signifies a challenge, the challenge of modernity and competition, a challenge to which I am certain that our workers, our businessmen, our scientists, our professionals, and society as a whole will rise up... I think we have the obligation to do so, and that we are going to comply with this obligation of leaving our children a Spain with a greater level of economic efficiency, a greater level of culture, and a greater capacity for solidarity. A Spain which, in Europe and with Europe, will play the role which is concordant with the history of Spain, of our own Spain, and which in Europe and with Europe will play the role which our collective will as a people, as a nation, will be capable of forging.[3]

I have quoted extensively from this televised political ritual,[4] because I think that González's emotionally charged discourse accurately sums up the dominant meaning of 'Europe' which was symbolically constructed in Spain in the aftermath of the Franco dictatorship, and which at the end of the twentieth century still coloured the attitudes of many Spaniards towards the European Union. 'Entering Europe' was indeed an achievement which, in the Spanish context, could confidently be announced with 'honour and satisfaction'. 'Europe' essentially represented the opportunity to leave behind what was known as *el atraso* – 'the backwardness' – of the Spanish past for good, and to recover a respectable status on the international stage. In a country where the very concept of *España* and notions such as *patria* and *patriotismo* had almost become moral taboos due to their symbolic association with the nationalist rhetoric of Francoism, the idea of a 'European Spain' – in other words, a modern, democratic, tolerant, and pluralistic Spain – was used by leaders such as González to redefine and relegitimate the project of Spanish nationhood.

3. *El País*, 30 March 1985.
4. On political rituals, see Lukes 1975 and Kertzer 1988.

Through accession into the EEC, it was believed that Spain could fortify its young democracy against the internal threats of right-wing extremism and nationalist separatism. Only four years earlier, on 23 February 1981, a group of armed civil guards had entered the Spanish Parliament firing gunshots in the air and shouting '*¡Todos al suelo!*' ('Everyone on the floor!'), in a shocking *coup d'etat* attempt that was ultimately blocked by the dramatic intervention of King Juan Carlos I. At the same time, the terrorists of ETA remained very active in their bloody struggle to achieve an independent Basque homeland. In the face of such dangers, 'Europe' represented a safeguard of peace and stability – an opportunity to overcome the polarized internal divisions of the past and to collaborate in the outward-looking project of European unification. At the same time, by joining the Common Market, it was hoped that the Spanish people would definitively jump on the train of Western modernity, prosperity, and progress. From this widely shared perspective, 'entering Europe' was seen as an ideal antidote against the so-called 'Africanism' of the nation's past (in other words, its political, economic, and cultural underdevelopment).

In his televised address, Prime Minister González also emphasized that the decision to opt for a 'European future' in no way implied a breaking of Spain's historic links with 'our South American brothers'. On the contrary, in opposition to the discredited imperialistic attitudes that had character-ized Francoist discourse, the 'new democratic Spain' was portrayed as a global-minded cosmopolitan nation which could act as a unifying bridge between Europe and Latin America, as well as between Europe and the Arab world. In this way, it was suggested, Spain would finally begin to play an honourable, worthwhile role in the international community.

One can see, therefore, how in the Spanish public sphere, 'Europe' became an appealing, emotionally charged symbol of national resurgence at the time of the country's adhesion to the EEC. Indeed, this was evident not only in the discourse of politicians such as González, but also in the language which the country's two leading national newspapers employed to describe the successful completion of the Brussels negotiations. For instance, in an article entitled 'Alleluia for Europe', the editor-in-chief of *El País* stated that the encounter with 'Europe' signified above all 'the discovery of a mental and ideological space still new to us, in which the words invoked for so long by Spanish intellectuals – tolerance, freedom, and rights – are deeply rooted in a way which will inevitably and happily benefit us'.[5] Similarly, an editorial in *ABC* entitled 'A Historic Day'

5. *El País*, 31 March 1985.

asserted that this achievement was 'a turning point which will anchor us, for a long time, in the orbit of the nations in which individual rights, free enterprise, and the freedom of ideas impose themselves upon any totalitarian temptation . . . a space which is still, in spite of everything, the geographic platform of reason and liberty'.[6] Another article in this same newspaper celebrated the way in which Spain had finally ceased to be 'African', by proclaiming that 'from yesterday, Europe no longer ends at the Pyrénées', and defining the accession into the EEC as a 'genuine democratic baptism' that had saved the dignity of the Spanish people.[7]

This impassioned 'Euro-enthusiasm' illustrates how national self-images have not only a cognitive, but also an emotional dimension. They not only classify individuals as members of nations, vis-à-vis other nations, but they can also ignite sentiments of superiority and inferiority, or pride and shame, in response to national successes and failures. As the German sociologist Norbert Elias pointed out, part of people's self-love and self-respect can become attached to the power and status of their respective nations (1987: xi–xii).[8] Hence, nationalized individuals may feel proud or ashamed, respected or humiliated, with regard to their country's shifting fortunes in the international arena. Sigmund Freud, who was one of Elias's chief sources of inspiration, similarly argued that feelings of narcissistic gratification can be experienced by individuals not only with regard to their personal triumphs, but also in relation to the collective achievements of groups to which they belong, such as nations (1952: 410). Indeed, the significance of these emotions was also recognized by Max Weber, who suggested that national communities were often motivated not by purely 'material interests', but rather by 'prestige-sentiments' and feelings of 'status honour' (1978: 921–6). More recently, the American sociologist Thomas Scheff has defined the varying sense of self-esteem felt by nationalized individuals as 'a sort of pride-shame balance', 'a moment-by-moment social status' (1994a: 285).[9]

On the basis of numerous criteria, such as political influence, military strength, economic prosperity, scientific excellence, technological advancement, artistic creativity, athletic success, historical accomplishment and so on, the world's nation states are all tacitly ranked on a hierarchic ladder of power and status.[10] National sentiments of pride and shame can

6. *ABC*, 29 March 1985.
7. Manuel Blanco Tobio, '¿Daremos la Talla?', *ABC*, 31 March 1985.
8. On this point, see also Elias 1991, 1994, 1996.
9. On national pride and shame, see also Scheff 1994b.
10. A more detailed discussion of this theoretical approach to the study of national identity can be found in Jáuregui 1999.

therefore be experienced in relation to many different spheres of international rivalry and competition. Indeed, although this is rarely noted, a nation's presumed moral worthiness can also become a crucial mark of 'distinction' or 'disgrace' in the global struggle for international prestige.[11] As Emile Durkheim, who also emphasized the emotional dimension of nationhood, suggested in his writings on patriotism:

As long as there are states, so there will be national pride, and nothing can be more warranted. But societies can have their pride, not in being the greatest or wealthiest, but in being the most just, the best organized, and in possessing the best moral constitution (1992: 75)

In this way, Durkheim suggested that nationalism and cosmopolitanism could conceivably be reconciled, as long as people's national pride became attached to their nation's respect for universal, humanistic values.

From this theoretical standpoint, one can observe how, in Spain, the idea of 'entering Europe' was experienced as a great collective triumph, a major promotion in the world's pyramid of international status. And this was true not only in relation to the spheres of political power and economic prosperity, but also, crucially, with regard to the nation's ethical respectability. To be accepted by 'Europe' was viewed as a just reward for the 'peaceful', 'civilized' way in which the Spanish people had managed to become 'a modern democracy' in which human rights were respected. To use the language of George Herbert Mead (1934), it was to receive the recognition and the acceptance of the national self's crucial 'significant Other': *Europa*. In short, it was to cease being a sort of moral outcast and to fully recover national self-respect after decades of rejection from the Western European establishment, symbolized by Spain's exclusion from the EEC throughout the Franco dictatorship.

'Europe', in this sense, had a powerful *affective* meaning[12] in Spain, because, as González asserted in his televised address, it symbolized the culmination of the struggle for the widely cherished, quasi-mythical ideals of *la transición*: 'freedom', 'democracy' and 'modernity'. From this perspective, a shameful national past of bloody civil wars, economic stagnation, political oppression, and international isolation were depicted as tragic disasters which should never again be repeated; and in opposition to these painful collective memories, a promising future of *convivencia pacífica* (peaceful coexistence), prosperity, liberty, and European solidarity

---

11. On struggles for social 'distinction', honour, and prestige, see Bourdieu 1984, 1990.
12. On the concept of 'affective meaning', see Barbalet 1999: 632.

were presented as the fundamental objectives of a new, self-confident Spain.[13]

## The Conflict Between 'European' Modernization and 'National-Catholic' Traditionalism in Early Twentieth-century Spain

The Spanish aspiration to become 'European' had quite a long history. To some extent, as Preston and Smyth (1984: 25) have noted, the debate over the desirability of reforming Spanish institutions and socio-economic structures by following European models 'had been the stuff of national political controversy since the second half of the eighteenth century', when the ideals of the Enlightenment were seen alternately by the country's elites as a recipe for civilized progress or as a dangerous foreign heresy. Indeed, at the time of the Napoleonic invasion of Spain in 1807–8, many of Spain's liberal reformists supported the occupation forces of post-revolutionary France, in the hope that this would lead to the radical transformation which they believed their country needed. One consequence of this, however, was that in the discourse of the country's conservative traditionalists, 'European modernization' was typically depicted as something alien and 'un-Spanish' (Preston and Smyth 1984: 26).

This dispute became particularly intense at the time of the so-called *desastre* ('disaster') of 1898, the year when Spain 'lost' Cuba, the Philippines, and Puerto Rico, the last remnants of its Empire, in a short war with the United States. At a time when 'the possession of colonies was seen as the hallmark of a vigorous nation' (Balfour 1996: 107), and when the fashionable theories of social Darwinism ranked nations into superior and inferior 'races', the disappearance of Spain's last overseas colonies was experienced as a devastating blow to collective self-esteem. The national mood was poignantly captured by the Andalusian poet Antonio Machado, one of the writers in the so-called 'Generation of 98', who lamented the way in which his country had become *la agria melancolía de una grandeza pasada*, 'the bitter melancholy of past greatness' (cited in Laín Entralgo 1997: 262).

The vast majority of Spain's American colonies had already won their independence as far back as the 1820s. However, this was originally

---

13. On the political symbolism and ritual of the Spanish transition, see Desfor-Edles 1998.

interpreted as a 'family quarrel' among Spaniards, rather than as an irreversible loss of imperial power. It was believed that the ties of blood, language, religion, and culture would ultimately guarantee the survival of a great Hispanic commonwealth of nations led by *la madre patria* (the 'mother country'). In any case, at the beginning of the nineteenth century, much of the population had little consciousness of Empire, and lacked any emotional attachment to it. By the 1890s, however, the honour of the *patria* had been instilled into the nationalized, urban masses, and the loss of Spain's last imperial fragments therefore became a source of widespread collective shame (Blinkhorn 1980: 5–6). Adding insult to injury, the British Prime Minister, Lord Salisbury, delivered a humiliating speech shortly after the Spanish defeat in which he described Spain as a 'dying nation' (Álvarez Junco 1998: 448).

A year later, the French anthropologist Georges Vacher de Lapouge published an influential study on the supposed biological diversity of European peoples, in which, on the basis of cranial measurements, national 'races' were ranked according to their different levels of cerebral intelligence. According to this 'scientific' classification, at the top of the list was the northern, blond *Homo Europeus*, in second place came *Homo Alpinus*, and finally, bringing up the rear, was the hopelessly inferior *Homo Mediterraneus* (Serrano 1998: 359). Hence, in the context of the times, the belief that the Hispanic 'race' was possibly inferior to other European peoples, perhaps as a result of contamination during the seven centuries of Moorish presence on the Iberian peninsula, inevitably disturbed Spanish intellectuals. From this perspective, the 'African' dimension of Spanish identity was considered a shameful stigma of backwardness and barbarity that had to be extirpated like a cancerous tumour, while the 'European' components were the only ones that were worth cultivating. Indeed, throughout this period, many writers of the so-called 'regenerationist' tradition often expressed their patriotic concerns employing the language of biology and medicine. They proclaimed that Spanish society was seriously 'sick', and desperately needed a radical therapeutic intervention in order to revitalize itself. It was in this context that the project of *europeización* ('Europeanization') was proposed by the influential intellectual Joaquín Costa (1981 [1900]) as the most effective remedy to cure the national disease. Costa was convinced that Spain would only be saved from its deteriorating condition if it assimilated Europe's rational mentality. What was absolutely indispensable, he proclaimed, was the 'deafricanization and Europeanization of Spain', and the 'remaking of the Spaniard in the European mould' (cited in Beneyto 1999: 23). 'Europe', in Costa's mind, was essentially the land of science, education, technology, and progress. In his view, this was the only medicine that would allow Spain to survive in the global struggle of rival national 'races'. Other important figures, such as the renowned Spanish neurologist Ramón y Cajal, similarly believed that 'the sickness of Spain is none other than its remoteness from Europe; in other words, from science' (cited in Serrano 1998: 190).

Not all intellectuals, however, agreed with this invocation of 'European modernity' as the ideal solution for Spanish decadence, since many saw the adoption of 'foreign' or 'alien' ideas as a dangerous threat to the unique traditions, and above all the Catholic spirituality, of the 'national spirit'. This was also a time when German Romantic theories of nationhood had spread to Spain, and began to inspire a number of literary attempts to define the 'soul' of the Spanish people through idealized depictions of the barren Castilian landscape and the pious stoicism of the rural peasantry (Abellán 1988: 37–8). The diplomat and essayist Angel Ganivet (1990 [1897]), for instance, was repelled by the irreligious, egoistic materialism of 'European modernity'. In his view, 'European civilization' was characterized by 'anti-human', 'anti-natural' and 'pitiless mercantilism', while Spain was a morally superior land of spirituality, generosity, and idealism (cited in Beneyto 1999: 83). Hence, according to Ganivet, the resurrection of Spain could only come from the inside, by looking for the truth and the strength that lay hidden in the depths of the national soul. In his view, Spain should fully resist the misleading temptation of European modernity, because with time it would ultimately be *them*, the Europeans, who would ultimately beg *us*, the Spaniards, to teach them the moral truths and the spiritual strengths of what he called *la España eterna, virgen y madre* ('the eternal Spain, virgin and mother').

One can see, therefore, the way in which during this difficult period of collective anxiety and uncertainty, 'Europe' was seen by some Spanish intellectuals as an 'inspiring Other', an ideal model which should be imitated to save the nation by modernizing it, while others viewed it as a 'threatening Other', a terrible danger which should be avoided at all costs to preserve the purity of the nation's Catholic soul.[14] Indeed, this opposition between *europeización* (European modernization) and *casticismo* (Hispanic traditionalism) led to a notorious public confrontation between the two most famous and influential philosophers of early twentieth century Spain, Miguel de Unamuno and José Ortega y Gasset. Both of these thinkers were fully 'Europeanized' Spaniards, in the sense

14. On the concept of inspiring and threatening Others, see Triandafyllidou 2000. On Europe as a utopia and a threat in Spanish literature, see Torrecilla 1996.

that they spoke several European languages and were very familiar with the intellectual currents of thought on the other side of the Pyrénées. However, while Unamuno ultimately developed a rather hostile attitude to the project of 'Europeanization', Ortega fully embraced it with passionate conviction.

Unamuno's fundamental philosophical concern was what he called *el sentimiento trágico de la vida*, the tragic sentiment of life. By this he referred to the feeling of anxiety which uniquely arises in human beings, as a result of their awareness of death. Man, said Unamuno, is *un animal enfermo* (a sick animal), because he is the only creature who is conscious of his own mortality (1988 [1912]: 22). This fundamental problem of the human condition was, in his view, the most important issue which philosophy had to address. As a Catholic who had bitten from the fruit of modern scientific reasoning, Unamuno himself was torn throughout his life between the need to believe in the immortality of his soul, and the rationalist denial of this longing for eternal life. In fact, it was precisely this inner struggle between scientific reasoning and Catholic faith which provoked his ambivalent stance toward the project of 'Europeanization'.

In some of his early writings, Unamuno had originally promoted the idea that the Spanish people could only reawaken if they opened the windows of their *patria* to the influence of 'European winds' (1966 [1895]: 866). Eventually, however, he turned against the project of 'Europeanization', because he identified this notion with a dogmatic scientific mentality that would completely wipe out the spirituality of the Spanish people, and the vital consolation offered by their religious belief in eternal life. In a famous essay against 'European modernizers', Unamuno wrote:

> I ask myself, alone with my conscience: Am I European? Am I modern? And my conscience responds: no; you are not European, that which they call European, you are not modern, that which they call modern . . . And if I do not feel European or modern, is that because I am Spanish? Are we Spaniards ultimately incapable of yielding to Europeanization and modernization? . . . I must confess that, the more I meditate on it, the more I discover the intimate repugnance that my soul feels towards everything that is supposed to represent the guiding principles of the modern European spirit, towards the scientific orthodoxy of today, towards its methods, towards its tendencies. (1983 [1906]: 926)

Hence, in opposition to the 'European' obsession with scientific knowledge, and the widespread denigration of Spain's so-called 'Africanism', Unamuno claimed that Spain had a valuable religious tradition with

African roots, represented by 'that great ancient African' Saint Augustine. He viewed this legacy as a treasure of spiritual wisdom that should never be abandoned.

Furthermore, Unamuno proclaimed that the national religion of the Spanish people was represented by their great literary hero, Don Quixote, who stood for an undying, utopian faith in the immortality of the soul – in opposition to all rationalistic, scientifically-minded 'Europeanizers'. Therefore, he concluded that a full-scale 'Europeanization' was simply incompatible with the spiritual needs of the quixotic Spanish people. Spain, in his view, was a land of mystics with a medieval soul, and therefore it could never become a 'modern' land of scientists unless it completely allowed its true national spirit to be conquered and swallowed up by the rationalistic European Other. In opposition to those who had turned modern technology and machinery into new objects of worship, Unamuno proclaimed, '¡*Que inventen ellos!*', 'Let them (in other words, the "Europeans") invent!' (1988 [1912]: 289–90). Hence, although to some degree Unamuno acknowledged that European modernization was undoubtedly a pragmatic necessity, he insisted that the Spanish people would betray their own national soul if they gave up their age-old religious spirituality, and above all their faith in personal salvation.

In contrast to Unamuno, Ortega fully took up Joaquín Costa's proposals for national salvation through 'European regeneration'. In his view, there were absolutely no doubts about what the Spanish *raza moribunda* ('dying race') needed to recover a respectable position in the world.[15] Only the adoption of Europe's scientific rationality could rescue Spain from the calamitous, humiliating condition in which it found itself. In opposition to those who continued to idealize the supposed spiritual and cultural virtues of the nation, Ortega promoted what he called *el patriotismo del dolor* ('the patriotism of pain'), which consisted in drawing attention to the miserable backwardness of Spain, in order to perceive, by contrast, the marvels of the 'magnificent European possibility'.[16] As he put it in a public lecture in Bilbao, delivered in 1910:

> Regeneration is inseparable from Europeanization; for this reason, from the moment in which the reconstructive emotion was felt – the anguish, the shame, and the desire – the idea of Europeanization was conceived. Regeneration is the desire; Europeanization is the means to satisfy it. It was clearly seen from

15. 'La Herencia Viva de Costa', *El Imparcial*, 20 February 1911, reprinted in Ortega y Gasset 1989: 18.
16. *Ibid.*

the beginning that Spain was the problem and Europe the solution. (1983 [1910]: 521)

Not surprisingly, therefore, a bitter conflict of rival national ideals erupted during this period between Unamuno and Ortega over the controversial issue of 'Europeanization'. One of its most famous episodes involved a heated exchange of insults in a series of letters published in the Madrid newspapers *ABC* and *El Imparcial* in September 1909. Unamuno initiated this intellectual duel by mocking the *papanatas* ('gullible simpletons'), who were dazzled by the supposed wonders of 'European modernity', and proclaimed that a nation which had produced the mystic poetry of Saint John of the Cross was preferable to one that had given birth to the cold rationalism of René Descartes. In response, Ortega called Unamuno *el energúmeno español* ('the hot-headed Spaniard'), and responded that in fact, 'without Descartes, we would be left in the dark and see nothing'.[17]

The contrasting attitudes towards 'Europeanization' in the work of these two philosophers can be explained by considering their divergent views towards Catholicism and its promise of eternal salvation. Unamuno, as we have seen, was a man tortured by the philosophical doubts that had largely eroded his own religious faith in the afterlife, and hence was terrified by the possibility that death signified the complete annihilation of the human person. Ortega, however, was an agnostic thinker who did not find the finitude of life particularly tragic. In his view, the consciousness of mortality was precisely what made human life an exciting, urgent task, a dramatic adventure, a voyage full of risks in which one should not waste a minute and always strive to do one's best, knowing that time is limited by the inevitable arrival of death (1972 [1939]: 132). Indeed, from this perspective, the urgent task that Ortega felt it was his duty to push forward as an intellectual was the political, economic, and cultural modernization of his country, a project which for him was encapsulated by the concept of 'Europeanization'.

Spain, in Ortega's view, was an 'invertebrate' nation threatened by internal, egoistic particularisms and ignorant, indocile masses (1975 [1921]). It was, in short, a decadent country in danger of self-destruction, which could only be saved by the rise of a new enlightened elite with a fully modern or 'Europeanized' mentality.[18] Ortega, furthermore, ultimately promoted the construction of a supranational European state in

17. The quotations from both letters are cited in Ortega y Gasset 1989: 36–7.
18. On Ortega's life-long concern for Spain's modernization, see Gray 1989.

his most famous book, *The Rebellion of the Masses* (1998 [1930]: 282–4) because he believed that it was the only project which could save European liberal democracy from what he saw as the twin threats of fascism and communism.

The discursive battle between Unamuno and Ortega was not, of course, a purely academic debate. On the contrary, these two intellectuals were very well-known public figures, and the issues they were debating with regard to the 'problem of Spain', and to whether or not 'Europe' was the best solution, were at the heart of the political conflicts of the time. Indeed, during the turbulent decades that preceded the ultimate rise to power of General Franco, the opposition between 'European' modernization and 'national-Catholic' traditionalism was one of the fundamental cleavages that divided Spanish elites and contributed in a crucial manner to the outbreak of the Civil War.[19] Some historians have illustrated this point by referring to the concept of the 'two Spains': 'the notion of a contest between the Spain of progress and free thought which looked to Europe and the inward-looking Spain of traditionalist Catholic values' (Carr 1980: 12).

To a great extent, what one eyewitness observer of the Civil War called 'the Spanish cockpit' (Borkenau 1974 [1937]) was indeed a clash between two radically opposed projects of 'national salvation', in which the contested issue of religion played a key role (Gifford 1997). Both the right and the left claimed to be passionately concerned with the health of their patient (the 'Spanish nation' or 'Spanish people'). However, while one side believed that the cure was to be found in the preservation of the nation's Catholic 'essence', as well as the maintenance of its traditional socio-economic and political structures, the other was convinced that the only possible remedy was 'European' secularization, democratization, and economic modernization – or, in the case of its more extreme factions, the success of a socialist revolution. As Álvarez Junco (1997: 62) has suggested, the Civil War can largely be seen as the last bloody confrontation of the two idealizations of the Spanish nation that had emerged in the nineteenth century: the liberal-progressive project, in which 'European modernization' was depicted as the example to be followed, versus the 'national-Catholic' one of Spanish traditionalism, which stood for the preservation of Spain's supposedly unique spiritual personality against the imposition of 'foreign', 'alien' models.

19. This was reflected, for instance, in the rival visions of national history promoted in school textbooks by the left and the right Boyd 1997.

## Franco's 'European Vocation' and the Emergence of a Rebel Discourse on 'European Democratization'

Not surprisingly, Franco himself originally defined his military uprising in 1936 as a 'national crusade' to protect the Catholic values of *la patria* from what he called the 'bastardized, Frenchified, Europeanizing' doctrines of modern liberalism (Franco 1975: 116).[20] Indeed, throughout the duration of his life-long rule, the fundamental 'threatening Others' of Francoist discourse were Communist 'reds' and liberal-minded 'Europeanizers', as well as Basque and Catalan nationalists. Franco proclaimed that he stood for *la España imperial*, the imperial Spain of the Catholic Kings, of Charles V, and of Philip II, the Spain of global prestige whose mission was 'to defend and extend all over the world a universal and Catholic idea, a Christian Empire' (Franco 1975: 116). In his view, 'Europeanizers' were directly responsible for the humiliating collapse of Spain's position in the world, and therefore only a return to traditional 'Hispanic' principles of order, hierarchy, and authority could ensure the recovery of her imperial greatness.

However, it would be inaccurate to define Francoist discourse as 'anti-European'. In fact, from his own particular standpoint, *el Generalísimo* actually claimed to be fighting for the authentic values of the 'true Europe'. Essentially, the crusade of 'national Catholicism' represented by his forces was placed within the larger context of a continental struggle for the preservation of 'Europe's Christian civilization', threatened by the 'evil forces' of liberalism and communism. In this way, Francoist discourse constructed a symbolic representation of the 'real Europe' which was said to coincide with the spirit of the 'real Spain'. As in earlier centuries, when Spain had successfully protected 'Europe' from Moorish invaders, it would now proudly continue this role against new infidels. Franco explained his position as follows, in a speech delivered during the Civil War in Burgos:

> This is a conflict for the defence of Europe, and, once again, Spaniards have been entrusted with the glory of carrying at the point of their bayonets the defence of civilization, the maintenance of a Christian culture, the maintenance of a Catholic faith. (Franco 1975: 49)

When the forces of *el Generalísimo* emerged victorious in 1939, his regime's discourse divided Spanish society into two camps: the *vencedores*

---

20. On Franco and the Francoist ideology, see Preston 1993 and Payne 1987.

(victors), who represented the 'true' Spain, and the *vencidos* (vanquished), who represented 'anti-Spain'. The very survival of *España* was thus symbolically identified with the maintenance of the regime, while all of its opponents were classified as 'traitors' or 'bad Spaniards'. Until the final years of his dictatorship, during which all media institutions of symbolic power were controlled by the Francoist state, only this exclusionist vision of the 'Spanish nation' and its foreign-inspired 'enemies' could be officially promoted in the public sphere.[21]

Although Spain remained formally neutral throughout the Second World War, Franco did not conceal his moral identification with the kind of 'European order' envisioned by Hitler and Mussolini. There were many occasions during the course of this conflict in which 'Europe' was invoked as a way of identifying the Francoist national project with the ambitions of the Axis powers. For instance, on 17 July 1941, the fifth anniversary of the outbreak of the Spanish Civil War, Franco delivered a public address in which he presented the World War as an interrupted sequence of Axis triumphs, and spoke of:

> these moments when the German armies lead the battle for which Europe and Christianity have for so many years longed, and in which the blood of our youth is to mingle with that of our comrades of the Axis as a living expression of our solidarity. (Cited in Preston 1993: 441)

In fact, it seems clear that until the victory of the Allies became increasingly obvious in 1944, Franco attempted to flatter the self-image of Spaniards by presenting himself as the leader who would wipe out the shame of 1898 and guide them to a new age of imperial splendour in which 'the nation' would finally recuperate its lost prestige in the world, through a powerful partnership with Hitler's Germany and Mussolini's Italy. Indeed, it was only in 1944, when the defeat of the Axis was clear for all to see, that Franco made the symbolic gesture of removing the pictures of *der Führer* and *il Duce* from his desk (Pollack and Hunter 1987: 13).

The Allied victory, however, radically altered Franco's plans of renewed glory for the Spanish *patria*. Instead, his regime's collaboration with the defeated totalitarian powers led to a harsh period of international ostracism and economic penury. Spain was excluded from the United Nations, as well as from the Marshall Plan for post-war recovery. Nevertheless, after this initial isolation, the Franco regime ultimately found a

---

21. On the concept of 'symbolic power', see Bourdieu 1991.

renewed source of wealth, prestige, and moral legitimacy through a cold war alliance with the United States in 1953. In return for allowing the establishment of American military bases on its territory, Spain would receive over one billion dollars of aid. Two years later, Spain was admitted into the United Nations, diplomatic relations were re-established with most Western countries, and hence the days of total international ostracism were over. The regime's propaganda now symbolically constructed a self-image of Spain as 'the sentinel of the Occident', an honourable partner in the Western family's struggle against Soviet Communism. Furthermore, its disastrous traditional policies of economic autarky were abandoned, and a successful, full-scale programme of capitalist development was implemented. Until the end of his life-long rule in 1975, Francoist propaganda therefore claimed that *el Generalísimo* had saved 'the nation' from economic ruin and transformed it into an advanced, prosperous 'Western society'.

Franco, however, was much less fortunate in his attempt to gain an additional source of moral legitimacy by trying to get accepted into the European Economic Community.[22] In February 1962, the Spanish state officially requested entry into the EEC. However, the authoritarian character of the Franco regime made this a futile pretension. Only a few days before the Spanish application was made, the European Parliament had approved a report which asserted that 'states whose governments do not have democratic legitimization and whose people do not participate in government decisions, either directly or through fully elected representatives, cannot aspire to be admitted into the circle of peoples which forms the European communities' (Pollack and Hunter 1987: 134). Hence, although the Spanish request received a sympathetic response from some conservative circles and sectors of European public opinion, accession into the EEC could not ultimately be allowed to an old ally of Hitler and Mussolini. To a great extent, Franco remained an anachronistic symbol of everything which the 'new Europe' was being constructed against, a shameful reminder of the Nazi and Fascist past.

Nevertheless, throughout this period, the official Francoist propaganda constantly proclaimed that Spain had a 'European vocation', that it wanted to participate in the great collective project of the Common Market. At the same time, however, it continued to classify the liberal politics of other European countries as 'dangerous' and 'inferior' (La Porte 1992: 396). In opposition to the so-called 'inorganic democracy' of other

---

22. On the Franco regime's attempt to enter the EEC, see Armero 1978 and La Porte 1992.

European countries, which were viewed as a dangerous first step towards Communism, Franco claimed to stand for 'organic democracy' – a 'natural', harmonious order based on traditional 'Spanish' institutions such as the Church and the family. The 'Europeanism' of *el Generalísimo* was thus limited exclusively to the sphere of economics – in other words, to a desire to share in the prosperity of the Common Market –, but in no way did it imply a conversion to the principles of Western liberal democracy.

However, in opposition to this official 'European vocation' which the regime tried to promote, many Spaniards who rejected Francoism began to unify under the symbolic banner of a very different 'Europeanism', which stood for the full modernization and democratization of their country (Tusell 1977). In fact, one of the most notable gestures of anti-regime protest which occurred during the Franco dictatorship took place in Munich during the IV Congress of the European movement in June 1962, when opponents of the regime from both within the country and abroad demanded that the EEC should reject the Francoist request to enter the Common Market, unless a full-scale programme of democratic reform was implemented in their country. One of the key interventions of this conference was that of the exiled Spanish writer Salvador de Madariaga, a veteran anti-Francoist and a passionate defender of European integration, who addressed the assembled delegates as follows:

Europe is not only a Common Market and the price of coal and steel; it is also and above all a common faith and the price of Man and of liberty . . . Should not Europe consider it essential for public life to circulate with full freedom among all its members? And if madame de Sévigné could write to her daughter: 'your stomach hurts me', cannot Europe say to Spain: 'your dictatorship hurts me'? (Cited in Tusell 1977: 395)

At the end of the session, all Spanish participants signed a joint manifesto in which they asserted that adhesion into the European Community should necessarily compel every member state to establish genuinely representative and democratic institutions, and to guarantee basic human rights. In opposition to the divisive Civil War rhetoric which Francoist discourse employed to legitimate its existence, these anti-Francoist rebels proclaimed that a democratic, truly 'European' nation in which Spaniards of all political tendencies could legitimately participate and live in peace with each other was possible.

Hence, for the first time since the Civil War, Spaniards from across much of the ideological spectrum joined forces at the Munich conference to oppose the Franco dictatorship and demand political reforms. In opposition to the regime's own official 'European vocation', a new rival 'Europeanism' therefore arose which openly stood for the rejection of a 'backwards' regime and the 'democratization' of Spain. Not surprisingly, the Francoist press branded all those Spaniards who had participated in this gathering as 'filthy conspirators' who had stabbed *la patria* in the back. Egged on by this official propaganda, thousands of people assembled to demonstrate in many Spanish cities to denounce these 'traitors', and Franco delivered several addresses to condemn their 'betrayal of the nation'. At that stage, the regime's monopolization of national symbolism and sentiment was still relatively effective.

Over the course of time, however, the legitimacy of Franco's version of Spanish 'patriotism' began to dwindle, and the rival national project of a modern, democratic, and hence 'European' Spain eventually gained the upper hand. By the 1970s, Spain had been transformed by Franco's own regime into a fully industrialized, better educated society. At this point, students, intellectuals, workers, Basque and Catalan nationalists, and even many representatives of the Catholic Church were publicly rejecting the official discourse of the regime.[23] A new national project was increasingly spreading, seeking the recovery of collective self-esteem through the achievement of the kind of 'freedom' and 'liberty' enjoyed in 'normal European countries'. Although the regime itself had repeatedly made the promise that it would satisfy the country's 'European vocation', the most it ever accomplished was a purely commercial trade agreement with the EEC in 1970. Full membership, however, always remained out of the question, and 'Europe' therefore remained an unfulfilled aspiration throughout the Franco dictatorship.

By the time *el Generalísimo* died in 1975, it had therefore become obvious, even among many of the elite within the authoritarian power structure, that if Spain truly wanted to become 'European', political democratization would be a necessary condition for this ideal to become a reality. By this stage, Francoism was increasingly seen as something which was still keeping Spain at humiliating 'African' levels of political backwardness. From this perspective, it was thus only through a complete 'Europeanization' of the country that national self-esteem could be fully regained.

Hence, after Franco's death, a new political discourse emerged in the Spanish public sphere which identified 'freedom' and 'democracy' with

23. On the gradual erosion of the Franco regime's legitimacy, see Carr and Fusi 1981 and Gilmour 1985.

the desire to achieve a 'modern' and 'European' status.[24] King Juan Carlos I, initially stigmatized among all the forces of the opposition for being Franco's appointed successor, clearly positioned himself on the side of 'European' democratization, and therefore managed to legitimate his rule among a population that was now overwhelmingly demanding political change. Indeed, it is interesting to observe how, in his inaugural address to the Spanish Parliament in November 1975, the new monarch proclaimed that 'a free and modern society requires the participation of all in the forums of decision-making', and went on to emphasize the 'Europeity' of Spain:

> The idea of Europe would be incomplete without reference to the presence of the Spaniard, and without a consideration of the acts of many of my predecessors. Europe should reckon with Spain, for we Spaniards are European. It is a necessity today that both sides understand that this is so and draw the consequences that derive therefrom.[25]

In this way, the King suggested from the beginning of his reign that his aim was to lead Spain to 'Europe', via the achievement of 'freedom' and 'modernity'.

Similarly, the leading politicians of the transition, such as the first democratically elected prime minister, Adolfo Suárez, often associated Spain's modernization and democratization with the idealized concept of 'becoming European' (Armero 1989). Indeed, the aspiration to become a full member of the EEC was one of the fundamental issues on which there was a broad consensus in Spain among the political forces which made the negotiated transition to democracy possible (Morán 1980: 289). It is undoubtedly significant, for instance, that at the time of the first elections in June 1977, the campaign slogans of the two parties that gained the most seats in the Spanish Parliament, Suárez's *Unión de Centro Democrático* (UCD) and Felipe González's *Partido Socialista Obrero Español* (PSOE) both made references to their capacity to satisfy the country's European ambition: 'Vote Centre. The ideologies that make possible a democratic Europe. The people that will make possible a democratic Spain'; 'The key to Europe is in your hands. Vote PSOE' (Desfor-Edles 1998: 57).

Indeed, when Suárez won these first elections, he triumphantly declared in his first press conference as Prime Minister that his government would do its utmost to get the country into the EEC, because, he

24. On this process, see Pérez-Díaz 1993; Ramón Arango 1995; and Holman 1996.
25. *ABC*, 23 November 1975.

proclaimed, 'Spain is Europe and forms part of it' (Bassols 1995: 187). The phrase 'Spain is Europe' could now be uttered with a renewed confidence in the public sphere. The nation's leaders had now been elected through democratic procedures, and it was this above all that was seen as the key component of a 'European' status. In all of this, one can observe how the concept of 'Europeanness' had become not so much something a country could *be* through mere geographical location, history, or culture, but rather something that had to be *achieved* through the accomplishment of certain moral and political conditions.

If, as Paloma Aguilar (1996) has shown, the Civil War was viewed as the collective tragedy of the past that had to be avoided at all costs during the Spanish transition to democracy, one could say that 'Europe' was the mythical aspiration of the future which the majority of Spaniards desired to reach. In opposition to the radical, extremist, violent 'two Spains' of the past, the symbolic ideal that was promoted in the dominant political discourse of this period was the notion of a 'third Spain' characterized by moderation, tolerance, and dialogue.[26] Only by respecting such values of mutual respect would the aspiration to 'European modernity' finally become possible. Hence, from the time of Franco's death to the triumphant televised address of Felipe González to which I referred early in this chapter, 'Europe' always remained the great collective goal, the great hopeful promise that would successfully put 'the nation' back on its feet after centuries of decadence and internal strife. As *El País* proclaimed in its editorial on the day after EEC membership became official and the Spanish national flag was finally hoisted in Brussels:

> We shall finally end our interior isolation and participate fully in the construction of the modern world . . . The European road responds to the imperative of reason and history. To assume it consciously and deliberately signifies one more step in the path of maturity. Good morning, Europe.[27]

## Conclusion: 'Europe' as a Unifying Prestige Symbol and a Potent Source of National Pride in Post-Franco Spain

In Spain, then, one could conclude by saying that 'Europe' functioned and has continued to function as a unifying prestige symbol and a potent source of national pride. After Franco's death, it became a common

26. The idea of the 'third Spain' was promoted in particular by the intellectual Pedro Laín Entralgo. See Beneyto 1999: 216–25.
27. *El País*, 2 January 1986.

national project that transcended the separate interests of different parties and ideologies across the political spectrum, because essentially it stood for all the widely shared ideals of the new, 'modern' and 'democratic' Spain. In contrast to the monolithic, divisive definition of *España* that had characterized Francoist discourse, the concept of a 'European Spain' was therefore a key ingredient in the symbolic construction of a more inclusive or 'multivocal' definition of the Spanish nation with which both Catholics and non-Catholics, progressives and conservatives, could conceivably identify.[28]

Nevertheless, it is important to note that even the successful transition to a 'European democracy', as well as the decentralization of state power through the creation of the regional autonomous communities, has never fully satisfied the demands of nationalist movements in Catalonia, the Basque Country, and Galicia. For such groups, the European Union has rather represented an opportunity to bypass the Spanish state and to ultimately achieve a new international status as separate 'nations in Europe'.[29]

At the same time, one should also point out that in today's Spain, the idea of 'Europe' has inevitably lost much of its affective potency, given that this achievement has now become a completely taken-for-granted aspect of Spanish life. As time has gone by, and the ghost of Franco has receded into a largely forgotten past, 'Europe' has ceased to be the emotionally charged ideal that it used to be. To use a Weberian phrase, the charisma of *Europa* has inevitably been routinized, as the image of Spanish leaders participating in European summits has ceased to be an exciting novelty, and instead has become a rather boring, mundane item in the news.

However, one can still observe that membership of the European Union remains a fundamental uncontested dimension of the national self-image in the world and its collective aspirations for the future. Even today, one can still hear references in popular and journalistic discourses to the old dichotomy between 'Africanism' and 'Europeanism'. For instance, news reports occasionally make statements such as that the AIDS epidemic is approximating dramatic 'African' proportions in Spain, or that the country has happily reached 'European' levels of mobile telephones and Internet connections. In this sense, one can observe that 'Europe' is still the yardstick of modernization, while 'Africa' remains the measure of backwardness, in the collective consciousness of Spaniards.

28. On the concept of multivocal symbols, see Cohen 1989.
29. On Spain's minority nationalisms, see Mar-Molinero and Smith 1996.

Indeed, as the project of European integration advances, particularly with regard to the process of monetary union, Spain's participation and its contribution to this objective is depicted in political and media discourses as an ongoing aspiration, as the permanent challenge that the country has to face in order to stay on the fast-moving train of Western progress and prosperity. Hence, the current conservative Prime Minister, José María Aznar has presented the country's successful incorporation into the Euro currency as a sign that Spain has fully recovered 'its place', 'its weight', and 'its influence'.[30] In many ways, therefore, 'being European' remains a key component of national self-esteem, and is widely viewed as the fundamental guarantee of Spain's continuing success in the international arena.

## References

Abellán, J.L. (1988), 'El significado de la idea de Europa en la política y en la historia de España', *Sistema*, 86–7: 31–43.

Aguilar, P. (1996), *Memoria y Olvido de la Guerra Civil*, Madrid: Alianza.

Álvarez Junco, J. (1997), 'El nacionalismo español como mito movilizador: cuatro guerras', in R. Cruz and M. Pérez Ledesma (eds), *Cultura y Movilización en la España Contemporánea*, Madrid: Alianza.

—— (1998), 'La Nación en Duda', in J. Pan-Montojo (ed.), *Más se perdió en Cuba: España, 1898 y la crisis de fin de siglo*, Madrid: Alianza.

Álvarez, Miranda, B. (1996), *El sur de Europa y la adhesión a la Comunidad: Los debates políticos*, Madrid: Siglo veintiuno.

Armero, J.M. (1978), *La Política Exterior de Franco*, Barcelona: Planeta.

—— (1989), *La Política Exterior de España en Democracia*, Madrid: Espasa.

Balfour, S. (1996), 'The Lion and the Pig: Nationalism and National Identity in Fin-de-Siècle Spain', in C. Mar-Molinero and A. Smith (eds), *Nationalism and the Nation in the Iberian Peninsula: Competing and Conflicting Identities*, Oxford: Berg.

Barbalet, J. (1998), *Emotion, Social Theory, and Social Structure: A Macrosociological Approach*, Cambridge: Cambridge University Press.

---

30. J.M. Aznar, 'La Hora de Europa, la Hora de España', *El Mundo*, 5 February 2000.

—— (1999), 'Boredom and Social Meaning', *The British Journal of Sociology*, 50(4), 631–646.

Bassols, R. (1995), *España en Europa: Historia de la Adhesión a la CE, 1957–85*, Madrid: Estudios de Política Exterior.

Beneyto, J.M. (1999), *Tragedia y Razón: Europa en el Pensamiento Español del Siglo XX*, Madrid: Taurus.

Blinkhorn, M. (1980), 'Spain: The "Spanish Problem" and the Imperial Myth', *Journal of Contemporary History*, 15: 5–25.

Borkenau, F. (1974 [1937]), *The Spanish Cockpit*, Ann Arbor: University of Michigan Press.

Bourdieu, P. (1984), *Distinction. A Social Critique of the Judgement of Taste*, London: Routledge & Kegan Paul.

—— (1990), *In Other Words: Essays Towards a Reflexive Sociology*, Cambridge: Polity Press.

—— (1991), *Language and Symbolic Power*, Cambridge: Polity Press.

Boyd, C.P. (1997), *Historia Patria, Politics, History, and National Identity in Spain 1875–1975*, Princeton: Princeton University Press.

Carr, R. (1980), *Modern Spain: 1875–1980*, Oxford: Oxford University Press.

—— and Fusi, J.P. (1981), *Spain: Dictatorship to Democracy*, 2nd edn, London: George Allen & Unwin.

Cohen, A. (1989), *The Symbolic Construction of Community*, London: Routledge.

Costa, J. (1981 [1900]), *Reconstitución y europeización de España*, Madrid: Instituto de Administración Local.

Desfor-Edles, L. (1998), *Symbol and Ritual in the New Spain*, Cambridge: Cambridge University Press.

Durkheim, E. (1992), *Professional Ethics and Civil Morals*, London: Routledge.

Elias, N. (1987), *Involvement and Detachment*, Oxford: Basil Blackwell.

—— (1991), *The Society of Individuals*, Oxford: Basil Blackwell.

—— (1994), 'Introduction: A Theoretical Essay on Established and Outsider Relations', in N. Elias and J. Scotson, *The Established and the Outsiders*, London: Sage.

—— (1996), *The Germans*, Cambridge: Polity Press.

Franco, F. (1975), *El Pensamiento Político de Franco*, Madrid: Ediciones del Movimiento.

Freud, S. (1952). 'On Narcissism: an Introduction', in *The Major Works of Sigmund Freud*, Chicago: Encyclopedia Britannica Inc.

Ganivet, A. (1990 [1897]), *Idearium Español con El porvenir de España*, Madrid: Espasa Calpe.

Gifford, P. (1997), 'La representación de la nación: El conflicto en torno a la identidad nacional y las prácticas simbólicas de la Segunda República', in R. Cruz and M. Pérez Ledesma (eds), *Cultura y Movilización en la España Contemporánea*, Madrid: Alianza.

Gilmour, D. (1985), *The Transformation of Spain: From Franco to the Constitutional Monarchy*, London: Quartet Books.

Gray, R. (1989), *The Imperative of Modernity: An Intellectual Biography of José Ortega y Gasset*, Berkeley: University of California Press.

Holman, O. (1996), *Integrating Southern Europe: EC Expansion and the Transnationalization of Spain*, London: Routledge.

Jáuregui, P. (1999), 'National Pride and the meaning of "Europe": A Comparative Study of Britain and Spain', in D. Smith and S. Wright (eds), *Whose Europe? The Turn Towards Democracy*, Oxford: Blackwell.

Kertzer, D. (1988), *Ritual, Politics, and Power*, New Haven and London: Yale University Press.

Laín Entralgo, P. (1997), *La Generación del 98*, Madrid: Espasa-Calpe.

La Porte, M.T. (1992), *La Política Europea del Régimen de Franco, 1957–62*, Pamplona: Ediciones Universidad de Navarra.

Lukes, S. (1975), 'Political Ritual and Social Integration', *Sociology*, 9: 289–308.

Mar-Molinero, C. and Smith, A. (eds) (1996), *Nationalism and the Nation in the Iberian Peninsula: Competing and Conflicting Identities*, Oxford: Berg.

Mead, G.H. (1934), *Mind, Self, and Society*, Chicago: University of Chicago Press.

Morán, F. (1980), *Una Política Exterior Para España*, Barcelona: Planeta.

Ortega y Gasset, J. (1972 [1939]), *El Hombre y la Gente*, Madrid: Espasa-Calpe.

—— (1975 [1921]), *España Invertebrada*, Madrid: Revista de Occidente.

—— (1983 [1910]), 'La Pedagogía Social Como Programa Político', *Obras Completas*, Vol. I, Madrid: Alianza, 503–21.

—— (1989), *Ensayos Sobre la Generación del 98*, Madrid: Revista de Occidente en Alianza Editorial.

—— (1998 [1930]), *La Rebelión de las Masas*, Madrid: Castalia.

Payne, S. (1987), *The Franco Regime: 1936–75*, Madison: University of Wisconsin Press.

Pérez-Díaz, V. (1993), *The Return of Civil Society: The Emergence of Democratic Spain*, Cambridge: Harvard University Press.

Pollack, B. and Hunter, G. (1987), *The Paradox of Spanish Foreign Policy: Spain's International Relations from Franco to Democracy*, London: Pinter.

Preston, P. (1986), *The Triumph of Democracy in Spain*, London: Methuen.

—— (1993), *Franco: A Biography*, London: Harper Collins.

Preston, P. and Smyth, D. (1984), *Spain, the EEC, and NATO*, London: Routledge & Kegan Paul.

Ramón Arango, E. (1995), *Spain: Democracy Regained*, Boulder: Westview Press.

Scheff, T. (1994a), 'Emotions and Identity: A Theory of Ethnic Nationalism', in C. Calhoun (ed.), *Social Theory and the Politics of Identity*, Oxford: Blackwell.

—— (1994b), *Bloody Revenge: Emotions, Nationalism, and War*, Boulder: Westview.

Serrano, C. (1998), 'Conciencia de la crisis, conciencias en crisis', in J. Pan-Montojo (ed.), *Más se perdió en Cuba: España, 1898 y la crisis de fin de siglo*, Madrid: Alianza.

Torrecilla, J. (1996), *El Tiempo y los Márgenes, Europa como utopía y como amenaza en la literatura española*, Chapel Hill: University of North Carolina.

Torregrosa, J.R. (1996), 'Spanish International Orientations: Between Europe and Iberoamerica', in G. Breakwell and E. Lyons (eds), *Changing European Identities: Social Psychological Analyses of Social Change*, Oxford: Butterworth Heinemann.

Triandafyllidou, A. (2000), *Images of the Other and the Reshaping of Collective Identities in a 'United' Europe*. Seminar Paper EUR/24 of the European Forum, Robert Schuman Centre, Florence: European University Institute.

Tusell, X. (1977), *La Oposición Democrática al Franquismo*, Barcelona: Planeta.

Unamuno, M. de (1966 [1895]), *En torno al Casticismo, Obras Completas*, Vol. I, Madrid: Escelicer, 773–869.

—— (1983 [1906)], 'Sobre la Europeización', *Obras Completas*, Vol. III, Madrid: Aguilar, 925–38.

—— (1988 [1912]), *Del Sentimiento Trágico de la Vida*, Barcelona: Ediciones B.

Weber, M. (1978), *Economy and Society*, Berkeley: Berkeley University Press.

# 4

# Us or Them? The Meaning of Europe in British Political Discourse

*Piers Ludlow*

To probe the meaning of the word 'Europe' in British usage is straight-away to appreciate one of the defining features of Britain's European debate, namely a profound ambivalence about whether or not Europe includes the United Kingdom. For while the exact connotations that the concept evokes have evolved considerably over the course of the last two centuries, it has always remained possible to both include or exclude Britain. This uncertainty will constitute the central theme of this chapter, starting with an examination of what 'Europe' has been taken to imply away from the political arena, before turning to investigate the layers of meaning involved in the political debate about Europe.

In everyday English, the most striking feature of the way in which 'Europe' is used is the manner in which it has often become synonymous with 'continental' – i.e. a geographical area which does not include the British Isles. A newspaper competition announcing 'Free Flights to Europe' is thus not to be taken to mean that air tickets between London and Edinburgh might be won. Instead it indicates that winners will travel to a variety of continental, and most probably Western European, tourist destinations. Similarly, a decision to take one's holidays 'in Europe' is more likely to mean that the merits of Italian sunshine prevailed over the charms of the English seaside than it is to suggest that Greece or Scotland is being preferred to Florida. 'Europe' is used as an alternative to Britain, not as a geographical area distinct from Africa, Asia or the Americas.

Used in this fashion, 'Europe', 'European' or the ubiquitous prefix 'Euro-' can of course carry negative overtones. It is not uncommon to hear fans of Anglo-American pop music speak somewhat derisively of 'Euro-pop'. Uninspiring car designs are on occasion dismissed as 'Euro-boxes', while cinema critics periodically denounce overwrought continental films as 'Euro-puddings'. One of Britain's television channels has for years broadcast a programme devoted to the more salacious aspects of continental European life entitled 'Euro-trash'. In each case the designation is uncomplimentary; in most cases, moreover, an implicit contrast is drawn with the more 'normal' British or Anglo-American fare to which British viewers and listeners have grown accustomed.

Just as often, however, the reference to Europe is designed to convey sophistication, exoticism or simply difference. Over recent years, many British companies have adopted the prefix 'Euro-' partly in an effort to sound distinctive and exciting. The Oxford telephone directory, for instance, lists no fewer than thirty-two companies so designated, ranging from the 'Euro Foto centre' to the intriguingly named 'Euroquip Automotive Ltd', by way of 'Euro Shred Ltd' and 'Euroclip Sheep Shearing Equipment'. Some, such as 'Euro-Industrial Plastics' or 'Europipes', presumably also intend to signal their ambition to capture a market that stretches beyond Britain. But others like 'Euro Fine Foods' clearly plan to trade on the implicit sophistication of the word 'Euro' – a particularly clever tactic in the field of gastronomy. Similarly bedding companies, trying to persuade the British of the merits of the duvet, consistently market their product as 'continental quilts'. In all of these cases 'European' or 'continental' is certainly meant to underline difference from plain 'Englishness' or 'Britishness', but it is done in a positive rather than negative manner.

In many further cases, the label 'European' is largely value-free, being simply intended to describe something which pertains neither to Great Britain nor to Asia, Africa, or the Americas. For many years, the Oxford University history syllabus required students to prepare three papers on 'English' history and two more on 'European' history – a terminology which eventually fell into disuse, not because of a recognition that Britain might be part of Europe, but instead out of the belief that some American, Asian and African history ought to be included as well and that the non-British papers should henceforth be called 'general' papers (cf. Robbins 1993: 50–6). In similar fashion the most widespread handbook for those interested in ornithology is entitled 'The Birds of Britain and Europe' (Gooders 1998). And the handbook to our current mobile phone notes that it can be used 'in Britain, Europe and beyond.' In none of these cases is 'Europe' intended to be interpreted favourably or unfavourably. As with the cases described above it is undeniably meant as somewhere foreign and distinct from Britain.

In other contexts, however, the term 'European' has been used by the English in a fashion which includes themselves as well as the French, Portuguese or Polish. Perhaps the most striking eighteenth- and nineteenth-century example comes from the Empire, and particularly India, where soldiers dispatched from Britain rather than recruited locally were routinely referred to as 'European' not 'British' or 'English', despite the fact that many, if not most, of them, almost certainly were of British origin. Similarly the 1844 survey *British India*, written by H.H. Wilson, spoke of 'Europeans in India rarely possessing . . . the inclination to invest capital in landed property' while E. Dicey in 1882 wrote of 'the gradual Europeanization of Egypt' (*Oxford English Dictionary* 1989). In none of these cases were the British intending to play down their own role; instead, they were both including themselves in the wider phenomenon of European colonial expansion and underlining the racial hierarchy upon which colonialism rested.

Likewise, a portion of the British-educated elite throughout the modern era have acknowledged some debt to a European culture which stretched back to Ancient Greece and Rome, but which also included the Renaissance, the Reformation, the Enlightenment and Romanticism. As a result, some at least of the artists, authors and intellectuals of Britain during the last two centuries have acknowledged that their own output belonged within a wider European tradition. Hence in part, the involvement of Lord Byron in the Greek struggle for independence, to which Constantine Tsoukalas refers in Chapter 1 of this volume. Furthermore, the leisure-travel patterns and the language-learning habits of the British elite for most of the last 300 years have reflected a sense of proximity to the continent, with France, Italy, Switzerland and Germany emerging as the favourite destinations, and French, followed by German and then Italian, as the most frequently studied modern language. The importance of the Grand Tour in the eighteenth century and the centrality of Latin and Ancient Greek to a 'proper' education up till the mid-point of the twentieth century also suggest that the British felt themselves to be the heirs of a European tradition stretching back to Classical antiquity (Hudson 1993: 13–25). This European bias has persisted even into the era of mass tourism, with the package-holidaymakers heading for Greece, Spain or Southern Italy confirming the European-centred pattern of travel set by the more moneyed travellers heading for Tuscany, the Algarve or the Dordogne. The *Cimitero degli Inglesi* in the middle of Florence is an eloquent reminder that even at the height of 'splendid isolation' the British never cut themselves off entirely from continental culture; the Volvo-loads of contemporary English families who descend on 'Chiantishire' each summer are testimony that links still remain strong.

In post-Second World War years, moreover, the British general public grew accustomed to the spectacle of British clubs and sports stars competing in European tournaments. Well before the 1990s, when the sudden flood of continental players and managers into English football led to a remarkable Europeanization of the British domestic game, British sports fans had become used to the notion that Liverpool or Manchester United should periodically take on Real Madrid, Inter Milan or Bayern Munich in competitions to decide the best football team in Europe, or that British runners such as Sebastian Coe or Linford Christie should compete for European titles to place alongside their Olympic, World and Commonwealth awards. In golf, indeed, viewers are even treated once every two years to the spectacle of a combined European team taking on the United States, although it has to be acknowledged that the sight of British fans so passionately backing Spanish or German golfers against US opposition was considered sufficiently unusual in the early 1990s to be the subject of at least one newspaper editorial.

In British domestic politics, moreover, the last decades of the twentieth century witnessed the steady rise in the number of references made to European standards, European growth rates, and European norms. Although the use of such comparative data has not displaced allusions to American, Australian or New Zealand examples, it nevertheless bears testimony to the way in which it has become commonplace to assume that Britain belongs in European league tables of wealth, pollution, defence spending, heart disease, crime or teenage pregnancy, and that such comparisons possess both intellectual validity and political weight. Tony Blair's recent pledge to raise British health spending to the European average within five years attracted much political comment (*Financial Times*, 17 January 2000). Nobody challenged the notion, however, that the comparison used by the government was a relevant one. To the extent that a country's identity is defined by the company that it sees itself as keeping, British domestic political discourse does suggest a surprising degree of consensus that Britain is indeed a European country.

Despite such recent developments, however, the fundamental ambivalence persists. Europe as both a place and as a concept may include Britain; alternatively, it may not. This linguistic and attitudinal uncertainty has been compounded by the presence, throughout the nineteenth and twentieth centuries, of a number of competing identities towards which the British felt themselves drawn. Prominent among these has been the idea of Empire or Commonwealth, the most frequently cited 'alternative' to European alignment in British political debate. But they also include the notion of an Atlantic Community, incorporating some of Europe certainly, but also extending to the United States and Canada, and the hazy yet oddly persistent appeal of 'the English-speaking peoples'. The presence of such rival communities and groupings means that the British have rarely seen themselves as having to choose between European involvement or isolation. Instead, participation in the affairs of the continent, whether economically, diplomatically or by means of institutionalized cooperation, has been seen by Britain as just one of several possible policy options.

Other European countries, of course, have also flirted with alternative alignments. But with a few exceptions – notably perhaps Nordic cooperation – these rival visions, while able to distract the energies and attentions of policy-makers during periods where ideas of European unity have been absent from the policy agenda, have not permitted their advocates to feel uninvolved whenever wider European vistas have opened up. Instead, imperial or subregional options have tended to have been ditched in favour of European cooperation, or at best, as with the case of the colonial arrangements France succeeded in incorporating in the Treaty of Rome, reconciled with a European strategy. Britain, by contrast, has periodically felt able to support both European integration for others and an alternative grouping for itself. Churchill was particularly representative of this view – both his famous 1930 article on 'The United States of Europe' and his 1946 Zurich speech advocated a united Europe living in harmony with a powerful British Empire. But this stance was far from exclusively Churchillian. The same assumption underpinned the attitude of 'benevolent neutrality' which characterized Britain's approach to integration among the Six in the period between 1950 and 1955, and recurs in the contemporary debate in the arguments of those opposed to Britain joining the euro. In public at least, most of those hostile to British membership assert that they wish no ill towards the single currency itself; they simply do not feel that it is the right choice for Britain.

The very multiplicity of policy options available to Britain has fuelled a further distinctive feature of the British debate, namely a recurrent tendency to attack regionalism in the name of global cooperation. Britain, one might argue somewhat cynically, has responded to its own unwillingness (or inability) to choose where and with which partners its own future belongs by accusing those more willing to press ahead with regional cooperation of threatening global harmony. Expressed more charitably, the worldwide nature of its own interests has encouraged Britain to champion global economic liberalism and the widest possible international cooperation. This attitude could have welcome effects: nineteenth-century Britain, for instance, pioneered the use of the 'Most Favoured Nation' clause in its trade arrangements, thereby attempting to spread the effects of bilateral commercial treaties as widely as was possible (Marsh 1999: 28). The same set of beliefs also lay behind less constructive episodes in British policy-making, however. Thus the 1930 Briand Plan was rejected by the British on the grounds that it would be contrary to the principles of free trade and would undermine the League of Nations (Salter 1933: 106–22). Similarly, the initial British response to the Messina conference was to condemn a step which, London claimed, would divide Western Europe economically, undermine the wider OEEC liberalization programme, and be contrary to GATT rules (Ellison 2000: 21). Enthusiasts for Commonwealth cooperation, meanwhile, often contrasted what Leader of the Labour Party Hugh Gaitskell could describe as 'this remarkable multiracial association, of independent nations, stretching across five continents, covering every race', with the narrow regionalism of 'Little Europe' (cited in Holmes 1996: 28). In similar fashion, one of the 'no' slogans in the 1975 referendum was 'Out of Europe and into the World' (Holmes 1996: 1). To many opponents of integration, it has been the self-styled 'Europeans' who have been guilty of a narrow and restrictive vision, not themselves.

Taken together, this fundamental ambivalence about whether or not Britain is a European nation at all, the presence of alluring alternatives to European cooperation, and a persistent belief that the widest possible global cooperation is preferable to action at a regional level, go a long way towards explaining why Britain has often reacted with uncertainty, perplexity and even hostility to the ideas of European cooperation which have been advanced by its neighbours, and hesitated profoundly about the extent to which it has wanted to be involved. So strong indeed have been the forces pushing Britain away from Europe that it is at first sight surprising that the question of involvement, let alone integration, has even arisen. And yet for all the temptations of detachment, the British have found themselves deeply entwined with nineteenth- and twentieth-century developments in Europe. Before 1900, the widespread rejection of active military engagement on the Continent did not preclude either extensive commercial ambitions – hence the British role in the spread of free trade (Howe 1997: 70–100) – or intense diplomatic participation in the rivalries and disputes which divided Europe. And in the twentieth century, Britain found itself acting as a major combatant in both World Wars, intervening frequently through diplomatic and economic means in the affairs of the continent, and, for the last thirty years of the century, playing a role as a central member state of the principal forum for European cooperation, namely the EC/EU. The actual reality of Britain's position, particularly in the twentieth century, was thus much closer to 'the heart of Europe' than the frequent talk of detachment or 'splendid isolation' implies.

In attempting to explain this apparent paradox, most British historiography has focused on a series of pragmatic calculations made by British governments. Involvement in European affairs, it has been argued, has not arisen out of sentiment, idealism or any powerful urge to be part of Europe. Instead it has reflected an assessment of the geo-political and economic advantages of throwing Britain's weight into European affairs. Hard-headed calculations of national interest have driven policy, not diffuse ideas about the meaning of Europe.

Britain's involvement in nineteenth-century diplomacy is thus most often portrayed as an attempt to ensure that a balance of power was preserved in Europe and that no single continental player became overly dominant. Similarly, nineteenth-century commercial involvement is seen as the product of economic self-interest: the fewer obstacles there were to European free trade, the greater the likely success of Europe's most industrialized nation. In much the same way, Britain's decision to go to war in 1914 tends to be explained in terms of London's assessment of how the balance of power in Europe would tilt against Britain in the case of British neutrality, while the hesitations and ambivalence about any 'continental commitment' during the inter-war years are attributed to a combination of economic and military weakness, a desire to avoid a new bloody conflict, and the placement of global and imperial interests above European ones.

The initial aloofness towards the Six is put down to the perceived difference in stature between Britain and the main continental powers in the immediate post-war years, a lack of economic interest in continental regional integration as opposed to Commonwealth free trade and global monetary liberalization, and the contrary pull of Empire, whereas the belated turn towards the EEC is explained in terms of Britain's diminished strength relative to that of the Superpowers, the ongoing disappearance of the Empire/Commonwealth option, and American pressure. Similarly, Britain's discomforts since it joined the Community in 1973 tend to be linked with the divergent economic and political interests of itself and its partners, as well as with its dislike of some of the institutional and policy characteristics of the EEC which had developed in the years before the British had been able to enter.

Policy-making of this sort would, prima facie, appear to be a rather poor hunting ground for 'meanings of Europe'. Totally pragmatic calculation should be grounded in objective geopolitical or economic realities, not value judgements about Europe's worth, appeal or meaning. But on closer inspection British decision-making can be seen to be influenced, at times even driven, by a variety of assumptions and attitudes toward Europe which have been much less than objective. And it is on these more subjective judgements which the remainder of this chapter will focus.

The first group of assumptions have centred on Europe's stability and on the likelihood of conflict or collapse either between or within the major states. Britain's readiness or otherwise to assume a major role in European diplomacy has, to a large extent, been influenced by judgements about whether or not European politics have been stable and likely to remain so. Such assessments, however, have often revealed more about Britain's underlying prejudices than they have about the real state of politics in continental Europe.

British nineteenth-century assessments of Europe's stability were deeply marked by the 'lessons' of the French Revolution and the Napoleonic era. Prior to 1789, a writer such as Edward Gibbon could argue that Europe as a whole was strengthened rather than weakened by its periodic disputes and wars. In a famous passage of *Decline and Fall* which asked whether eighteenth-century Europe might succumb to the fate which had befallen the Roman Empire, the British historian asserted that such a fate was unlikely. Rome's great weakness, he maintained, had been its enormous centralization; misrule in the centre thus had far-reaching effects throughout the empire. Furthermore, the combination of peace and Christianity sapped the will of the many peoples living under Roman tutelage to defend the Empire against the barbarian hordes. Modern Europe, by contrast, although comparable to Rome in the extent to which it stood 'above the rest of mankind', was unlikely to be affected by the same frailties, primarily due to its very diversity and decentralization.

> The abuses of tyranny are restrained by the mutual influence of fear and shame; republics have acquired order and stability; monarchies have imbibed the principles of freedom, or, at least, of moderation; and some sense of honour and justice is introduced into the most defective constitutions by the general manners of the times. In peace, the progress of knowledge is accelerated by the emulation of so many active rivals: in war, the European forces are exercised by temperate and indecisive contests. (Gibbon 1963: 277–9)

Far from the embattled Occident of which contemporary Austrians spoke, Englishmen such as Gibbon hence perceived Europe as a dynamic and confident civilization, free from imminent danger (cf. Weiss in Chapter 11 of this volume).

The French Revolution swept away such comfortable assumptions, however. The progressive ideas of the revolutionaries – Europe as 'civilization' – made less impression on British consciousness than did the barbarity of their methods. And the lengthy wars which ensued undermined any notion of European stability. Gibbon, it appeared, had been wrong to anticipate that the danger to Europe came from the barbarian without; instead, the greatest threat arose from its internal divisions, whether of class or of nation. To many in Britain this prompted two interlinked conclusions. First, direct involvement in European wars should be avoided wherever possible. And second, continental politics were to be regarded as an object lesson in how not to govern rather than something to be imitated. Bolstered in time by the events of 1830 and 1848 when once more Britain appeared a lone outpost of stability as a wave of unrest swept the continent, this mistrust of European politics gradually developed into the belief that Britain and its neighbours had taken fundamentally divergent political paths. By 1849, another distinguished historian, Thomas Macaulay, could draw a contrast between Britain and the rest of Europe as stark as that which Gibbon had perceived between Modern Europe and Ancient Rome:

> All around us the world is convulsed by the agonies of great nations. Governments which lately seemed likely to stand during ages have been on a sudden shaken and overthrown. The proudest capitals of Western Europe have streamed with civil blood . . . Europe has been threatened with subjugation by barbarians, compared with whom the barbarians who marched under Attila and Alboin were enlightened and humane . . . Meanwhile in our island the regular course of government has never been for a day interrupted. (Macaulay 1849: 655–64)

The horrors of the first half of the twentieth century only seemed to reinforce both this notion and the attraction of British detachment. The Great War produced an understandable desire, both among the public at large and within the political elite, to ensure that no comparable carnage could occur again. It also further cemented the perceived link between Europe and bloodshed. Even such an observer as Winston Churchill could write of continental European developments in deeply blood-tinged language. In his 1930 article, 'The United States of Europe', which compared the idea of European unity to a fire which had smouldered for years but which was only now at a stage where it was likely to set alight the 'rubbish heap' of Europe, he wrote:

> We must regard this heap a little more closely in the glowing light. It has been the growth of centuries, and even millenniums have passed since some of its still-existing materials were deposited. In the main, it is made up of the bones

and broken weapons of uncounted millions who brought one another to violent death long ago. Upon these, three or four centuries have cast masses of rotting vegetation, and latterly an increasing discharge of waste paper. But in it, mixed up with all this litter, scattered about and intermingled, are some of the most precious and dearly loved of treasures of the strongest races in the world. All the history books of Europe are there; its household gods; all the monuments and records of wonderful achievement and sacrifice; the battle flags for which heroes of every generation have shed their blood; the vestments of religions still living and growing in the minds of men; the foundations of the jurisprudence still regulating their relations one with another – all flung and blended together. (Saturday Evening Post, 15 February 1930)

For Churchill the conclusion to be drawn from this mix of barbarity and civilization was that Britain should do all in its power to encourage Europe to unite – without itself taking part – thereby putting an end to the continent's endemic bloodshed. But it was unsurprising if other statesmen, while sharing with Churchill the association between Europe and bloodshed, drew rather different conclusions.

Fear of further European war also threw into sharp relief the fundamental uncertainty about whether or not Britain was European. For Imperial statesmen such as W.L. MacKenzie King, the Canadian Prime Minister, the best response to the underlying dangers of European involvement was clearly disengagement: Canada, he asserted, should take advantage of the fact that 'We live in a flame-proof house, far from inflammable materials' (Howard 1974: 75–6). Many other statesmen from the Dominions – influential figures in inter-war Britain – shared this view. Yet for Britain itself the decision to disengage from European affairs was much harder to take, particularly at a time when the emergence of air power was increasing Britain's vulnerability to attack from the continent. The flammable material was much too close, the house itself far from flame-proof. The story of Britain's military and strategic planning between the wars thus centres on an agonizing debate about how European – or how Imperial – Britain could afford to be. Through most of the 1920s and the first part of the 1930s, guided by politicians such as Austen Chamberlain and Stanley Baldwin, Britain opted primarily for the politics of European involvement. As Baldwin put it to the House of Commons in 1934: 'When you think of the defence of England you no longer think of the chalk cliffs of Dover; you think of the Rhine. That is where our frontier lies' (Howard 1974: 112). But neither public opinion nor all of Baldwin's Conservative colleagues were wholly convinced. Two years later, the Chancellor of the Exchequer, Neville Chamberlain, could respond to an army plea for greater resources, by noting that public opinion, 'strongly opposed to continental adventures . . . will be strongly suspicious of any preparation made in peace time with a view to large scale military operations on the Continent and they will regard such preparations as likely to result in our being entangled in disputes which do not concern us' (Howard 1974: 116). From such views to the belief that the Sudeten crisis was 'a quarrel in a far away country between people of whom we know nothing' was but a short step. Accordingly, appeasement was in part a function both of attitudes about how European Britain should be and of assessments of how dangerous and unstable continental politics were likely to prove.

Britain's disinclination to involve itself too deeply in 1930s Europe was bolstered by an equally-strong suspicion of domestic continental politics. Distaste at the Italian Fascist and Nazi German regimes was of course deeply comprehensible, as were the equally strong misgivings about Soviet Russia. But British dislike of European politics extended also to countries which had remained democratic, such as France. The perpetual comings and goings of Third Republic governments were looked at with a mixture of dismay and contempt, and even as Anglophile a French leader as Leon Blum had to struggle in order to establish a close rapport with London. The inter-war failure to build a strong Anglo-French alliance against Adolf Hitler was hence intertwined with a sweeping British judgement about the nature of European politics.

British dismissiveness toward the stability of the continent was much in evidence after 1945 as well. Although the late 1940s were an era when Britain did take the lead in building a variety of trans-European bodies, designed both to distribute American Marshall Aid and to put in place defensive structures which might help repel a Soviet attack, it did so with misgivings, unwilling either to see itself reduced to the level of 'just another European country' or to allow its own survival to become dependent on continental armies which were as likely to collapse in the face of a Soviet challenge as they had been in the face of the Germans in 1940. The British military, in particular, continued to feel that continental Europe was indefensible without American assistance, and made no effort whatsoever to plan for ways in which Britain might honour the defensive obligations that its politicians had decided to assume by means of the Dunkirk and Brussels treaties (Baylis 1993: 76–91). British European policy-making in the first years of the cold war was thus deeply influenced by the 'lesson' of 1940, namely that no continental country could be considered militarily reliable (Reynolds 1993: 315–20). Both its military strategy, which went on being centred on the Middle East and

Commonwealth defence long after NATO's creation in 1949, and its attitude towards European projects such as the Schuman Plan, reflected this dismissive judgement of Europe's prospects in the event of war with the Soviet Union.

As during the inter-war period, question marks about Europe's strategic reliability went hand-in-hand with uncertainty about the domestic politics of the major continental countries. Britain admittedly was not alone in taking time to regain its trust of Germany, but by the 1960s the tone of caution, mistrust and ill-concealed hostility which still characterized some of Britain's approaches to Bonn looked increasingly anachronistic (Schaad 2000: 169–71). Relations with France were also less than ideal. Britain has never been good at understanding the intricacies of coalition politics, and its attitude towards the rapid rotation of governments under the Fourth Republic only confirmed this rule. French governments were seen as transient, weak and totally unreliable, the policy consistency which sprang from the powerful French Civil Service usually being totally overlooked. But matters did not improve with the advent of the Fifth Republic, since dismissiveness about weak governments was replaced with near paranoia about de Gaulle's maverick foreign policy. Italy, meanwhile, was treated with scant respect, its politics and economy considered backward, even long after it at least had begun its remarkable post-war boom (Ludlow 2000: 383–404). As one senior British diplomat recalled:

> We were highly sceptical about Europe. Europe was a collection of aliens and foreigners . . . who were erratic. They were unreliable. Some of them had let us down. Some of them had fought against us. All of them were seen, in 1948, to be liable to communist subversion and they were, quite frankly, not the sort of area that we – in contrast to the Commonwealth and all its glittering prospects as we saw it – wanted to tie ourselves down to. (Charlton 1983: 62)

This dismissiveness fed through into Britain's early European integration policy-making. For a start it tended to cast doubts about the viability of the whole enterprise. Despite the success of the ECSC, the British would remain unpersuaded of the effectiveness of integration until very late in the 1950s, and were still expressing doubts, even as they prepared for Community membership in the early 1960s, about whether it would survive after the demise of the French and German leaders, Charles de Gaulle and Konrad Adenauer. But dismissiveness also led to both a strong sense that full participation, as opposed to association, would somehow be demeaning for a country such as Britain and also the unfounded expectation that Britain had only to say the word to be able to assume control over the process. Expectations that Britain could push Europe where it willed were to reach their apogee in the mid-1950s with the Free Trade Area scheme and would subsequently fade somewhat. The belief, however, that Britain's negotiating position was much stronger than it really was continued to shape British policy-making under both Prime Ministers Harold Macmillan and Harold Wilson. Its most famous expression after all, in the form of Foreign Secretary George Brown's reported outburst to West German Chancellor, Willy Brandt 'Willy, you must get us in so we can take the lead' dates from the end of the 1960s rather than from the previous decade (Brandt 1978: 161).

A vein of dismissiveness towards much continental politics has continued up until the present day. Fully-fledged attacks on the viability of continental democracy, along the lines of the former Prime Minister Clement Attlee's full-page newspaper advertisement in 1962 in which he spoke of Europe being 'politically unstable' and asked whether France, Germany and Italy would still be democracies in twenty years time, have faded somewhat (*The Daily Telegraph*, 15 August 1962). But the sentiments arguably live on, both in the recurrent attacks on the undemocratic structures of the Community itself and in the repeated questioning of the honesty and freedom from corruption of most continental politicians – and indeed of continental life. Conservative politician Michael Portillo's off-the-record comments about how easy it was to buy educational qualifications in most European countries were indicative of a widespread mistrust of continental fairness (Financial Times, 5 February 1994).

Suspicion of Germany, in particular, has frequently bubbled to the surface. As early as 1956 Harold Macmillan was warning that the Messina project could constitute 'an instrument for the revival of German power through economic means. It is really giving them on a plate what we fought two world wars to prevent.' Similar sentiments have been expressed more recently by Nicholas Ridley, the Conservative Secretary of State for the Environment under Margaret Thatcher, who described the EEC as 'a German racket designed to take over the whole of Europe' – as well as by Thatcher herself in the notorious 1990 Chequers study day (Young 1998: 359–62). In all cases, the aggressiveness of the Germans and the political unreliability of the remaining 'Europeans' has been contrasted, normally implicitly, sometimes explicitly, with the reliability, fairness, honesty and respect for democracy of the British. (Kaiser 1996: 221–5). Although extreme, an outburst by the by-then Lady Thatcher illustrates the basic attitudes well, with the former Prime Minister telling a gathering of Scottish Tories that: 'We are quite the best country in Europe . . . I dare say it – I'm told I have to be careful about what I say and I don't like it – in my lifetime all our problems have come from mainland Europe and all the solutions have come from the English-speaking nations of the world that have kept law-abiding liberty alive for the future' (*The Times*, 6 October 1999).

This long tradition of British criticism of the military and political reliability of its continental neighbours is most usually associated with those opposed to closer ties between Britain and the Continent. The prominence in the preceding paragraphs of Eurosceptics such as Attlee, Thatcher or Portillo only reinforce this linkage. But the fact that men such as Churchill and Macmillan have also been prone to denunciations of the state of continental politics underlines the fact that unhappiness at the state of Europe has not necessarily been an argument for indifference or detachment. On the contrary, some of the most powerful advocates of British involvement have drawn much of their zeal from the twin beliefs that, first, Britain could not but be affected by instability among its nearest geographical neighbours, and secondly, that British involvement would be the best means of stabilizing the situation and ensuring that matters were not allowed to slip out of control. Thinking of this sort has been observable in the British political and policy-making debate throughout the twentieth century. In what might perhaps be termed its weaker variant, such thinking has not necessarily overcome British doubts about whether European cooperation is suitable for itself, but has led British politicians and diplomats to feel that Britain should play an encouraging role from the sidelines. Churchill's advocacy of such an approach has been noted above. In similar vein, the initial Foreign Office response to the Briand plan, while ruling out British participation, counselled against too negative a reply on the grounds that British dismissiveness might harm the French Foreign Minister. Briand was, in the view of the Foreign Office, 'an old and valued friend of this country . . . almost alone among French politicians he has in recent years consistently shown himself a good European, the friend of peace, and of the improvement of international relations' (Boyce 1987: 247–8). The poor state of French and European politics generally was, in other words, being advanced as a strong reason for mitigating British criticism of the plan. In the post-war era comparable anxieties about the adverse effect of British hostility tempered both Labour and Conservative attacks on the Schuman and Pleven Plans. Anthony Eden, in particular, became so convinced that the EDC was vital for European stability, that he was prepared to go to great lengths in his efforts to salvage the project (Mawby 1999: 73–103).

In its stronger form, the perceived need for British encouragement has been superseded by the belief that the stability of Europe can only be achieved through actual British participation. The best known inter-war manifestations of this line of thought were of course the arguments of those who opposed appeasement and denounced the Munich agreement. In their eyes, Britain, France and Russia would have to act together in order to curb German aggression and preserve peace in Europe. Full-hearted British involvement in the politics of Europe was essential if war was to be avoided and the dictators held in check. Since 1945, comparable reasoning has been applied with regard to European integration. The 1960 Lee Committee report, for instance, a major milestone on Britain's road to EEC membership, noted the strong foreign policy pressures which would be brought to bear on Britain should the Six succeed in their collective endeavour, and then went on:

> If on the other hand, the Six 'fail', there would be great damage to Western interests, and the weakening of Europe which would follow would be a serious matter for the United Kingdom; it would be too late for us to go in to prevent failure when a breakdown was seen to be coming, but if we were already in, we could probably strengthen the European bloc and prevent its disintegration. (PRO. CAB 134/1853, ES(E) Cttee, June 1960)

The potential for European instability was once more being turned into an argument *for* rather than *against* British involvement.

Throughout the last two hundred years, the British have thus been recurrently drawn into making sweeping generalizations about the stability, reliability and honesty of European politics. Such judgements when made have rarely, if ever, been the product of a genuine pan-European survey, ready and able to differentiate between different tendencies across the differing parts of the continent. On the contrary, they have most often been snap judgements, based on a patchy knowledge of Western Europe in general, and France and Germany in particular (Deighton and Warner 1993: 60–2). But despite their questionable reliability, such assessments have played a central role in the determination of the British government's policy toward its neighbours, at times forming the basis of arguments for isolation and detachment, at others underpinning the belief that Britain needed to become more deeply involved.

The second cluster of attitudes which need to be considered in under-standing the assumptions that have underpinned Britain's European policy are questions surrounding the idea of Europe and modernity. In common with judgements about stability, these have a long pedigree. Indeed, links between the two were strong, and both appear to have undergone a major shift in the course of the eighteenth and nineteenth centuries. In the twentieth century they have become still more vital, with assessments about the extent to which participation in European cooperation would drive Britain forward, or hold the country back, playing a notable and telling role in virtually all of Britain's intermittent debates about Europe.

For Britain's eighteenth-century elite Europe, and France in particular, represented civilization and modernity. The French language was widely learnt, French manners were imitated, and continental travel was seen as a vital, and civilizing, part of a young man's education. So cosmopolitan indeed did members of the British elite feel, that Edmund Burke could write that Europe was 'virtually one great state, having the same basis of general law with some diversity of provincial customs and local establishments'. Britain's wealthiest citizens felt fully part of this civilization (Newman 1997: 1–18).

In the course of the eighteenth century, however, three distinct trends undermined this situation. The first was the rise of literary and artistic culture highly critical of the 'fashion' for all things foreign. The drawings of Hogarth and the novels of Fielding were just two manifestations of this revolt against cosmopolitanism (Newman 1997: 50–76) Secondly, British political radicalism came to place ever greater emphasis on the way in which alleged 'Saxon freedoms' had been crushed by the 'Norman Yoke'. The language of political protest, in other words, began to associate Englishness with freedom and progress, and 'foreign' (i.e. French) rule with oppression (Newman 1997: 117–91). And thirdly, the spectacle of the French Revolution, far from impressing with the modern and progressive ideas which it invoked, instead repelled much of the British elite with its violence and brutality. The same Edmund Burke, indeed, who had earlier written of Europe as 'one great state', could denounce events in Paris in language which borrowed liberally from the ideas of political radicals. Others who followed a similar trajectory from cosmopolitan Francophilia to nationalistic Francophobia during much the same period included both Wordsworth and Coleridge (Newman 1997: 228–41).

By 1815, therefore, the British elite not only had seen many of its continental ties cut by two decades of war, but also had lost the habit of looking to Europe for progressive ideas. This pattern was reinforced by both economics and religion. Britain's growing industrial self-confidence meant less heed was paid to outside models, while secular judgements about Europe were reinforced by Protestant misgivings about the Catholicism which characterized so many of Britain's neighbours (cf. Stråth, Chapter 5 in this volume.). A widespread assumption of superiority therefore emerged which all but destroyed any link between Europe and modernity. There were isolated exceptions of course. Richard Cobden, for instance, came back from an extensive continental tour impressed with land-tenure patterns in France, Spain and Italy, and eager to see Britain follow suit (Taylor 1994: 12–18). Similarly, Matthew Arnold urged his fellow countrymen to copy continental approaches to education (Arnold 1868: v–xxii). And within the university world there were multiple instances, whether in history, classics or theology, of British scholars borrowing profitably from their European and especially German counterparts (Goldstein 1990: 141–53; Wilson 1987: 54–5; Morgan and Barton 1988: 57–9). But such exceptions, while enough to puncture the myth of total detachment, were not sufficient to alter a general belief that Europe would do well to borrow from Britain rather than Britain from Europe.

Such views remained prevalent in the first half of the twentieth century. A few on the extreme left were admittedly attracted by the example of Soviet Communism. And toward the opposite end of the political spectrum there were some who spoke highly of the methods employed by Mussolini and Hitler, and advocated their use in Britain. But the total failure of such notions in the British context was indicative not only of a society the problems of which were not serious enough to warrant such drastic remedies, but also of a British political class which had fallen entirely out of the habit of looking across the Channel for inspiration. Even those who sought large-scale reform seldom used European examples to bolster their case. Harold Macmillan's The Middle Way, for instance, is remarkable for containing virtually no references to habits or methods employed elsewhere. Two passing allusions to Swedish policy – one about a milk-distribution scheme, the other about unemployment benefits – are the sole foreign examples used (Macmillan 1938: 80–1, 334). On the contrary, the pattern of German, Italian, French and Russian politics merely seemed to confirm the belief that continental politics were of a deeply unattractive variety.

It is thus only in the post-war period that the idea of looking to Europe for progressive notions has begun to gain some credence. And even after 1945 the initial experience seemed to indicate that little had changed. For many on the Left of British politics, one of the most persuasive reasons to look askance at the whole integrative project was the belief that Western Europe was primarily reactionary and conservative and that, as such, British involvement could only impede Britain's own path towards the construction of a socialist state. 'Europe' in this sense became not an alternative to 'Commonwealth' or 'Atlanticism' but instead a barrier to 'that New Jerusalem which the post-war Labour Party wished to build. In April 1948, for instance, the Labour-leaning *Daily Herald* urged Labour delegates to boycott the Hague Conference since the gathering would merely provide a platform for Churchill and others who desired 'the old order of things' (Moon 1985: 107).

During the 1960s and the great debate about British membership of the EEC, there was a similar subtext about the compatibility of European integration and socialism. Gaitskell's 1962 party conference speech, in which he attacked the Macmillan government's headlong rush into Europe, displayed strong doubts about whether or not joining the Community would be progressive:

> For although, of course, Europe has had a great and glorious civilisation, although Europe can claim Goethe and Leonardo, Voltaire and Picasso, there have been evil features in European history too – Hitler and Mussolini, and today the attitude of some Europeans to the Congo problem, the attitude of at least one European government to the United Nations. You cannot say what this Europe will be: it has two faces and we do not know yet which is the one which will dominate. (Holmes 1996: 21)

This sense of general unease was compounded by more specific doubts about whether EEC membership would allow Britain the economic freedom to tackle local unemployment and the extent to which economic planning would be permitted. For those on the Labour left, such as Barbara Castle or Richard Crossman, the choice between Europe and socialism was much more clear-cut, as the latter's diary account of 1967 Cabinet discussions of the issue reveal:

> Those who are in charge – Michael Stewart, George Brown, Harold Wilson, Jim Callaghan – all now feel that the attempt to have a socialist national plan for the British Isles keeps us balanced on such a terribly tight rope that it really has got to be abandoned and that of course is the main reason why they favour entry into the Market. Today Barbara [Castle] made a tremendous speech saying that entry would transform our socialism and make us abandon all our plans. In a sense she's completely right. If anybody wanted, apart from myself, Britain to be a socialist off-shore island, entry to the Market would mean the abandonment of that ideal. (Crossman 1977: 335)

The way to the left's vision of modernity and the path to Europe were thus seen as utterly divergent. To the Labour left, the Wilson government's espousal of Common Market entry signalled its abandonment of fully-blown socialism. In the light of such views, it is unsurprising that the apogee of left-wing power within the Labour Party saw the party fight the 1983 General Election on a platform of withdrawal from the European Community.

By the mid- to late-1980s, however, it had become the Thatcherite right, not the socialist left, who felt that their opportunity radically to transform Britain was being obstructed by the European Community. The tension between the ideals espoused by the European Community and the free-market vision of the British Prime Minister was nowhere better expressed than in Thatcher's 1988 Bruges speech:

> I want to see us work more closely on the things we can do better together than alone. Europe is stronger when we do so, whether it be in trade, in defence, or in our relationship with the rest of the world. But working more closely together does *not* require power to be centralised in Brussels or decisions to be taken by an appointed bureaucracy. Indeed, it is ironic that just when those countries such as the Soviet Union, which have tried to run everything from the centre, are learning that success depends on dispersing power and decisions away from the centre, some in the Community seem to want to move in the opposite direction. We have not successfully rolled back the frontiers of the state in Britain, only to see them re-imposed at a European level, with a European super-state exercising a new dominance from Brussels. (Holmes 1996: 91–2)

As had been the case with the Labour left during the years between 1945 and 1983, the most radical members of Britain's political class thus regarded the notion of collective European action as something which would at best dilute and at worst altogether remove their capacity for a far-reaching transformation of the British economy and society. To those with the most extreme visions of modernity, 'Europe' was a regressive rather than a modernizing concept.

The alarming radicalism of both the left and the Thatcherite right may equally have led some with more centrist convictions to a more favourable position towards European integration. That same capacity to obstruct or dilute far-reaching change which so appalled the radicals would appear rather attractive to those hostile to socialist or Thatcherite ideals. There is some evidence of this happening in the 1950s and 1960s. For instance, the *Daily Telegraph* editorial, entitled 'Socialism vs Europe', which advocated observer status at least for the British at the Schuman Plan negotiations, may well have been born in part out of the belief that the worst excesses of the post-war Labour government might be contained by European involvement (Moon 1985: 108). And it is sometimes claimed that one of the unspoken arguments behind the Tory volte-face on Europe of the early 1960s was the need to make Britain safe from the socialism of any future Labour government (Holmes 1996: 116–18). But it is in the 1980s that this phenomenon is most easily observed. The swing towards pro-Europeanism of the TUC and the majority of the British Labour movement, for instance, was strongly related to the growing conviction among British trade unionists that Europe, far from posing a danger to their aspirations, instead represented the most effective means of protecting the conquests of the past from a right-wing British government which appeared instinctively hostile to trade unionism. To beleaguered British trade union officials, who had come to dread virtually all economic, social and fiscal policy-making under Thatcher, Jacques Delors's sweeping (and ill-founded) prediction that 'in ten years time, 80 per cent of economic, and perhaps social and tax legislation, will be of Community origin' sounded like a promise of liberation (Delors 1988). Similarly, there is much to suggest that the transformation of Scottish opinion towards European integration in the course of the 1980s – which saw what had been the part of the British electorate in the 1975 referendum most hostile to the idea of remaining inside the EEC become, by the late 1980s, consistently more pro-European than the national average – had much to do with Scotland's antipathy to Thatcherism. For many in Edinburgh, Brussels represented the best protection available from the excesses of London.

It would, however, be unfair to those who have occupied the centre ground of British politics to suggest that their pro-Europeanism sprang merely from the belief that Europe would act as a restraining force on either or both of the political extremes. Instead, there has always been a strong strand of argument within the moderate centre of British politics which has equated European involvement with the modernization of the country. For example, the Labour MP, Roy Jenkins, one of the most articulate exponents of this view-point, could write in 1961:

> Looked at in more practical and more specifically European terms, would joining the Six be likely to inhibit the rate of social progress in this country? Only those who are still living in the world of 1949 could answer with a firm yes, for no one who has observed the world of the 'fifties can believe that Britain is a less Tory nation than the dominant powers of the EEC. For rapidity of economic growth (France, Germany and Italy), for the fullest of full employment (Germany and France), for highly successful nationalized industries (France), for a model system of economic planning (France), and for a most imaginative and generous system of retirement benefits (Germany), the Six have far more to show the Left than anything which this country has achieved for years past. (Jenkins 1961)

In the course of the 1960s debate a large number of other 'progressive' benefits were linked to the European cause. These ranged from metrification to decimalization, from Parliamentary reform to the building of a Channel Tunnel. At its most extreme, Lord Gladwyn could conclude a 1961 newspaper *plaidoyer* in favour of EEC membership with the invocation: 'Somehow we must get out of our present nineteenth-century rut and join the main stream of mid-twentieth century history' (*The Guardian*, 31 July 1961).

Much the same process has occurred during the 1980s and 1990s when Europe was seen as a powerful means to an end by those pursuing any number of 'progressive' goals. Probably the two reforms of the British political system most frequently linked to European integration have been electoral reform – it was often argued that pressure to devise a single uniform electoral system for European elections would, by inexorable logic, strengthen the case for the whole British system to move in the direction of proportional representation – and the decentralization of power. A more flexible approach to the sovereignty of Westminster which recognized the need to pool some sovereignty at a European level would, it was maintained, go hand in hand with a greater readiness to devolve power within the United Kingdom itself. But both the mechanism of European integration and the example of numerous continental countries have also been invoked by those pressing for better public transport, higher public spending, a more liberal criminal justice system (the role of the European Court of Justice and the European Court of Human Rights have reinforced this tendency), more equal treatment of men and women, and a more 'enlightened' attitude towards sex education or the use of soft drugs. Debates about Europe among politicians from the centre ground of British politics, whether Liberal Democrats or moderate Labour and Conservative figures, have thus tended to convey more than just an attitude toward Britain's place within the EC/EU; they have instead been about a whole-scale modification of Britain's approach to a wide range of political, social and economic issues. From the standpoint of the political centre, embracing Europe has also implied an embrace of 'modernity' defined in centrist terms.

The extent to which Europe has been seen as a modernizing force has thus depended greatly on the standpoint of the observer. For those on the political left or the political right it has rarely been seen as modernizing, appearing instead as a regressive force, more likely to thwart than to promote change. But those more centrist in their ideal have repeatedly looked across the Channel and invoked the ideal of Europe both in the hope of blunting the more dangerous zeal of some of their compatriots and in the belief that European involvement would encourage a welcome Europeanization and therefore modernization of British life. At the risk of caricature, it is often the case in Britain that the socially-permissive, bike-riding Liberal Democrat who calculates his or her height in centimetres will more likely be pro-European than will a Toyota-driving, six-foot-three Tory, who is strongly in favour of capital punishment.

Despite the tendency of much of the current historiography to present Britain's attitude toward Europe as one of calculating pragmatism and hard-headed realism, the concept of Europe in British political discourse has been far from value-free. Britain's fundamental uncertainty about whether or not it is part of Europe, geographically, culturally or politically, has certainly given the British debate about Europe a distinctive twist, as has the rival pull of both Empire and the English-speaking world. But rather than permitting a detached and dispassionate objectivity, the question mark over Britain's Europeanness has in fact allowed Britain's policy-makers to let their choice for or against European involvement be guided by assumptions about the stability, reliability and modernity of continental political life. In circumstances where a choice to participate or not to participate in any form of European activity has never been automatic, both the ferocity of the debate and the diversity of possible views have always been increased. The concept of Europe has acquired multiple layers of meaning as a result. Thus while a large portion of the British population still gives the impression that it has not made up its mind whether Britain belongs in the heart of Europe, it has become abundantly clear on the basis of twentieth-century history that the concept of Europe has come to occupy a position at the heart of British political discourse.

## Acknowledgement

The author would like to thank the editors, Arne Westad, Robert Boyce, Anthony Howe, Linda Colley and Peter Ghosh for their help, comments and advice.

## References

Arnold, M. (1868), *Schools and Universities on the Continent*, London: Macmillan.

Baylis, J. (1993), *The Diplomacy of Pragmatism: Britain and the Formation of NATO, 1942–9*, London: Macmillan.

Boyce, R. (1987), *British Capitalism at the Crossroads 1919–1932: A Study in Politics, Economics and International Relations*, Cambridge: Cambridge University Press.

Brandt, W. (1978), *People and Politics: The Years 1960–1975*, London: Collins.

Charlton, M. (1983), *The Price of Victory*, London: BBC.

Churchill, W. (1930), 'The United States of Europe', *Saturday Evening Post*, 15.2.1930.

Crossman, R. (1977), *The Diaries of a Cabinet Minister*, Vol. II, Book Club Associates.

Deighton, A. and Warner, G. (1993), 'British Perceptions of Europe in the Post-war Period', in R. Girault and G. Bossuat, *Les Europe des Européens*, Paris: Publications de la Sorbonne.

Delors, J. (1988), 'Europe 1992: The Social Dimension', Address to the TUC Conference, Bournemouth, September 1988, Brussels: European Commission.

Ellison, J. (2000), *Threatening Europe: Britain and the creation of the European Community*, 1955–58, London: Macmillan.

Gibbon, E. (1963 [1776–88]), *The Decline and Fall of the Roman Empire* (ed. H.R. Trevor-Roper), London: Sadler & Brown.

Goldstein, D. (1990), 'History at Oxford and Cambridge: Professionalization and the Influence of Ranke', in G. Iggers and J. Powell (eds), *Leopold von Ranke and the Shaping of the Historical Discipline*, Syracuse, NY: Syracuse University Press.

Gooders, J. (1998), *Birds of Britain and Europe*, London: HarperCollins.

Holmes, M. (ed.) (1996), *The Eurosceptical Reader*, London: Macmillan.

Howard, M. (1974), *The Continental Commitment: The Dilemma of British Defence Policy in the Era of Two World Wars*, London: Penguin.

Howe, A. (1997), *Free Trade and Liberal England 1846–1946*, Oxford: Clarendon.

Hudson, R. (ed.) (1993), *The Grand Tour 1592–1796*, London: The Folio Society.

Jenkins, R. (1961), 'From London to Rome', *Encounter*, August 1961.

Kaiser, W. (1996), *Using Europe, Abusing the Europeans: Britain and European Integration*, 1945–63, London: Macmillan.

Ludlow, N.P. (2000), 'A Slow Reassessment: British Views of Italy's European Policy 1950–1963', *Storia delle relazioni internazionali*, xiv (1999), (1): 385–406.

Macaulay, T.B. (1849), *The History of England from the Accession of James the Second*, Vol. 2, London.

Macmillan, H. (1938), *The Middle Way: A Study of the Problem of Economic and Social Progress in a Free and Democratic Society,* London: Macmillan.

Marsh, P. (1999), *Bargaining on Europe: Britain and the First Common Market 1860–1892,* New Haven: Yale University Press.

Mawby, S. (1999), *Containing Germany: Britain and the Arming of the Federal Republic,* London; Macmillan.

Moon, J. (1985), *European Integration in British Politics 1950–1963: A Study of Issue-Change,* Gower.

Morgan, R. and Barton, J. (1988), *Biblical Interpretation,* Oxford: Oxford University Press.

Newman, G. (1997), *The Rise of English Nationalism: A Cultural History 1740–1830,* London: Macmillan.

Reynolds, D. (1993), 'Great Britain and the Security "Lessons" of the Second World War', in R. Ahman, A.M. Birke and M. Howard, *The Quest for Stability: Problems of European Security 1918–57,* Oxford: Oxford University Press.

Robbins, K. (1993), *History, Religion and Identity in Modern Britain,* London: Hambledon.

Salter, A. (1993), *The United States of Europe and Other Papers,* George Allen & Unwin.

Schaad, M. (2000), *Bullying Bonn: Anglo-German Diplomacy on European Integration, 1955–61,* London: Macmillan.

Taylor, M. (ed.) (1994), *The European Diaries of Richard Cobden 1846–9,* Aldershot: Scholar Press.

Wilson, D. (1987), *Gilbert Murray OM 1866–1957,* Oxford: Clarendon.

Young, H. (1998), *This Blessed Plot: Britain and Europe from Churchill to Blair,* London: Macmillan.

# –5–

# The Swedish Demarcation
# from Europe
## *Bo Stråth*

The Greek foundation myth – where Greece is seen as the cradle of Europe, and where the meaning of Europe is derived teleologically from its Greek origin – was, as Constantine Tsoukalas demonstrates in Chapter 1 of this volume, not invented in Greece but in its European periphery. Europe took on the meaning of Greece – and vice versa – in this construction of a historical heritage. This myth was mobilized in particular during the Ottoman expansion in the Balkans.

At about the same time as the Ottomans consolidated their positions in the Balkans, Gustavus II Adolphus launched his campaign against the Roman Catholic Church, where religious rhetoric also contained clear elements of political power. The Swedish king presented himself as a Protestant lion on the bulwark against the Pope in a European *mission civilisatrice*. Many of the rhetorical figures in the propaganda used against the Turks recurred in Swedish war propaganda, with the difference being that the Pope was substituted for the Turks.

Further, an element in the Swedish allusion to the light from the north was the impudent attempt to appropriate the idea of the Greek origin of Europe and to make it Swedish. Sweden, like so many other dynastically-ruled states in medieval Europe, staked its claim to be the oldest state in the world – that is to say, in Europe. As early as at the council in Basle in 1434, the Swedish representative Bishop Nicolaus Ragvaldi claimed, in a dispute with Spain, that Sweden was the world's oldest state. Ragvaldi made his barefaced claim at a time when both Sweden and Poland were included under the banner of the German nation within the organization of the Roman Catholic Church. Equally, both Ragvaldi and his Spanish counterpart referred to the (Visi)Gothic heritage of their respective states.

This mythical field was then further cultivated in sixteenth-century Sweden by Johannes Magnus. During the reign of Gustavus II Adolphus, who was King of Sweden from 1611 to 1632, Gothic rhetoric was developed into a veritable campaign for a Gothic heritage. This *göticism* served as a royal propaganda instrument in the build-up of Swedish military power and was used in support of the claim to the Baltic as a *mare nostrum*. Archaeology and the excavation of burial mounds supported the promotion of Gothic ideology and the proclamation of a grandiose past. This Gothic rhetoric represented national self-assertion as produced through the merging of the Gothic language with classicism by means of locating the origin of the antique world in *Norden*, the North. The patriotic speculations on this Gothic heritage culminated with the *magnum opus* written by the Uppsala professor, Olof Rudbeck. The first volume of his *Atlantis* was published in 1679, but the work was still unfinished when he died in 1702 (*Olaus Rudbecks Atlantica: Svenska*). With arguments based on the diligent study of both ancient authors and newly discovered Icelandic literature, Rudbeck drew far-reaching conclusions about Swedish antiquity. Accordingly, Plato's Atlantis was identical with the realm of the Goths, the king's castle had been situated in Old Uppsala, and it was from there that the gods of antique culture had emigrated. As a Swedish scholar of the history of ideas has put it, Rudbeck's 'patriotic gospel meant that he appropriated the whole Greek and Roman culture and provided it with a Swedish label' (Lindroth 1955; cf. Stråth 2000a: 376–8).

In this scenario, Europe was Christian unity through Protestant progression. History was progression and Europe was the goal of this Protestant progression. This is without doubt an alternative view of Europe to that which Gilbert Weiss attaches to Austria in Chapter 11 of this volume. This Swedish image of Europe was not mobilized as a nostalgic defence against the propagation of the values of the French Revolution, but rather it was an early edition of the French *mission civilisatrice* – certainly Protestant Christian instead of revolutionary enlightened, but with the same core of utopian quest entwined with power politics and military ambitions.

This idea of a Protestant Europe built on the battlefields in the fight for the just belief constituted the core of a missionary trope that, with the Thirty Years War, resulted in the final collapse of the idea of a European Christian *res publica*. The Swedish production of meaning disentangled itself from the European unification discourse in a process of national consolidation, although for another three-quarters of a century after the Westphalian Treaty, it retained high-powered political ambitions in the European arena.

The Swedish Protestant *mission impossible* was ever more accentuated after the loss of political and military power in the European arena in

1718. The trope survived, however, and surfaced much later after the Second World War as a third-way world conscience which bypassed Europe, as I will demonstrate later in this chapter. This rebirth had, as one important point of departure, a Social Democratic mobilization of Protestant values in the 1930s, in demarcation from an imagined Catholic and conservative Europe. Protestant virtues and rhetoric – and belief in progress – remained, although the missionary quest was halted in the form that Gustavus Adolphus had given it.

The ending of Sweden's position as a big power in Northern Europe in 1718 was painful, and the loss of Finland in 1809 was traumatic. The central part of Finland, along the Baltic, had been considered to be as integral a part of Sweden as the central areas around Stockholm, while the Finnish periphery had been perceived as no more peripheral than the Swedish periphery itself. For this reason, the geographical orientation of Sweden had been understood in east–west rather than north–south terms (Klinge 1983; and, for a critical discussion of Klinge's thesis, Nordin 1998). From 1809 on, a new mental map was gradually projected along an imagined north–south axis. Mentally, the loss of Finland was coped with in terms of the motto: 'Reconquer Finland within Sweden's borders'. In this therapeutic political consolidation of the smaller state, a glorious past was invoked ever more strongly. In 1811, patriotic intellectuals, each with a greater or lesser degree of Romanticism, founded an association based on imagined Gothic values and rites, the *Götiska Förbundet*. Gothic heritage and rhetoric were reclaimed, having been largely overlooked during political and military decline, and during the emerging Enlight-enment discourse of the eighteenth century. The Gothic myth merged with an invocation of the Vikings, making the myth appear more concrete, and with a mythical peasant figure, *odalbonden*, who, particularly in the writings of historian and poet Erik Gustaf Geijer emerged from a dim past. The peasants in Sweden had constituted a separate diet estate since the fifteenth century, and in the historiographical tradition that had become established by the nineteenth century they were the carriers of national freedom and equality. The peasants were the core of the *folk*, not as a passive crowd, but as the incarnation and manifestation of the general will. The free peasants were historically derived from the Viking Age and a mystical past in which, when they met at the *thing* (judicial council), they were not only free but equal. There was a clear continuity with this idea when the Social Democrats redefined themselves as a *folk* party rather than as a class party in the 1930s. The free and equal peasant became a trope that represented a progressive historical force much more than the bourgeoisie did, as the Marxist scheme suggested. Progression in Swedish foundation mythology passed from the peasants to the workers (Sørensen and Stråth 1997: 7–8).

The superimposition and the overlapping of the memories of the Goths and of the Vikings through the figure of the peasant was a rather harmless and inoffensive instrument by which to build up collective self-confidence after 1809 without indulging in expansive dreams of revenge. The 'great power' period was certainly present in the collective memory, but it was consigned to a less prominent position in a past almost as dim as that of the Vikings. Bishop and poet Esaias Tegnér's 1818 ode for the centenary commemoration of the death of Charles XII ('King Charles, the Young Hero') offers a good illustration of this. Gothic escapism long survived the doomsday atmosphere of 1809, and only disappeared after the First World War (when the Gothic and ancient Norse myths experienced a period of greatness in the context of Nordic studies at German universities). What survived even longer was the image of Protestant progression. This idea of progression was palpable not least in the dreams of Scandinavian unification, where one source of inspiration was the Danish clergyman, Grundtvig, who developed Rudbeckius's fanciful imagination of Atlantis and formulated the idea of the Nordic countries as the new Greece. Here, Scandinavians were 'natural' peoples with their own mythology and folklore, as opposed to the 'artificial' peoples of the rest of Europe. In Grundtvig's civilization view, all that connoted Roman and Catholic was excluded. His adoration of a Nordic heroic past with the free peasants as the carriers of culture made a deep impression in Sweden. It was in this mythological scenario that Geijer and Tegnér made their contributions to the nineteenth-century Swedish construction of community, externalizing lost territories like Finland and the Baltic and German-speaking provinces from Swedish history and culture, and reinventing a Nordic peasant community based on a glorified past. Later, in the nineteenth century, poverty and privation were invoked as specific Swedish virtues added to the peasant morals of freedom, equality and moderation. For instance, the Swedish poet Carl Jonas Love Almqvist wrote the novel *On the Importance of Swedish Poverty* (Stråth 2000a). By implication the demarcation from this Protestant peasant culture was an imagined European and Catholic bourgeois high culture.

National consolidation after 1809 meant a definite end to Sweden's military ambitions. The foreign policy changed in a more defensive direction aiming at maintaining peace and the territorial status quo. When Napoleon's Field Marshal Jean-Baptiste Bernadotte acceded in 1818 to the Swedish-Norwegian throne (Norway taken from Denmark and imposed a union with Sweden in the wake of the Napoleonic Wars) as

Karl XIV Johan, he proclaimed a policy which made a clear break with the tradition of military interventions in European politics: 'Separated as we are from the rest of Europe our policy and our interests will always lead us to refrain from involving in any dispute, which does not concern the two Scandinavian peoples [of Sweden-Norway]' (Blidberg and Wahlbäck 1986; af Malmborg 2001: 43–7, 53–5).

During the military and political decline of the eighteenth century, interest in French culture had increased. The language of the Enlightenment was quite compatible with the Protestant ethic and penetrated the Swedish elite. Through architecture and Enlightenment discourse in the Lutheran vicarages, and in the manor-houses of the rural iron mills, this French style had a much deeper popular impact than just as an elite phenomenon in Stockholm. After the French Revolution, the French image peeled off. France became the point of reference more exclusively for the liberal left. French Republican values never really made it to the fore of modern Swedish society. Intellectuals of the left could easily embrace Kantian and Mazzinian ideas of a reform of the European state system, although they rarely did it in the revolutionary spirit and with that sense of urgency that often characterized the movement in continental Europe. For these Swedish reformists 'Europe' rather signified the old system that should be overthrown. The new order to come was rather depicted in national, constitutional and universal liberal terms. They thought of Swedish reforms much more than of European unification for peace (af Malmborg 2001).

The view on that German-speaking territory which had not yet become Germany was ambiguous. Sweden was certainly seen as part of a larger Germanic community, a view which was underpinned by Romanticism. During the twenty-five years of Scandinavianism around 1850, Prussia emerged as an increasingly great threat, however. Prussia's wars against Denmark in 1848 and 1864 promoted feelings of hostility in Sweden. That war in 1864 effectively crushed the Scandinavianist dream. The absence of an agreed principal enemy was crucial to the decline of Scandinavianism. For Sweden the main enemy was Russia and for Denmark it remained Prussia/Germany. Few Swedes were prepared to die for Scandinavia on its southern borders in a war against Prussia/Germany, and as few Danes were prepared to die for Scandinavia against Russia. While the German and the Italian unification projects succeeded the Scandinavianist movement failed. Later, after 1870, the Scandinavian demarcation from Prussia was gradually transformed into a Swedish identification with Germany, which replaced France as a point of reference in elite discourse, which became more Conservative and less liberal.

The emulation of a German model of society was not conceptualized in terms of European civicness, but was based on ideas of a cultural and ethnic community. Somewhat later, the German Social Democrats became a point of reference for the Swedish labour movement. They did not see the same Germany as the Conservatives, of course, but although the image of Germany was contested it was nevertheless a source of inspiration for Swedish organization of society. While the identification with Germany was particularly strong in the royal court and the upper class, the Germanism of the Left was blended with a considerable assimilation of Western liberal and socialist ideas.

This German orientation became more problematic and contradictory after the First World War, although in general terms it remained strong among the Conservatives. Immediately after 1905, which was as traumatic a year as 1809, due to the Norwegian dissolution of the union with Sweden which had been established in 1814, a new modernization discourse strongly emerged. In this, the United States was a generator of utopian energy, and a source of inspiration for political, economic and social reform. The difference between the crisis therapy of 1905 and that of 1809 was that the Utopia was linked to future-oriented ideas of rationalization and modernization rather than to an idealized past. The common denominator in both cases was the missionary quest.

The Russians represented the negative image of the Other in Sweden. Around 1900 there were clear signs of a real Russophobia. In the decades before the First World War, military planning had a Russian threat as its point of departure. These perceptions of fear of Russia and friendship with Germany were embedded in a racial and social Darwinian Enlightenment discourse involving a 'natural' opposition between Slavs and Germans, where the Swedes belonged to the German tribe. This idea of the German tribe did not disappear with the German defeat in 1918 and was not an exclusive Conservative phenomenon. The Social Democrat, Värner Rydén, in his much-used school textbook published in fifteen editions between 1923 and 1959, argued that the Swedes belong to the German part of the Aryan tribe, and had been influenced only to a limited extent by Europe and Rome.[1]

In this development the concept of European had various meanings, from a neutral description of being an inhabitant in Europe ('I am a human being, European, Swedish, Smålander and nobleman', Schröderhielm 1794) to a civilization project, in which Sweden partook. A

1. I am grateful to Oscar Österberg, European University Institute, for having drawn my attention to this example.

European was, in this latter view, somebody who considered the whole of Europe as a *patria*, and whose education had 'a more European stamp' (*Göteborgs Handels-och Sjöfartstidning*, 6 1898: 2). Europeanization was a derivative concept in this view: the Europeanization of the Russian state (Arfwidsson 1842; Kjellén 1905), the Europeanized continents of America and Australia, or the idea of taking on a European look (*Svensk Litterär Tidning*, 1820: col. 396). *Europeism* was defined as a European way of living and culture, a European cultural community (*Polyfem*, IV(30), 1811: 1).[2] Witness, also, the proclamation by Karl XIV Johan in 1818, where he talked about Sweden as separated from *the rest of* Europe: European, but nevertheless separated from Europe. However, it should also be emphasized that the kind of Finnish polarization between industrialization based on a Western-oriented liberalism and an ethnicified agrarianism that Henrik Meinander refers to in Chapter 6 of this volume never emerged in Sweden. The Western/European influence in industrialization and economic relations was too strong. (For all references in this and the following paragraphs, see *Swedish Academy Dictionary*, editorial office, Lund.)

In order to get clarity in this conceptual ambiguity and to express Swedish demarcation from – rather than belonging to – Europe, the concept of the continent was used early on. The continent was the European mainland as demarcated from the British islands and Scandinavia (*Stockholms-Posten*, 54, 1809: 2). The king of Sweden was, after the peace in Tilsit in 1807, 'alone with England, and, after having left Pommern to its fate, excluded from the Continent' (Geijer 1844: 266). On the Continent absolutism prevailed (Bolin 1871: 83; Hellström 1931: 35) In a certain sense, also, Sweden was isolated from the Continent: 'At this time Sweden did not receive continental mail every day' (Ord och Bild 1932: 156). In the tension between the two concepts of Europe and the continent, the Swedish meanings of Europe were formed. The concepts were not synonymous as in England, where to go to Europe and to go to the continent means the same thing: to cross the Channel. A Swede would say that he is going to the continent, but not that he is going to Europe, because in that sense he feels European, although in political and cultural terms a demarcation has often been obvious.

The Swedish sense of belonging to Europe was expressed in a particular way in encyclopaedias such as *Nordisk Familjebok*, which, as a

---

2. I am grateful to Anki Mattisson, the editorial office of the *Swedish Academy Dictionary*, Lund, for assistance with the excerpts of the office on the concepts of 'Europe' and 'continent', and derivations from these concepts.

matter of fact, did not change much from the 1880s to the 1930s.[3] According to the edition of 1881, Europe was the smallest of all the three continents of the Old World, and just a little bigger than the smallest of all, Australia. However, Europe 'occupies as the hearth of the whole of the modern development of mankind the first place, and that time cannot yet be discerned when it would have to retreat from this its ruling position' (*Nordisk Familjebok* 1881: 822). Europe had become the point of departure and the hearth for all higher life in the fields of science, art and statesmanship. Europe's high 'material as well as spiritual development' could be ascribed not only to its central geographical position with longer coastlines than all other continents, but, particularly, to the 'natural superiority of the population'. Sweden was quite clearly a part of this Europe. Among the three European tribes, the Roman people had made the start in the cultural development of the continent. Then the Germanic tribes took over, standing over the most important innovations in modern times, while the Slavic peoples had not yet held 'the place they no doubt in future are called to fill'. The culture in spiritual terms – '*andlig odling*' – revealed great differences. The Germanic peoples, to the rise of whom the Reformation had given mighty impulses, stood, in particular where popular education was concerned, as far above the Roman tribes, as these latter stood over the Slavic ones. Further, 'Highest on the scale [among the Germanic peoples] come the Scandinavians and the Germans' (*Nordisk Familjebok* 1881: 832). No wonder that the encyclopaedia identified Sweden so clearly as a part of a Europe defined in such terms.

In the edition of 1907 the description of Europe's geography, geology and climate was considerably extended. The language of the article was somewhat more moderate and sober in the judgements about European superiority in comparison to other cultures, although there was no doubt about who was number one. The internal division and classification of the European population into races and religions remained the same (*Nordisk Familjebok* 1907: 1067–95). The edition of 1927 problematized more fully the concept of Europe. In geographical terms the article discussed whether Europe should not more properly be considered one continent together with Asia. Through a distinction in geography, history and culture, European uniqueness stood out as before, however. The linguistic division of Europe was elaborated on much more. In the division of the population, tribes ('*stammar*') had become peoples

3. I want to express my thanks to the library staff at Malmö University College for assistance with excerpts.

(*'folk'*). The peoples were defined in linguistic rather than ethnical terms. A new entry was made for 'Europe's races', however, where it was reckoned to be difficult to give clear information about Europe's present race conditions. An undisputed scientific basis for how to divide human beings in races did not exist. Academic opinion was divided and the whole terminology was confusing. Still another problem was the mixture of races. On these grounds, full of reservations rather than doubts, the encyclopaedia nevertheless provided six main races with four sub-races. The list began with the Nordic race, *Homo europaeus* (*sic!*) – which was also labelled with a German term, *Reihengräbertypus* – who had 'high stature, blond hairs, blue eyes, oval head and face, and a heavy, straight nose'. The other races were described in corresponding terms (*Nordisk Familjebok* 1927: 1190–93). In all the editions since 1881 five million Jews, who were scattered all over Europe, in particularly in Germany and Eastern and Central Europe, received mention, as did the roaming *zigenarna*. Both groups were seen as in – but not of – Europe.

Images of modernity and rational organization of society based on liberal principles broke through early in the Swedish case. Through the two concepts of 'Europe' and 'the continent', ambiguous and contradictory images could be expressed . The emphasis between them shifted with context and over time and the meanings were contested. This was particularly obvious after the First World War. In the wake of the Versailles Treaty, the contours emerged of a New World based on peace and international cooperation. Three imperial thrones had imploded and American President Woodrow Wilson provided a prescription for how to make the world safe for democracy; his instrument was the League of Nations. The socialist experiment in the Soviet Union also contributed to the optimistic scenario of a peaceful world. During the 1920s in Sweden, the Social Democrats, in the wake of the progressive introduction of universal suffrage between 1907 and 1919, began to establish their position of parliamentary power. They participated in a coalition government with the Liberals from 1917 to 1920 and formed their first minority government thereafter. Social Democrat governments held power during the periods 1921–23 and 1924–26. In the prevailing mood of optimistic expectations for a better future, Social Democrat leaders invested much hope in the League.

Throughout the 1920s, the Social Democratic leadership in Sweden was made up of true internationalists, in contrast to the inward-looking Swedish Conservatives, who argued for Swedish neutrality based upon a strong army. In the formulation of Swedish politics and Sweden's external relations, Europe as a concept was mobilized against the concept of the continent. The Social Democrats believed that they could obtain peace and follow progressive policies of social justice through international cooperation and disarmament. The League of Nations was their political instrument. Social Democrat leaders – such as Hjalmar Branting, Arthur Engberg, Richard Sandler, and others – spoke English, French and German fluently and went on frequent party political and government missions to Europe, which once again became an arena for Swedish politics. In action and practice they tried to override the prevailing demarcation. The train to Geneva became a true bridge with Europe. The Swedish Social Democrats were part of, and active participants in, a new Europe which was perceived as being politically progressive. As a matter of fact, they invested much more political energy and expectations in international cooperation at that stage than they had done during the Second International prior to 1914 (Stråth 2000b). They did it in the same spirit that made the German Socialists (SPD) speak about a United States of Europe in their Heidelberg programme of 1925 or which drove Aristide Briand and Eduard Herriot to deliver their federalist visions (Orluc 2000; Marcussen and Roscher 2000).

In the 1920s, the Swedish Conservatives emphasized Swedishness rather than their German point of reference, which dated from the 1870s and which no longer worked. A strong Swedish army should be the basis of a Swedish policy of neutrality, according to the Conservative view. It was not the case that everything suddenly became Social Democratic in Sweden at this time. On the contrary, although a clear left-wing political trend was discernible, as in so many other countries, this trend was opposed by a strong conservative alternative. The frequent crises and changes of government in Sweden during the 1920s are an expression of this political situation, where mobilization of the electorate occurred in polarized form. In this framework, the Social Democrats stood for the international orientation in Swedish politics. The image of a victorious Left was projected onto the new Europe. With international cooperation, new wars would be prevented and a new democratic world would be built. The Social Democrats regarded a collective security order as the instrument for general European disarmament. Supranational authority being vested in the League of Nations would create the preconditions for disarmament. This approach connoted Protestant progression and commitment to missionary civilization for a better world with obvious similarities to the French revolutionary quest, although Swedish pecularity was clear at the same time. The role, not least the role of religion and religious values, transformed to a larger or smaller extent for political purposes, was different in the two missionary approaches.

Confronted by the developments which took place to the east and south of Scandinavia in the 1930s, and the collapse of the League of Nations, the Social Democrats were forced to reconsider their hopes and political dreams, and to transform them into a consolidated image of Sweden through the construction of a European Other. Instead of Sweden as a member of a progressive Europe, as one in a European 'Us', Europe emerged in the 1930s ever more as the Other in Social Democratic strategic thinking. In the Social Democratic self-image of Sweden constructed in the 1930s, a Protestant, progressive and labour-oriented Sweden emerged, juxtaposed against a xenostereotype of a Catholic, conservative and capital-oriented Europe ('the continent').

The framework of this deep transformation, under considerable continuity in value patterns, was the experience of crisis in two areas, which coincided with – and reinforced – the feelings of a state of emergency. In the labour market a slow process of modernization had begun after 1905 with the building of institutions designed to facilitate conciliation and compromise, but the 1920s were still filled with industrial conflict. In 1931 military troops shot on a peaceful demonstration rally against strike-breakers and killed five people. The shootings provoked national shock and an acute feeling of crisis which was underpinned by the economic depression at the time and the associated mass unemployment. The trauma prompted social energy in the direction of national conciliation and consolidation. The second area of crisis was in international relations, where the initial hope surrounding the Soviet Union slowly turned into perceptions of threat. The same shift from hope to jeopardy was discerned for the Weimar Republic, where the Social Democrats seemed increasingly marginalized from high politics and the signs of social and political polarization grew. The friendly world of the 1920s was, at least from 1933 onwards, seen in much less optimistic colours. Here, though, the experience of crisis was less acute than in the field of industrial relations and was more something that gradually emerged as a dark sideshow, which turned down the glossy language of the 1920s and promoted national consolidation and political peace.

Immediately before the emergence of this scenario the Social Democrats had redefined their role in Swedish politics from one of being a class party to that of a people's party in its self-examination after painful defeat in the elections in 1928 (*kosackvalet*), which had stirred up an anti-socialist mood of hate. The sense of crisis together with the ongoing Social Democratic reorientation made them key actors of the political scene. The Social Democrats became the agents of national consolidation through the establishment of considerable continuity with the Conservative modernization programme, which had emerged in response to the events of 1905 (see p. 130 above). One of the key instruments in their appeal for national reconciliation was the demarcation from Europe. In all, continuities and discontinuities were interwoven during this phase of political reorientation (Stråth 2000 a, b).

The demarcation between a progressive (and by implication Social Democratic) Protestant Sweden and a Conservative Catholic Europe had its point of departure in specific Social Democratic policy on Church. Swedish popular culture not only contained calls for revivalism and Free Churches, but also a Lutheran State Church capable of adjustment and being accessible to Social Democratic politics. Another important factor was the role of the peasants and the fact that the nobility played a declining role after their military losses in 1718.

This decline had begun even earlier. As a matter of fact, coalitions in the seventeenth century between the king and the estate of the peasants in the *Diet* against the nobility not only highlighted the latter's decline, but also resulted in at least some popular confidence in the state. The king-peasant coalition and the Lutheran State Church made the Swedish people well-disposed towards a strong state and corporative interest representation, as well as the establishment of centralized infrastructural power in combination with a strong local administration. As in Germany, it is possible to see social democracy in Sweden as a kind of secularized Lutheranism. However, owing to the old king-peasant coalition, the relationship between social democracy and the state developed completely differently. Instead of the Social Democrats coming out against the throne-altar coalition, as in Germany, the Swedish Social Democrats in the interwar period definitively transformed the old State Church into a modern *folk* Church – under a Social Democrat government and based on liberal theology. They thereby appropriated the concept of *folkkyrka*, the people's Church, that was developed during the 1910s by a conservative reformist tendency within the State Church, while it was trying to respond to the pressures emanating from the protesting popular movements. The Social Democrats integrated and skilfully canalized the popular protests by connecting them to a historical heritage. They bridged the opposition between revivalism and the calls for free Churches on one side, and the Lutheran State Church organization on the other, between peasant individualism and state corporatism.

In this framework, the Social Democrats drew the image of a Catholic threat. The main architect was Arthur Engberg, who had also been prominent in the League of Nations internationalism of the 1920s. Early in that decade, he had already developed a Social Democratic policy on

Church which, instead of crushing the State Church, had taken it over as its aim. A key instrument was political control over the teaching of theology at the universities and the guarantee of a liberal theology through this authority. In this environment, the perception of a Catholic threat was developed and, as a matter of fact, was contradictorily used in parallel with the international commitment during the 1920s. However, use of the threat was much more pronounced in the 1930s, when it became an active instrument – indeed, the key instrument – in the reorientation of Swedish politics towards a demarcation from Europe. Engberg warned of an expansive and greedy Catholicism which was beyond every form of political control. A Lutheran State Church, under political control, was a guarantee against this 'Catholic lust for power' and an instrument in making 'the nation invulnerable against the weapons of Papism' (Stråth 2000b).

In a parliamentary debate in 1930, Engberg constructed a wall between Swedish/Lutheran and alien/Catholic. In pursuit of the contrasting effect he wished to achieve, he connected his depiction of Swedish to the *folk* concept. The Swedish *folk* culture and the Swedish *folk* Church would – through the political representatives of state power and as the last resort responsible for Church policy – ward off catholicizing tendencies within the folk Church (Stråth 2000b: 368–9). This was at the same time that the Social Democrats were moving to redefine themselves from a class to a people's party. As a real threat, Catholicism was, of course, no more than the creation of a vivid imagination, but as an instrument of rhetoric to emphasize Swedishness – in an international situation which was apparently becoming ever more menacing, one where it was dangerous to speak out against the real dangers presented in the south and to the east – the Catholic threat was effective. The hazard of Catholicism was played off against the Swedish cultural heritage. This demarcation, built in the 1930s, had a long-lasting impact, not least in the puritan Free Church environments in the popular movements. When Parliament debated a Bill in 1951 regarding the freedom of religion, Members of Parliament of Free Church origin saw the threat of Catholic monasteries as being almost as dangerous as secularization and de-Christianization (Stråth 1992: 211). The mental demarcation between progressive Protestant Sweden and conservative Catholic Europe thus remained beyond 1945, and Europe took on proportions of being synonymous with Catholicism.

After the Second World War, the Social Democrat government developed an approach in international politics which was very much a continuation of the neutrality policy followed during the war and the self-imposed demarcation from Europe. This approach had clear elements in common with the politics in the early 1950s of the German SPD under

Kurt Schumacher (Marcussen and Roscher 2000). Schumacher was against Western integration and argued for a third-way policy somewhere between the two emerging blocs. Indeed, he counselled rhetorically against an alignment with Western Europe by making reference to the four dangerous *C*s which, according to him, prevailed there: Capitalism, the Cartels, Conservatism, and Catholicism. This threatening picture of Europe was found to be attractive by Swedish Social Democrats. The Catholic instrument of demarcation to Europe was supplemented by new elements, in the form of Conservatism and Capitalism. However, the Swedish Social Democrats absorbed these elements of demarcation at about the same time that the German SPD was about to abandon them through the Bad Godesberg Programme of 1959. This demarcation has been described as a kind of *Berührungsangst* (Misgeld 1990), while continued demarcation from Europe was reinforced by yet another factor after the Second World War. Germany and France were weakened as cultural and political points of reference, and the Anglo-American orientation was intensified; the United States became the model to emulate and English quickly replaced German or French as the principal spoken foreign language among educated Swedes.

The threatening picture thus broadened out from the religious argument to include capitalism and political conservatism. Both of these new elements fitted well into the Social Democratic self-understanding. However, to this extended threatening scenario, a further self-image was added, one which also appealed to those other than the Social Democrats; this explains the relative political concord regarding the demarcation from Europe. The fact that Sweden had managed to avoid active participation in the war was legitimized by reference to the neutrality concept, which came to fill the same heroic function as the resistance movement in other countries. The need for theoretical legitimatization of the pragmatic politics of adjustment during the war years, together with the emerging dictates of the cold war, gave form and content to the neutrality doctrine; this form and content was greater than the politics that had actually been pursued during the war, when more concessions had been made to Germany before 1943, to be followed by a more restrictive approach thereafter. The dictates of the cold war meant that the Swedish perception of threat was now immediately relocated to the intersection between conflicting big-power interests.

The neutrality concept had been historically deduced from 1834, when Sweden's King Karl XIV Johan had used it for the first time in order to keep his country apart from a difficult foreign political situation. Despite subsequent and frequent deviations from this very contextually conditioned first use of the concept, a line of continuity was established in historical and social sciences. A modern Swedish foundation myth emerged around the concept of neutrality, mediating feelings of Swedishness and historical continuity (Stråth 1992: 198–215). When the neutrality doctrine was formulated, the UN was an important point of departure. The neutrality policy was perceived as fitting the framework of a functioning international legal order. The bone of contention in the 1920s, regarding compulsory participation in collective sanctions decided upon by the League of Nations, caused less dispute now. The government argued that the veto instrument in the UN Security Council was the guarantee that Sweden would never risk becoming involved in a conflict with one of the big powers. Therefore, Swedish participation in the UN was also compatible with its neutrality.

The neutrality concept in the 1950s gave rise to a kind of 'third-way identity'. The image of Sweden and the Swedes reflected in the concept of the third-way contained supporters of liberation movements in the Third World (cf. for this concept Erik Tängerstad 2000), peace angels, arbitrators, conciliators, and disarmament managers, in contrast to colonial powers, such as Great Britain and France, that economically and politically exploited poor countries. In the 1960s the 'imperialistic USA' and the 'rich man's club of the EC' took over this role of the Bad Other in the construction of a Swedish self-image. The third-way identity radiated a feeling of standing outside 'big power' ties. The third-way, or the third standpoint – which was the title of a series of articles in the daily *Morgon-Tidningen* at the beginning of the 1950s – where the belief was laid out, meant a strong critique of the United States, whereas criticism of the Soviet Union was pushed aside, although this did not necessarily mean that views about the Soviet Union were very positive. There was a wide range of opinions, from a naive view of communism and the liberation movements in the Third World to a more critical attitude to the *realkommunismen* under Josef Stalin. The connection to the image of a *mission civilisatrice* was obvious.

On the whole, it was a matter of having a third point of view between East and West, the origins of which can be seen as a reaction to the vehement campaign for Sweden's membership of NATO in and around 1949. This third-standpoint reaction was interpreted in that campaign as crypto-communism. There was a polarizing and fundamentalist/puritanist element in the third-way debate despite the name's allusions to mediation and conciliation which was quite compatible with the Protestant ethic of moralism and revivalism in Swedish popular movements. Initially, the concept of *alliansfrihet*, i.e. a policy of non-alignment, was used to describe this bridge-building self-image. When this became the collective concept of self-image used by a number of recently independent former colonies, the neutrality concept became the key term.

Almost from the beginning, the Social Democrat government appropriated priority over interpretations of the concept of neutrality. If the government argued in the political debate that something was incompatible with neutrality, the issue was removed from the agenda. This priority was reinforced by a similar development concerning the concept of welfare. Neutrality connoted welfare, and vice versa, and the Social Democrats emerged as the architects of this success story too. Support for NATO membership disappeared rapidly, while overly sharp criticism of the Soviet Union was considered irresponsible in this discursive scenario. In 1959, the Leader of the Conservatives, Jarl Hjalmarson, was banned from the Swedish parliamentary delegation to the UN, because he had 'ardently and constantly' taken sides with 'one of the political deployments', thereby neglecting to 'work for peaceful cooperation and real international conciliation' (Stråth 1992: 202). The background to this decision was the repeated criticism directed by the Conservative Party Leader at the brutal crushing of the Hungarian revolution in 1956.

Ideological ties with the Western democracies were there all the time, but this example demonstrates that, when it came to 'standing free between the blocs', criticism of the Stalinism being practised in the Peoples' Democracies was not going to be allowed to be too acute. This self-restriction also demonstrates how problematic neutrality was when it departed from a distant Third World situation and was applied to Sweden's immediate surroundings. Thus, the third-way identity found its biggest outlet in far-away lands where Swedish security political interests were not so immediately connected with the East–West conflict. In its support of the Third World's endeavours for political and economic emancipation, the Swedish government could verbally develop its role as an independent scrutinizer and mediator, indeed, as a kind of world conscience. In doing so a connection was built to the Social Democratic internationalism of the 1920s, which was much more Europe-oriented, however.

After 1969, with Olof Palme, the policy of neutrality became more active, i.e. less reactive and more independent in relation to the international situation. However, this increased activity, as a rule, concerned questions which did not touch upon Sweden's immediate surroundings. In this respect, the active policy was not so new. It has been argued that the aim of this more active policy was at least as much to integrate radicalized domestic opinion in the wake of '1968' as it was to achieve a better world order. It is probably impossible to put the problem in this way, because belief in this peace mission was an integrated element of the Swedish, or at least the Social Democratic, self-image of an earlier origin, and because this self-image was only mobilised with more emphasis in the political attempts to respond to a wave of radicalism and social criticism. However, it can be argued that Palme's moralism was something new compared to the caution and low profile maintained by the architect of the neutrality doctrine after the Second World War, Östen Undén (Swedish Foreign Minister, from 1945 to 1962), who, paradoxically enough, was a much more rigorous moralist than Palme. The moralism and interventionism of the 1970s could thus exploit the capital of trust, which had been built up during the earlier more cautious period (Andrén 1991).

This activist phase culminated with the Vietnam War. The preconditions for the Swedish self-image as mediators and conciliators slowly decreased following the American withdrawal from Vietnam in 1973, with increasingly direct contacts between the United States and the Soviet Union, as well between the United States and China from 1972. A more definitive step in the erosion of these original preconditions was the period of détente between the Soviet Union, under Mikhail Gorbachev, and the United States from 1985.

The central attribute of Swedish 'neutrality' was adjustment and pragmatism. Its basis was the aim to keep Sweden out of any military conflicts between the big powers. The content of the neutrality concept changed with the requirements of the situation. Since 1834, the concept has been pregnant with many varied meanings. During some periods, it has been attractive to believers in the need for a strong army, in others for pacifists, and in still others for both these tendencies at the same time. The attractive power of the concept has been not least because of its ambiguity, although in general it held a positive value charge. The consolidation of the concept in the 1950s and 1960s was based on an almost hegemonic unification under Social Democrat leadership of both its more defence-oriented and its pacifist elements.

In his whole political approach and throughout his career, Palme was an internationalist. Indeed, his active commitment through the Vietnam War was an expression of this internationalism. However, for Palme, internationalism did not exist in opposition to Europe. With his mastery of German and French, he was in many respects reminiscent of the Social Democratic League of the Nations' generation in the 1920s, wherein Europe and the larger international sphere overlapped. Not least the fact that Willy Brand became German chancellor in the same year that Palme became Swedish Prime Minister might have encouraged the latter in his attempt to reorientate Sweden's European policy. However, Palme was actually a *Realpolitiker* with *Fingerspitzgefühl* more than an idealist. When he realized that the party base was refusing to go along with his U-turn regarding Sweden's EEC policy, he withdrew the Swedish 'open' application in March 1971 and declared that Sweden would not seek membership, irrespective of what Britain, Denmark, Norway and Ireland did.

With this step, he avoided a development such as the one that took place in Norway, where the leadership of the Norwegian Labour Party offered the country a referendum on the issue of EEC membership, which the population then rejected. The consequences of this included a deep and long-lasting split in the Labour Party in that country. For the Swedish Social Democrats, Norway acted as a illustrative warning. After 1972, the old demarcation from Europe was as solid as it had been ever since the 1930s. It was a political approach, motivated by Catholicism, capitalism and conservatism, but dictated by the cold war. Only with the arrival of Gorbachev and the prospect of a post-cold war world did this situation change. Another, and probably even more decisive, factor for the changed framework for Swedish European policy was the growing insight in the 1980s that the preconditions of welfare politics under national auspices had changed dramatically. The new 'globalization' language in the 1990s was but one of the late expressions of this insight. Still more, the warning presaged by the French government's experiences – in its policy of 'socialism in one land' between 1981 and 1983 (Marcussen and Roscher 2000) – had made an impression.

From the mid-1980s, the political attempts to increase the degree of market integration in Western Europe were intensified. The Single European Act, with the creation of the internal market without borders and border controls, was decided upon in 1986. More or less remote future images, as expressed in the Treaties of Rome, became immediate political goals. In the face of this development, Sweden could, as with the other EFTA countries, only remain passive. Cooperation with the EEC was intensified and expanded to new areas not covered in the free-trade agreement of 1972. Neo-liberal market rhetoric, under the key concept of market, had by then also influenced the Swedish Social Democrats; this much was obvious from their political approach when they came back to power in 1982. An insight developed which saw that the room for manoeuvre of the nation state was decreasing and that the solution would have to be found in international co-ordination. The neo-liberal language provided powerful sound effects for the beginning of the new orientation in Sweden's European politics. The Luxembourg Agreement of 1984 was an early expression of the efforts to step up cooperation. This cooperation would be extended to new fields, such as economic, monetary and industrial policies, research and technology, and the environment, as well as fishing and transport policies. The Luxembourg Agreement was soon considered insufficient, however.

In a Swedish Bill in December 1987, a reinforcement and expansion of the government's administration was announced in order to bring greater efficiency to the government's relationship with Europe. A Council for European Issues was established, with leading figures from the government, industry and business, and the trades unions as members. The aim was to establish 'a cooperation with the EC as close and as extensive as possible in as many areas as possible under considerations to the Swedish neutrality policy'. (*Riksdagens Protokoll* 1987–88: 117). The Bill, and the parliamentary debate on it, demonstrated that the neutrality concept as such maintained its position, but the interpretations of its content were beginning to pull apart. The Conservatives considered EEC membership to be compatible with neutrality; it was only in order to create a broad political movement for intensified cooperation with the EEC that they abstained from arguing for membership. Swedish sovereignty was, according to the Social Democrat government, self-chosen and nothing would be allowed to nibble away at it. The neutrality concept was the guarantor of this sovereignty. Neutrality provided more than protection against military threat, however. In the debate on the bill in parliament, it was obvious that welfare politics and culturally dist-inctive features – such as alcohol policies – just as much as concern with any military threat were what the neutrality concept involved (Stråth 2000b).

The precondition of the entente between the Social Democrats, the Conservatives, the Liberals, and the Centre Party on the European question, and their agreement on intensified European cooperation, was that the issue of Swedish membership was not addressed. However, a process of reconsideration through self-examination had begun in the Social Democratic Party and the trade union movement. In the process, the EEC was seen in a more positive light and the old Catholic-conservative-capitalist image faded away. The EEC was even said to have realized many of the early dreams of the labour movement regarding a new and different Europe (Misgeld 1990: 195–6). In January 1989, the President of the European Commission, Jacques Delors, responded to the appeals of the EFTA governments for intensified cooperation, by suggesting the establishment of the European Economic Area; just like the Luxembourg Agreement five years earlier, it was soon judged as insufficient by several of the EFTA governments. In this respect, for instance, Austria applied for membership of the EEC in July 1989. The Swedish government realized that there was an obvious risk of Sweden becoming isolated. The fall of the Berlin Wall in November 1989 changed the preconditions of the whole rhetoric of neutrality. Consequently, in the spring of 1990, a cautious redefinition of the neutrality concept also began among the Social Democrats. One line of thought which emerged was a tightening of the concept of security politics in the strict sense, with the repression of its earlier welfare-political connotations. The EEC was no longer seen as a threat to Social Democratic welfare politics.

In October 1990, the Swedish currency came under severe speculative pressure. Swedish political tradition saw the solution to such problems in the form of devaluation through which the problems were then exported. This had been the solution reached in 1931, 1949, 1976, 1977, 1981 and 1982; this solution was not applied in 1990. The government had been impressed by the neo-liberal globalization rhetoric about the narrowing scope for political management of the economy in a national framework. This rhetoric was translated to specific Swedish experiences, as for instance with the ongoing flight of capital: investment capital was going abroad and the political debate centred on whether Sweden risked de-industrialization. The Social Democrats generally acknowledged that capacity to promote economic growth through the provision of favourable conditions for industry appeared to have come to an end. The solution to the Swedish currency crisis – and the crisis in the Social Democrats' shrinking confidence– was to apply for membership in the EC.

From this point, developments moved quickly. It was like a dyke that had burst. Everybody in the political elite convinced one another of how correct this historical decision was, and the media sang from the same songsheet. What had been wrong up to a few years earlier was suddenly right. Swedish political leaders competed with one another regarding who was most European. The political conflict was directed towards this competition. The Conservative leader, Carl Bildt, proposed a referendum on Swedish membership of the EEC, although not because he had any doubt about the outcome, however. On the contrary, he was sure that a vast majority of the people would support the proposition. With Sweden 'becoming European', he saw the end of more than fifty years of Social Democratic power; thus, he wanted the solemn and formal confirmation of this change by the people through a free election. Bildt and the Swedish Prime Minister, Ingvar Carlsson, quarrelled over who was to submit the Swedish application in Brussels. Bildt only wanted this act to take place after the parliamentary elections in September 1991, which he hoped to win and thus succeed Carlsson as the head of government. However, Carlsson submitted the application to the EEC on 1 July 1991, himself hoping to profit from this act in the elections. It was difficult to discern deviant meanings or interpretations other than from the small communist and environmental parties during this European euphoria (Stråth 2000b).

Things changed quickly, however. The fact that Carlsson's party lost the election, and that Carl Bildt became the Leader of a Coalition Government, gave many Social Democrats something to think about. The Conservative-Liberal appeal was to 'Europeanize Sweden' after too many years of Social Democratic rule; Sweden had lost too much during these years of its demarcation from Europe. The Social Democratic counter-appeal was to advocate the missionary task to 'Swedenize Europe' – that is, to translate and transfer the Swedish welfare model into Europe (Stråth 2000b).

The discussion about these two alternatives became ever more vociferous, at the same time as the initial popular astonishment at the elite consensus regarding membership changed. General popular passivity shifted to activity through resistance. A popular movement against the EEC was formed and aroused great support. The anti-EEC movement made deep inroads into the Social Democratic Party. As a matter of fact, it paralysed both the party and the trade union confederation (LO); whereas the male-dominated unions in manufacturing industry were for Swedish membership, the female-dominated unions in the public sector were massively against, because they feared that Swedish membership would mean neo-liberal budgetary politics and lost job opportunities. The party told its members that it did not have any position on the European issue; the members and party adherents could vote for what they wanted in the referendum and still be good Social Democrats, irrespective of how they voted. The LO did not give its members any voting recommendation either.

The outcome of the referendum was almost a dead heat; 51 per cent of the voters were for Swedish membership, while 49 per cent voted against. The figures could be interpreted as a severe polarization of the population. Rather than a polarization, however, the outcome was the fruit of general confusion. A considerable proportion of the voters determined how they would vote only very late in the day and were very uneasy and uncertain about their choice. The paralysis of the Social Democratic Party and the LO was another expression of this confusion.

The people had disarmed their leaders and imposed on them a general and ongoing poltical passivity in dealings with Europe. One expression of this passivity was that Sweden did not join Economic and Monetary Union. At the same time, however, membership of the EU meant that something *had* indeed changed. The view of Sweden as part of Europe grew in strength. Europe lost the connotation which it had held since the 1930s of being more or less synonymous with Catholicism, and took on its earlier meaning of a bigger 'Us'. The new emerging division in the production of meaning around the concept of Europe is whether Europe is equal to EU or whether it, as in the conceptualization of the anti-EU movement, should be seen in a broader cultural context, including Eastern Europe and political and religious pluralism, but cut off from the connection to a specific political project.

## References

Andrén, N. (1991), 'Den mångtydiga neutraliteten', in *Internationella Studier*, 2, Stockholm.

Blidberg, K. and Wahlbäck (eds) (1986), *Samråd i kristid: protokoll från den Nordiska arbetarrörelsens samarbetskommitté 1932–1946*, Stockholm: Samf. för utg. av handskrifter rörande Skandinaviens historia.

Henningsen, B. (1997), *Die schwedische Konstruktion einer nordischen Identität durch Olof Rudbeck*. Working paper 9 from the research project 'The Cultural Construction of Communities in Modernisation Processes in Comparison', in cooperation between the European University Institute, Florence and the Humboldt Universität zu Berlin, Berlin.

Klinge, M. (1993), *Runebergs två fosterland*, Helsinki: Söderströms.

Lindroth, S. (1955), *Reformation och humanism. Ny illustrerad svensk litteraturhistoria 1:* Stockholm.

Malmborg, M. af (2001), *Neutrality and State-Building in Sweden*, Basingstoke: Palgrave.

Marcussen, M. and Roscher, K. (2000), 'The Social Construction of "Europe": Life-Cycles of Nation-State Identities in France, Germany and Great Britain', in B. Stråth (ed.), *Europe and the Other and Europe as the Other*, Brussels: PIE-Peter Lang.

Misgeld, K. (1990), 'Den svenska socialdemokratin och Europa från slutet av 1920-talet till början av 1970-talet: Attityder och synsätt i centrala uttalanden och dokument', in B. Huldt and K. Misgeld (eds), *Socialdemokratin och svensk utrikespolitik: Från Branting till Palme*, Stockholm: Utrikespolitiska Institute.

Nordin, J. (1988), 'I broderlig samdräkt? Förhållandet Sverige-Finland under 1700-talet och Anthony D Smiths *ethnie*-begrepp', in *Scandia: Tidskrift för historisk forskning,* Lund, Sweden.

*Nordisk Familjebok,* Articles 'Europa' and 'Kontinenten' 1881, 1907, 1927, Stockholm.

*Olaus Rudbecks Atlantica. Svenska originaltexter* (ed. by Axel Nelson on behalf of Lärdomshistoriska Samfundet. 5 vols) Uppsala, Stockholm: Almqvist & Wiksell 1937–1950.

Orluc, K. (2000), 'Decline or Renaissance: The Transformation of European Consciousness after the First World War'; in B. Stråth (ed.), *Europe and the Other and Europe as the Other,* Brussels: PIE-Peter Lang.

*Riksdagens Protokoll* (Minutes of the Swedish Parliament) 1987/88:114, proposition 1987/88:66.

Sørensen, Ø. and Stråth, B. (eds) (1997), *The Cultural Construction of Norden,* Oslo: Scandinavian University Press.

Stråth, B. (1992), *Folkhemmet mot Europa: Ett historiskt perspektiv på 90-talet,* Stockholm: Tiden.

Stråth, B. (2000a), 'Poverty, Neutrality and Welfare: Three Key Concepts in the Modern Foundation Myth of Sweden', in B. Stråth (ed.), *Myth and Memory in the Construction of Community: Historical Patterns in Europe and Beyond,* Brussels: PIE-Peter Lang.

Stråth, B. (2000b), 'The Swedish Image of Europe as the Other', in B. Stråth (ed.), *Europe and the Other and Europe as the Other,* Brussels: PIE-Peter Lang.

Tängerstad, E. (2000), '"The Third World" as an Element in the Collective Construction of a Post-Colonial European Identity' in B. Stråth (ed.), *Europe and the Other and Europe as the Other,* Brussels: PIE-Peter Lang 2000.

# – 6 –

## On the Brink or In-between? The Conception of Europe in Finnish Identity
### Henrik Meinander

Finland has often been characterized as the most western country in Eastern Europe and the most eastern country in Western Europe. The reason for this is not only its geographic situation. An even more important reason is its cultural and political development which has followed an interesting, sometimes even a contradictory, mixture of eastern and western patterns. Being for over six centuries (1150–1809) an eastern periphery of the Swedish kingdom, Finland was strongly tied up with Western Christianity and was thereby thoroughly imbued with its values and traditions. However, its position as a lengthy borderland next to Russia meant that Finnish territory was often threatened and occasionally also invaded by the eastern power.

Twice occupied by Russian troops in the eighteenth century, Finland's strategic status became increasingly troublesome for Sweden, and when the kingdom was dragged into the Napoleonic Wars in 1808 Finland was once again overrun by the Russian army. This time it came to stay. Consequently, the land was transformed into a Grand Duchy within the mighty Russian Empire and remained as such until 1917 when, due to the Russian Revolution, these ties were cut and national sovereignty was achieved. The next chain reaction of European aggression struck Finland in the Second World War, but thanks to geographical position and fighting spirit, independence was maintained – even throughout the cold war, when Russian dominance in Europe in the form of the Soviet Union reached its peak. Thus, when Finland joined the EU in 1995 many Finns felt as if history had come full circle. Once again the land had become integrated within a greater power.

What impact did this geopolitical drift between East and West have on the Finnish national identity? And more crucially, how did these changes of borders and rulers influence the Finnish conception of Europe as a political and cultural framework for its own nation and state? In other words, has Finland been on the brink of Europe or rather somewhere in the middle? In the following I shall discuss this topic by analysing a number of public statements which in one way or another exemplify the shifting views and opinions about Finland and Europe.

In 1872 the famous Finnish author, Zacharias Topelius, became very upset by a rhetorical question posed by a peasant member of the Finnish parliament. The background was the following: a political language feud was emerging and a key question was what role the Finnish language should have in public life and culture which previously had been totally dominated by Swedish, the administrative and elite tongue since the Middle Ages. The Russian Emperor Alexander II, Grand Duke of Finland, had decreed in 1863 that Finnish should have equal status with Swedish in public affairs within the following two decades. The initiative for this decree came from those Finns who wished to replace the Swedish language with Finnish in public life. By the beginning of the twentieth century they had in practice won the battle, not least owing to the Russian authorities, who understood that support for these so-called Fennomans was an efficient form of *divide et impera* policy in the increasingly nationalistic Grand Duchy.

Now, what did this straightforward parliamentarian say, then? He referred scornfully to the often-mentioned claim that Finland was in debt to Sweden for its Western civilization and asked if anyone could show him the original promissory note of this debt. By this he wanted to emphasize that Finns already stood on their own two feet and had bowed enough to the domestic Swedish-speaking elite. Topelius, both an author and an influential history professor at Helsinki University, stood close to the Fennoman camp on many questions and often emphasized in his writings that the Finnish people were predestined to a great future. Similar messianic visions were put forward by nationalists throughout Europe, but according to Topelius, Finland had a unique mission, namely, to spread civilization to the outskirts of the inhabited world and function as a bulwark for Europe and the whole of mankind (Forsgård 1998: 113–25).

The Parliamentarian's ironic request, therefore, was in Topelius's eyes nothing less than blasphemy. As a reply he wrote the poem 'The original promissory note' [*Originala skuldsedeln*], in which he robustly argued that, although Finland had gradually grown apart from Sweden, it would be stupid to deny the mutual cultural roots that essentially showed a debt to Western civilization. The whole of Finnish society was this promissory note, since what would the country be without its Swedish past, asked Topelius, and pointed at the other, much less wealthy or fortunate Finno-Ugrian peoples in north-eastern Europe. Finland could rip up its cultural debt, but by doing that it would also rip apart its own history. This was of course impossible, or to use the elaborate metaphors of the poem's finale (Söderhjelm 1939: 14–15):

> Tear your note to pieces, but on one condition!
> I release you from all your former ties,
> when the stem grows rootless, when the ear of corn
> no longer praises the labour of its sower,
> when the past is no foundation of the present,
> when memory is no cradle of hope,
> when the rambler tramples on his faithful staff,
> when the grown man denies his youthful years,
> when peoples arise without light and warmth,
> like mushrooms springing up in the misty night,
> and when history, tired of reconciliation,
> rewards ingratitude with a crown of glory.

The dispute continued in other contexts, but spelled out already were many questions crucial for the understanding of Finnish identity and its European dimension. Topelius' position in this rather dualistic discourse was somewhere in the middle. As mentioned before, he wrote touching historical fiction about Finns as heroic and loyal subjects of the Swedish Crown, but he also claimed that the nation had a bright future within the Russian empire which implied that the historical path of Finland would follow the routes of the more powerful neighbours. On the other hand, he was keen to underline the inborn singularity of the Finnish destiny. In that way Topelius could describe Finland as both a bulwark of the West and a cooperative western borderland of the Russian realm.

Contrary to most of the Fennoman nationalists, Topelius thus did not see the expanding cultural and economic contacts with Western Europe as a serious threat to the emergence of a Finnish identity. And contrary to many Finnish Western-minded liberals, who would continue to see the Russian rule as troublesome, he would not play with the thought that Finland could loosen its ties with St Petersburg and its immense provinces behind the horizon. In short, instead of remaining a potential battlefield between the two civilizations, Finland should become a bridge between them (Tiitta 1994: 313–19).

The difference between the Fennoman and the liberal conception of Europe in the Finnish identity became even more apparent during subsequent decades when the national image faced two main challenges. The first challenge was a consequence of the accelerating industrialization and urbanization in Western European societies which step by step would also involve Finland and integrate it into the industrial world. The liberals, who usually belonged or, for ideological reasons, stood close to the old upper class, welcomed this development with full hearts, as it was in line with their notion of Finland as part of, if not Western Europe, then at least Western civilization. They were not in principle opposed to the promotion of the Finnish language in public life, but saw no reason to give it highest priority in domestic politics, which however, as the Fennomans rightly remarked, in practice meant that they defended the hegemony of the Swedish language.

In the eyes of these liberals, societal modernization and national maturation could be best achieved by applying Western solutions in politics, social planning and culture. As such they were by definition in favour of stimulating the international exchange of ideas and goods. They thought essentially in the same way as contemporary Russian *zapadniki* (Westernizers) and British Whigs, who believed in the blessings of free trade, free opinion and close contacts to centres of culture in Central Europe. And for the same reason as those kindred spirits, the Finnish liberals tended to draw the eastern and northern borderline of European civilization according to the countries and cultures that fulfilled these requirements. Europe was thus essentially synonymous with Western civilization and from that sprang a natural desire to remove all obstacles to westward integration (Klinge 1983: 169–82).

The other main challenge which motivated Finnish liberals to propagate the maintenance and enforcement of links with Central and Western Europe from the 1880s onward was the changing priorities in Russian security policy. As the threat of German eastward aggression grew, Russian military strategists had to take into account the possibility that Finland would be used as a bridgehead in a German attack against the nearby St Petersburg. Consequently, Russian authorities gradually tightened military and administrative control over the Grand Duchy which again, due to the westward integration of its industry and culture, saw even greater cause to emphasize its national characteristics and legal rights. The situation was further heated by demands for integration from Russian Slavophiles and this resulted in lengthy political conflict. Not surprisingly, the conflict would enforce the impression among many Finns that they lived at the eastern limits of Western civilization, that is 'Europe'.

The Fennoman understanding of these two challenges was rather different. The first leading Fennoman politician, the Hegelian thinker and professor J.V. Snellman, stated in the late 1850s that the success of the national movement in Finland was ultimately dependent on the success of agricultural production. Only in this way could the peasants, who constituted the great majority of the Finnish-speaking population, acquire sufficient wealth to educate their children to become politically aware patriots and citizens. Snellman admitted that positive development in rural Finland was not possible without parallel advances in domestic industry. Industrialization was needed, but it should be controlled by the Finnish state, with strict limitations on foreign investment and ownership. Otherwise, Finland would soon be invaded by new languages and cultures which would eventually destroy the dream of a Finnish Finland (Kuisma 1993: 188–90).

Some of Snellman's influential followers went one step further by claiming that an industrial culture in Finland was unnecessary and that it would only become a burden to its agriculture. From the 1870s onwards many Fennomans saw industrialization also as the Trojan horse of Socialism, which would twist the heads of the people and destroy their inherited feeling for the homeland. Following from this, the Fennomans eagerly defended the image of an agrarian Finland and were opposed to the image of an industrial Finland that the liberals wanted to promote in international arenas (Liikanen 1995: 119–49). The clash of opinions became apparent in connection with the great world exhibitions that forced the parties to articulate and propagate their vision of Finland and its cultural context. The first time such a quarrel occurred was before the Scandinavian exhibition in Stockholm in 1866, when the Fennomans were against participation, because it would enforce the impression that Finland belonged culturally to the Scandinavian realm. This was not in line with their nationalist conception which included the idea that Finland had also had its own history before 1809 and was not first and foremost a periphery of Western civilization.

On this particular occasion Finland participated and gained much admiration, but the conflict continued. When the country was denied its own pavilion at the world exhibition in Paris in 1878, the international audience was not attracted by the Finnish industry exhibits found in the Russian section. It was rather the ethnographic collection and the proofs of Finnish political autonomy within the Russian Empire that drew attention. In other words, it was the rural and less Western layers of Finnish culture that were on show and this was of course annoying for the industry-oriented liberals, who wanted to spread an impression of a Westernized Finland. It was a decade later, at the Paris world exhibition in 1889, when the liberals were in power, that Finland got the chance to set up its own pavilion. Not surprisingly, the international audience was now confronted with a totally different exposition of Finland, a well organized nation in its own right with promising industry and Western customs (Smeds 1996: 107–58, 249–68).

The ideological tug-of-war between the Fennomans and the liberals, therefore, was only on the surface a language feud. Beneath the bold slogan 'One language – one consciousness' existed a much more fundamental polarization of opinions which ultimately was dependent on how the parties understood Finland in a wider European context. For ideological reasons the Fennomans were already obliged to point out that the destiny of Finland and its own culture would be dependent on how efficiently its 'national individuality' could be nourished and crystallized. In this Hegelian cultural campaign they were, of course, not alone in Europe. The Fennomans regularly referred to the national movements in the Baltic provinces and the Austrian Empire in order to underline that each people who wanted to become a nation worthy of its name ought to choose its own path. Their conception of Europe thus was not inspired by a vision of a civilizational frontier between a 'real Europe' and a 'pseudo-Europe'.

From this followed also the fact that the Fennomans reacted in the beginning rather differently to the second of the challenges to the national image, that is, to the increasing signs of a systematic Russification policy in Finland. One natural reason for their more compliant, sometimes even intriguingly flexible, attitude towards the Russian authorities was that they greatly benefited from it during their struggle for political and cultural power in the Grand Duchy. Yet it would be wrong to argue that this was their only or even their foremost reason for keeping a low profile when Russian demands began to harden in the late 1880s. Truly exalted by nationalist ideology and its function as a civic religion, leading Fennomans systematically gave priority to the cultural development of Finland. They characterized the equally hardening voices of liberal politicians in defence of the institutional autonomy of the Grand Duchy as a deliberate overreaction, which aimed at accelerating the inflamed political situation, arousing sympathies in Europe and thereby linking Finland's destiny closer to the West. This political conflict is one of the most studied and debated crises in Finnish history. (For recent discussions, see *Historiallinen Aikakauskirja* 1999: 97–130 and *Historisk Tidskrift för Finland* 1999/4.)

It was not that the Fennomans had any illusions about the political or cultural motives behind the Russification programme. But it would clearly have been against their long-term interests to let the liberals take advantage of the situation, which in their opinion was superficially exaggerated. As hinted before, in the traditional Fennoman conception of Finland in a wider context, Russia was in a cultural sense not outside Europe. Russia was undeniably a threateningly strong and autocratic empire that could be dangerous for Finland, but its people had the same inborn strivings and right to national consolidation as any other vigorous people on the European continent.

In this way the domestic disagreement between the Fennomans and the liberals, although charged with intriguing political rhetoric, uncovered two fundamentally different notions of Europe. When the Russification actions became more bold at the turn of the nineteenth to the twentieth century, a growing number of Fennomans saw themselves obliged to join the liberals in their fight against the integration policy. This shift of political strategy especially among younger Fennomans was of crucial importance for the success of Finnish resistance. It also paved the way for an ideological shift among them, that is, towards the notion of Finland being 'The Bulwark of the West' and of Russia, in fact, being outside Western civilization (Jussila 1994: 42–50).

Nevertheless, despite social pressure a number of Fennoman officials held that public resistance towards Russification would only deepen the conflict, further stimulate the separatist urge and thereby grow into a major obstacle to the Fennoman project. A similar outlook was also common among the numerous Finns who had made a career in the Russian imperial army, or who as industrialists or tradesmen had made considerable profits in the huge Russian markets. In the writing of Finnish history, this interpretation was strongly condemned in the 1920s and 1930s, when the new-born republic of Finland was absorbed by the idea that the independence achieved in 1917 had been a historical necessity. This implied also that the liberal and young Fennoman tradition of constitutional and conspiratorial resistance should be understood as the main national strategy and that Finland was on the eastern edge of Western civilization (Tommila 1989: 177–200).

The impression of standing at the very edge of Europe had been enforced not only by the tragic incidents during the Finnish Civil War, a chain-reaction to the Russian Revolution. An equally traumatic experience was the birth of the Soviet Union, a political system totally different from the bourgeois order that existed in most of the other European countries. Russophobia had of course been strong in Finland before 1918, but thereafter it reached almost pathological dimensions (Ahti 1999: 171–94).

But as has been emphasized, such a clear-cut conception of Finland's exposed geographical position in Europe would become a widely accepted 'truth' only after national sovereignty had been gained. A revealing example of the ambivalent attitude which many patriotic Finns had towards Russia at the onset of the twentieth century was the famous composer Jean Sibelius, who stood close to the young Fennomans and was therefore understood to express sympathy for the resistance against Russification in all his compositions from that epoch. Sibelius certainly supported the autonomy of the Grand Duchy and its Western traditions, but as an artist also sought inspiration from many different sources. He spent long periods in Central European metropolises and it was actually during one of his stays in Vienna that his romantic interest in Eastern Karelia and its archaic Kalevala-culture fully blossomed, not least due to the influence of national romantic compositions by Wagner, Smetana and Weber (Kvist Dahlstedt 1999: 15–75).

This Central European source of inspiration was willingly noticed by later music historians, since it could be smoothly combined with the notion of Finland as a cultural nation, which despite some of its partly Eastern archaic roots certainly belonged to Western civilization. There are, however, equally clear signs that the young Sibelius was strongly influenced by renowned Russian composers, not least by Tchaikovsky, whose impact on Sibelius's first two symphonies was obvious and willingly acknowledged by the Finnish composer. It is naturally questionable whether the elite imperial culture of Russia could truly be animated by a set of national aesthetic values. Nevertheless, Sibelius would later declare that his early production was closer to Slavonic than to Western music, and added that he had been directed by the same urge to express a sense of national originality as had the great Russian composers. It is not surprising therefore that the much praised first performance of his composition 'The Daughter of Pohjola' took place in St Petersburg in 1906 and that his third symphony, released in the following year, was eagerly debated in Russian high society (Murtomäki 2000).

After the final closure of the Finnish-Russian border in 1918, such acknowledgements became sparse indeed. Instead, expressions of extreme hatred toward Russia became fashionable, especially among those Fennoman student radicals who had joined the White Army in the civil war. This Army had defeated the revolutionaries, and subsequently became convinced that it was the 'historical mission' of Finland to defend Western civilization. Mostly unconsciously, but sometimes outspokenly, many radical nationalists would hereby also express a fear of the dangerous and uncivilized, some would even dare to call it the eastern and 'Russian' layers of the Finnish identity, which in their opinion had caused the Civil War and explained why ten per cent of Finns were still devoted communists (Högnäs 1995: 165–81).

This latent layer had to be constantly cured and harshly guarded against, almost like a life-threatening congenital disease. When in the late 1920s the Finnish communists tried to organize some political provocation, the nationalist networks were bewildered and the country was thrown into a chain of chaotic right-wing demonstrations and terrorist actions. The Finnish democratic system eventually managed to calm the situation down, but the crisis in itself restored fears of the Finns being an immature and unpredictable lot. Scornful remarks to that effect by Scandinavian and West European commentators, however, enforced another dimension of the imagined historical mission of Finland. When Finns were accused of overreacting, many of them took these accusations to be a reminder of how alone they were as defenders of Western civilization.

The poet, Uuno Kailas, described this solitary task with the following frantic lines:

The border cracks open
facing Asia and the East.
With the West and Europe behind me,
I, the guard, protect it.

Inspired by such images, the Finnish notion of Europe became increasingly polarized. On the one hand was the proud guardian attitude towards the West, but on the other was the permanent fear of being left alone with the Russian bear which, once recovered, would try to get back the Baltic provinces it had lost in the First World War (Klinge 1972: 158–88).

In that situation some radical nationalists made a virtue of necessity and emphasized that Finland should not even bother about the West. It was as if Western Europe had been reduced in scale, or alternatively, had been transformed into an irresponsible and impotent civilization, which had become corrupted by its passion for democracy and an individualistic lifestyle. This opinion was naturally not shared by the more moderate elites, which maintained their admiration of – and attachment to – Western Europe and the Nordic realm. But since the radical nationalists had a strong grip on the academic youth, it was often this arrogant attitude which attracted the public attention. The view, naturally, was rooted in the inferiority complex of the young nation, but also took undoubted inspiration from Oswald Spengler's fashionable notion of the decline of Western civilization. According to this nationalist interpretation, the young and vigorous Finland was the bright exception to the European rule (Mikkeli 1999: 20–5).

Another vision of these sturdy nationalists was the hope of expanding Finnish cultural and political dominance in all directions. The national rights of Finnish-speaking minorities in northern Sweden and Norway had to be secured; the brotherhood with the Estonians in the south, who also spoke a Finno-Ugrian language, ought to replace the Finnish-Swedish cultural contacts; and last but not least, the large Karelian realm behind the eastern border was predestined one day to become part of the Great Finland (Nygård 1978: passim). As the Soviet Union began to recover, these eastbound fantasies looked even more naive, but not for those who saw in Hitler's Germany the solution to the problem. Had Hitler not in *Mein Kampf* promised to mobilize a crusade against the Bolsheviks, and could this not also serve the dream of a Greater Finland (Uola 1982: 108–19, 264)?

Although seldom expressed in public, this hope of a German rescue sustained those among the radical nationalists who in the 1930s drifted sharply toward the extreme right. In fact, a defensive version of the same thought was also nourished among moderate conservatives, who still had fresh in their memories the German intervention on the White side in the Finnish Civil War of 1918, and who, despite the obvious vulgarization of German culture during Hitler's regime, would continue to value Germany as the leading European nation in both science and art. Exactly like the *Bildungsbürgertum* in Scandinavian countries, the educated class in Finland had for centuries thought of Lutheran and Baltic Germany as a natural counterpart in Central Europe. This explains, at least partly, why many evidently moderate Finns showed so much tolerance and understanding toward the Third Reich (Hiedanniemi 1980: *passim*).

One of these intellectuals was the author Olavi Paavolainen, who after a well-staged journey through the 'rejuvenated' Germany in the summer of 1936 wrote an impressionistic book of his experiences. The work reflected the strongly ambivalent attitude which many Finns had toward what they understood to be, both for better and for worse, the very *Kraftwerk* of Europe. He did not neglect what he characterized as the strongly barbarian energy behind the German recovery; he pointed at the dark sides of the Nazi dictatorship, but added in the following lines that, perhaps, this was the price to be paid for the birth of Germany and the whole of Europe. By saying this, Paavolainen evoked not only Spenglerian associations. An equally strong notion behind these words was the slogan of the 'New Europe', which the Nazi ideologue Alfred Rosenberg charged with dreams of an Aryan hegemony, but which of course originated from the much older Pan-European vision (Paavolainen 1937: *passim*).

It is obvious that Paavolainen's comprehension of the 'New Europe' was closer to the German interpretation than to the more French and universal understanding of the concept. One pragmatic reason for this was, as already mentioned, the belief that a strong Germany could keep away the Russian bear from the Baltic region. And furthermore, looked at from a North European perspective, it was almost inevitable that Germany should be understood to be the heart of the European body. Although Nordic liberals and social democrats looked with disgust on what was happening in Germany and put their hopes in Great Britain, France and the United States, they tended to see German development as a key question for both Finland and the whole of Europe.

And yet, this did not mean that liberal and leftist intellectuals, who often constituted a silent majority, shared the radical nationalist view of the New Europe. Their admiration of French and British democracy grew even stronger in the shadow of Hitler's Germany. Some of these intellectuals, such as the later internationally famous architect Alvar Aalto, expressed their dismissive attitude towards Nazi rule by showing an almost provocative interest in the modern art of the Soviet Union. It was not that Aalto and his kindred spirits had any illusions of what happened behind the eastern border of Finland. But when they were faced with what went on in Germany, it was not unthinkable that they should understand much of the huge societal and building project in Soviet Union as rational and modern (Meinander 1999: 119–20).

The grim experiences of the Second World War would naturally enforce the impression that Germany played a crucial role in the European continent. In most European countries the most horrific fears came true, whereas the Finnish case was more complicated, since the two countries actually fought together against the Soviet Union, before turning their weapons against each other in autumn 1944. How did the Finnish conception of Europe shift in the shadow of these drastic changes?

The first traumatic experience for Finland was naturally the outbreak of the Winter War in late autumn 1939, when the country was left alone to fight for its very life against the Soviet Union. The attack was a direct consequence of the unholy alliance between Germany and the Soviet Union, which gave Moscow a free hand to take back its imperial provinces on the east coast of the Baltic. Although the invasion was hindered and a peace treaty was signed in March 1940, the Finns were left with a deep wound in the heart. The war had shown how correct all the fears of being left alone with Russia actually were. From then on the political leadership of Finland would always remember that it was not only naive, but also fatally irresponsible, to believe that any Western country would ever seriously try to rescue Finland – that is, if it did not serve their own military interests (Meinander 1995: 181–94).

This bitter insight was expressed with maximal clarity by the Commander-in-Chief, Field Marshal Gustaf Mannerheim, in his classic order of the day, given one day after the Peace Treaty in March 1940. Mannerheim declared his deep gratitude to his soldiers and people for their patriotic deeds and contrasted their heroism with the passivity of the West, which despite its rosy promises and emphatic encouragement had done very little for Finland. Referring to the traditional notion of Finland as the 'Bulwark of the West', Mannerheim stated that the Finnish people was naturally proud of this task. But he added, with an obvious allusion to Topelius's 'The Original Promissory Note', that Finns also knew that, by shedding their blood alone for the West, they had to the last penny paid off their debt to Western civilization (*Överbefälhavarens dagorder* 14 March 1940; N:o 34).

This feeling, of course, was not new, but now it impinged on the collective consciousness of the Finns with such brutal force that it became a crucial dimension of Finnish national identity up until the 1990s. When the West turned its back and the Germans showed signs of defending Finnish interests against the Soviet Union in autumn 1940, the government of Finland did not hesitate to align itself with Germany, and take part in Operation Barbarossa, the momentous crusade against the Soviet Union. The Finnish President, Risto Ryti, made a triumphant radio broadcast on 26 June 1941, in which he declared that this time Finland would fight against the Soviet Union alongside a victorious comrade-in-arms and thus rid Finland of the eastern threat forever (*Hufvudstadsbladet* 27 June 1941).

In this situation, and for natural reasons, Hitler's Germany and his conception of a 'New Europe' overshadowed other Finnish notions of the continent. However, when Finland's sturdy fighting spirit had been crushed, and the Finnish government began to seek a way to cut its ties with Germany and reach an acceptable peace with the Soviet Union, it was confronted with a totally different Europe. It was not only the concept of German Europe that would soon belong to the past. Equally alarming was the knowledge that democratic Western Europe, despite the predicted victory of the Allied Forces, would be a much weaker player in international politics than it was before 1939.

In fact, the only thing that was certain was that the Soviet Union would become the leading power in Europe. To this harsh conclusion came, among others, Dr Urho Kekkonen, a rising star in Finnish politics, who in a speech given in Stockholm in early December 1943 pointed out three alternative directions for Finnish security policy after the war. The first alternative, an exclusive neutrality, had already been shown to be a failure. Finland was too weak and too close to Leningrad to keep the great powers away from its territory in the event of international crises. The second alternative, a membership in some kind of Western military alliance, was equally troublesome, since it would transform the Finnish borderland into a permanent military camp and make it a major battlefield in every clash with the Russian Empire. Kekkonen would thus stress the third alternative, which, he admitted openly, required almost the impossible. The Finns should leave behind their animosity toward their hereditary foe, Russia, and instead try to build up a constructive and friendly relationship.

Kekkonen reminded his listeners of the considerable societal advances Finland had made as a Grand Duchy within the Russian Empire, and tried to convince the audience that a rather similar relationship could be possible only if the sovereignty and established democratic system of Finland could be fully guaranteed (Kekkonen 1967: 122–34). When the war against the Soviet Union ended nine months later in a harsh armistice treaty, similar thoughts of reconstructing the Finno-Russian relationship were put forward by many other politicians. Not surprisingly, they were repeatedly accused of being opportunists by more cautious compatriots, and naturally the selfish power motive was an unavoidable fact.

But the threatening dominance of the Soviet Union spoke for itself and soon Kekkonen became a leading figure in Finnish foreign policy. Together with the old Fennoman J.K. Paasikivi, who had begun his political career as a compliant official in the Grand Duchy and in 1946 was elected President of the Republic, Kekkonen rose to be the foremost proponent of this line and in 1956 succeeded Paasikivi as president. In 1948 Finland signed a 'Treaty of Friendship and Cooperation' with the Soviet Union in which Finland promised to defend its territory against every attack by Germans or their allies. The treaty constituted a cornerstone in Finnish policy – both in foreign and domestic affairs – through the whole of the cold war, and would thereby also have a clear impact on Finnish identity and its conception of Europe (Meinander 1999: 264–6).

Reluctantly, but nevertheless increasingly, the Finns began to admit that Russia in its new manifestation of the Soviet Union was a part of European civilization. Owing to Russia's Communist order, the great majority of Finns, of course, would not classify it as a Western culture. But on the other hand, up until the 1970s many Finns were impressed by the economic and technological progress of this superpower and were inclined to believe that it could eventually overtake even the United States. One such impressed Finn was President Kekkonen, who during his amazing 25 years as head of state (1956–1981) was a leading spokesman for the notion of Finland as a small but clear-sighted nation which had learnt to balance itself between the two competing superpowers and their mighty military forces.

One of Kekkonen's favourite expressions was the 'Finnish paradox'. It included the claim that Finland, despite its military and diplomatic obligations to the Soviet Union, was able to sustain its political system and even strengthen its ties to the West. This meant, however, that the Finnish–Soviet relationship should be based on mutual trust. Otherwise the Finns would be forced to put all their energy into improving the eastern connection, and this would freeze its Western ties. Although never fully accepted by the NATO hawks, who pointed to Finland as a warning example of a Western democracy that gradually lost its independence to the Russian bear, the Finnish paradox was nevertheless a concept which had a certain credibility (Kekkonen 1967: 143–8; Meinander 1999: 334–40).

The political culture in Finland was clearly complicated by the primacy of the eastern connection. Yet, equally obvious was the fact that the Finnish export industry, due to a stable foreign policy and favourable trade agreements with EFTA and the EEC, achieved firm footholds in the west European and overseas markets. This brought wealth, Western consumer goods and mass culture to Finland at a pace that gradually outstripped development in Central and Western Europe. In other words, the economic and cultural gains of the diplomatic balance between East and West were real. Simultaneously, it paved the way for a conception of Europe with Finland, if not exactly in the middle, then at least not on the brink. When tourism to the Soviet Union expanded in the 1970s, Finns became acquainted with the world-class high culture and historical monuments in Leningrad and Moscow, which further strengthened the impression that Russia, despite all its less attractive characteristics, was part of European civilization.

This is not to say that the Finns would forget the bitter past or that they had any illusions of what plans the Soviet Union had for Finland if war should break out. But what realistic alternative could Finland have had? The Winter War had taught the Finns a grave lesson. Since that time, the Finnish government had only been occasionally disturbed by moral objections to the businesslike cooperation with Hitler's Germany and the Soviet Union. If that was the price Finland had to pay for its independence, then so be it! Despite the cynicism which this attitude undeniably nourished, it steadily gained ground among the Finnish people, even if it required a considerable amount of indulgence towards the obscure talk about the trustworthy and honest relations between Finland and the Soviet Union.

Oversimplifying this complex relationship we can say that throughout the cold war the Finns floated as if they were at the same time 'on the brink' and 'somewhere in-between' in Europe. The first conception was for strategic and psychological reasons often repressed, whereas the other was actively supported by the government and progressive intelligentsia, which from the 1960s onward began to dismantle the nationalist historical paradigm and its inborn Russophobia (Meinander 2000: 195–208). This goal was also noticeably facilitated by the heated criticism from student radicals and the New Left in Western Europe and North America against the United States's involvement in the war in Vietnam, which supposedly revealed the evil imperialist motives behind the slogans of defending 'the Free World' and 'the market economy'. Affected by these accusations against the political and economic order in NATO-sheltered Western Europe, the younger generation of Finnish academics, journalists and artists seriously questioned the characterization of Western Europe as the 'real Europe' (Alapuro 1997: 194–8).

This dissociation from the Western order was of course idealistic and far-fetched, and yet it could serve the interest of the Finnish government, which regularly underlined its aim of upholding a policy of neutrality in international affairs. The Soviet Union would never fully accept the Finnish claim to neutrality, and true enough, when the security interests of the Soviet Union were at stake, Finland kept a very low profile. But when attention turned to issues which were important in ensuring mutual understanding between the United States and the Soviet Union, Finland eagerly took initiatives to smoothen the process and visibly participated in arranging international conferences and superpower negotiations. The high point of this policy was the Final Act of the European Security Conference, arranged in Helsinki in 1975, which served two purposes. Apart from temporarily calming the cold war in Europe, it gave the Finns a chance to advertise their independent position – not least in relation to the Soviet Union (Jakobson 1998: 80–4).

When President Kekkonen in his welcoming speech to the gathering of thirty-four European and North American heads of states proclaimed that the Act would function as a cornerstone in international politics, because it would nail down the principle of sovereign equality between all states (Suomi 1998: 672), he must have regarded his own words with scepticism. And yet the words were in perfect accord with the rhetoric of Finnish foreign policy, which had as its main task the strengthening of belief in a united Europe that was capable of overcoming the animosities which had arisen from the World Wars and the cold war. It was of course an illusionary conception of Europe, but it provided a more optimistic perspective on the Finnish position than the dualistic cold war conception, which inevitably awoke questions of whether Finland actually was a part of the West.

How did this tightrope-walking succeed? As far as political rhetoric is concerned, it is disputable if either Western or Soviet analysts ever swallowed the bait. But as emphasized earlier, if the measures are economic growth, social welfare and cultural liberalism, Finland undeniably reached West European standards during the cold war. This twofold development was recognized early both in Western and Eastern Europe, and although some would condemn the Finnish foreign-policy liturgy as grotesque, others were truly impressed by its practical consequences. For example, in 1955 the Polish Communist Party daily characterized the Finnish export trade as a kind of Janus capitalism, and pointed at how its forest industry was westbound and metal industry predominantly eastbound.

As the Polish commentator noticed, this did not bother Finnish capitalists, who wanted to take advantage of the huge markets in the Soviet Union. Although the diplomatic Pole went on to add that the Finns did not wear two faces, this was indeed what many leading capitalists were doing. They would give steadfast support to the official friendship between Finland and the Soviet Union, and if necessary, even get drunk with influential *apparatchiks*. However, among reliable compatriots, Western diplomats and businessmen they spoke out and did what they could to weaken domestic Communism and defend the bourgeois order in Finland (Kuisma 1997: 99–101).

When the Soviet system became increasingly shaky in the late 1980s, this double protocol gradually lost its rationale. It was replaced with an equally smooth attitude toward the leading members of the European Community, especially toward Germany, and efficiently paved the way for Finnish membership of the EU. Some critics claimed that Finnish flexibility as an EU member did not differ markedly from the traditional servility toward Imperial Russia and the Soviet Union. These accusations were uttered especially by domestic EU opponents, who feared that membership would have fatal consequences for Finnish agriculture and the policy of neutrality. Sometimes similar thoughts were also put forward by Scandinavian politicians and journalists, who had difficulties in comprehending why the Finns, as it seemed, so easily accepted the national interests of the large EU states and were even prepared to speak openly of transforming the union into a centralized federation state.

As such, the critique was well-founded. Finnish agriculture had by the end of the twentieth century begun a thorough transformation, and the Finnish policy of neutrality belongs to the past. But it would be misleading to explain this remarkable shift in Finnish foreign policy and the general attitude toward Western Europe only from a strictly economic or diplomatic point of view. Why did 57 per cent of the Finns vote to enter the EU in the referendum in autumn 1994, when the margin in favour of the Union was much smaller in the Swedish referendum? This was because the Finns, contrary to the Swedes, did not think in the first place of their welfare state and, ultimately, had no serious difficulties in leaving behind the neutrality rhetoric of the cold war (Tiilikainen 1999: 212–18).

Not surprisingly, it all boiled down to the traumatic experiences in Finnish history, which had taught the Finns how dangerous it could be to trust in a better future and leave hard questions of security policy unsolved. Joining the EU meant for the majority of Finns a step toward a more secure position in Europe. Developments in Russia were fearfully chaotic in 1992–1993 when the question of joining the Union became a public issue in Finland, and thus awoke many unpleasant associations to earlier large-scale crises in Europe. In that specific context the EU was understood to offer a more secure future, not least since the EU member states had declared in the 1992 Maastricht Treaty that the common aim was not only monetary union, but also an integrated foreign and security policy.

The Finnish government avoided emphasizing this motive on the eve of the referendum, but trusted that the people would understand what actually was at stake. Some commentators would later accuse President Mauno Koivisto of playing a risky game but, as he replied, the situation could have become even more unsafe if the security motive had been boldly underlined and the Finns then for some reason had voted against membership (Koivisto 1995: 531–48). Koivisto's remark was widely accepted and it enforced the impression that the Finns have maintained their strong trust in political leadership. Building on the cold war tradition of reticence, crucial questions in Finnish security policy are seldom discussed in public, although numerous Finns have decisive opinions about the issue, and on rare occasions outspoken statements are made by the President or Prime Minister.

There are already many signs that membership of the EU has affected the Finnish identity and its conception of Europe. The first Finnish President of the EU-era, Martti Ahtisaari, spoke about the European Community and its potential in a clearly more optimistic tone than had his predecessor Koivisto. One reason for this rhetoric shift was clearly Ahtisaari's background as a renowned UN diplomat and his natural ability to verbalize a vision of a brighter future. But more importantly, the rhetoric shift is a sign that Finnish public opinion at the end of the twentieth century had a more open mind toward a deepening political integration in Europe than had, for example, Swedish or Danish public opinion (Ahtisaari 1998).

The changes on this front are naturally also an outcome of the diffusion of the new information technology, which is swiftly dismantling the state monopoly in national culture and macroeconomics. However, it is equally clear that membership of the EU has been felt to be not only a significant improvement in national security but also a kind of emotional homecoming. Admittedly, this sounds pathetic, and yet it is perfectly understandable that many Finns feel that EU membership is like closing a wide circle, a circle that began when Finland, after 700 years under Swedish rule, became in 1809 a Grand Duchy within the Russian Empire. After at least two centuries of uncertainty and ideological searching, the Finns are no longer continuously asking themselves whether their country belongs to Western Europe and, if that is actually the case, whether they are 'on the brink' or rather 'somewhere between' where European civilization is concerned.

This increasingly relaxed attitude toward Europe and its own national identity has opened many new perspectives on Finnish history and culture which further uncover the limits and anachronisms of the writing of nationalistic history. Still, it would be wrong to believe that the national history of Finland is completely finished. The Finns have today a relatively strong confidence in the EU and are less and less explicitly troubled by their historical traumas. But beneath the surface, Russophobia and the fear of being left alone by the West will continue to form the Finnish identity for many generations and perpetuate the notion of a heroic – and tragic – Finland.

## Acknowledgement

I wish to thank Professor Bo Pettersson, University of Helsinki, for the comments on and corrections of the translations of poetry on pp. 151 and 157, and for help with the translations.

On the Brink or In-between?

# References

Ahti, M. (1999), *Ryssänvihassa. Elmo Kaila 1888–1935: Aktivistin asevomien harmaan eminenssin ja Akateemisen Karjala-Seuran puheenjohtajan elämänkerta*, Helsinki.

Ahtisaari, M. (1998), 'Suomi kannattaa vahvaa EU:ta', *Helsingin Sanomat* 18.6.1998.

Alapuro, Risto (1997), *Suomen älymystö Venäjän varjossa*, Helsinki.

Forsgård, N.-E. (1998), *I det femte inseglets tecken: En studie i den åldrande Zacharias Topelius livs- och historiefilosofi*, Helsingfors.

Hiedanniemi, B. (1980), *Kulttuuriin verhottua politiikkaa. Kansallissosialistisen Saksan kulttuuripropaganda Suomessa 1933-1940*, Helsinki.

*Historiallinen Aikakauskirja* 1999.

*Historisk Tidskrift för Finland* 1999.

Högnäs, S. (1995), *Kustens och skogarnas folk: Om synen på svenskt och finskt lynne*, Stockholm.

*Hufvudstadsbladet* 27.6.1941.

Jakobson, M. (1998), *Finland in the New Europe*, London.

Jussila, O. (1994), 'Nuor- vai vanhasuomalainen Suomi?', in T. Mällinen (ed.), *Nuoren Suomen ytimessä*, Helsinki.

Kekkonen, U. (1967), 'Naapurisopu "perivihollisen" kanssa', in *Urho Kekkonen: puheita ja kirjoituksia I*, Tapiola.

Klinge, M. (1972), *Vihan veljistä valtiososialismiin: Yhteiskunnallisia ja kansallisia näkemyksiä 1910- ja 1920-luvuilta*, Porvoo.

—— (1983), *Runebergs två fosterland*, Helsingfors.

Koivisto, M. (1995), *Kaksi kautta: Historian tekijät II*, Helsinki.

Kuisma, M. (1993), *Metsäteollisuuden maa. Suomi, metsät ja kansainvälinen järjestelmä 1620–1920*, Helsinki.

—— (1997), *Kylmä sota, kuuma öljy: Neste, Suomi ja kaksi Eurooppaa 1948–1979*, Porvoo.

Kvist Dahlstedt, B. (1999), 'Nationell hängivenhet: Sibelius Kareliamusik och den västeuropeiska identiteten i 1890-talets Finland', in B. Kvist Dahlstedt and S. Dahlstedt (eds), *Nationell hängivenhet och europeisk klarhet*, Stockholm.

Liikanen, I. (1995), *Fennomania ja kansa*, Helsinki.

Meinander, H. (1995), 'Vinterkrigets lärdom', in *Historiska och litteraturhistoriska studier 70*, Helsingfors.

—— (1999), *Tasavallan tiellä: Suomi kansalaissodasta 2000-luvulle*, Espoo.

Henrik Meinander

—— (2000), 'Stiff Trends, Soft Turnings: Remarks on Finnish historical research in the twentieth century', in F. Meyer and J. Eivind Myhre (eds), *Nordic Historiography in the 20th Century*, Oslo.

Mikkeli, H. (1999), 'Tornin pidot – korkokuva 30-luvusta?', in P. Karkama and H. Koivisto (eds), *Ajan paineessa: Kirjoituksia 1930-luvun suomalaisesta aatemaailmasta*, Helsinki.

Murtomäki, V. (2000), 'Juna Pietariin meni juuri: Helsingin-Pietarin-rata kuljetti musiikkiväkeä ja vaikutteita vaikeinakin aikiona', *Helsingin Sanomat*, 26.3.2000.

Nygård, T. (1978), *Suur-Suomi vai lähiheimolaisten auttaminen*, Helsinki.

*Överbefälhavarens dagorder* 14.3.1940; N:o 34.

Paavolainen, O. (1937), *Kolmannen valtakunnan vieraana: Rapsodia*, Jyväskylä.

Smeds, K. (1996), *Helsingfors-Paris: Finlands utveckling till nation på världsutställningaran 1851–1900*, Helsingfors.

Söderhjelm, H. (1939), *Finlands svenska arv* (småtryck), Göteborg.

Suomi, J. (1998), *Liennytyksen akanvirrassa. Urho Kekkonen 1972–1976*, Keuruu.

Tiilikainen, T. (1999), 'Finland och Sverige: Skillnader och likheter i sätten att förstå världen efter det kalla kriget', in T. Suominen and A. Björnsson (eds), *Det hotade landet och det skyddade: Sverige och Finland från 1500-talet till våra dagar. Historiska och säkerhets-politiska betraktelser*, Stockholm.

Tiitta, A. (1994), *Harmaankiven maa. Zacharias Topelius ja Suomen maantiede*, Helsinki.

Tommila, P. (1989), *Suomen historiankirjoitus. Tutkimuksen historia*, Porvoo.

Uola, M. (1982), *Sinimusta veljeskunta: Isänmaallinen kansanliike 1932–1944*, Helsinki.

# –7–

# Europe's Eastern Outpost? The Meanings of 'Europe' in Baltic Discourses
## Klas-Göran Karlsson

In the vast literature written since the 1980s on the transition of East and Central Europe, the general focus has been political and economic. Hundreds of scholarly and other works have been devoted to analysing the change from single-party dictatorship, command-administrative economy and power state to something else in post-Soviet Russia, or the much more unequivocal development towards democracy, market economy and state of law in post-communist Poland. In contrast, the most important theme of the 'transitology' literature on the Baltic republics – not least the part written by ethnic Balts – has been *identity* or, rather, various collective *identities*. Marju Lauristin, one of the major scholarly and political actors of the Estonian independence movement, has synonymously talked about Baltic transition as an issue of 'changing mental sets' (Lauristin 1997: 26), and other observers have also testified to the predilection of many Balts to analyse their conditions in terms of 'identity' (cf. Lieven 1994: 17).

If the ideal unit to identify with in the Baltic republics has been somewhat indistinct, changing between the ethno-national, the civic, the Baltic, the Nordic, the European and the Western – or rather, if there have been conscious Baltic identity policies not to 'put all their region-building eggs in one basket' (Neumann 1999: 135) – the unit to distance oneself from has been more unambiguous. The Other has been the Soviet Union into which the Baltic republics were forcibly integrated as a result of the 1939 Molotov-Ribbentrop pact: the German-Soviet agreement to divide Eastern Europe into two power spheres which served to trigger the Second World War and to map post-war East and Central Europe. Soviet Baltic identity has never been regarded as 'normal' or 'natural', but as an anomaly or a parenthesis. In important aspects, Russia has created the role as the successor of the Soviet Union as the Baltic Other since the latter's demise in 1991.

It is often generally stated that the essence of collective identity is an awareness of commonality and distinctiveness. Political scientist Samuel Huntington, author of the book that more than any other brought issues of cultural identities back to the front of international relations studies, has for example stressed that 'we know who we are only when we know who we are not and often only when we know whom we are against' (Huntington 1996: 21). In an era of dramatic international change and of ethno-national and regional revival, when old certainties are gone and 'a multitude of identity-possibilities are put on display' (Megill 1998: 38–40), identity needs have often brought macro-historical perspectives of cultural refigurations and civilizational orders to the fore.

This seems to be especially true in cultural border areas where, with Huntington's words, the clash of civilizations has been most perceptible. This has most certainly been the case in the Baltic republics, which are situated where Western civilization meets the Eastern, Orthodox one. However, in Baltic discourse being 'Western' or 'European' is not primarily a matter of geographical qualifications, but a superior cultural, political and moral objective to be perceived and interpreted from macro-historical perspectives of cultural continuities, absolute chronologies and black-and-white collocations of the past. The struggle for 'Westernness' is only comparable in importance to the simultaneous struggle to secure national identities in the Baltic area.

## The Baltic Struggle for Identity: Present Concerns

A widespread awareness of the precarious civilizational or geopolitical position of the Baltic territory as an intermediary between West and East is obviously an important factor behind the present Baltic engagement for identity formation and identity politics. In part, this awareness is based on contemporary concerns. One is demographic: the indigenous populations are very small, which obviously raises fundamental questions about Baltic cultural survival. Another is geographical, or rather geopolitical: the post-cold war Baltic states are not normally considered part of Central Europe or *Mitteleuropa*. However, they do not belong to Eastern Europe either, often not even to a vaguely outlined East Central Europe. Naturally, this problem of cultural cleavages challenges Baltic endeavours to form well-defined supranational identities (cf. Lagerspetz 1996: 45–51).

Another factor that probably spurs identity issues is the ongoing Baltic integration into Western and European networks such as NATO and the EU. One Western observer hits the nail on the head by asking whether traditional Baltic song festivals will hold up against rock concerts (Clemens 1994: 185). It goes without saying that questions of whether the Balts might bring their own perspectives and safeguard their own interests in these networks, or if they will be reduced to members of secondary importance are about identity. Most ethnic Balts associate the latter position with the abominable Soviet period, but some are reminded of the peripheral and marginal positions of the independent Baltic states in the period between the two World Wars as well (cf. Ruutsoo 1995: 15).

Another concern is the Baltic republics' relations to their eastern neighbour, Russia. In Huntington's civilizational map of the post-Soviet era, Estonia, Latvia and Lithuania are the only former Soviet republics outside Islamic Central Asia which have ended up outside the 'orthodox' civilizational bloc, the latter more exactly defined as Russia and its 'near abroad'. Whether Huntington's assumption is reasonable, or whether it is more realistic to assume that the Balts bear the stamp of a half-century of integration into Soviet networks with regard to central mental or psychological features such as political culture, economic behaviour and working ethics, is in itself a challenge for identity debates.

In Baltic political discourse, there is a suspicion that the Baltic area is not yet removed from the 'near abroad' concept, with its intimations of continuous Russian influences and legitimate interests in *Pribaltika*. The Russian military forces have withdrawn from the Baltic area but are still close, in the militarized Kaliningrad enclave, the Baltic Sea and Russia proper. Russia in the late 1990s openly opposed eastward expansion of NATO, particularly vis-à-vis the Baltic republics. Political disputes arose round the drawing of borderlines between Russia and all three Baltic states. By proving their non-orthodox identities, the Balts obviously intended to reinforce – or rather perpetuate – toward Russia a border not regarded as politically negotiable.

Compared to the situation in the Caucasian area, the disintegration of the Soviet Union has certainly not lead literally to a 'clash' between the Baltic republics and the Russian centre. The divorce has, however, not been altogether unproblematic. The sorest problem has been the perceived discrimination against the large ethnic Russian and Russian-speaking minorities in Estonia and Latvia, which at times has provoked strong opposition among Russian nationalist groups and brought down international criticism on the Baltic states. The state of tension between the core Estonian and Latvian nations and the Russian minority groups, as well as various direct or indirect threats from Moscow toward the governments in Tallinn and Riga, probably served to intensify further the Baltic identity concerns. These tensions were (and may remain) related to the 'European' question, but in a paradoxical way; while the latter threats increase the Baltic will to integrate into Western networks – both 'soft' networks such as the EU or the NATO network which can provide the Baltic states with a 'hard' security guarantee – the accusations of discrimination against the Russians might have a disturbing effect on the same process of integration. This paradox will be further elaborated later on.

## The Baltic Struggle for Identity: History, Memory and Culture

In part, early twenty-first-century Baltic awareness of cultural identity has stemmed from historical experiences and relatively well-established collective memories. Until the twentieth century, the Balts were subordinated to several foreign regimes in the Baltic Sea area. The sea itself, in German the *Ostsee*, in Estonian *Läänemeri*, the Western Sea, mainly served the purpose of integrating the different Baltic Sea areas, especially during the Middle Ages when the Hanseatic League brought the Baltic Sea coastal areas together into a tight mercantile network in which Riga, founded in 1201, became an important eastern hub. The northern Baltic territory that is now Estonia and Livonia was part of the military monastic German Teutonic Order, and the Danish and Swedish dynastic states. Estonia was a province of the Swedish Baltic Sea empire from 1561 until it, together with Livonia, was annexed by the Russian empire as a result of the Great Northern War, 1700–1721.

In the south, Lithuania successfully resisted German conquest and formed an extensive dynastic state of its own in the high Middle Ages at the same time as Muscovite Russia laboured under the Mongol 'yoke'. Partly as a result of an increased threat from the east, the Grand Duchy of Lithuania became a partner of initially equal rights in a Polish-Lithuanian dynastic union from 1386, which was later converted into a joint-Commonwealth in which Lithuanians were subject to 'cultural Polonization'. As a consequence of partitions of Poland in the late eighteenth century, imperial Russian rule was imposed also on Lithuania, including the southern parts of today's Latvia – that is, Latgalia and Kurland.

The imperial Russian policy in the West included military conquest of the strategically vital eastern Baltic Sea area, followed by cultural assimilation, abolishment of local institutions, ruthless enserfment of the rural population, exploitation of internal splits between the nobility and the rest of the population, and co-optation of local elites, which gave the loyal Baltic German nobility considerable economic and cultural autonomy. The methods of imperial incorporation gradually met with growing resistance, however, especially from the core ethnic groups, which could profit from a relatively high level of culture and education, spurred not least by the spirit of broader European intellectual trends at Dorpat and Vilnius universities, and from a relative openness of the empire to the surrounding technically and culturally more advanced Western world.

During the second half of the nineteenth century, when the German Romantic conception of the *Volk* swept through Europe, and when modernization resulted in a gradual improvement in the economic position of the peasants, and in industrialization and urbanization, resistance to a more persistent tsarist Russification policy found a new expression and a new social base in the growth of national consciousness and nationalist movements in the entire Baltic territory. National awakening sparked off demands for autonomy primarily in relation to the Baltic German aristocracy, but also to the Russian imperial authorities. Demands for the establishment of independent Baltic national states outside the Russian imperial realm were not made, however, until under the very last Romanov years. Nevertheless, it has been convincingly argued that this development was much more dynamic in the Baltic area than in adjacent Russian, Belorussian and Ukrainian parts of the tsarist empire (Thaden 1985: 411–21).

In spite of the relative lack of political independence and the frequent occurrence of war and conquest, relatively clear-cut ethno-linguistic and culturally differentiated identities have occurred in the Baltic area since prehistoric times. Tacitus wrote about 'Aesti' living on the Baltic coast even in the first century AD. To be certain, this did not mean that the vast majority of the Baltic population, the peasants, had a national consciousness until in the mid-nineteenth century, but rather that the way toward the emergence of Baltic nations was cleared by means of cultural factors such as widespread literacy and affiliation to Western Christianity. Another push factor was the relatively successful modernization process which separated the Balts from their eastern imperial neighbours. An additional factor that gradually promoted ethnic consciousness was that class affiliations coincided with ethnic boundaries; while the land-owning nobility, the merchants and the clergy were predominantly Germans and Poles, the lower peasant classes consisted almost exclusively of Estonians, Latvians and Lithuanians.

These Baltic identities have quite clear Western or European outlooks. Among the core ethno-nations, Estonians belong to the Finno-Ugric language family, which make them closely linguistically linked to their Finnish and Karelian neighbours. Culturally, there have been close relations between the Estonians and the Finnish through history. The Estonian national epic *Kalevipoeg*, written by F.R. Kreutzwald, was prohibited by the Baltic Russian censor, but was accepted by the censor in Russian Finland and was printed there in 1862 (Raag 1999: 102–3). The epic hero himself, Kalevipoeg, swam over the Gulf of Finland in search of his mother. Later in the poem, a giant oak fell to form a bridge from Estonia to Finland. This bridge symbol has been widely used to prove Estonia's European orientation.

Latvians and Lithuanians speak old Indo-European languages of a Baltic language group, but nothing like the Slavic languages spoken by their eastern neighbours. Several other ethnic groups have formed considerable Baltic minorities, such as the Poles, the Jews, the Swedes and the Baltic Germans, and these still more have supported cultural relations with Central and Western Europe. Of special importance in this context were the wealthy Germans who, through their aristocratic corporations, the *Ritterschaften*, had a dominant administrative and cultural position until the Russification processes were initiated in the late nineteenth century (Hosking 1997: 382–5). The only larger Baltic minority group that has strengthened cultural relations with Eastern Orthodoxy is the Russian and Russian-speaking one, of whom the absolute majority migrated to the Baltic republics during the Soviet postwar era. In the liberation period of the late 1980s, many of them enrolled in hardline Communist so-called intermovements, struggling reactively, but in vain, to preserve Moscow's dominance over the Baltic republics.

Furthermore, Baltic emigrant groups in the West have served to maintain cultural and other relations between their new and old homelands even in periods when official relations between the Soviet Union and the West were strained. Several thousands of Estonians and Latvians left their homelands at the end of the Second World War to create influential exile communities in Sweden. Several hundreds of thousand of Lithuanians left Eastern Europe between the 1860s and 1940 to form a strong minority group in the United States. These *emigré* groups have been much involved in re-establishing Western institutions and values in the late Soviet and post-Soviet Baltic societies and states (Hallik 1989: 73).

What is more, the Christianization of the Balts from the thirteenth century was mainly a result of missionary activities from the Western Church, even if a considerable number of princes and noblemen, especially Lithuanian ones, adopted Orthodox faith. With the spread of the Reformation in the first half of the sixteenth century, the Lutheran faith became predominant in Estonia and Latvia, despite the fact that large numbers of Latvian and Estonian peasants in Livland, probably for socioeconomic reasons, converted to Russian Orthodoxy in the mid-nineteenth century. A strong Pietist current within Baltic Lutheranism emphasized individualist responsibility and everyday religiousness, which clearly contrasted it with Russian Orthodoxy's collectivist, authoritarian and unworldly underpinnings. In Lithuania the Roman Catholic counterrevolution was victorious, largely due to the efforts of the Jesuits. It should be added that the Estonians and Latvians at least became secularized during the twentieth century, but that Christianity and the Church nevertheless has kept its grip over large Protestant Baltic groups, since it has symbolized national and European values different from those of Soviet communism. In Lithuania, the Roman Catholic Church kept its position as an important religious and cultural institution throughout the Soviet period. In the late Soviet era, influence from the Polish Catholic Church combined in transforming the Lithuanian Church into a significant political institution (Senn 1990).

These historical, linguistic and religious descriptions obviously point to another factor which may be important to explain the anxious search for identity and identities in the Baltic area, especially in a period in which regional cooperation is highly estimated: the Balts are, even among themselves, ethnically different and do not have that many common cultural experiences to share, the precarious geopolitical situation notwithstanding. Through history, Lithuanians have generally had a Polish–Central European–Roman Catholic, Estonians a German–Scandinavian–Protestant, and Latvians a more divided cultural orientation. As mentioned above, a certain American orientation should be added to the Lithuanian case. Also, economic developments diverged: while the northern parts of the Baltic area became centres of industry and trade in the modern era, Lithuania remained mainly an agrarian country.

The common – negative – memory of most Balts concerns incorporation into and life within the eastern Russian and Soviet empires. This means that the Balts to a great extent have been kept together by the perception of a common enemy. An American scholar of Estonian origin has summed up the predominant Baltic perception by claiming the existence of 'a basic pervasive mistrust of all Russians and Russian intentions' (Misiunas 1994: 99). This is certainly true when analysing the period since the 1920s, but less so in earlier history.

The more positive equivalent that the Baltic national liberation movements could and did benefit from was a 'European' or 'Western' otherness which was both factual and imagined. As a matter of fact, it has been suggested – especially from commentators of Baltic origin – that the distinction between 'factual' and 'imagined' is less relevant when analysing the Baltic situation, because the basic cultural 'Europeanness' of the Balts is in accord with both the self-perception of the Balts themselves and the perception of observers from the outside (Prazauskas 1994: 161), or that the Baltic situation is objectively 'the striving of society, as an organic entity of material, social and mental structures, reacting against 'non-historical' (i.e. inauthentic) forcefully imposed economic, social and political deformations' (Ruutsoo 1995: 168).

Such essentialist propositions notwithstanding, implying that certain identities are to be understood as organic, perpetual and 'good', and others as transitory, momentary expressions of power relations and 'evil', it should be underlined that the perceptions of European identities of the Balts have been changing in intensity. They have been most cherished in periods of imperial weakness, when there have been living expectations and prospects for the Balts to leave the Russian and Soviet empires. The 'European' or 'Western' components have seldom been accurately defined, other than as an absolute antithesis to the 'Russian' or the 'Soviet' components, and as being in total concert with Baltic national projects.

The first appearance of such 'European' prospects was in the first decades of the twentieth century, the second in the late 1980s. This does not mean that they were totally absent in the interval, but merely that expectations are crucial for explaining Baltic national awakenings. The matrix of this subjective explanation of revolutionary breaks dates back to Alexis de Tocqueville, who as early as 1856 pointed out that the most dangerous moment for a poor government arises when it starts to reform itself: 'The evil that you patiently carry within you as long as it seems inevitable, becomes unbearable as soon as you think that it will be possible to escape it' (Tocqueville 1856: 292).

## The Baltic Turn and Return to Europe

Not only relatively well co-ordinated national movements, but also the First World War, the German intervention and the ensuing breakdown of political and social order in tsarist Russia combined in establishing independent Baltic states in 1918, including ones in Estonia and Latvia for the first time ever. After a turbulent period when the Bolsheviks and the Red Army tried to establish Soviet republics in the Baltic area, the new states were recognized *de jure* in separate peace treaties by Soviet Russia in 1920.

The Balts were allowed to practise state-building and society-making in freedom for two decades, until they were forcibly brought back into a Russian empire, this time in a Soviet Communist framework, in June 1940. The Soviet era ended in 1991, when the Soviet Union – economically weakened by decades of mismanagement and the burdens of empire, and politically shaken by the liberal reform endeavours of the last Communist party chief, Mikhail Gorbachev – disintegrated into fifteen independent states. Among these were three Baltic republics. By serving as intellectual *avant-gardes*, the Baltic independence movements, called popular fronts, were instrumental in first generally supporting the Gorbachev reform programme, then de-legitimating the entire republican and union-wide Communist leadership, and also in establishing national and civic values.

It goes without saying that the two Baltic liberation processes cannot be compared with reference to relations to Europe and the West, or any other aspect, without taking into consideration the time factor. As has been stated by one authority on modern Estonian history, no country will be able any more to establish the independent status of the inter-war era. In the current context of globalization, the alternative to independence is a status of European and global interdependence (Taagepera 1993: 215).

There is also another, less objective, time factor involved. In *The Poverty of Historicism* and *The Open Society and Its Enemies*, Sir Karl Popper once argued that history never repeats itself because of the simple fact that when we are getting close to repetition, a new factor intervenes in the historical process the second time: the memory of the first time. That this memory phenomenon is crucial is evident from the Baltic experiences. On the first occasion, most Western powers, including the Nordic neighbours, hesitated in diplomatically and politically recognizing the new Baltic states and tended to subsume upcoming Baltic problems as 'Russian problems', which, according to two initiated analysts, 'may have lessened the chances of keeping the Baltic free from conflict' (Hiden and Salmon 1991: 63). When the second time drew nearer, it became apparent that Western politicians and others, especially those of Nordic origin, had learned their lesson, because since the late 1980s the Western states have been much more alert in supporting in various ways the Baltic liberation and reconstruction processes.

Inclusion into a European or Western framework was an important political, economic and cultural objective for leading circles in the new Baltic states in instances both of independence struggle and of state-building. To be sure, this was also the case in the Soviet era, although less so in high politics and ideological attitudes than in social lifestyles

(Misiunas and Taagepera 1993: 218–21). It was intimately related to the principal goal of large Estonian, Latvian and Lithuanian groups to promote the development of national identities and to secure the survival of the independent nation states. It is obvious that the two objectives were considered mutually strengthening. The Baltic struggle for independence from the Russian and Soviet imperial power was initially pursued as a battle for 'nation' and 'Europe', against 'national subjugation' and 'empire'. What is more, 'Europe' as a cognitive frame and a mobilizing metaphor has twice provided many Balts with expectations of future civic societies characterized not by Eastern authoritarian rule and centralization, but by 'European' democracy, economic prosperity and state of law.

In the first instance, enlightened ideas of European origins of national self-determination, land reform, constitutional rule, the creation of free, compulsory national education systems, social welfare provisions, cultural autonomy for minority groups and parliamentary democracy were realized in the new republics. As a matter of fact, such ideas gained ground even in the period before independence. In the more relaxed socio-political conditions after 1905, a group of liberal Estonian writers, organized in the Young Estonians movement, wanted to promote a 'European' modernist orientation, attained through increased Estonian contacts with Finland (Alenius 1998: 131–2). This orientation was, however, far from unequivocal. In Estonian and Latvian national discourse, the Baltic Germans were mostly regarded as the main enemy, whose cultural and socio-economic dominance interfered with national aspirations more directly than did the imperial Russian power. Consequently, the main threat against national autonomy came from the West, which brought the Baltic nations closer to Russia, while constructing an 'anti-European' border against Germany and the Germans. Nor was the meaning of an increased autonomy unambiguous. The dilemma as to whether it meant a focus on questions related to national, cultural identities, to social and economic development or to a more definitive political independence divided moderates and radicals in the years before and during the First World War (Lehti 2000: 74–82).

In the newly established Baltic republics, these differences of orientation initially became less urgent. Civil societies rapidly developed, including some five hundred new voluntary organizations annually in Estonia in the first independent decade (Aarelaid-Tart and Tart 1995: 153–4). By enrolling teachers from many countries, the Baltic universities became centres for the diffusion of European culture (von Rauch 1995: 128–34, cf. Karling 1988: 55–64, Alenius 1998: 146–7). The traditional eastward trade diminished radically and had been reduced almost to nil within a few years, while economic relations with Germany, Britain and Scandinavia were magnified. Generally, foreign policy was aimed at establishing cooperation with Baltic neighbours and with the Western powers while, in contrast, relations with the Soviet Union deteriorated, especially after an aborted Communist putsch in Tallinn in 1924 and the assumption of power of right-wing political parties in all the Baltic republics. In September 1922, the Baltic states were admitted to the League of Nations.

For many Balts, contacts with Europe were thought to be best mediated through intensified cooperation with the Nordic countries. In scholarly and intellectual discourse, the concept 'Baltoscandia' was introduced, originally to denote an area kept together by similar geographical and geological conditions, but gradually also to demarcate a politico-cultural entity (Lehti 1998: 23–6). Large-scale political projects to establish a Baltic League, including the Baltic and Nordic states and Poland, were debated from the end of the First World War onward. For Jaan Tönisson, a prominent liberal politician and Estonian Premier four times in the inter-war years, the main motive for forming a Baltic-Nordic 'union of thirty million people' would be to prevent the Balts from being subjugated by the greater powers in the Baltic Sea area (Jaanson 1995: 79–80). The 'league of nations' concept was generally supposed to provide a framework for the new Europe after the First World War. For the small Baltic nations, squeezed between the two Baltic Sea great powers, the USSR and Germany, and lately and hesitantly recognized by the Western powers, it was obvious that a European mission could best be fulfilled within the framework of a league of small nations round the Baltic Sea.

If the purpose of the first Baltic liberation process was to turn to European institutions and values, and the result a mere response to European development, the second liberation was apprehended as a return to Europe, after fifty years of forced absence, and was carried out by an active cultural and political struggle. However, unlike the first time, Europeanization was in itself part of the reform idea that made Baltic national mobilization and liberalization possible. As noted by Iver B. Neumann in Chapter 8 of this volume, one of Gorbachev's pet reform projects was the 'common European house', in which even the Soviet citizens were supposed to move in. The project, obviously closely related to the main *perestroika* reform, was primarily initiated to render economic management more effective. In this process, the Balts in the 'Soviet West' were considered a key group as a skilled and disciplined labour force with an efficiency markedly above the Soviet average.

Andranik Migranian, a prominent intellectual who was close to Gorbachev in the early *perestroika* period, pointed out the Baltic republics as the reform engine which 'helped by Western technology and financial support, a relatively well-developed labour culture and the occurrence of necessary resources will relieve the other territories of immobility and stagnation' (Migranian 1989: 173). According to Gorbachev's main reform architect, Aleksandr Yakovlev, the reason was their association with a civilization other than the predominant Russian Orthodox one, which obviously was considered incompatible with the desirable reform spirit. Echoing Max Weber's idea of a Protestant ethic which fosters reason, diligence and industry and other necessary qualities of reformist development, Yakovlev pointed out the Estonians and Latvians, influenced by the European Reformation, as an example for *perestroika*. In his *Kommunist* article of 1990, he also mentioned Western historical phenomena such as the Enlightenment, Roosevelt's New Deal and social democracy as necessary models for a successful Soviet economic reform. In Russian and Soviet history, according to Yakovlev, no precedents for *perestroika* were to be found, only dogmatism, passive waiting and 'worship of holy texts, in the service of an authoritarian regime' (Yakovlev 1990: 10).

Turning to the Baltic side, the 'return' concept, together with frequently used similar 're-' concepts such as 'recovery', 'rebirth', 'restoration', 'restitution', 'reawakening' and 'release', indicate that the second Baltic national awakening was meant to be linked not to a Soviet context, not even a liberal reformist one, but to the inter-war Baltic states and, indirectly, to Europe. The memory of national statehood, and the fact that the Balts could and did draw upon pre-Soviet culture and symbols of democracy and market economy, gave them a unique position among the peoples of the USSR. This goes a long way to explain the preparedness and radical stance of the Baltic popular fronts on national self-determination. Moreover, historical structures and cultural prerequisites are probably important to explain also the reformist, non-violent, 'Scandinavian' liberation process in the Baltic states, so essentially different from the bloody and uncompromising internal wars in Transcaucasia, or Ukrainian and Belorussian division and irresoluteness.

## Europe as an Alternative

In fact, an important part of the Baltic liberation struggle was devoted to reinterpreting these historical and cultural structures. The accomplishments of the inter-war Baltic states in introducing 'European' cultural values were emphasized by Baltic intellectuals and politicians. The myth of the Balts' voluntary dissociation from Europe and incorporation into the Soviet Union that had been hegemonic in Soviet historiography since the 1940s was effectively crushed (Kakhk and Siilivask 1987: 155–64, cf. Karlsson 1999). Instead, there was general agreement that the Soviet-ization of the Baltic republics was part of Nazi and Stalinist aggression and arbitrariness during the Second World War, and that the war in Europe was not entirely overcome until the Baltic states had regained their independence.

A concept which was of crucial importance for the liberation move-ments to indicate the desirable national and European status of the Baltic republics was 'normalcy', and 'normalization' for the ongoing process which was expected to lead to a 'normal' situation. The basis for the debate was the abnormalcy of communist rule after 1940, and the implicit assumption that the ongoing efforts to 'normalize' the Baltic territories by establishing national independence and gaining admission to Europe was legitimate, good – and normal. Marju Lauristin used an argument inspired by the French *Annales* school to dismiss Communist party rule and five-year plans as examples of superficial, changing and 'abnormal' Baltic *événements* and *conjonctures*, respectively, while sparing what was considered more profound and 'normal' Baltic cultural institutions and values for the extremely durable level of *longues durées* (Lauristin 1989: 72; cf. Stukuls 1997: 131–6).

*Alternativnost'*, counterfactuality, constituted another central, closely related theme in the *glasnost'* debate on Soviet history. By focusing on what positives might have occurred, if the negative aspects of the Soviet system had not prevailed, critics of the system could effectively demon-strate the drawbacks of Communist and imperial rule and where it went wrong, while simultaneously mentally transcending it. For these critics, historical alternatives were to be found not only within the system, but also in other societies and countries whose history could serve as positive, desirable objects of comparison. The sociologist Klara Hallik, a Popular Front activist and Estonian delegate at the First Congress of People's Deputies in 1989, underlined in this connection that national development is not only internal, but the result of 'the richness and diversity of our inter-national and inter-ethnic ties' (Glebov and Crowfoot 1989: 39). The favourite Baltic alternative to Russian and Soviet rule was European affiliation. The main question was: what could have happened if the favourable inter-war development toward national stability and social welfare had continued, instead of being interrupted by Soviet dictator-ship?

In answering the question, the Nordic intermediary dimension was once again highly useful. For Estonians, who had access to several Finnish television channels and had had ferry connections with Helsinki since the 1960s, Finland played the crucial role as an *alter ego*, whose existence 'sustained the idea of a Republic of Estonia, keeping alive the Estonians' vision of what the country might have been had they stood up to the Russians' (Ruutsoo 1995b: 177). Based on statistical information, it was often stated that Finns, Estonians and Latvians lived under comparable economic conditions in the last years of the inter-war era, only for this to be drastically changed to the advantage of the Finns in the postwar era. For Baltic Popular Front activists, who generally painted their inter-war years in bright colours, it was obvious that the conditions of the post-war republics would have been much better, comparable to Nordic development, if history had been more favourably disposed to the Baltic area. At the First Congress of People's Deputies, the Latvian writer Janis Peters, chairman of the Writers' Union of the Latvian republic, answered a comment which hinted at the proposition that the Russians had a more exposed position within the Soviet state than the Balts, in the following characteristic way:

> The proposition that the Russians are worse off is no consolation for the Latvians, Lithuanians and Estonians, or a reason for waiting for a deteriorating situation also in the Baltic area. Why compare us with less developed regions? Compare us instead with Finland, Sweden, Norway and Denmark. (Peters 1989: 6)

For Algirdas Brazauskas, Lithuanian president from 1993, the latter connection ensured that the Lithuanian future was constructed on 'the historically proven model of Western democracy, economy, and culture' (Vardys and Sedaitis 1997: 220). On Independence day in February 1993, Lennart Meri, President of Estonia, similarly asserted that Estonia had reached its rightful and final destination west of the only relevant border in Europe: 'Our border is the border of European values' (Meri 1993: 9; cf. Meri 1999). And indeed, compared with the other post-Soviet republics, transition to Western political, economic and juridical institutions has been rapid and effective after liberation in 1991. The Baltic states in general, and Estonia in particular, have skilfully adjusted to meet several political and economic European standards, and although there might have been at least short-term advantages in upholding traditional trade relations with other post-Soviet states within a Russian-dominated CIS, trade has been directed westward. Civil society has been restored; in

Estonia, thousands of grass-roots and local movements, most of them with cultural and educational tasks, have been created (Aarelaid-Tart and Tart 1995: 157–8). In September 1991, a few weeks after independence, the Baltic states were admitted to the United Nations and the CSCE, a few years later to the Council of Europe. They have all enthusiastically expressed their interests in deepening integration by becoming members of the EU and NATO.

## Nation versus Democracy, or Nation and Democracy?

As has been noted earlier in this chapter, a frequent point of departure for Baltic observers of transition in their own countries is that national processes of change and processes of 'Europeanization' have been and are working well together, mutually reinforcing each other. There is, however, also some empirical evidence to prove that the dual objectives of national consolidation and European integration have been a great deal harder to bring together in both instances of independent Baltic statehood, when the immediate liberalization from empire has been completed. When discussing Baltic 'normalcy' it has been argued convincingly that, while in the immediate period of liberation and transformation from communism to post-communism the 'normal' was 'a space where diverse elements could unite against a common adversary, specifying a goal without defining it', Baltic independence has opened a period when the normalcy concept has become 'a site of contestation where allies in opposition struggled to define what normalcy meant and how it could be realized' (Stukuls 1997: 133).

The two processes of nationalization and Europeanization have sometimes rather appeared as communicating vessels: more of one, less of the other. This perspective must be put together with two historical conclusions that have been somewhat anathema in Baltic discourse during the liberation from the Soviet Union. The first is that the inter-war period of Baltic independence was not wholly positive, but also in some important respects problematic and conflict-ridden. The second conclusion is that the Soviet period and its influence on the post-Soviet societies cannot be totally disregarded when judging current Baltic developments.

As mentioned above, the tension between the 'European' and the 'national' can be traced back to the period of national awakening in the Baltic territory from the mid-nineteenth century. The 'European' trait was the German culture and language, representing progress in socio-economic and educational matters but also nationalist ideas of a Romantic coloration for a developing liberal Baltic middle class and intelligentsia.

On the other hand, nationalist ideas, as expressed for example in the leading Latvian nationalistic periodical *Peterburgas avizes*, became more and more opposed to German cultural and political domination in the eastern Baltic area. In the Latvian national epic from 1888, *The Bearslayer*, the forces of darkness were represented by colonizing German knights who threatened to destroy ancient Latvian independence. Aiming at strengthening national identities by means of an ideological use of history, the same social strata chose to glorify a pre-German, pre-Christian Baltic period by turning it into a golden 'national' age of Baltic 'normalcy' (Plakans 1974: 469–73, Plakans 1995: 89–100). In Lithuanian nationalist discourse, the relation to Poles and Polish culture was similarly contradictory.

The political systems of the Baltic inter-war republics oscillated between what has been called democratic idealism (Raun 1987: 112–13), that is, parliamentary democracies with strong egalitarian colouring, and authoritarian governments of a corporative, nationalist and presidential kind. After a large number of short-lived, weak governments, a swift popular rejection of liberal democracy occurred in Lithuania as early as 1926, while in Latvia and Estonia democracy was overthrown in the 1930s in situations of impending civil war. In all the Baltic states, the authoritarian rulers and their military advisors were identical with the political and military actors who had played leading roles in the liberation struggles. But while minority rights were sanctified in the early independence period, slogans such as 'Latvia for the Latvians' indicate a different policy in the 1930s, which the authoritative historian Georg von Rauch in the case of Latvia has described as 'a determined attempt . . . to "Latvianize" the economic, educational and cultural life of the country' (von Rauch 1995: 156).

The Lithuanian inter-war crisis was furthermore aggravated by international military conflicts. After a military operation in 1920 in which the Polish army seized Vilnius, diplomatic ties with Poland were severed until 1938. Partly to compensate for the loss of Vilnius, partly to have access to a Baltic Sea port, a few years later Lithuania seized the German town Memel, or Lithuanian Klaipeda. Memel had been controlled since 1919 by the League of Nations.

The political crisis had an obvious economic counterpart. The inter-war international economic system was characterized by protectionism and a concentration of trade in a few highly developed states. The Baltic states with their relatively undifferentiated agricultural economies had been allowed admission to this economy after the First World War, when they were mainly assigned the roles of suppliers of raw materials and agricultural goods. These were products which most European countries seldom demanded and in many cases exported themselves. In this context, the inter-war change in Baltic trade relations from Russia to the West was not economically advantageous, since, in stark contrast, export to Russia had mostly involved more valuable industrial goods. When economic crisis followed by a deep depression hit worldwide in 1929, the Baltic states suffered heavily. This obviously caused European values, including both liberal market economy and political democracy, to lose their status among many Baltic politicians and ordinary citizens. Corporative economic performance improved in the 1930s, especially in Estonia, but the undemocratic accession to power of right-wing, nationalist and anti-communist groups, and the rejection of European or Western political and economic institutions and values, incurred the antipathy of their Baltic Sea neighbours, especially the Social Democratic governments in Denmark and Sweden. This finally ended all discussions on any pan-Baltic foreign-policy cooperation.

What is more, a stereotype that the Balts generally have authoritarian or fascist leanings grew and proved hard to eradicate. This probably was conducive to providing the Balts with limited European support during the Sovietization process. Sweden recognized de facto the Soviet appropriation of the Baltic republics as early as 1940. A few years later, Swedish Social Democratic Foreign Minister Östen Undén alluded to the same stereotype when he claimed that the Baltic incorporation into the Soviet Union should be accepted, since the 'political maturity' of the Balts was 'not particularly marked' (Carlgren 1993: 94). The official Swedish attitude did not change until late 1989, when Social Democratic Foreign Minister Sten Andersson, pressured by the dramatic Soviet disintegration process and an internal Swedish public debate which became increasingly sympathetic to the Baltic cause, suddenly admitted that the Baltic states had been occupied by and later unrighteously incorporated into the Soviet state.

There is some reason to believe that Baltic political and economic transition since 1991 has finally set aside this stereotype and a corresponding critical Baltic attitude toward this Western stereotyping of three entire nations on the basis of historical patterns, with its possibly negative implications for the integration of the Baltic states into European networks. The current regionalization of the Baltic Sea area, which has dramatically expanded the opportunities for physical contacts, may reinforce this positive development.

An important question is, however, whether the old factual problem is finally solved, or whether it has survived in a partly new, more pronounced ethno-national garment and, therefore, can still disturb the newly re-established relations between the Baltic states and Europe in the post-Soviet era. One could, as did the French sovietologist, Hélène Carrère d'Encausse, ask whether the Baltic states have entered a phase of development of 'nation versus democracy', or 'nation and democracy' (Carrère d'Encausse 1993: 231). The problem subsequently concerns the relationship between, on the one hand, particularist vertically-historically motivated national values and, on the other hand, horizontal universalist civic virtues, when handling a Soviet heritage of institutionalized multinationality (a concept borrowed from Brubaker 1996: 23–40) and building the new Baltic nation states. Both can be considered necessary ingredients of post-Soviet Baltic state-building and society-making, but the balance between them is not definite. As argued by Graham Smith, the Baltic aspect of this general post-Soviet and post-communist problem must be understood in connection with a post-colonial discourse, and with the question of whether Russians and Russian-speaking minority groups as the 'colonial Other' should enjoy the same rights of citizenship as the titular nations, or whether history – that is, both the imperial heritage and the fact that the absolute majority of Russians and Russian-speakers were not citizens in the interwar Baltic republics – disqualifies them from an equal status with the residents of the national homelands (Smith 1998: 93–5). Expressed the other way around, the basic question is whether the titular nation, with its special relation to a Baltic home territory, can claim special historical rights and automatic access to citizenship, while Russians have to earn it.

Throughout the post-Soviet period, a narrow, historically based advance toward ethnocracy, defined as a political system which 'accords an institutional superior status to the core nation beyond its numerical proportion within the state territory' (Smith 1996: 164), has competed with the development toward 'European' ethnic accommodation, multiculturalism and democracy. The former style of politics has been most successful in Latvia and, to a lesser extent, in Estonia, where the numerous Russian minority, perceived as a manifest threat to national development, has encountered difficulties in obtaining citizenship and political rights. In the 1989 Soviet census, the ethnic Russians constituted 30.3 per cent of the entire Estonian population. The corresponding number for Latvia was 34 per cent. As part of de-Sovietization, centre-right and right-wing political parties in Estonia and Latvia have successfully worked for the establishment of citizenship laws based firmly on descent, qualifications of residency and language skills, and for loyalty oaths as requirements for citizenship for Russians. Non-citizens who have served in foreign armed forces, such as the Soviet army, cannot apply for citizenship. When the Latvian state propounds its idea of the 'one nation-state community' (Smith 1998: 103), in which a single Latvian culture will be hegemonic, there is an evident and problematic continuity from the inter-war slogan 'Latvia for the Latvians' in a country with a substantial Russian minority. The Estonian and Latvian politics of exclusion have alarmed various Russian nationalist groups in Moscow, but also European organizations. Latvia was criticized by both the OSCE and the Council of Europe in 1993 for adopting naturalization quotas that were too restrictive, and it was understood that such politics could jeopardize Latvia's application to be a member of the Council. Simultaneously, the Estonian parliament's restricted 'aliens' law received widespread European criticism. In both cases, presidential interventions resulted in more moderate legislation, which enabled Estonia and Latvia to be member states of the Council of Europe in 1995.

Together with the fact that no physical confrontations between Balts and Baltic Russians have taken place so far, this increased Baltic pragmatic political will to achieve ethnic conciliation and compromise probably creates better opportunities for a coincidence of perception and position in Baltic relations with Europe. If the political situation in Russia does not turn into aggressive, expansionist nationalism, the Baltic states will, to all appearances, unequivocally stand out as 'European' in the relatively near future, even if henceforth there probably will be differences in 'Europeanness' between the three states concerning the institutional integration timetables and, more generally, in the cultural meanings of 'Europe'. No doubt, it will be both factually and psychologically beneficial for the Balts. As has often been written between the lines in this chapter, 'Europe' does not merely represent traditional civic values such as democracy, market economy and state of law for them. 'European' also communicates more abstract values that transcend traditional borders between civic nationalism and ethnic nationalism, values that clearly distance the Baltic states from Eastern chaos, disruption and uncertainty. Among them are continuity, harmony, persistence, prosperity, stability and unity.

## References

Aarelaid-Tart, A. and Tart, I. (1995), 'Culture and the Development of Civil Society', *Nationalities Papers*, 23(1): 153–65.

# Klas-Göran Karlsson

Alenius, K. (1998), 'The Cultural Relations between the Baltic Countries and Finland 1917–1997', in K. Hovi (ed.), *Relations between the Nordic Countries and the Baltic Nations in the XX Century*, Turku: University of Turku.

Brubaker, R. (1996), *Nationalism Reframed: Nationhood and the National Question in the New Europe*, Cambridge: Cambridge University Press.

Carlgren, W. (1993), *Sverige och Baltikum: Från mellankrigstid till efterkrigsår. En översikt*, Stockholm: Publica.

Carrère d'Encausse, H. (1993), *The End of the Soviet Empire: The Triumph of the Nations*, New York: BasicBooks.

Clemens, Jr., W. (1994) 'Baltic Identities in the 1990s: Renewed Fitness', in R. Szporluk (ed.), *National Identity and Ethnicity in Russia and the New States of Eurasia*, Armonk: M.E. Sharpe.

Glebov, O. and Crowfoot, J. (1989), *The Soviet Empire: Its Nations Speak Out*, Chur: Harwood Academic Publishers.

Hallik, K. (1989), 'Slychat' drug druga', *Kommunist*, 6: 62–80.

Hiden, J. and Salmon, P. (1991), *The Baltic Nations and Europe. Estonia, Latvia & Lithuania in the Twentieth Century*, London and New York: Longman.

Hosking, G. (1997), *Russia: People and Empire 1552–1917*, Cambridge, Mass. Harvard University Press.

Huntington, S.P. (1996), *The Clash of Civilizations and the Remaking of World Order*, New York: Simon & Schuster.

Jaanson, K. (1995), 'Estonia and Baltic Sea Cooperation: From Idea to Reality', *Nationalities Papers*, 23(1): 79–84.

Kakhk, Ju. and Siilivask, K. (1987), *Istoriia Estonskoi SSR: Populiarnyi ocherk*, Tallinn: Periodika.

Karling, S. (1988), 'Kulturförbindelser mellan Estland och Sverige', in R. Raag and H. Runblom (eds), *Estländare i Sverige. Historia, språk, kultur*, Uppsala: Uppsala University.

Karlsson, K.-G. (1999), *Historia som vapen: Historiebruk och Sovjet-unionens upplösning 1985–1995*, Stockholm: Natur och Kultur.

Lagerspetz, M. (1996), *Constructing Post-Communism: A Study in the Estonian Social Problems Discourse*, Turku: Turun Yliopisto.

Lauristin, M. (1997), 'Contexts of Transition', in M. Lauristin, P. Vihalemm (eds), *Return to the Western World: Cultural and Political Perspectives on the Estonian Post-Communist Transition*, Tartu: Tartu University Press.

—— (1989), 'Slychat' drug druga', *Kommunist* 6: 62–80.

Lehti, M. (1998), 'Baltoscandia as a National Construction', in K. Hovi (ed.), *Relations between the Nordic Countries and the Baltic Nations in the XX Century*, Turku: University of Turku.

—— (2000), *A Baltic League as a Construct of the New Europe: Envisioning a Baltic Region and Small State Sovereignty in the Aftermath of the First World War*, Frankfurt am Main: Peter Lang.

Lieven, A. (1994), *The Baltic Revolution: Estonia, Latvia, Lithuania and the Path to Independence*, New Haven and London: Yale University Press.

Megill, A. (1998), 'History, Memory, Identity', *History of the Human Sciences*, 11(3), 30–52.

Meri, L. (1993), *Baltic Independent*, March 5–11.

—— (1999), 'Estonia: Heading West and Relating with the East', http://ceip.org/programs/ruseuras/meri.htm

Migranian, A. (1989), 'Dolgii put' k evropeiskomu domu', *Novyi mir*, 7: 166–84.

Misiunas, R. (1994), 'National Identity and Foreign Policy in the Baltic States', in S.F. Starr (ed.), *The Legacy of History in Russia and the New States of Eurasia*, Armonk and London: M.E. Sharpe.

—— and Taagepera, R. (1993), *The Baltic States: Years of Dependence 1940–1990*, Berkeley: University of California Press.

Neumann, I.B. (1999), *Uses of the Other: 'The East' in European Identity Formation*, Minneapolis: University of Minnesota Press.

Peters, J. (1989), Argument without headline at the First Congress of People's Deputies, *Literaturnaia gazeta*, 7 June.

Plakans, A. (1974), 'Peasants, Intellectuals, and Nationalism in the Russian Baltic Provinces, 1820–1890', *Journal of Modern History*, 46(4): 445–73.

—— (1995), *The Latvians: A Short History*, Stanford: Hoover Institution Press.

Prazauskas, A. (1994), 'The Influence of Ethnicity on the Foreign Policy of the Western Littoral States', in R. Szporluk (ed.), *National Identity and Ethnicity in Russia and the New States of Eurasia*, Armonk and London: M.E. Sharpe.

Raag, R. (1999), *Från allmogemål till nationalspråk: Språkvård och språkpolitik i Estland från 1857 till 1999*, Uppsala: Uppsala University Library.

Raun, T. (1987), *Estonia and the Estonians*, Stanford: Hoover Institution Press.

Ruutsoo, R. (1995a), 'Introduction: Estonia on the border of two civilizations', *Nationalities Papers*, (23)1: 13–16.

—— (1995b), 'The Perception of Historical Identity and the Restoration of Estonian National Independence', *Nationalities Papers*, 23(1): 167–79.

Senn, A.E. (1990), *Lithuania Awakening*, Berkeley: University of California Press.

Smith, G. (1996), 'Latvia and the Latvians', in G. Smith (ed.), *The Nationalities Question in the Post- Soviet States*, London and New York: Longman.

—— (1998), 'Nation re-building and political discourses of identity politics in the Baltic states', in G. Smith, V. Law, A. Wilson, A. Bohr and E. Allworth, *Nation-Building in the Post-Soviet Borderlands: The Politics of Nation Identities*, Cambridge: Cambridge University Press.

Stukuls, D. (1997), 'Imagining the Nation: Campaign Posters of the First Postcommunist Elections in Latvia', *East European Politics and Societies*, 1: 131–54.

Taagepera, R. (1993), *Estonia: Return to Independence*, Boulder: Westview Press.

Thaden, E. (1985), 'Baltic National Movements During the Nineteenth Century', *Journal of Baltic Studies*, 16(4):411–21.

Tocqueville, A. de (1856), *L'Ancien Régime et la Révolution*, Paris: Michel Lévy Frères.

Vardys V.S. and Sedaitis, J.B. (1997), *Lithuania – The Rebel Nation*, Boulder: Westview Press.

von Rauch, G. (1995), *The Baltic States: The Years of Independence 1917–1940*, New York: St Martin's Press.

Yakovlev, A. (1990), 'Sotsializm: ot mechty k realnosti', *Kommunist*, 4: 8–21.

# From the USSR to Gorbachev to Putin: Perestroika as a Failed Excursion from 'the West' to 'Europe' in Russian Discourse

*Iver B. Neumann*

In the mid-1980s, the attempts at reforming (or rebuilding, *perestroika*) the Soviet model had exposed the vacuum at the centre of the state. Further, discourse on how what was increasingly referred to as 'Russia' should relate to contemporary Western models – *in casu* pluralism and capitalism – was coming to the fore of general politics. As part and parcel of this process, Mikhail Gorbachev raised the issue of the Soviet Union's relations with Europe, and thereby also sanctioned the legitimacy of debate, a legitimacy that had been at best tenuous in the preceding sixty-odd years of Soviet discourse. In the English-language version of his book *Perestroika*, Gorbachev made the following representations of the terms 'the West' and 'Europe':

> Some in the West are trying to 'exclude' the Soviet Union from Europe. Now and then, as if inadvertently, they equate 'Europe' with 'Western Europe'. Such ploys, however, cannot change the geographic and historical realities. Russia's trade, cultural and political links with other European nations and states have deep roots in history. We are Europeans. Old Russia was united with Europe by Christianity . . . The history of Russia is an organic part of the great European history (Gorbachev 1988: 190).

A long decade later, the Russian Prime Minister, Vladimir V. Putin, greeted the country in a long speech celebrating the incoming Millennium by drawing up the following assessment:

> The main thing is that Soviet power did not let the country develop a flourishing society which could be developing dynamically, with free people.

First and foremost, the ideological approach to the economy made our country lag increasingly behind (*otstavanie*) the developed states. It is bitter to admit that for almost seven decades we travelled down a blind ally, which took us away from the main track of civilization . . . The experience of the 1990s vividly shows that the genuine and efficient revival of our Fatherland cannot be brought about on Russian soil simply by dint of abstract models and schemata extracted from foreign textbooks. The mechanical copying of the experiences of other states will not bring progress. Every country, Russia included, has a duty to search for its own path of renewal. We still have not made much headway . . . Society has been in a state of schism (*raskol*) . . . Russia will not soon, if ever, be a replica of, say, the US or Great Britain, where liberal values have deep-seated traditions. For us, the state, with its institutions and structures, always played an exclusively important role in the life of the country and its people. For the Russian (*rossiyanin*), a strong state is not an anomaly, not something with which he has to struggle, but, on the contrary, a source of and a guarantee for order, as well as the initiator and main moving force of any change. Contemporary Russian society does not mistake a strong and effective state for a totalitarian one. (http://www.government. gov.rus/government/minister/article-vvp1.html)

In this speech, 'Europe' was gone, but what remained was 'the West' (*zapad*), and the great historical powers of the West (the United States, Britain). This chapter will be devoted to tracing this shift, and to interpret it in the light of Russian conceptual history. In this history, the central concept is precisely Запад – 'the West'. I bring a discursive method to the task, and the first part of the chapter is devoted to demonstrating where this method comes from and how it works. The second part argues that the representations of Russia, and its relationship with Europe which surfaces in this quote, are the result of a compromise which has settled, at least temporarily, the struggles which broke out when Gorbachev became General Secretary of the Union of Soviet Socialist Republics (USSR). The third part demonstrates how the struggling parties have emerged out of path-dependent Russian traditions. The concluding part presents a model of Russian discourse on Europe.

## Presuppositions: The Copenhagen School on Discourse

The two basic suppositions of discourse analysis in the Copenhagen School of International Relations are that each collective is constituted in terms of visions of itself, and that each collective will attempt to make its visions of the outside world and of themselves come together. A main figure of the School, Ole Waever, makes specific reference to Henry Kissinger's 1957 analysis of how Metternich and other statesmen restructured international order after the Napoleonic Wars, and explicitly builds on the Kissingerian formulation of these two presuppositions:

> [W]hile powers may appear to outsiders as factors in a security settlement, they appear domestically as expressions of a historical existence. No power will submit to a settlement, however well-balanced and however 'secure', which seems totally to deny its vision of itself [Why did Metternich try to preserve Austria's vision of itself by changing the structure of Europe rather than its vision of itself?] Why not attempt to adapt the Austrian domestic structure to the national *élan* sweeping across Europe? But a statesman must work with the material at hand and the domestic structure of Austria was rigid, much more rigid, paradoxically, than the international one. (Kissinger 1957: 146, 28)

One notes that the Copenhagen School identifies the border between the domestic and the international as the locus of 'the statesman' and as the most promising locus in which to study the evolution of foreign policy. Rationalistic theorists often assume that because a particular foreign policy proposal from say a Russian nationalist is 'irrational' by the light of American, British or international diplomatic discourse, it will *for this reason alone* not be able to make it to the status of official Russian foreign policy. In refutation of this, discourse analysis may show how such a proposal may be rational by the lights of Russian discourse, and therefore may make it to official Russian foreign policy.

Granted that human collectives try to perpetuate visions of themselves, and granted that this undertaking can be conceptualized in terms of discourse, the question arises of how to conceptualize discourses of foreign policy. Waever (2001) suggests that, for purposes of studying the changing French and German Europe-oriented foreign policies, it is vital to conceptualize discourse as *layered*. The reason is obvious: since at stake are processes which involve different degrees of change, only a layered conceptualization of discourse will be able to catch change in its various discursive depths. One point which is not made explicit, but which should be, is that we are talking here of a generative model, where the deeper layer generates the more shallow one. A three-layered conceptualization is proposed. The basic layer consists of constellations of the ideas of state and nation. In both the German and the French cases, Waever (2001) postulates that one basic constellation has generated discourse on Europe over the last two hundred years. In keeping with the discreteness of discourses as stressed by Winch and others, however, it is stressed that there can be no set structuralist formula for how this should be done. The analysis of each human collective must be grounded in the specific historical conceptualizations by the terms of which that collective negotiates its identities and foreign policies.

So, the suggestion is that 'the domestic' or inside must be treated as a layered structure, on a par with 'the international' or outside. In each case, a three-layered structure is proposed. The three layers are made up by discursive structures concerning, (1) the constellation of state and nation which constitutes the collective in question; (2) the structural relations between these constellations and the collective's conceptualizations of Europe; and (3) the collective's specific European policies. That, in its barest outlines, is one version of the ongoing attempt of the Copenhagen School to reconceptualize foreign policy as discourse. I now turn to the actually modelling of the case at hand in terms of this theory.

## Russia

With Gorbachev coming to power in 1985, the slogan 'common European home', which had its roots in diplomatic practice of the early 1980s, became central to Russian political discourse. The new representations of Russian identity involved a political struggle over how to differentiate Russia from Europe (as well as from Asia, cf. Hauner 1990). The Russian discourse on Europe pitted Westernizers against nationalists.

The Westernizers emerged from both the dissident movement and Gorbachev's entourage of reform communists. The framework within which they represented Europe was a cultural one, stressing liberal ideas about the integrity of the individual and the limited rights of the state vis-à-vis the citizen as the common political goals of all mankind. Russia was not held to be morally superior to Europe, but as its potential equal and in certain respects contemporary inferior.

To quote but one example of many, Boris Pankin, who served as Foreign Minister of the Soviet Union from the August coup of 1991 until the disintegration of the Union, wrote in his memoirs that the country's foreign policy at this time reflected an 'obsession . . . with the idea of becoming a civilized state' (Pankin 1996: 104). This was the main representation in relation to which all others had to act.

The idea of a 'Eurasian' destiny for the Soviet Union cropped up in the writings of foreign affairs specialists. In groping for a strategic goal for Soviet foreign policy to take the place of the defunct ideological struggle with the West, Vladimir Lukin came up with the formation of a European community from the Atlantic sea to the Ural mountains in the west and the joining of the Pacific integration process in the east: 'If that succeeds, we would become the bridge between the two "Europes". It may sound Utopian today, but this variant seems highly realistic to me, perhaps the only way our country may enter the upcoming Millennium in a worthy manner' (Bovin and Lukin 1989: 67).

Westernizers proposed relationships with Europe based on two different variants of partnership. Whereas some advocated a 'return to civilization' – that is, a relationship with Europe where Russia was seen as an apprentice with no clear additional and specific identity – others saw this as a poor way of rallying mass Russian support behind a programme based on individual rights, market economy and political pluralism. Instead, they evolved the slogan of 'Eurasia' as a proposed group identity for a Russian-based state which should secure the electorate's support for closer relations with Europe. The feeling of being left in the lurch is tangible between Westernizers as well. For example, in February 1996 Russian Deputy Defence Minister Andrey Kokoshin attended an annual conference on security sponsored by the German Ministry of Defence and argued that 'we have pulled back to the East, while NATO is turning in this direction and is pushing us further and further eastward' (quoted in Lynch 1997: 82).

If Westernizers dominated Russian discourse on Europe in the late 1980s and into the 1990s, a nationalist opposition was also clearly present. Already in December of 1987, a group which called itself *Pamyat'* put out an appeal. El'giz Pozdnyakov complained that 'The disease of "Europeanism", of "Westernism", came to Russia' with Peter the Great (Pozdnyakov 1991: 46). Since then, he charged, a number of Russians have seen Russia through the eyes of an outsider, and not of an insider. These 'Westernizers' have either held that Russia's destiny lay with European civilization, or they have not seen a destiny for it at all. In either case, they have been wrong. Russia's particular destiny is to maintain a strong state so that it can act as the holder of the balance between East and West, a task 'vitally important both for Russia and the entire planet' (Pozdnyakov 1991: 46). And Pozdnyakov goes on to write that

Russia cannot return to Europe because it never belonged to it. Russia cannot join it because it is part of another type of civilization, another cultural and religious type . . . Any attempt to make us common with Western civilization and even to force us to join it undertaken in the past resulted in superficial borrowings, deceptive reforms, useless luxury and moral lapses . . . in nature there does not exist such a thing as a 'Common Civilization'. The term in fact denotes the pretention of Western European civilization to the exclusive rights to universal significance. (Pozdnyakov 1991: 49, 54)

Other nationalists presented a rhetoric which was grounded not in the need for a strong state but in the need for spiritual regeneration. For example, in 1990 Aleksandr Solzhenitsyn published a long Philippic against modernity: Russia should not spend its force being a superpower, but on attaining spiritual clarity; free elections and a multiparty system were harmful onslaughts against the organic Russian nation; Russia should concentrate on restructuring its own house rather than any common European one (Solzhenitsyn 1990).

The years 1992 and 1993 were pivotal for Russian discourse on Europe. Given that so many aspects of the political were being re-presented so thoroughly, the stakes were very high, and given the radical incompatibility of the two representations of the European Other, the question was how the relationship between these representations would play itself out. The two extreme (and for that reason rather unlikely) possibilities seemed to be that there would arise a monological situation whereby one representation swallowed the other, or there would be a civil war. What ensued instead was a twofold dialogical development. First, the regrouping of communism as a political force took the shape of infusing the nationalist representation with a number of key ideas and institutional resources out of the former communist regime. The Russian Communist Party took the idea of a 'nationally comprehended, spiritually grounded statehood' as its starting point (Zyuganov 1994: 42). This re-presentation of Russia was set out in books by the party chairman Gennadiy Zyuganov whose very titles underlined this nationalist starting point. Witness, *Great Power; Russia – My Motherland: The Ideology of State Patriotism* (Zyuganov 1996).

The view that new partitions are developing between East and West in Europe is a common denominator of Russian discourse. Typically, in trying to come up with an answer to NATO expansion, Russian nationalists and communists avail themselves of elements which historically have been part of Russian nationalist *and* communist discourse (Williams and Neumann 2000). Indeed, the entire operation of reorganizing the Russian Communist Party on a nationalist-communist platform may be viewed in this light, as when Zyuganov argues that 'The empire is the form which both historically and geopolitically has been closest to the development of Russia' (Zyuganov 1996: 223), and that 'Soviet culture' represented an important manifestation of this development. Russia is specifically cast as a bulwark against Western civilization, whose essence is 'extreme individualism, warlike atheism, religious indifference, mass mentality and mass culture, contempt of traditions and subscription to the principle of quantity before quality' (Zyuganov 1996: 149). Building on this general approach, it may be argued that Russia is an independent civilization which is threatened by the cultural encroachment of NATO and should answer by pursuing a policy of isolationist consolidation. Such an answer was offered by the Vice-chairman of the Duma Committee on Foreign Affairs, Aleksey Podberezkin, when he argued that

> NATO's intense insistence on . . . gobbling up new strategic territory and showing its muscle outside the borders of an unstable state with an economy which is in tatters will, I think, not have a deterring effect on the people of that state . . . The idea of once again being 'a besieged fortress' will knit the Russian people closer together than the many agreements and insurances by the West about peace and freedom. (Podberezkin 1996: 64)

Further, 1992 and 1993 saw the end of the stand-off between the Westernizing and the nationalist representations as the political strength of this nationalist re-presentation began to work on the Westernizing representation, shearing it of what came to be known as its 'romantic' tendency to hold up 'the West' as an entity to be unequivocally copied. This was the beginning of the compromise which, as I am going to argue in the conclusion to this chapter, the Putin regime embodies. Thus, although Westernizers sat on a number of key material and institutional resources, the Westernizing representation of Russia did not crowd out the nationalist one. Of course, the European discourse on Russia is one factor which may help us understand why this did not come to be: despite Gorbachev's discursive work, Russia was not recognized as a European country in a number of key social, political and economic contexts. One reason why Russian Westernizers were not able to carry the day in Russian discourse relates to how their efforts to have Russia accepted as a 'normal' European country in overall European discourse came to nought. Aleksey Pushkov (*Nezavisimaya gazeta,* 29 January 1998) is one of many to have signed texts which argued along the lines that 'Our democrats and liberals argued that weakening the all-powerful, non-effective, rotten state was a blessing and a part of the democratic process of this country . . . However, as a result we now have a demoralized, disorganized and weak apparatus which ignores the national interests'. A change of this magnitude, however, may hardly be understood if one does not see it against a historical background which provided a benchmark against which developments were represented in the first place. In order to understand that, it is necessary to grasp what happened in Russian discourse itself, how it was that the nationalist representation could maintain such a strong position in lieu of a relative dearth of institutional and material capital. The reason, I will argue, is that the nationalist representation came complete with references back to an unbroken and proud national history, which had been propelled by – among other things – nationalist sentiments allegedly of the same kind as those which constituted that nationalist representation which now, in turn, presented those historical references. It was the symbolic capital that the nationalist representation was able to draw on in its discursive work which first forced the Westernizing representation into a dialogue, and then transformed it to become more compatible with the nationalist representation. Put another way, there was a stiffness in Russian discourse which the Westernizing representation could not break down, and so it happened that it was transformed itself instead. Since the nationalist representation drew its strength from the narratives it told about itself and its role in Russian history, one must look to those narratives and that history, and not only to the wider European discourse, in order to understand the shift in Russian discourse.

## Two Representations of Europe, Two Traditions

It would be a mistake to see either the Russian debate about Europe which emerged in the 1980s and the 1990s or the shift from Gorbachev to Putin as a unique response to post-Soviet challenges. On the contrary, the conflict between Westernizers and nationalists can be traced in the *samizdat* writings of the 1960s and 1970s, as well as in writings of the tsarist period. This part will trace these two traditions. As any categorization, the one used here serves a purpose, namely to prop up the central claim of this chapter, which is that Russia under Putin is a polity which has arrived at a political compromise. If the purpose had been to illuminate, say, Russian defence policy or its policy on globalization, then other categorizations would have served better. Those who want a more fine-grained categorization of Russian European discourse are referred to Neumann (1996).

### Nationalists

The most striking thing about Solzhenitsyn's piece from 1990 mentioned above is, arguably, its almost verbatim repetition of the views set out in the *samizdat* articles collected in *From under the Rubble*. Of course, even if it had been the very same article, that – in and of itself would not have meant that it would have been 'the same' in other respects, since its discursive context would have been brand new. Nonetheless, there is a continuity here which should be highlighted, even at the risk of over-stressing how things stay the same as against how they change.

Solzhenitsyn's *samizdat* articles attacked Westernizers, and particularly Andrey Sakharov, for parroting false Western ideas about freedom:

> The West has supped more than its fill of every kind of freedom, including intellectual freedom. And has this saved it? We see it today crawling on hands and knees, its will paralysed, uneasy about the future, spiritually racked and dejected. Unlimited external freedom in itself is quite inadequate to save us. Intellectual freedom is a very desirable gift, but, like any sort of freedom, a gift of conditional, not intrinsic, worth, only a means by which we can attain another and higher goal (Solzhenitsyn 1975: 18).

Where Sakharov's suggestion for introducing the multiparty system was concerned, Solzhenitsyn wanted nothing to do with it: '[A] society in which political parties are active never rises in the moral scale . . . can we not, we wonder, rise above the two-party or multiparty parliamentary system? Are there no *extra-party* or strictly *non-party* paths of national development?', Solzhenitsyn asked, and lamented that the 'almost perfect' Westernizing unanimity in circles outspokenly critical of Soviet power was

> an example of our traditional passive imitation of the West: Russia can only recapitulate, it is too great a strain to seek other paths. As Sergei Bulgakov aptly remarked: 'Westernism is spiritual surrender to superior cultural strength' (Solzhenitsyn 1975: 20).

Solzhenitsyn, however, does insist that not just any nationalism is worthy of support. A harsh, cold current of opinion

> has become discernible of late. Stripped to essentials, but not distorted, it goes like this: the Russian people is the noblest in the world; its ancient and its modern history are alike unblemished; tsarism and Bolshevism are equally irreproachable; the nation neither erred nor sinned either before 1917 or after . . . God need not be written with a capital letter, but [*Gosudarstvo*, that is, the state] must be. Their general name for all this is 'the Russian idea'. (A more precise name for this trend would be 'National Bolshevism.)' (Solzhenitsyn 1975: 119–29)

As witnessed by Solzhenitsyn's attack on the 'national bolsheviks', today's statist nationalists also have their precedents in the 1960s. Yet this internal nationalist debate between spiritual and statist nationalists has a much longer history. Traces of it can be found in the semi-official Russian life of the 1920s, and it was a fixture of the political debate in tsarist times. In the early post-revolutionary years, spiritual nationalism was represented by Nikolay Berdyaev – whose thinking now enjoys a far from incidental revival in Russia – and other former contributors to the volume which had appeared in 1909 as *Vekhi* and instantly became a common point of reference for the debate (and which also has been republished recently). Statist nationalism was represented by among others the original Eurasianists, a coterie of Russian émigré intellectuals.

In a closely argued book published in 1920, *Europe and Humanity*, Prince Nikolay Sergeevich Trubetskoy delivered a blistering attack against the very idea that Russia and other non-European countries should look to Europe for political and economic models. Before the revolution, Trubetskoy wrote, it had been almost 'organically inadmissible' for most people, educated as they were in the European manner, to grasp the idea that Russia's involvement with Europe was a historical mistake (Trubetskoy 1920: III–IV). Europe does not equal civilization; this is merely a 'formula of chauvinistic cosmopolitanism' (Trubetskoy 1920: 2). A country which tries to copy it will come to a bad end. No matter *how* hard it tries, some of its specific traits will remain, and it will, 'from the European point of view, always look "backward" (*otstalyy*)' (Trubetskoy 1920: 64). The result is that 'only the government and the ruling political circles' will retain a national outlook, while the rest of the people will be demoralized and self-loathing (Trubetskoy 1920: 65).

This state of affairs will be aggravated by the sporadic events of the backward people mustering its forces and making a dash to catch up, trying to take in its stride developments which the Romano-Germans may have undergone over a prolonged period of time: 'The result of such "evolution" by fits and starts is indeed horrific. Every leap is inevitably followed by a period of seeming (from the European point of view) stagnation (*zastoy*), during which the results of the leap must be made to dovetail with the backward elements of the culture' (Trubetskoy 1920: 67). The inevitable result is a cycle of 'progress' and 'stagnation'. 'And so', Trubetskoy (1920: 69–70) concludes, 'the upshot of Europeanization is so heavy and horrible that it cannot be considered a good, but a bad thing'.

One notes throughout these exchanges that 'Europe' and 'the West' tend to be used interchangeably, and that little effort is put into pinpointing different Europes. There are other exchanges during the nineteenth century which largely hinge on which kinds of 'national spirits' animate the respective great powers; nonetheless, the major representation is of 'the West' as such. As can be seen, for example, in Trubetskoy's lumping together of German and French elements, the political emphasis is firmly on Europe understood as a civilizational entity with political powers.

The same goes for the previous generation of debating Russians. The differences of opinion and emphasis between the spiritual and the statist nationalists in the 1920s echoed the debate between Nikolay Danilevskiy and Vladimir Solov'ev in the 1880s. Danilevskiy presented his views in another recently republished volume, *Russia and Europe*, which he sums up in the following manner:

> Europe's interests cannot be ours, but not only that: in most cases they will be in direct opposition to one another . . . Dealings will have to be close, yet they must not be intimate, hearty, as if between kindred. Where political relations are concerned, the only rule must be an eye for an eye, and a tooth for a tooth – tit for tat . . . What stands in our way, however, we must fight in all ways possible, whatever the consequences for Europe itself, for humanity, for freedom, for civilization. (Danilevskiy 1888: 480–1)

Solov'ev retorted that Danilevskiy was mistaken in ascribing Europe's hostility to Russia in terms of the envy of a dying culture upon beholding its successors. Rather, Europe's hostility is to a large extent of Russia's own making, provoked by things such as Danilevskiy's book:

> Europe looks at us with hostility and fear because they understand that the Russian people is a dark and elementary power, whose spiritual and cultural preconditions are frightfully small, but whose aspirations know no boundaries. (Solov'ev n.d., probably 1905: 137)

Russia, Solov'ev continues, should grasp that its relations with Europe are fraternal. Instead of railing against Europe, it should confess its sins and put its own house in order. Bearing in mind history's intention, it should brace itself for the path toward spiritual perfection. Indeed, since the early Russian nationalists adopted German romantic nationalist thinking to their own uses, there has existed a tension between those who have focused on the divine strength of the people, and those who have focused on the strength of the state (von Schelting 1948; Walicki 1975; this difference may be even older, cf. Cherniavsky 1958). Thus, for the revamped Russian communists to splice together a representation of Russia with explicit references to both these traditions, and to put it to good discursive work despite the aggressively non-spiritual history of the communist movement itself, is indeed no mean feat.

## Westernism

Turning now to the precedents of today's Westernizing representation of Russia, one is immediately confronted by the question of how to categorize Stalinism. From Bukharin and Trotsky onward, anti-Stalinist communists have insisted that Stalin was certainly no Westernizer, but an Asian despot, a Ghengis Khan. Bukharin, for example, attacked Stalin's programme of super-industrialization as a policy 'in line with old Russia', and referred to it on a number of occasions as being 'Asiatic'. Stalin himself was privately referred to as a 'Genghis Khan' (see Cohen 1974: 291). This representation is present in contemporary discourse: for example, Starikov (1989) argues that Stalin's Asiatic paternalistic model for society crowded out a European one based on a civil society.

The Stalinist representation of Soviet Russia and the Soviet Union, on the contrary, put itself forward not as 'Asiatic' but as the epitome of European thinking. Yet there is a passage in that basic statement of Stalinism – the *Short Course of the Party History* – which explicitly states that Stalinists saw themselves as fighting Westernization inside the party. According to the *Short Course*, the Bolsheviks tried

> to create a *new* Party, to create a party of a *new type*, different from the usual Social-Democratic parties of the West, one that was free of opportunist elements and capable of leading the proletariat in a struggle for power. In fighting the Bolsheviks, the Mensheviks of all shades, from Axelrod and Martynov to Martov and Trotsky, invariably used weapons borrowed from the arsenal of the West-European Social-Democrats. They wanted in Russia a party similar, let us say, to the German or French Social-Democratic Party. They fought the Bolsheviks just because they sensed something new in them, something unusual and different from the Social-Democrats of the West. (*Short Course* 1948: 171–2)

Indeed, E.H. Carr has suggested that the Bolsheviks were the 'Westernizers' of the Party, and the Mensheviks the 'slavophiles', and has drawn up the following catalogue of examples of how this internal social democratic debate proceeded:

> A Menshevik journal which appeared spasmodically in St Petersburg after the 1905 revolution dubbed the Bolsheviks 'Slavophilizing Marxists'. Plekhanov, as well as the Mensheviks, denounced Lenin's attitude towards the peasantry as non-Marxist and a revival of *narodnik* heresies. In 1912 the Menshevik, Axelrod, was preaching the need 'to Europeanize, i.e. radically to change, the character of Russian social-democracy, . . . and to organize it on the same principles on which the party structure of European social-democracy rests';

and Lenin angrily retorted that 'the notorious "Europeanization" about which Dan and Martov and Trotsky and Levitsky and all the liquidators talk in season and out of season' was 'one of the chief points of their opportunism' . . . Axelrod was like 'a naked savage who puts on a top-hat and imagines himself for that reason European'. (Carr 1958: 18)

At the very least, one may note that communists of all shades invested large amounts of energy in presenting themselves as the true Europeans – in Stalin's case, indeed as the only true European. One also notes that Carr, in his catalogue of examples, refers to the late nineteenth-century debates between Marxists and populists as paradigmatic of the debate between Westernizers and nationalists. This is not entirely accurate, inasmuch as many populists, too, saw themselves as Westernizers in at least some senses of that word. For example, someone like Nikolay Ivanovich Sieber, a Marx scholar, could hardly have been clearer in his insistence on the necessity of Russian industrialization for individualization when he wrote even in the early 1870s that 'We shall have no sense in this country until the Russian *muzhik* is cooked up in the factory boiler' (quoted in Kindersley 1962: 9). But the populists, who still preferred their peasants raw, also argued in terms of European precedents. Writing in 1869, for example, Tkachev maintained that individualism, as espoused by Russian Westernizers, was first formulated by Protagoras and the Sophists, the ideologists of the urban bourgeois civilization of Athens. Against this individualism, he set the anti-individualism of the Sparta celebrated by Plato (Walicki 1969: 41–5). Tkachev's intervention is interesting not least for the choice of comparative case. At this time, ancient Greece was almost universally held to be not only the 'proto-European' phase of history, but also the cradle of European civilization as such. By choosing this particular point of reference for a comparison of Russia and Europe, Tkachev is able to present his own programme as a European one.

The debates between Marxists and populists were preceded by the debates between liberals and 'Russian socialists'. There exists an almost paradigmatic exchange of letters between Turgenev and Herzen from the early 1860s, where Herzen held that Russia was a cousin of Europe, who had taken little part in the family chronicle, but whose 'charms were fresher and more commendable than her cousins" (Hertzen 1968: 1747). Turgenev (1963 [1862]: 64–65) begged to differ: 'Russia is not a mal-treated and bonded Venus of Milo, she is a girl just like her older sisters – only a little broader in the beam'. Indeed, both Herzen and Turgenev saw the relationship in terms of family metaphors, but when it came to degree of kinship and to relative desirability, they parted ways. Actually, as early as in 1847–48, Botkin and Herzen discussed the pros and cons of industrialization and the need for an indigenous working class in Russia. Botkin, a tea merchant, prayed: 'God give Russia a bourgeoisie!', only to be met with a counter-prayer from Herzen: 'God save Russia from the bourgeoisie!' Belinskiy, in a letter to Botkin declared: 'So far all I have seen is that countries without a middle class are doomed to eternal insignificance' (Gerschenkron 1962: 164–6).

## The 'why' question

Without elevating being over becoming, or universalism over particularism, structural pressure must be acknowledged as being one of the strongest, if not the strongest, contexts which may help us understand the continued centrality of Westernizing and nationalist representations in Russian discourse on Europe, as well as in overall political discourse. Russia's political and economic backwardness – that is, its low degree of functional differentiation of power between politics and economy and between state and society – meant that the country continuously had to face up to the challenge posed by the more highly differentiated and therefore more efficient political and economic order in Western Europe. I avoid the word 'advanced' here because of its normative and modernist connotations: in its starkest and most immediate form, the challenge was to do with the need for Russia to maintain an economic base which would make it possible to sustain its military power and thus its role in international politics. Inasmuch as West European models were seen to be more efficient in performing this than was the Russian model, it meant that Russia's strength relative to that of West European states was in decline, and so the question of what was to be done was deemed to be unavoidable.

Of course, the possibility always exists that some new idea may emerge and spawn a specifically Russian model for economic and political organization. It would indeed be an overstatement to conclude that the inventory of the debate is given once and for all. Yet it is difficult to see how this can happen in any other way than by negating some aspect of thinking which could be referred to as 'European'. Russians are too caught up in their country's relationship with Europe to think entirely independently of it. When a contemporary, anti-modern, romantic nationalist such as Solzhenitsyn rails against Western civilization, he does so within what is routinely referred to as *European* literary genres such as the novel and the essay, availing himself of a European-developed medium such as the newspaper, in a public debate upheld by conventions developed in Europe, in a formal language with its roots in Europe, availing himself of linguistic archaisms in the way pioneered by German romantic nationalists. In short, it is the fate of Russians and others who have wanted to forge a non-European, anti-hegemonic debate that such debates cannot fail to maintain ties to Europe, if only inversely so, because of the very fact that they are patterned as attempts to negate the European debate, and therefore remain defined by it. Globalization means that 'Europe' may be nowhere, in the sense that it no longer has one and the same centre in all contexts, but it also means that 'Europe' is everywhere, in the sense that discursive elements such as the ones mentioned are permeating more and more discourses.

The most acute participants in Russian debate on Europe have acknowledged the structural pressure exerted by Western hegemony, and predicated their thinking on it. Herzen, Trotsky and Trubetskoy all acknowledged that Russia could not simply disregard Europe's dynamism. Yet, characteristically, except for communism, Russian discourse has not been able to produce any models which could take the place of the European ones. If Trubetskoy drew up an impressive and depressing catalogue of the disadvantages for Russia of copying European models – the humiliation conferred on it by Europe's arrogance in usurping the term 'human civilization' for itself, the handicap incurred by competing on somebody else's 'home turf', the imbalance caused by Russia's recurrent breakneck attempts at 'catching up' and the concurrent split between a 'Westernized' elite and its people – his alternatives to further copying were far from equally impressive. Westernizing representation has shed its romantic aspect. 'The West' is no longer unequivocally something to be copied, and there is no longer an expectation that Russia can become part of Europe as the result of a five-year plan or two. As so many aspects of Russian politics and society have changed since the advent of *perestroika*, however, the centrality of Russian discourse on Europe has only increased. It is this lingering centrality, and not the uniqueness of each of the constellations of representations of which it is made up, which I wanted to highlight in this reading of Russia in terms of its European Other.

## *A semiospheric model of Russian European policy*

One may try to capture discourse in its synchronicity, understanding the state of discourse at any one point in time as a semiosphere in Yuri

Lotman's sense of the term. The basic layer may be conceptualized as the *constellation* of the human collective's ideas about itself. Whereas Waever (2001) very parsimoniously settles for one single basic constellation in the cases of France and Germany – a republican constellation and a constellation built on the *Kulturnation,* respectively – the Russian case does not seem to lend itself so easily to parsimonious modelling. It will simply not do to operate only with the relations between conceptualizations of state and nation. The conceptualization of *the leader* is equally basic; contrary to circumstances in France and Germany, Spinoza's dictum that the king's documents must be binding on all, including the king, has not been incorporated in Russian discourse to such an extent that the king/leader may be subsumed under the state. The very concept of state in Russian – *gosudarstvo* – comes from *gosudar,* which translates as head (of an extended household). The well-known reference to the tsar as 'little father' (*batushka,* grandfather) further underlines the parallel between the idea of the household and that of the state, and between those of the *paterfamilias* and the head of state. This link, so important in West European countries particularly before the coming of modernity (see, for example, the classic debate between Filmer and Mill), also existed in a Russian variant, and maintains strength to this day. Given the stature of the leader in Russian political discourse, it is no coincidence that, following the demise of the Party, Yeltsin's administrative entourage quickly grew to encompass a tremendous number of people, and that Putin's seems to have been scaled back to around 5,000.

In the Soviet period, furthermore, the State was penetrated by the Party. In order to capture the basic constellation of that period, the party must also be included. The first constellation on the basic layer of Russian European discourse (1-1) is the one of the Slavophiles, where the state is treated as an alien – and, indeed, evil – feature which intrudes on the organic ties between the leader and the nation. It can be shown how the Slavophile formulation of this constellation drew on early German romantic ideas about relations between the realms of the cultural and the political, and so we have here one example of discursive overlap between all-European and Russian discourses (Neumann 1996). It is true that this basic constellation has yielded less specific European policies than the others. When I nonetheless venture to include it, it is because it is frequently invoked in its own right, and furnishes Russian political discourse with a dimension which is nonetheless real for being represented as 'irrational', perhaps even apolitical, by most Western analytical lights (see comments above on p. 193 about the need to apply the discourse's own ideas about rationality when modelling it). What is at stake here is the modelling of Russian discourse as it unfolds, not a censoring of it to make it fit with rationalistic models of the political.

The second constellation on the basic layer (1-2) is a monolithic one, where the leader is the state is the people is the party, or where the leader is the state is the nation. The state is conceptualized not as an arbitrator between groups, but as the organic embodiment of the sum total of the human collective that is Russia. Soviet official discourse included the genre of slogans – huge red cardboard hoardings which filled public space with inscriptions such as 'The plans of the party are the plans of the people'. Politics, then, was not conceptualized as mediation between groups, but as a struggle by a monolithic human collective – the Soviet Union – for objective emancipation. Contradictions in politics were relegated to the outside – to relations between the Soviet Union and other collectives, to relations between the international proletariat led by the Soviet Union and other collectives, to contradictions between collectives other than the Soviet Union. I have conflated this overwhelmingly dominant constellation of the Soviet period with the standard nationalist conceptualization of the state and the nation as two sides of the same coin, where the state is the shield of the nation just as the party is the shield of the people. The structural similarity at the root of this is to do with an *organic* way of thinking about relations between human collectives; the constellation is not monolithic in the sense that state and nation are the same thing, but in the sense that they are organically interlinked so that contradictions between them cannot be thought of as anything else than *illness* in the body politic. To the tsarist regime, the nation was the body to which the state was the head – to the Soviet one, the people was the body to which the party was the head. For both regimes, the leader was leader exactly because he *embodied* the state and the nation/people. So, in conflating the basic constellations of tsarist and Soviet state discourse, I heed Nikolay Berdyaev's famous dictum about the events of 1917, that instead of the Third Rome, we got the Third International. That, of course, does not in any way imply that there were no differences whatsoever, that things could not have developed otherwise, or that one may not make differing normative assessments of the two different regimes. The point is a structural one, not in the sense of a deep structure unreachable, inaccessible and therefore unchangeable, but in the sense of offering constellations which are similar enough to warrant modelling conflation for our specific purpose. The capping argument in favour of conflation, however, is an empirical one: witness the way discursive elements of these two strands *themselves* combined in the 1990s under the heading of the Red-Brown alliance. What is at stake here is not the tenuous organizational combination in blocs, etc. but the arguably much less tenuous discursive combination.

The third constellation on the basic layer (1-3) should be readily identifiable and not in need of much explanation – it is a generic *Rechtsstaat* model. The fourth basic level-one constellation (1-4) is the radical Other of Russian political discourse – the spectre of a stateless situation, almost invariably associated with the Time of Troubles (*smutnoe vremya, smuta*) of the first decade of the seventeenth century. One of the basic resources of Russian political discourse is to invoke this spectre and argue that if not a specific layer-one constellation is adopted as a model, the alternative will be a new Time of Troubles: there will be no strong hand/law, foreign powers will come in to feast on the cadaver of Russia, etc. The English equivalent would be to argue that life will be poor, nasty, brutish and short, but that only involves invoking the artificial construct of a state of nature. Hobbes's specific historical references to Ancient Greece and the English Civil War are drowned out by universalistic claims. In Russian discourse, on the other hand, the phrase is rife with the historical echoes of the Time of Troubles, the Civil War of the early twentieth century and the Tatar (i.e. Mongol) Yoke from the thirteenth through the fifteenth centuries all rolled into one.

Gorbachev's reform drive was launched under three different headings: *perestroika, glasnost, uskorenie*. One could argue that these three slogans referred to rather different basic constellations. Perestroyka was very much an 'away from here is my goal' undertaking, with the slogan *tak nel'zja zhit'* – it is impossible to live like this – being indicative of a recognized malaise to which there was no widely acknowledged cure. Beginning in 1990 and culminating in 1992, an attempt was made to reorient discourse in the direction of the basic constellation of the *Rechtsstaat*, which was seen by some as a possible cure. For a short moment, Yeltsin even adopted this as a position alternative to Gorbachev's, not least since Gorbachev himself manifestly made a point of not adopting it and thus left it free for the opposition to use. Gorbachev's invocation of the two other slogans further showed the depth of the political crisis. *Glasnost* was sometimes interpreted as a call for freedom of the press, that is, a phenomenon with a clear affinity to a *Rechtsstaat* constellation. Etymologically, however, it may be traced back to Slavophile thinking, where it referred to how the tsar might allow the voice of the people (in the singular) to reach him without having it tampered with on its way. That is, it may be seen as a pincer movement whereby the leader appealed to the people for help in checking the shenanigans of the presumably infidel state. On such a reading, it belongs to discourse rooted in the Slavophile-style constellation on the basic layer (1–1). The thrust of the last slogan, of *uskorenie* (acceleration) indicated that the basic constellation of the Soviet period (1–2) was fine, and that all that was needed was an overhaul. This slogan was quickly dropped, thus furnishing more discursive evidence for the depth of the ongoing political crisis. I mention this here to show how changes initiated by the onset of the Gorbachev years set in motion all three basic constellations at level one.

That was level one explained. Let me return to the relations between the different layers of Russian political discourse. As a corollary of the fact that the political sphere has also enveloped the first and deepest layer of the discursive structure, what may be called the *depth span* of the three levels of Waever's model – state-nation constellation, structural relations between this constellation and the collective's conceptualizations of Europe, specific European policies – seems to be more shallow, conflated and truncated, than in the German and French cases. There is an obvious reason for the pervasiveness of the political and the correspondingly more shallow span between the levels of discourse, and it is to do with a key factor which Waever et al. have not paid heed to because it has not been active in recent French and German history to the same extent. This is the hegemonic pressure exerted by those conceptualizations of state and nations active at the core of the international system onto conceptualizations of state and nature in the rest of the system.

In the case of Russia, the Russian deliberations about the basic state-nation-leader constellation have been inextricably entangled with the debate over 'Europe'. Indeed, since as a rule it has been politicized, it has more often than not been directly observable, in the form of a call for a law-governed state, a *pravovoe gosudarstvo*. It is hardly accidental that the idea is often referred to by the German loan word of *Rechtsstaat* (although not too much should be made of this, inasmuch as it is a loan word in European languages spoken by collectives which have made the concept a basic feature of political discourse also). I would like to stress particularly that the key point here is *not* to do with any normative pull that this idea may or may not have. Rather, it is to do with the fact that it signals a bundle of ways of organizing the state and state/society relations which are seen by some as more effective in building up a power basis for state policy in the long run than are other and competing constellations. Thus, any modelling of Russian political discourse must include this hegemonic pull of what is sometimes (but not very often) seen in Russian discourse as specific French, German, British ways of organizing the state, but most often as a generic European or even Western way of doing so. In the Putin quote on p. 192, liberalism as a general European and Western phenomenon is of the essence – specific countries are by the way.

I now turn to the proposed second layer of discourse, consisting of variously proposed structural relations between the basic constellations of the first layer and the collective's conceptualizations of Europe. Historically, there have evolved two such possible relations from basic constellations one: Russian leadership (2-1) and Russia versus Europe (2-2).

There is a very good reason why the ways in which the structure of Russo-European relations emerges in the second layer of Russian European discourse (with one exception) involve the two entities Russia and Europe, and not the whole gamut of great powers. This is that Russia, alone of the European great powers, adheres to a political discourse which is generated first and foremost by a constellation of state, nation, etc. which is of another kind than the generic one shared by all other European great powers; if those constellations are indeed different, they may all be subsumed under the heading of *Rechtsstaat*. It could be argued that the entire Western policy of containment was about this; to sit back and wait until the hegemonic force of the *Rechtsstaat* model and its associate economic model of capitalism permeated Russian discourse and worked the demise of the Soviet Union. It could also be argued that, when the slogan of the Gorbachev era became 'we cannot live like this', that signalled the success of this policy. And yet, as has been demonstrated above, if the model of the *Rechtsstaat* enjoyed a heyday in Russian discourse between 1990 and 1992, that heyday was not halcyon enough to establish the *Rechtsstaat* as the major new generative constellation of political discourse. Thus, when Russia finds itself marginalized in the central discourses about the EU and NATO, and time and again is confronted with such a high degree of co-ordination among the other powers that what emerges is a Russo-European dialogue rather than an all-European heterologue, it is for a very good reason. It is among other things in recognition of this that Russia has tried to make the OSCE a two-tiered (NATO and CIS) central locus of European security discourse, and it is first and foremost because Russia is not recognized as a heavy enough dialogue partner that the other powers refuse to treat this proposal seriously. This refusal, in turn, fans Russian anxieties about not being recognized as a great European power. The rest of Europe's responses to these fears have been to treat Russia as a great power by courtesy (for example as a less-than-full addition to the G-7, thus underscoring that its status as a great-power is indeed in doubt), to acknowledge Russia's nuclear capacity as a vital great-power credit (thus underscoring that its great power status is unidimensional) and, at least in the early 1990s but in an ever-diminishing degree, to acknowledge Russia's maintenance of a sphere of influence in the Asian CIS countries (thus drawing into doubt its recognition of Russia's similar presence as a great power in Europe). The point is this: by dint of being the hegemonic model in European (and international) discourse, the basic constellation of the *Rechtsstaat* enhances its presence in Russian discourse as well.

## Conclusion

Seen in the light of Russian conceptual history, the shift in representations of 'Europe' and the fading of its centrality from Gorbachev to Putin was overdetermined. The Putin quote given at the outset carries within itself so much of the Russian discursive universe, and sets it in motion in such a way that it is seen to evolve around the pivotal figure of Vladimir Putin.

The compromise between the two basic representations of Europe – those of the nationalists and the Westernizers respectively – is brought about from a sound institutional basis, viz. the FSB, inheritor of the KGB. It is hardly historically unique that an institution of force steps into the breach and forges a political compromise when the basic political question of who we are and who the enemy is cannot be settled by other political actors. The major problem is that, in a situation where the EU and NATO are hegemonic political forces in Europe and post-sovereignty is the name of the game, Putin's representation of Europe as a system of sovereign states which are perched uneasily between conflict and cooperation is a lonely one. It is not Russia which developed a domination representation of Europe which is *outré* relative to representations which are to be found in other countries. On the contrary, having emerged from the communist discourse which set it apart, Russia has embraced the litany of national interests, great powers, *Realpolitik*, etc. – that is, a classical Realist position. The problem is that, as can be seen from the other chapters of this book, this is a representation which seems to be weakening in most other quarters. It is everybody else who moves away, and Russia which embodies the European Tradition. Even this has been seen before: after the Napoleonic wars, as seen from St Petersburg, it was everybody else which abandoned the Europe of *l'ancien régime*, while Russia was left as true Europe's sole defender. At the present juncture, as seen from Moscow, everybody else is abandoning the game posited on sovereignty for a new one based on integration, networks and other dangerous pursuits. In the sphere of economics, as the Putin quote indicates, Russia must broaden its interface with Europe in order to immerse itself in a market economy. In the sphere of politics, on the other hand, Russia is likely to become the last guardian of the Europe of the nation state. As long as this conceptual framework reigns, the quicker European integration will be, and the more problematic Europe's relations with Russia are therefore likely to become.

# References

Baudrillard, Jean (1977), *Oublier Foucault*, Paris: Galilée.

Borisov, Vadim, (1975 [1974]), 'Personality and National Awareness', in A. Solzhenitsyn et al. (eds), *From Under the Rubble*, London: Collins & Harvill: 194–228.

Bovin, A.E. and Lukin V.P. (1989), 'Perestroyka mezhdunarodnykh otnosheniy – puti i podkhody,' *Mezhdunarodnaya Ekonomika i Mezhdunarodnye Otnosheniya*, XXXIII(1): 58–70.

Brown, A. (1990), 'Perestroika and the Political System', in T. Hasegawa and A. Pravda (eds), *Perestroika: Soviet Domestic and Foreign Policies*, London: SAGE, Royal Institute of International Affairs, 56–87.

Carr, E.H. (1958), *Socialism in One Country 1924–1926*, vol. I, London: Macmillan.

Cherniavsky, M. (1958), '"Holy Russia": A Study in the History of an Idea', *American History Review*, LXIII(3): 617–37.

Cohen, S.F. (1974), *Bukharin and the Bolshevik Revolution: A Political Biography 1888–1938*, London: Wildwood.

Danilevskiy, N.J. (1888 [1869]), *Rossiya i Evropa: Vzglyad na kul'turnyya i politicheskiya otnosheniya Slavyanskago mira k Germano-Romanskomy*, 3rd edn, St Petersburg: Strakhov.

Duncan, P.J.S. (1989), Russian Messianism: A Historical and Political Analysis. PhD thesis, University of Glasgow, Glasgow, mimeo.

Gerschenkron, A. (1962), 'Economic Development in Russian Intellectual History of the Nineteenth Century', in *Economic Backwardness in Historical Perspective: A Book of Essays*, Cambridge, Mass.: Harvard University Press.

Gorbachev, M. (1988 [1987]), *Perestroika: New Thinking for Our Country and the World*, 2nd edn, London: Fontana.

Hauner, M. (1990), *What is Asia to Us? Russia's Asian Heartland Yesterday and Today*, Boston: Unwin Hyman.

Herzen, A. (1968), 'Ends and Beginnings: Letters to I.S. Turgenev (1862–1863)', in *My Past and Thoughts: The Memoirs of Alexander Herzen, 1680–1749*, London: Chatto & Windus.

Kindersley, R. (1962), *The First Russian Revisionists: A Study of 'Legal Marxism'*, in *Russia*, Oxford: Clarendon.

Kissinger, H.A. (1957), *A World Restored: Castlereagh, Metternich and the Restoration of Peace, 1812–1822*, Boston: Houghton Mifflin.

Lotman, Y.M. (1990), *Universe of the Mind: A Semiotic Theory of Culture*, London: I.B. Tauris.

Lukin, V. (1996), 'Russia's Entry to the Council of Europe', *International Affairs*, (Moscow), 2: 25–9.

Lynch, A.C. (1997), 'Russia and NATO: Expansion and Coexistence?', *The International Spectator*, 32(1) January–March 1997, 81–91.

Neumann, I.B. (1996), *Russia and the Idea of Europe: A Study in Identity and International Relations*, London: Routledge.

Novikov, A. (1991), 'Ya – rusofob.', *Vek XX i mir*, XXXIII(7): 12–14.

Pankin, B. (1996), *The Last Hundred Days of the Soviet Union*, London: I.B. Tauris.

Podberezkin, A. (1996), 'Vyzovy bezopasnosti Rossii: Rasshirenie NATO', *Svobodnaya mysl'*, no. 12.

Pozdnyakov, E. (1991), 'The Soviet Union: The Problem of Comning Back to European Civilization', *Paradigms*, V(1–2): 45–57.

Said, E.W. (1985 [1978]), *Orientalism*, Harmondsworth: Penguin.

Schelting, A. von (1948), *Russland und Europa in Russischen Geschichtsdenken*, Bern: A. Francke.

Shafarevich, I. (1989), 'Rusofobiya', *Nash sovremennik*, LVII(6): 167–92.

Shevtsova, L. (1990), 'The Chances of Democracy', *New Times*, 52: 4–6.

Short Course (1948 [1938]), *History of the Communist Party of the Soviet Union (Bolsheviks): Short Course*, edited by a Commission of the Central Committee of the CPSU (b), authorized by the CC of the CPSU (b) 1938, Moscow: Foreign Languages Publishing House.

Solov'ev, V.S. n.d., probably 1905 [1888/1891], 'Natsional'nyy vopros v Rossii', *Sobranie sochineniy*, V, St. Petersburg, Obshchestvennaya pol'za, 1–368.

Solzhenitsyn, A. (1975 [1974]), 'Repentance and Self-Limitation in the Life of the Nations', in Alexander Solzhenitsyn et al. (eds), *From Under the Rubble*, London: Collins & Harvill: 105–43.

—— (1990), 'Kak nam obustroit' Rossiyu: Posil'nye soobrazheniya', Enclosure to *Literaturnaya gazeta*, Moscow, 19 September 1990.

Starikov, E. (1989), 'Marginaly, ili razmyshleniya na staruyu temu: "Chto s nami proiskhodit?"', *Znamya*, LIX(10): 133–62.

Trubetskoy, Prince N.S. (1920), *Evropa i chelovechestvo*, Sofia: Rossiysko-bolgarskoe knigoizdatel'stvo.

Turgenev, I.S. (1963 [1862]), Letter to A.I. Herzen of 23 October/4 November 1862, reprinted in *Polnoe sobranie sochineniy i pisem v dvadtsati vos'mi tomakh: Pis'ma v trinadtsati tomakh*, vol. V, Moscow: Akademiya nauk, 64–5.

Waever, O. (2001), 'Discourse on Europe', in L. Hansen and O. Waever (eds), *Between Nation and Europe: The Nordic States and the EU*, London: Routledge.

Walicki, A. (1969), *The Controversy over Capitalism: Studies in the Social Philosophy of the Russian Populists*, Oxford: Clarendon.

—— (1975), *The Slavophile Controversy: History of a Conservative Utopia in Nineteenth-Century Thought*, Oxford: Clarendon.

Waltz, K. (1979), *Theory of International Politics*, Toronto: Addison Wesley.

Williams, M. and Neumann, I.B. (2000), 'From Alliance to Security Community: NATO, Russia and the Power of Identity', *Millennium*, 29(2): 357–87.

Zyuganov, G. (1994), *Derzhava* [Great Power], Moscow: Informpechat.

—— (1996), *Rossiya – rodina maya* [Russia – my motherland]: The Ideology of State Patriotism, Moscow: Informpechat.

# –9–

# The Complex of an Unwanted Child: The Meanings of Europe in Polish Discourse

*Barbara Törnquist-Plewa*

This chapter undertakes a historical analysis of the discourse on Europe in Poland, an analysis delimited of course by the scope allowed in this publication. One of the main theses argued for here is that despite changing meanings of Europe there are some stable elements in the Polish discourse on Europe: stereotypes, categorizations and representations of relations between Poland and Europe, which are extremely tenacious. Their recurrence in Polish political and intellectual debates through centuries justify our viewing them, in the spirit of Braudel, as 'tenacious mental structures' and looking at them from a *longue durée* perspective. The longevity of these representations is to a considerable degree namely due to the political and geographical situation of Poland and its place in the European economic system, i.e. factors of almost geo-historical nature, which have hardly changed through the ages. On the level of *les événements* and *les conjonctures* a lot has changed since the Middle Ages: the political map of Europe has been redrawn many times, empires have come and gone, political systems and trade routes have been modified, but the relationship between periphery and centre in Europe has remained (cf. Jedlicki 1993: 84). Those nations that today form the core of the EU are largely the same that were part of the Western Christian empire of Charlemagne, and already in the Middle Ages had become leaders of European cultural and economic development. The idea of Poland's peripheral position permeates Polish thinking about Europe. It is all the more visible in eager Polish attempts to deny this fact through the constant formulations and reformulations of Poland's mission in Europe and Polish yearning to be called the 'Heart of Europe'.

Barbara Törnquist-Plewa

# Poland's Place in *Republica Christiana* – Polish Discourse on Europe During the Pre-modern Period (AD966–1600)

The first documented use in Poland of the term 'European' is found in the *Tractatus de duabus Sarmatiis, Asiana et Europiana* of 1517 by Matthew of Miechow (Maciej Miechowita), a principal of Cracow University. He claimed that the River Don constitutes the border between Europe and Asia – an idea largely shared by the European elite of his time (Tazbir 1998: 8–20). This placing of the border tells us that the idea of 'Europe' was at that time synonymous with the Western Christian world. Outside Europe were first and foremost Muslims (Turks and Tartars) but also Eastern Christians – that is, the Byzantine world. Europe went as far as the influence of Western Christianity. It corresponded to an area where Latin was the *lingua franca* of the elite, where the heritage of Antiquity was an obvious reference and where ideas circulated that originated at Western Christian universities and at the courts of Western Christian monarchs. The borders of this sixteenth-century idea of Europe thus coincided, with among others, the borders of the Polish state. This naturally had implications for the way the Polish elite viewed the relations between Poland and Europe. Since AD966, the year it was founded as a Christian state, Poland had been the periphery and outpost of Western Christianity/Europe.

The periphery–centre relation appears clearly in the fact that the elite of medieval Poland viewed the Pope in Rome as the highest authority, and turned to Italy, France and the Holy Roman Empire for education and scientific and aesthetic ideals. Foreigners from these countries (German farmers and craftsmen, Jewish merchants, Italian scientists and artists) were welcomed by Polish monarchs in order to develop the economy and culture of the state. We may wonder if this status of a periphery developing through impulses from the centre led to a kind of inferiority complex among the Polish elite. No medieval sources confirm such a possibility; however, it is not excluded (Zientara 1973). If it had been so, it most probably disappeared during the fifteenth and sixteenth centuries. Written sources from that time suggest in fact that the Polish elite was self-confident and proud of the status of its state. From the end of the fourteenth century, the next two hundred years saw a dynamic economic development (Geremek 1989: 109–32). The union of Poland and the Grand Duchy of Lithuania under one monarch in 1385, as well as the victory over the Teutonic Knights in the fifteenth century, led to an enlarged territory and increased political significance. Polish culture developed as well, with the first universities in Cracow and in Vilnius.

From being primarily the receiver of Western Christian culture the Polish elite became one of its creators and its exporter to Lithuania and the Orthodox Eastern Slavs. The Lithuanians converted to the Christian faith when the Union with Poland was sealed. Those Orthodox Eastern Slavs who because of the Union found themselves inside the joint Polish-Lithuanian state became the subjects of papal authority two hundred years later through the Church Union of Brest-Litovsk 1596. The majority of the Orthodox in Poland thus became so-called Greek-Catholics, recognizing the Pope as the head of their Church but maintaining their own rites. The view of Poland as the periphery of Western Christianity was gradually, with growing self-confidence of the elite from the fourteenth century onward, transformed into a view of Poland as the outpost of Western Christianity, its shield against 'infidels': primarily Tartars and Turks, but also Orthodox Muscovites. The sixteenth and seventeenth centuries saw rivalry between Poland, Hungary, Austria and other powers as to which of them was *Antemurale Christianitatis* – the bulwark of Christianity. After the Polish victory over the Turks at Vienna in 1683, the Pope called Poland-Lithuania *Antemurale Christianitatis* in a number of official documents. This image of Poland as the bulwark of Christianity/ Europe was strongly assimilated by the political and cultural elite of the Polish state – that is, the numerous gentry – and it was transmitted to further generations and levels in Polish society (Krzyżaniakowa 1992: 3–24). A more or less articulated idea that Poland had a special role to fulfil in Europe was from then on recurrent in Polish political discourse.

The Polish political rhetoric of the sixteenth and seventeenth centuries describes Poland's role in Europe in terms of 'outpost', 'bulwark' or 'shield', but in reality the Polish-Lithuanian state was rather a 'bridge' between Western and Eastern Christianity and also between Christianity and Islam. The Polish-Lithuanian State was inhabited by several confessional and ethnic groups: Catholics, Orthodox, Protestants, Tartar Muslims, Jews and others.

The elite created a culture that was a mixture of Western and Eastern elements. This became especially clear in the seventeenth century when the gentry, with reference to its origins in a mythical *Asian* tribe, called themselves 'Sarmatians' and cultivated the Oriental elements in their dress in order to emphasize their particular collective identity and position in society. Through the *Sejm* (Parliament) the Polish-Lithuanian gentry had full control of the politics of the state. They might have said 'the state – it is we'. The Sarmatian gentry considered Poland's political system, the so-called 'gentry democracy', the best in the world. Yet the seventeenth century brought violent wars, occupation and crises that led to the economic collapse of the state, further aggravated by political disint-egration. When Russia after its victory in the Nordic War of 1721 began to control Polish politics, the country's sovereignty was threatened. The image of Poland as the 'knight of Europe' or 'the granary of Europe' (referring to Poland's role in the grain trade in the sixteenth century) prevented the self-complacent Sarmatian gentry from perceiving this danger. Many members of the gentry were convinced that the continued existence of Poland was in the interest of Europe, that Europe could not let this state disappear at least for the sake of the balance of powers (Tazbir 1987: 20–1). The first partition of Poland in 1772 between Russia, Prussia and the Habsburg Empire clearly demonstrated that this idea was no more than an illusion, which was a terrible shock for the Polish political élite. At last all the gentry realized that Poland was weak, vulner-able and reduced to a peripheral position in Europe. This was a painful insight, all the more so as the Polish intellectual elite began to judge Poland according to value scales from Paris and London, i.e. the centres of the Enlightenment.

## The Enlightenment: A New Meaning of 'Europe' and the Concepts of 'East' and 'West'

During the Enlightenment the meaning of Europe as synonymous with Western Christianity was gradually replaced by a new, secular, under-standing of this term. The intellectuals of this time identified Europe with 'civilization' and 'progress', which were two basic concepts emerging from the Enlightenment. According to the philosophers of that current, Europe was the cradle and the leader of the progress of the whole of mankind toward new higher stages in material, spiritual, intellectual and societal development. This idea spread to Poland in the course of the eighteenth century. The Polish thinkers of the Enlightenment could not help perceiving big differences in the material and societal development in France and England on the one hand and in Poland on the other. One of the leading intellectuals of that time, Stanisław Staszic, wrote:

> How far away stands Poland! How far ahead are other countries . . . Poland is only in the fifteenth century. The whole of Europe completes its eighteenth century . . . This land, the most fertile in Europe, which should be the richest today . . . this great land is Europe's poorest' (1790: 253–4. translation).

This view of Poland-Lithuania as economically backward and retarded in its civilization shows that the Polish elite had adopted the standards for civilization and economy set in France and England and perceived them as universally valid. By these standards, the thinkers of the Enlightenment divided Europe into two parts: civilized West versus uncivilized East. Larry Wolff describes this 'mental mapping' in his book *Inventing Eastern Europe* (1994). Yet the Enlightenment did not 'invent' the 'East', as Wolff somewhat radically puts it. The image of 'barbarians' in the East and the North existed already earlier in Western European discourses (Möller 1999). However, during the Enlightenment these concepts were modified. The barbaric North disappeared as a relevant category, while the East remained and its belonging to Europe was questioned in an age when Europe became synonymous with 'civilization'. Since it was Western Europe that set the standards for civilization (such as material prosperity, level of industrialization, transport systems, education, hygiene, etc.) and only Western Europe lived up to them, Europe was more and more identified with the 'West'. From the second half of the eighteenth century onward the term 'West' has been often used as synonymous with 'Europe' in the Polish political and cultural debate (Wierzbicki 1984: 50–66). Sometimes the 'West' has been used in a larger sense, referring to both Western Europe and the United States of America. In any case, at the end of the eighteenth century, the Poles began to identify the 'West' and 'Europe' with 'modernity' and 'modern civilization'.

What was, then, the place of Poland in a Europe understood as 'modern civilization'? As the statement by Staszic quoted above shows, its status was extremely uncertain. As for space, Poland was within Europe (as its poorest country, according to Staszic) and as for time, it was outside Europe (300 years behind Europe as to civilization). This was a dilemma the Poles have had to deal with.

The Polish Enlightenment elite was firmly determined to 'Europeanize' Poland, i.e. to implement a series of reforms in politics, culture and economy in order to modernize the Polish state. These reforms encountered resistance from the Sarmatian gentry, who in the reform proposals saw an imitation of foreign models and a threat against native Polish customs and values. The advocates of reform countered this reaction by maintaining their political orientation, yet adhering to the Sarmatian criticism about parroting of foreign dress, etiquette, customs, etc. The Polish literature of the Enlightenment (works by Niemcewicz, Zabłocki, Naruszewicz, Bogusławski) ridicules people who blindly admired and followed foreign lifestyles and fashion (Micińska: 1999).

Behind these campaigns against foreign influence we can discern a fear that the native culture might lose its originality in the encounter with patterns from Western Europe. This in turn reveals a lack in self-confidence as to the strength of the native culture. This is a characteristic feature of cultural peripheries. It emerged in Poland in the eighteenth century and came to stay until our own times.

## The Emergence of the Modern Polish National Idea and the Discourse on Europe

At the end of the eighteenth century, under the influence of French, English and American ideas about nations, a new modern concept of the Polish nation began to take shape. The old idea that *Natio Polonica* was a political community of the entire gentry (and only the gentry) in Poland-Lithuania gradually gave way to the modern notion of a nation encompassing all citizens of the state, regardless of social level. Around 1793 (the year the so-called Constitution of 3 May was adopted) the Polish political elite began to define the Polish nation as a political community which included all citizens of the state, regardless of social group, confession or ethnic background – i.e., ethnic Poles, Lithuanians, Ruthenians, Jews and others. The community was to be based on the institutions, laws and history of the Polish-Lithuanian State. Poland-Lithuania was at that time losing its federal character and moving toward becoming a unitary state. This development was, however, cut short in 1795 with the final partition of Poland-Lithuania between Russia, Prussia and the Habsburg Empire. The state disappeared, but the process of nation-building continued nevertheless in the nineteenth century in the lands of the partitioned Poland. This process implied that the Polish cultural and political elite was given the task of defining the meaning of 'Polishness'. They had to find arguments which legitimized the existence of the Polish nation in spite of the fact that there no longer was a Polish state. In political and intellectual debates on the 'to be or not to be' of the Polish nation, two concepts were recurrent, namely 'Europe' and 'Russia'. In relation to these concepts attempts have been made to define Poland and its place in the international order.

When analysing the Polish discourse on Europe of that time we cannot speak of any clear agreement among the Polish elite as to Polish identity and its relation to Europe and Russia (cf. Jedlicki 1999; Walicki 1994; Wierzbicki 1984). Still, as Jedlicki suggests (1999), two directions can be discerned in the discussion that has now been going on for two centuries. The first may be called 'occidentalist'. According to this viewpoint, Poland is clearly part of Europe defined as a Latin, Western Christian civilization – i.e., a Europe without Russia or any Islamic

countries. Most 'occidentalists' considered that Poland in its seventeenth-
and eighteenth-century development had taken a different course from
that of Europe, but this could be explained among other things by
pointing to Poland's vulnerable position in the periphery of the European
civilization and its role as Europe's shield against 'Asian barbarism'. This
deviation from the European model could and must be overcome.

The other direction in Polish political thinking turned against this
occidentalism, but yet it cannot be called 'oriental'. It never presented
an Eastern, Asiatic civilization as a possible alternative for the Poles.
Instead, there was the choice between 'occidentalism' and a kind of
'ethnocentrism' , i.e. the idea that the native culture is unique and should
be defended and developed along its own tracks. However, there was no
agreement as to what was unique about Poland. During Romanticism, i.e.
the first half of the nineteenth century, the unique was seen among other
perceptions in the fact that the Poles were the Slavic people living furthest
to the West. The Slavophile element in the ideology of the 'ethnocentrists'
made them consider Russia part of Europe. This Europe was, however,
divided into West and East. To the east there were all the Slavs, including
the Poles. The Polish Slavophiles accepted the view of German historians
that the Slavic peoples were 'younger as to civilization' but they turned
the tables on this essentially disadvantageous judgement and claimed that
it implied that the future belonged to the Slavs, while Western Europe was
bound to fall. The role of the Poles in such a Europe was to carry further
to the Russians and other Eastern Slavs those values and ideals that could
be salvaged from the degenerate West. It was the destiny of the Poles to
do this, since they, because of their particular development and geopolitical situation, constituted a bridge between East and West. The 'Act
of Foundation' of the first Polish democratic party TPD from 1831, states
that:

> The only calling of Poland, her only duty to mankind, is to bring to the depth
> of the East true enlightenment and the understanding of the rights of man. This
> is why the existence of Poland is needed for the civilization, happiness, and
> peace of Europe. (Walicki 1982: 82)

This quotation is characteristic of Polish thinking in terms of a mission
which the Poles are destined to carry out in Europe. The most extreme
expression of this thinking was Polish Romantic Messianism as formulated by the poet Adam Mickiewicz and widely spread by literature and
iconography in the nineteenth century. According to this idea Poland
was the 'Christ of nations'. Its destiny was to suffer in order to bring

'salvation' – in the form of freedom to all nations in the world (cf. Walicki 1982: 237–322; Törnquist-Plewa 1992: 42–5, 136) .

This recurrent seeking for a mission should not be seen as an expression of national megalomania - quite the contrary. Psychologists would call this tendency a 'compensatory idea', a way of counteracting profound inferiority complexes and the humiliation the Polish elite felt after the loss of the state. However, one cannot help noticing that this idea to some extent also was a political strategy for convincing European opinion of the necessity for the restoration of a Polish state, of the fact that Europe needed the Poles and should therefore support them in their struggle for freedom. Behind recurrent ideas about Poland's special role in Europe there is a tenacious Polish tendency to treat the relations between Poland and Europe in the terms of creditor and debtor. In the eyes of the Poles it is Europe that has a debt to Poland, 'the knight of Europe' and 'the Christ of nations', a debt never paid back.

## Polish Slavophiles, Anti-occidentalists and their View on Europe

The 'Slavophile' direction in Polish political discourse emerged after the Napoleonic Wars, when the hopes of restoring a Polish state with the help of France were shattered. The Congress of Vienna in 1815 established the Kingdom of Poland as a Russian vassal state. This made the Poles first seek a kind of modus vivendi with Russia, and therefore the ideas of the Slavophiles gained some popularity. According to Polish Slavophiles, the Poles would become like the Greeks of Antiquity. Just like the Greeks, they were politically subjugated to an Empire that was materially superior, but they would have an important moral and civilizing influence on that empire (Kizwalter 2000: 176).

One reason for the emphasis of the Slavic element was that the Polish elite under the influence of Romanticism was trying to define the Polish nation in cultural terms – a task seen as important for a nation stripped of its state. However, Latin Christianity could not work as a base for the cultural community of the Polish nation, since it excluded the Orthodox and the Greek-Catholic Ruthenians. In order to include them it was preferable to emphasize the linguistic and ethnic community of all Slavic people.

Another reason for the 'Slavophile' and 'ethnocentric' tendencies was the disappointment of Polish Romantics in Western Europe. After the fall of the Polish revolt against Russia (November Uprising 1830–31) a large part of the Polish intellectual elite lived in exile in the West. Many of them never felt at home in their host countries. Moreover, they waited in vain for the Western powers' commitment to the Polish issue. The West became for them a synonym for egoism, cold rationalism, pursuit of economic gain, materialism and superficiality, a civilization doomed to go under. Such declarations can be found in many works by the leading Romanticists: Mickiewicz, Słowacki, Krasiński (Krasucki 1980). As a contrast to Western Europe, Slavic Eastern Europe was described as first and foremost embodying spirituality, love of freedom, equality and a solidarity between social groups with its roots in 'ancient Slavic communalism' (Walicki 1994: 20–1). Joachim Lelewel, a historian and the leading ideologist of Polish democrats at the beginning of the nineteenth century claimed that it was wrong to view the history of seventeenth- and eighteenth-century Poland as the period when the country deviated from Western development. There were no universal standards for development. Every nation should follow its own path and cherish its individuality. The progress of humankind had, according to Lelewel and the Romantics, nothing to do with material prosperity, but was all about development toward greater freedom and democracy. The Polish Gentry Republic and its political system anticipated modern democracy and thus was ahead of the rest of Europe. Lelewel and his disciples considered Western European influences in Poland more detrimental than advantageous for the nation. The West was a threat against the originality of the nation, its high ideals of freedom and moral values (Wierzbicki 1984: 126–41).

It must be pointed out that the Polish 'anti-occidentalism' and Slavophilism on many points differed from Russian Slavophilism. Polish Slavophiles wanted to compete with the Russians as to which nation was to be 'the leader of the Slavic peoples'. They kept their distance from the Russian ambitions of unifying the Slavic world. At the same time, however, they wanted the Poles to view the Russians as their Slavic brethren, which met strong resistance in a political situation where the Russians were seen as the oppressors of the Poles. This made Polish Slavophilism much weaker than Russian, and pan-Slavic ideas never saw much following. Moreover, it should be emphasized that Polish Romantic anti-occidentalists and Slavophiles never excluded Poland from Europe, and they were even ambivalent as to distancing themselves from Western Europe. Time and time again they declared their adherence to all revolutionary forces in Western Europe. Their declarations were confirmed by deeds, as many exiled Poles during the first half of the nineteenth century took part in French, German and Italian revolutionary movements and fought on the barricades under the rallying cry 'For your freedom and for ours'.[1] In difference to Russian Slavophiles, Polish Romantics never had a thought of 'pulling out of Europe'. They were most committed to the fate of Europe. An expression of this commitment was the idea of Count Adam Czartoryski to create a Pan-European organization, *L'Association Européenne*, aiming at peaceful solutions of conflicts between nations according to international laws and generally accepted moral principles.[2]

It is important to bear in mind that the Polish 'anti-occidentalists' accused Western Europe of betraying values such as freedom, solidarity, democracy, etc., but they considered these values to be universal for the whole of Europe, for both East and West. This means that the Polish 'anti-occidentalists' criticized Western Europe harshly, but never left its community of values. Moreover, their critical arguments had much in common with viewpoints that at the same time were put forth by Western critics of society. Compare, for example, with Scandinavianism described by Bo Stråth, in Chapter 5 of the present volume. The attacks of Polish intellectuals on industrial civilization and the attacks of the Polish Left on capitalism can thus be seen as part of the criticism of society made by European Romanticism. The difference lay in the fact that Western European intellectuals criticized the situation existing in their own society, while the criticism made by Polish Romantics was of a preventive character. The point is whether their attempt to present the lack of industrialization in Poland as a virtue and privilege was not, in fact, caused by a complex due to the economic backwardness of the country.

The Polish Romantics created a dark stereotype of Western Europe. This stereotype was especially used by politicians from the Agrarian Left and the Agrarian Right and writers with strong Catholic orientation. What united these groups was their fear of the ideology of Western liberalism. Catholic writers in particular expressed an ambivalence between their acceptance of Western *culture* identified as the Latin-Christian heritage and their suspicion of Western European *civilization* identified with liberalism and rationalism. However, this dual understanding of Europe has never resulted in such strong juxtaposition of cultural and civilizational concepts of Europe, as happened in the Austrian Empire, where a German *Mitteleuropa* stood for a cultural concept of Europe with its

---

1. A good example thereof is the creation of the organization called *Young Europe* in 1834 by Polish, Italian and German refugees. The organization was led by Mazzini and was a kind of 'Nationalist International.'

2. Czartoryski presented this idea in his 'Essay on Diplomacy', written in connection with the Greek Uprising 1830 (Walicki 1982: 85).

positive connotations and a French Europe for civilizational concept with its traps and dangers (see Weiss in Chapter 11 of the present volume). Such a contrapositioning of Germany and France was unacceptable for the Poles. Germans seen by the Poles as traditional enemies, occupiers and oppressors were frequently perceived as the violators of European cultural values. German nationalism was seen as alien to European culture and the Poles wanted to protect Europe from it (see declarations of this kind quoted in Wapiński 1992: 221). In this respect there was a clear parallel between the Poles and Czechs (see Hroch in Chapter 10 of the present volume). At the same time, for political and cultural reasons, the Poles felt strong links with France. France and England were essential parts in the Polish modern conceptualization of Europe.

The majority of the participants in Polish political life felt themselves connected with Roman Catholicism but they did not emphasize the contrast between their religious values and the heritage of the French Enlightenenment. On the contrary, they tried to reconcile the gospel with the idea of material progress, Christian moral philosophy with economics. The writings by Cieszkowski, Supiński and Kamieński can serve as examples (for an analysis see Jedlicki 1999: 103–65). It was especially striking among those writers who did not go into exile after the Polish uprisings (1830, 1863) but remained in the country. They could experience how the hunger-ridden Polish countryside badly needed economic, social and technological reforms. This made their criticism of the West moderate. Most of the Poles who committed themselves to the social modernization of the country took for granted that it meant development according to the Western European model (Walicki 1994: 26–8). This line of thought was adopted also by the whole intellectual elite after 1863 when the January Uprising was suppressed and the ideas of Polish Romantics lay buried together with the victims of the revolt.

## Changes in the Process of Polish Nation-building and the Discourse on Europe

The intellectuals of the next generation, whose ideas guided Polish society after 1863, called themselves 'Positivists' because of their interest in the Positivist philosophy of Auguste Comte. They were deeply influenced by Western European scientism and Darwinism. They claimed that the only way the Polish nation could survive was by modernizing. This implied developing industry, introducing new agricultural methods, giving access to education for all groups in society and secularizing and democratizing society. For the Positivists, modernization was not a simple imitation of the West, yet the 'originality' of the nation did not hold the same value for them as for the Romantics. They were clearly steering westward. Modern Western Europe was for them a challenge. One of their main ideologists, A. Świętochowski, wrote in 1883:

> There is no choice here; we have only one road left to us: To join in the stream of general civilization, to adapt ourselves to it, to subject our life to the same impulses, the same rhythms which govern the development of other nations. Otherwise, they will never recognize our rights and our needs, and will continue to regard us as if we were some ancient relic which can be comprehensible only with the help of an archaeological dictionary. (Quoted from Jedlicki 1999: 225)

By the end of the nineteenth century Europe became for the Poles a 'civilizational idea', a matter of civilization and modernization. On the other hand, Europe as a 'political idea' lost its significance. This was the time when established state nationalisms and young ethno-nationalisms were fighting each other and began to tear Europe apart. In such a political situation there was no room for dreams about the brotherhood of nations. The idea of Poland's special mission in Europe, the Romantic Messianic belief that the task of the Poles was to sacrifice themselves on the altar of freedom for the sake of all nations, now appeared ridiculous. The Positivists had no sympathy for this kind of thinking. In 1881, A. Świętochowski wrote:

> Then, what was the purpose of all our efforts to make Europe safe, when this Europe does not need us? . . . Let us forsake the illusionary thought that we are an indispensable condition for European equilibrium, an indispensable dam checking the waves of Asian barbarity, the bulwark of the world . . . We should try to justify the Poles' right to existence not by claiming that Europe cannot sleep peacefully without them, . . . but by the fact that they exist for themselves and by themselves, that they form a separate quite numerous nation, that they have their own reasonably well developed civilization, which adds to mankind's progress and enriches it with significant original elements. Those whose right to life stems from these sources, will be understood and finally respected by the whole world. (Quoted from Jedlicki 1999: 224)

Europe identified with a civilization of Western type was also frequently a point of reference for Polish historiography at the end of the nineteenth century. The 'Cracow school of history' of that time (with Szujski, Kalinka and Bobrzyński as leading figures) distanced itself from the Romantics' view on Polish history and historiography. For the Cracow scholars, Europe was synonymous with Western Christianity and Latin civilization. Kalinka wrote in 1879: 'Just as Latin divides Europe from Asia and where knowledge of Latin ends, there was the border of real Europe, thus the difference in alphabets has pushed the nations which adopted them in different directions as to history and civilization' (Quoted from Wierzbicki 1984: 224. Own translation). According to the Cracow school, Poland was a given part of a Europe thus defined. In the seventeenth and eighteenth centuries the country had deviated from the Western model of development because the institutions of the Gentry Republic had degenerated into anarchy. This was the cause of the fall of Poland, thus seen as largely self-inflicted. The Cracow school became extremely important for the future development of Polish historiography. It instilled in the Poles the thesis of the fundamentally Western and Latin character of Polish culture. The subsequent twentieth-century history schools criticized the Cracow school on several points. The 'Warsaw school of history' (with Aszkenazy, Balzer and Halecki) for instance turned against the theory about the anomalous development of the Polish Gentry republic and claimed that it was only one of many variations within Western European development. They were very critical of the thesis of the 'self-inflicted fall'[3] and some historians (for instance those influenced by the popular Neo-Romantic Chołoniewski) went instead for an apologetic line and claimed that the tragic fate of Poland was the consequence of the part played by the country in Europe as a shield and bridge toward the East. The history schools continued to argue whether the development of Poland was partly different from that in Western Europe or completely in line with it, and whether Russia was part of Europe or not, but from the end of the nineteenth century to the Second World War, no one questioned the thesis of Poland's belonging to Western European civilization.

This victory of the occidentalist view of Poland's history was connected with the changes in Polish nation-building. The idea that the Polish nation was a multi-ethnic community, based on memories of the fallen Polish-Lithuanian state, became anachronistic by the end of the nineteenth century. Many factors contributed to this change. One of the most important was the emergence of modern ethnic nationalisms among Lithuanians, Ukrainians and Belorussians, who no longer had any interest in a political community with the Poles. Another important factor was the

3. The historian Konopczyński wrote in 1911: 'We don't want anything in common with a sect of self-floggers, who ascribe to the Poles . . . suicidal perversions' (quoted from Wierzbicki 1984: 305). Author's translation.

social emancipation of Polish peasants and the need to mobilize them for national issues, which could be achieved by turning the ethnic and religious symbols into national symbols. This, however, led to a narrower delimitation of the Polish national community (Törnquist-Plewa 2000). By the end of the nineteenth century the Polish political scene saw the emergence of national ideologists who defined the Polish nation as an ethnic community, based on the Polish language, Catholic religion and common ethnic roots. This new idea soon became popular among broad sections of Polish society and gradually superseded the old political Romantic nationalism, in the end ousting it completely.

The Polish nation, defined as an ethnic community, no longer included Orthodox and Greek-Catholic Slavs, and therefore could without reservations be inscribed into the Western European cultural sphere. It is therefore hardly surprising that the ideological fathers of Polish ethno-nationalism (Dmowski, Popławski, Baliński) were 'occidentalists'. They saw Europe divided into an Eastern and a Western part. East meant Russia, which belonged to Europe geographically but not culturally. Europe meant Western civilization which implied technological progress, prosperity, order, work ethic, respect for the law and refined manners. The East and Russia on the other hand meant economic backwardness and stagnation, poverty, disorder, sloth, lawlessness, alcoholism and debased manners.

The Polish ethno-nationalists were convinced that the place of Poland was in Europe (i.e. in the West), but that the Polish state had disappeared because during the seventeenth century it had deviated from the European norm. Roman Dmowski (1864–1939), the author of the ideology of Polish integral nationalism and the leader of the National-Democratic party, wrote 'Poland fell . . . because . . . it had derailed from its development' (1989: 53). Therefore, the Poles should make all efforts to recover from their civilizational backwardness and again become a complete and respected European nation. The West was a model, but not to be imitated blindly, since national values and traditions were to be respected, and first and foremost the forces of the Polish people were to be relied upon.

It is interesting that Dmowski was able to combine his strongly occidentalist attitude with an acceptance of Polish political dependence on Russia. This was a consequence of his conviction that Russian culture was so alien and unattractive for the Poles that it did not threaten Polish national identity. On the other hand, Poles had to be on their guard with respect to German culture. It was closer to Polish culture and it was a greater danger for the survival of the nation, since it might be attractive. These views express a typical ambivalence in Polish national discourse:

Europe is a model and at the same time a threat for the survival of the national culture.

It is worth pointing out that the strongly occidentalist thinking that dominated from the end of the nineteenth century was discernible among all political groupings from the right to the left.

Occidentalists dominated both among conservatives (e.g. the Cracow School) and nationalists (e.g. National Democracy), and also among socialists. An example of the latter is the literary and social critic Stanisław Brzozowski. He clearly expressed a wish that Poland should modernize with Western Europe as its model. However, he did not, as Dmowski, perceive the force that could generate the dynamics for development in the national idea, but in the ideas held by the working class and socialism. Brzozowski formulated an extremely radical criticism of Polish society and claimed that the Poles had distanced themselves from Europe through their 'degenerated' culture, intellectual laziness and messianic myths. The images of Poland as 'the shield of Europe' or 'the first freedom fighter of Europe' he considered political 'alibis' in order to justify failures and dodge work and responsibility for the economic and cultural development of Europe. He wrote: 'We live with Western culture as a background, but we are not conscious of the hard collective work which is the base for this culture' (1907: 264–5). He called on the Poles to relinquish this role of parasite and in an active and creative way contribute to the development of European culture.

Brzozowski was, however, a child of the turn of the century and well acquainted with Marx's and Nietzsche's criticism of modern society. Therefore, in spite of his occidentalism he did not share the enthusiasm of the Positivists for modern civilization but saw through its pitfalls, contradictions and paradoxes. He did, however, see it as a necessity and a tragic challenge for the Poles. It was only in this way that they could take on their responsibility for the future of humankind.

## The Meanings of Europe in Inter-war Poland

The occidentalist view on the relationship between Poland and Europe gathered strength after the First World War with the rebirth of the Polish state. With independence in 1918 it seemed pointless to continue the discussion that had been going on for over a century about the causes of the fall of the Polish state. The theories that Poland in its development had side-tracked from the West were discarded. The Warsaw School of History was at the forefront with its view that Poland was an integrated part of the Western European cultural sphere. One of its representatives, Oskar Halecki, did want to qualify the thesis of Poland's occidental character with a theory of Poland belonging to Central Europe, a particular region between East and West. Yet this viewpoint did not gain many followers in the inter-war years.[4]

The victory of the occidentalist thesis was largely supported by the outcome of the Polish–Russian war in 1920. The newly-won Polish independence was seriously threatened by Bolshevik Russia. The unexpected victory of the Poles over Russian forces at the battle of Warsaw not only saved the Polish state, but also prevented the Bolshevik Revolution from spreading to Germany. This event was interpreted by the Polish elite as a confirmation of the renewed role of Poland as the bulwark of Europe, as the shield of free, democratic Europe against Eastern barbarism. For the Poles, Bolshevik Russia and later the Soviet Union did not belong to Europe. During the whole inter-war period the Soviet Union constituted a political and military threat against Poland, which within its border held several million Ukrainians and Belorussians. They were exposed to constant calls from Moscow. The praise of Western European civilization in political rhetoric, in schools and in the media, and the stressing of Poland belonging to Europe therefore undeniably had an anti-Soviet and anti-Russian component. It was also intended to give the Ukrainians and Belorussians a 'Western European' identity and thus turn them into loyal subjects of the Polish state. At the same time the old image of Poland as a European bridge between 'West' and 'East' was taken up.

To get an idea about how Europe at that time was presented to the Polish public, we can look at the encyclopaedias that were used in schools. One of the most popular ones, *Świat i Życie* from 1934, shows that Europe was considered a 'cultural and geographic concept', with emphasis on 'cultural'. The basis for the cultural community that was Europe was the Antique and Christian heritage. The most important features of European culture were, according to the encyclopaedia, rationalism, belief in reason linked to the awareness of its limits, a balance between idealism and realism, belief in human dignity. This distinguished European culture from the Far East 'where spirituality and the impressive philosophical depth coexisted with the contempt for efforts in everyday life and for the individual, as well as from the United States of America, where the pursuit of money pushed aside thoughts about moral and

---

4. The 'Central Europe' concept revived among the oppositional circles in communist Poland in the 1980s, but its popularity diminished radically during the 1990s (i.e., in the post-communist period) .

spiritual values' (Encyclopaedia *Świat i Życie* 1934: 280). The authors of this encyclopaedia declared that the term 'European culture' first and foremost referred to the culture created in Western Europe, i.e. the old Western Roman Empire. Thus Russia and the Balkans, belonging to the Eastern Roman, Byzantine sphere, were outside the European cultural sphere. Poland was declared to belong to the West because of its 'culture type'. At the same time, however, the authors pointed out that the border between Eastern and Western Rome ran through Poland's territory. The task of Poland was then to spread the ideas of Western European culture in the East (ibid: 278–9). The information on Europe in inter-war encyclopaedias was not only in the occidentalist spirit but also extremely Eurocentric. One could for instance read that every educated inhabitant in Europe 'is proud and honoured to be European'. It was pointed out that it was a considerable compliment to call somebody 'a genuine European'. Moreover the idea was promoted about the need to create a United States of Europe in order to counterbalance 'growing powers outside Europe' (ibid: 273–4).

Europe was thus an important reference in the shaping of the identity of the Polish reborn state. The relationship with Europe and European culture was, however, not so easy as the encyclopaedias and schoolbooks made it. Two dilemmas still haunted the Polish élite. One was the question as to whether it was possible to create a culture which was national and at the same time 'European' in the universal sense. Most considered these two factors difficult to combine. Therefore, there were those who advocated a national native culture, inspired by Romanticism and peasant culture (cf. Jedlicki 1995) and those who, like the innovative writer Witold Gombrowicz, were of the opinion that a Polish artist or writer could become universal only if he managed to liberate himself from the burden of the Polish cultural heritage (cf. Stala 1999).

The other old question that preoccupied the Polish elite was that of the economic, technological and educational modernization of Poland. When the independent state and national institutions finally were in place this goal appeared realistic. During the twenty years between the wars the educational level was significantly raised and important investments were made in industrial development. The starting point, however, was so low and the consequences of the depression of 1929 so harsh that growth was very slow. Poland on the eve of the Second World War was therefore a semi-modern country, where islands of modern industrial centres were surrounded by an agrarian society with subsistence agriculture (cf. Jedlicki 1993: 83) The big difference in economic development between Poland and Western Europe made the Poles feel that they were the periphery of Europe, which contributed to their inferiority complex. A testimony of how an educated Pole during the inter-war years experienced the encounter with what he called Europe (Western Europe) can be found in Czesław Miłosz's *Native Realm*. This book was written in the 1950s but it contains Miłosz's reminiscences of his first travels in Western Europe in the early 1930s. He describes how he as a poor young student arrived in towns and places that he had read much about. Enraptured he entered cathedrals and museums, read Latin inscriptions, and felt everywhere that the surroundings were familiar. He also attended lectures at the Sorbonne and followed cultural debates in Paris, and he concluded that these activities very much resembled those in Warsaw. The cultural community stretched far, but that could not prevent his strong feelings of alienation. As a visitor from the distant periphery of Europe he felt both 'native and alien':

> Undoubtedly I could call Europe my home, but it was a home that refused to acknowledge itself as a whole . . . it classified its population into two categories: members of the family (quarrelsome but respectable) and poor relations (Miłosz 1981: 2).

The feeling of being an unwelcome poor relative from the forgotten countryside grew when he saw the treatment given to Polish seasonal labour by the French police in the streets of Strasbourg, and the poverty of Poles looking for work in Paris, and when he noticed on a bridge near Basle a sign with the text: 'No entry for Gypsies, Poles, Romanians and Bulgarians'. The contrast between the prosperity, order and security in the West and the poverty, disorder and insecurity in Poland was very painful for a Polish intellectual. Miłosz writes: 'Poland weighed upon us' (ibid: 138). The humiliation was so profound that it led to the yearning to change homeland, to become someone else. Miłosz claims in his book that this feeling comes to many Poles (and to other Eastern Europeans) and may find expression in a 'spasmodic patriotism' which is compensation for an inner betrayal.

The well-ordered and prosperous states of Western Europe caused admiration in the Polish intellectual, but also anger that these riches were built upon the profit from others – by conquests and exploitations of colonies – and that no one seemed to remember that fact (ibid: 139–40).

Can Western Europe be a model for Poland? Is its culture, its ideas a universal model that can be followed everywhere?

For Miłosz and many other Polish intellectuals in the 1930s this was not an obvious truth, especially as the political events in Europe at that time and the cultural atmosphere (as expressed in the writings of Ortega y Gasset or Spengler about the 'decline of the West') contributed to the feeling of an approaching catastrophe. The universal value of the Western European model became even less obvious after the horrors of the Second World War and the communist dictatorship in Poland. Therefore Miłosz could, in a poem written much later, in 1980, summarize his – i.e., the Polish intellectual's – encounter with Europe as follows:

> Bypassing rue Descarets
> I descended toward the Seine, shy, a traveler,
> A young barbarian just come to the capital of the world
>
> We were many, from Jassy and Koloshvar, Wilno and Bucharest
> Saigon and Marrakesh,
> Ashamed to remember the customs of our homes,
>
> I had left the cloudy provinces behind
> I entered the universal, dazzled and desiring.
>
> Soon enough, many from Jassy and Koloshvar, or Saigon or Marrakesh
> Would be killed because they wanted to abolish the customs of their homes.
>
> Soon enough their peers were seizing power
> In order to kill in the name of the universal, beautiful ideas.
>
> Meanwhile the city behaved in accordance with its nature,
> Rustling with throaty laughter in the dark . . .
>
> (the poem *Bypassing Rue Descartes*, in Miłosz 1996: 271–2)

## The Meanings of Europe During the Years of Communist Rule

During the Second World War the Poles experienced all the horrors of war: terror, mass death and mass destruction. But the end of the war, too, brought with it new shattering experiences. The Allies left the decision about the fate of Poland to Stalin, which implied changes of borders, population transfers, loss of sovereignty and the introduction of the communist system. The inter-war image of Europe as consisting of concentric circles of nations with a centre in the West was replaced by a representation of Europe sharply divided into two separate parts, West and East, each with its separate centre. The Iron Curtain had 'descended on the continent'. Without having been consulted, the Poles landed up in the East under the control of Moscow, which for them meant landing up outside Europe.

All these events led to a deep crisis in the European consciousness of the Poles, noticeable in the political and cultural debate in the years 1945–1950 (Gosk 1985). The inter-war idea, in which Poland's belonging to Europe and Poland's role as the shield of Europe had been taken for granted was declared a tragic illusion. Their Western European allies had left Poland and other Central and Eastern European countries to their fate. A prevailing opinion was that Europe had betrayed the ideals and values it always had defended, i.e. freedom and democracy. Obvious expressions of this treason were the concessions to Hitler at Munich 1938, military passivity when Poland was attacked in 1939 and the division of Europe at Yalta in 1945. Europe as a political authority was just a memory. The Continent became an object for horse-trading between the great powers. Moreover, the image of Europe as a model of civilization was crushed. The admired 'civilized' Europe had during the twentieth century given birth to one of the greatest barbarisms, nazism. After the Second World War, there was everywhere in Europe a moral crisis and a crisis of the values that had been considered 'European': democratic institutions, rationalism, education, humanist culture. These had not been able to resist the ravaging of 'barbarism'.

This crisis of the European value system, extremely acute in Poland which had suffered severely from the war and its consequences, facilitated the establishment of the communist regime. The prevailing feeling among the Poles that they had been 'deserted' by Europe contributed to an inclination to listen to communist arguments that only the Soviet Union could guarantee the new Polish borders. The collapse of European values had a particularly strong effect on intellectuals, and many later analyses have demonstrated that this fact contributed to the support that a part of them gave to the communist system. (Kowalczyk 1990, compare with Miłosz 1980). For some, Marxist ideas appeared a possible alternative to the compromised democracy, a remedy against the nihilism of values or a historical necessity after all the events of the war. Moreover, the communists promised a speedy reconstruction and modernization, as well as full employment and free health care and education. Almost everyone could accept such a programme. However, in the 1950s it became clear that the only and absolutely primary goal for the regime was to monopolize power for the Communist party, not to strive towards social justice or economic progress (Jedlicki 1993: 84). The speedy industrialization of the country did not bring the expected higher living standards. The economy stagnated and the gap between Eastern and Western Europe regarding economic development increased significantly. Thus, the communist system increased the old difference between the centre and the periphery in Europe. The communists tried to prevent Western influences reaching the Poles. Until 1970 it was almost impossible for ordinary Poles to travel to the West. The isolation was further strengthened by limiting the teaching of Western languages only to the theoretical sections in upper secondary schools. In historiography and teaching of history, the inter-war Eurocentrism and the 'dogma' of Poland as part of the Western European culture was sharply criticized. However, no thesis about Poland's belonging to the East was offered instead (it was probably judged as provoking for the large part of the society and considered too difficult to defend), but an ethnocentric line was advocated. Poland was the focus of interest in education and research, and nationalistic ideas were propagated in forms controlled by the regime. In addition, as a kind of lip-service to the Soviet Union, the Russian language and culture were promoted.

However, the Russian-Soviet culture was in Polish minds strongly linked to the political system that had been imposed by Moscow. It was seen as alien and thus rejected. Moscow was reluctantly accepted as the political centre, but never as the cultural one. When the Poles looked for cultural inspiration and models they looked not eastward, but still toward Paris, London, Rome and New York. Through the Roman Catholic Church, which continued to stand for the fact that Poland was part of Western Christianity, through relatives that had emigrated and sometimes through their own travels, the Poles kept in touch with the West. The contrast they experienced between prosperity and individual freedom in the West on the one hand, and misery and oppression in the East on the other, turned them strongly pro-Western. The concept of Europe – often referred to as 'the West' – became for the average Pole a symbol for prosperity and freedom, a dream and an unreachable goal. There were many expressions for this in the popular culture of communist Poland, in popular jokes, in texts of semi-official or underground character, such as cabaret texts and rock lyrics.[5] It should however be stressed that the 'pro-European' attitude of the Poles was often accompanied by scepticism as to the will of Western Europeans to commit themselves to their cause.

---

5. One example of it is a rock lyric 'My street' from 1980, which says: 'My street is divided by a wall/The right side is shining with neon signs/The left side is darkened days and nights/I watch both sides from behind the blinds'. Quoted from Micińska (1999: 57).

The longing for Europe was not for the average Pole linked to a deeper reflection upon the meaning of the concept of Europe. Such a reflection can be found among Polish intellectuals: in articles, essays and literary texts, often published abroad or underground. The limits of this chapter allow us to mention only one such text, 'A High Wall' from 1987 by Adam Zagajewski. The text is a concise analysis of the development of the Polish oppositional intelligentsia and its views on Europe. Zagajewski writes about 'the therapeutic value of slavery' which helped Polish intellectuals to overcome value relativism or value nihilism. 'In order to endure slavery you need armour, you need values and the hope to survive in them and through them' (1987: 13). This intelligentsia claimed that it found in the European cultural heritage such values as belief in truth and justice, freedom, human dignity and democracy. In the name of these values the opposition fought against the regime, and the bravest were ready to give their lives for them. The belief in these values meant for them the belief in Europe and the yearning for Europe. At the same time they were not naive and knew that Western European intellectuals questioned those very values and looked for new ideals, for instance in China, Nicaragua or Vietnam. They were conscious of invoking 'a figure of Europe from days gone by, . . . a model to live by, as an ideal' (ibid: 27). Europe meant for them a community of culture and values, and as such, it was the ground for their hopes.

## After 1989 – The Concept of Europe in Times of Transformation

With the understanding of Europe as a moral community, as described above, the Polish elite entered a new phase of Polish history after the fall of communism in 1989. The head of the first Polish non-communist government Tadeusz Mazowiecki said in his speech to the European Council (in Strasbourg):

> What do we [the Poles] bring to Europe? . . . The fact that we managed to survive as a community is among others due to our deep attachment to certain institutions and values that belong to the European norm. It is due to religion, Church, attachment to democracy and pluralism, to human rights and citizen rights, to the idea of solidarity. Even if we could not practice these values wholly . . . we cherished them, loved them and fought for them, . . . we know their price. We know the price of the European norm . . . Thus we bring to Europe our belief in Europe. (1992: 4)

Mazowiecki formulated also a slogan about Poland's 'return to Europe' which became extremely popular. The return was not interpreted as a sudden event, as a result of the fall of the Iron Curtain, but as a process that was launched, a project that was to be implemented in several areas. From a political viewpoint it meant the return of Poland to the European arena of independent and democratic states. For the economy, it referred to the introduction of a market economy and economic modernization. For culture, it meant a settling of accounts with the mental and social heritage of communism and a broad opening towards the West (intensive cultural contacts, adoption of educational models, etc.). The slogan 'return to Europe' thus became linked to the transformation, and because of the unavoidable difficulties and social problems it brought, the enthusiasm it had originally stirred up gradually diminished. There were also other reasons for this. The image of the earlier so idealized Europe became more realistic. With intensified contacts with the West, many Poles became painfully aware both of their economic backwardness and provincialism and of the lukewarm reception Western Europeans gave to Eastern Europeans knocking at their door, the contempt for 'illegal Eastern labour' and the fear of the Eastern European 'Mafia'. These experiences led to the feeling of being Europe's 'unwanted child', and to the deepening of the latent Polish inferiority complex. A series of sociological inquiries from the 1990s showed that the Poles carried strong negative stereotypes about themselves. When asked to rank Poland in Europe according to economy and civilization, they tended to place it far down and often underestimated their own country (Skotnicka-Iliasiewicz 1998: 109–25). This lack of self-confidence was also noted in the Polish attitude in the debate on the future adhesion to the European Union. (For an extensive overview of this debate see Kolarska-Bobinska, 1999.)

Polish 'Euro-enthusiasts' who advocate a speedy integration into the EU are deeply critical of Polish society and accuse it of being conservative, limited, fanatically religious, nationalistic, burdened with the heritage of the past and immature. Every negative or indifferent attitude toward the EU is interpreted as a sign of Polish ignorance and backwardness.[6] Polish 'Euro-sceptics' on the other land, who are either against Poland's adhesion to the EU or want to postpone it into an undefined future are afraid that Poland will be 'degraded' in the EU and completely controlled both politically and economically by Western powers. Some 'Euro-sceptics' also fear that the Poles, once they are in the EU, will lose

6. This kind of statement is for example to be found in the daily *Gazeta Wyborcza,* the main forum for the Euro-enthusiasts.

those values traditionally associated with Polish national identity, e.g. the cult of national history and tradition, Catholic piousness, etc.[7] Thus the 'Euro-sceptics' bring up questions that we recognize from earlier on in Poland's history, for instance how the modernization with the West as a model threatens Polish originality, or what function Poland has had and still has in Europe. They are eager to stress Poland's merits for the sake of Europe.[8] There are groups still on the look-out for a mission for Poland in Europe. Catholic intellectuals grouped around the *Fronda* review claim for instance that Poland's role is to be a vehicle for Eastern European spirituality directed towards the materialistic West. Thus they create a new version of the role of Poland as a bridge between East and West. Other groupings, such as the KPN party, seek for Poland a political mission that consists in setting up, together with the Baltic states and the Ukraine, a security system against Moscow, a kind of new 'bulwark'.[9] The attitudes of both Euro-enthusiasts and Euro-sceptics reveal a profound inferiority complex and insecurity with regard to the status of Poland in Europe and the strength of Polish identity.

There are, however, many moderate attitudes in Poland as well, even if they are not the loudest ones in the debates. Those that express such attitudes could be called 'Euro-rationalists'. They view Poland's adhesion to the EU as necessary in order to save the country from marginalizing and speed up its modernization. But they want to prepare the adhesion both through advanced economic transformation and firm support for adhesion among the society at large. For them Europe is a model, yet not to be imitated thoughtlessly but modified in a creative way, in a way that fits Polish society. This 'Euro-rationalistic' attitude is discernible in the Polish Catholic Church's official view on Poland's accession to the EU (cf. articles in Dylus 1999) even if there is no lack of Euro-sceptics within the Church on the grass-root level. The 'Euro-rationalists' do not want to identify Europe with the EU. Referring to the statement by Pope John Paul II on 7 June 1991, they express the opinion that Poland needs to join the EU, but not 'Europe', since the Poles 'always have taken part

---

7. The main medial channels for Euro-sceptics are the radio station 'Maryja' and the daily *Nasz Dziennik*, both connected with fundamentalistic Catholic circles.

8. Skotnicka-Iliasiewicz quotes interviews containing such opinions as 'It was we who defended . . . who bled . . .' (1998: 142).

9. This refers to the so-called 'Inter Sea initiative' – League of Political Parties in the Inter Sea Countries from 1993. It received considerable interest in Lithuania and the Ukraine, but the Polish governing circles did not support it and the initiative had no larger political significance (Zarycki 1997: 103).

in the creation of Europe' (Życiński 1999: 208). The attitude of 'Euro-rationalists' can be seen as an attempt to overcome the Polish inferiority complex.

The Polish discourse on Europe changed in the course of the 1990s. In the beginning of the decade the intellectuals' definition of Europe as a cultural and moral community prevailed. In such a Europe there was room for the Poles as creators and defenders of European values. However, by the end of the decade politicians and economics experts began to set an agenda for the European debate and the concept of Europe began to be synonymous with that of the EU. The debate on Europe became a debate about adjusting to the EU and about Polish–EU relations. In this way the identifications of the Poles with Europe was once again put on trial. What will Europe mean for the Poles during the first decades of this new century? It probably depends whether Poland joins the EU and on what terms, or if it remains outside.

## Concluding Remarks

East and West, Europe and Russia have been permanent points of reference in Polish national discourse. They can be seen as marks of identity and have been well used in Polish-nation building. While the delimitation against Russia is sharp, Europe remains something that Poles want to be part of but never quite are. The identification with Europe is made difficult by the fact that Poles do not feel accepted by those they want to identify with. The consequence is that the Poles get a status of 'strangers', and land up somewhere 'in-between'. This leads to a considerable ambivalence towards Europe. It is expressed among other things in the two attitudes presented above, occidentalism and ethnocentrism, which exist side by side in spite of their inner contradictions. While the occidentalists see the past and future of Poland as part of Europe, the ethnocentrists express their fear of Europe. The ambivalence is often painful and can lead to feelings that may complicate the communication between individuals, groups and communities. The Polish attitude to Europe presents whole emotional syndromes described by psychologists as 'the complex of an unwanted child'. There is longing and unrequited love, distrust, fear, inferiority feelings and a compensatory need for self-assertion. In view of the future cooperation in Europe it is important not to forget these socio-psychological aspects in the relations between the EU and Poland, between the 'European core' and its periphery.

# References

Brzozowski, S. (1910), *Legenda Młodej Polski*, Lwów: Księgarnia Polska Bernarda Połonieckiego.

Dmowski, R. (1989), *Myśli nowoczesnego Polaka*, Warsaw: Grunwald. First edition 1904.

Geremek, B. (1989), 'Średniowiecze w rozwoju kultury polskiej', in J. Kłoczowski, (ed.), *Uniwersalizm i swoistość kultury polskiej*, Lublin: R.W. KUL.

Gosk, H. (1985), *W kęgu 'Kuźnicy': Dyskusje krytyczno-literackie lat 1945–1948*, Warszaw: IBL.

Jedlicki, J. (1993) 'Poland's perpetual return to Europe', *Cross Currents: A Yearbook of Central European Culture*, v. 12.

—— (1995) 'Polish Concepts of Native Culture', in Goldblatt, Harvey (eds), *National Character and National Ideology in Interwar Eastern Europe*, New Haven: Yale University Press.

—— (1999), *A Suburb of Europe. Nineteenth-Century Polish Approaches to Western Civilization*, Budapest: Central European University Press.

Kizwalter, T. (2000), *O nowoczesnoœci narodu. Przypadek Polski*, Warsaw: Wyd.-SIC.

Kolarska-Bobińska, Lena (ed.) (1999), *Polska Eurodebata*, Warszaw: Instytut Spraw Publicznych.

Kowalczyk, A.S. (1990), *Kryzys świadomosci europejskiej w eseistyce polskiej lat 1945–1977*, Warszaw: IBL.

Krasucki, J. (1980), *Obraz Zachodu w twórczości romantyków polskich*, Poznań: Wyd. Poznanskie.

Krzyżaniakowa, J. (1992), 'Poland as *Antemurale Christianitatis*: the Political and Ideological Foundations of the Idea', *Polish Western Affairs*, XXXIII(2).

Mazowiecki, T. (1992), 'Powrót do Europy' in O.S. Międzynarodowych (ed.), *Polska w Europie*, April 1992.

Micińska, M. (1999), 'The Dual Image of the West in the Eyes of the Poles', *Slavica Lundensia*, 19.

Miłosz, C. (1980), *Captive Mind*, London: Penguin.

—— (1981), *Native Realm*, London: Penguin.

—— (1996), *Poezje wybrane: Selected Poems*, Kraków: Wyd. Literackie.

Möller, P.-U. (1999), 'Russian Identity as an East-West Controversy', *Slavica Lundensia*, 19.

Skotnicka-Iliasiewicz, E. (1998), *Powrót czy droga w nieznane: Europejskie dylematy Polaków*, Warsaw: Centrum Europejskie Uniwersytetu Warszawskiego.

Stala, K. (1999) 'Inventing the Wheel? The Postmodern Catching up with Witold Gombrowicz', in B. Stråth and N. Witoszek (eds), *The Postmodern Challenge: Perspectives East and West*, Postmodern Studies 27.

'Świat i życie. Zarys encyklopedyczny współczesnej wiedzy i kultury', Lwów – Warszaw: Książnica – Atlas.

Tazbir, J. (1987), *Polskie Przedmurze chrześcijańskiej Europy: Mity i rzeczywistość*, Warszawa.

—— (1998), *W pogoni za Europą*, Warsaw: Wyd. SIC.

Törnquist-Plewa, B. (1992), *The Wheel of Polish Fortune*, Lund: Slavonic Department, Lund University.

—— (1998), 'Cultural and National Identifications in Borderlands – Reflections on Central Europe', in K.-G. Karlsson, B. Petersson and B. Törnquist-Plewa (eds), *Collective Identities in the Era of Transformation*, Lund: Lund University Press.

—— (2000), 'Contrasting Ethnic Nationalisms: Poland, Hungary, Slovakia and Czech Republic', in S. Barbour and C. Carmichael (eds), *Language and Nationalism in Europe*, Oxford: Oxford University Press.

Walicki, A. (1982), *Philosophy and Romantic Nationalism: The Case of Poland*, Oxford: Oxford University Press.

—— (1994), *Poland between East and West*, Cambridge, Mass.: Harvard University Press.

Wapiński, R. (1992), 'The Question of Civilizational Options in Polish Political Thought', *Polish Western Affairs*, XXXIII(2).

Wierzbicki, A. (1984), *Zachód w koncepcjach dziejów Polski*, Warsaw: PIW.

Wolff, L. (1994), *Inventing Eastern Europe: The Map of Civilization on the Mind of the Enlightenment*, Stanford: Stanford University Press.

Zagajewski, A. (1987), 'A High Wall', *Cross Currents*, 6.

Zarycki, T. (1997) 'Attitudes Towards West and East as a Main Element of the Central European Identity', in G. Gorzelak and B. Jałowiecki (eds), *The Identity of Central Europe*, Warsaw: Europejski Instytut Rozwoju Regionalnego I Lokalnego.

Zientara, B. (1973), 'Cudzoziemcy w Polsce X–XV wieku: Ich rola w zwierciadle polskiej opinii średniowiecznej', in Z. Stefanowska, (ed.), *Swojskość i cudzoziemszczyzna w dziejach kultury polskiej*, Warsaw: PWN.

Życiński, J. (1999), 'Koncepcja zjednoczonej Europy w nauczaniu Jana Pawla II', in A. Dylus (ed.), *Europa: Fundamenty jedności*, Warsaw: Wyd. Fundacji ATK.

# –10–

# The Czech Discourse on Europe, 1848–1948

*Miroslav Hroch*

To analyse the meaning of Europe in the Czech national context, it is vital to distinguish two levels: first, the general placement of 'Us' into a broader, macroregional and continental context, and secondly, the discourse on Europe, which is explicitly oriented to the term itself. For this reason, this contribution is divided into two parts, the first giving an overview of Czech history, the second based on sources.

## A Czech Overview

Similar to all European national movements, the Czech national movement offered a new, modern identity and had to define this identity in order to place the Czech nation into the broader regional and continental context. This search was complicated by the fact that the definition of the Czech place in Europe was characterized by severe ambivalence borne from history and geography. This involves a number of factors.

First, since the Middle Ages, the Czech lands were included in the Holy Roman Empire, but they were never fully integrated into this Empire and kept their status of state. As a result of this, German historians, who identified their national history with the history of the Holy Roman Empire, regarded Czech history as a part of German history, while Czech historians, for their part, constructed their own national history independent of Germans.

Second, from a linguistic point of view, the Czechs were a Slavic nation and had their own literary language from the late Middle Ages, but they were entwined in the German linguistic environment and culture. Third, Czech lands, and especially Bohemia, constitute a historical and closed geographical territory with an extraordinary stable political border and administrative structure, but this territory has been inhabited not just by the Czech-speaking majority, but also by a German-speaking minority which in the mid-nineteenth century opted for German national identity.

Fourth, the Czechs inhabited a territory that could be classified neither as the 'West' nor as the 'East' of Europe. Fifth, almost all the population of Bohemia were Roman Catholics, but in the fifteenth and sixteenth centuries there was a Protestant majority which was forced to convert to Catholicism after 1620. Under these conditions, it is not surprising that we can distinguish five competing identities in Bohemia at the threshold of the inauguration of the Czech national movement:

- an Austrian dynastic state identity
- an identity with the historical land of the kingdom of Bohemia
- a Slavic identity
- a linguistically-defined Czech (originally ethnic) identity
- a linguistically-defined German (originally ethnic) identity.

The decisive turn came with the 1848 Revolution, when only two of these identities survived – the Czech and German ones – and were no longer defined as ethnic but as political identities. Since then, one can observe in Bohemia a competition and political struggle between the German element, represented by a wealthy bourgeoisie and a section of the old elites, and the Czech element. In opposition to the apparent cultural and material superiority of Germans, Czech intellectuals and politicians tried as early as the 1860s to find spiritual inspiration and cultural support in non-German parts of Europe, first in Russia and France, and then later also in the Anglo-Saxon world. Further, before the end of the nineteenth century, the literature of other 'small nations' was systematically translated and reviewed, including that of Scandinavian and Polish writers. This naturally predestined the European orientation of Czech culture – or better, that of leading Czech intellectuals and artists. They did not accept the alternative of becoming merely 'translated Germans' but rather demonstrated their ability to create an original national culture.

Some kind of cultural syncretism emerged, where the Slavic component was also strongly represented. Nevertheless, the position between East and West often drew the reflection: are we Eastern or Western people? We are partially Western and partially Eastern but we inherited from both parts their feebleness, wrote the poet J.S. Machar at the threshold of the twentieth century. It was not easy to solve the problem by introducing the construct of Central Europe because this term was, at least until the First World War, filled by the German nationalist concept of 'Mitteleuropa'.

At the end of the nineteenth century, Czech society achieved a full social structure and was differentiated into several political streams corresponding to the general trend of European political development. Czech politicians, like the politicians of all Europe's fully-formed nations, regarded their nation as a 'personality' and demanded full equality with other nations irrespective of their size, including also the German nation. This demand was unacceptable to the German 'Herrenvolk' mentality, which resulted in an increasing national tension. In spite of this high self-consciousness, Czech politics did not formulate any demand for political independence until 1914.

This changed with the First World War: increasing numbers of intellectuals and politicians joined the group around T.G. Masaryk who decided to emigrate and to support the entente powers in order to fight for national independence. The Czech syncretism of Western and Eastern cultural orientation seemed to be confirmed by political developments. Nevertheless, Masaryk won the acknowledgement of independence after the October revolution, only through the decision of the Western powers and under condition of the waging of an open war between the Czech legions and the Bolshevik troops in Siberia. This fact was decisive for the political and cultural orientation of the Czechoslovak state after 1918 in favour of the Western powers and, above all, in favour of France. To the large majority of Czechs the meaning of Europe was limited to the West.

It is in this sense that one must interpret the strong accentuation of the need for the improvement of Czech culture in order to correspond to 'European criteria'. Nevertheless, some relics of Slavism remained after the October revolution: cultural contacts with the Soviet Union were rather strong and even if political sympathy with the new regime were originally limited to the extreme left, the defence treaty with both France and the Soviet Union from 1935 was accepted by the majority of the population.

The 1938 Munich Conference and Agreement severely challenged the Czech sense of Western identity: people felt betrayed by the Western powers. This caused a new revival of Slavism manifested in sympathy for the Soviet Union among the majority of the population and by no means only among leftists. These sympathies seemed to be confirmed by the results of the Second World War.

New reflections concerning the Czech place in Europe emerged. The slogan, originally formulated by President Beneš, was very influential: under present conditions, we are not living between the West and the East, but between Germany and Russia (Soviet Union). This concept was accompanied by the myth about the Czech mission in post-war Europe:

to become a bridge which could mediate an exchange of both cultural and political values between West and East.

Events turned this in a very different way. Europe was divided by the cold war and Czechoslovakia was included in the Soviet sphere and classified, above all in the West, as a part of the East. This was not accepted by the Czech population: the concept of Central or Middle Europe was used, even though in a very unreflective sense. Even the official state ideology never dared to qualify Czechs as part of Eastern Europe. The Eastern orientation was substituted by Slavism (itself becoming increasingly artificial) and by the construct 'community of socialist countries'.

During the 1980s, some dissenting intellectuals formulated a new version of the myth of Central Europe. It was based on reflection on one aspect of the 'tragedy' of the region: the West's non-acceptance of the Czechs, who were not a part of the East, but maintained Western traditions under Soviet rule, which was itself the historical mission of Central Europe. In the early 1990s, to be European meant also to be above all Central European (as a part of Western culture).

After 1990, this ideological concept lost its political anti-communist connotation, but it survived transformed in two fashions. For the main part, it contributed some feelings of value to the general consciousness of the self-evident allegiance to Central Europe, but for the other part, it degenerated into a nostalgic conception of Central Europe, which was interpreted as a lost Habsburg heritage and is still presented as such in the revue *Střední Evropa* (Central Europe) by a group of conservative intellectuals. Some of this group use the concept of Central Europe not as a complementary element of the European identity as represented by the EU, but on the contrary, according to their opinion, the traditional, 'true' European values, represented by the Central European heritage, are violated by EU technocracy and centralism. It is difficult to say just how strongly these ideas influenced Czech public opinion.

## The 'Narrow' Meaning of Europe

The second part of this contribution aims to analyse the meaning of Europe in the narrow sense by concentrating on the term 'Europe', itself. Only those texts are included wherein 'Europe' is explicitly verbalized and defined, above all in relation to the emerging modern Czech national identity. What will not be included is the general 'European horizon', the interest of Czech writers and politicians in other countries, and in the European context of their writings, translations and other activities.

A specific limitation concerns the fact that the word 'Europe' was very frequently used as *terminus technicus* of geography or even politics, without being conceptualized as a classificatory scheme. Reflections on Europe as a quality, as a dimension of national identity were rather rare in Czech discourse, compared for instance to similar reflections on the relationship with Germans, or on the Slavic identity. This under-representation did not change until the 1990s when, on the contrary, the concept of Europe became a very fashionable component of cultural and political rhetoric.

The presented results are not based on an exhaustive study of all manner of sources, but rather on a selection of texts, which include the most important politicians and intellectuals between the mid-nineteenth and mid-twentieth centuries. For this reason, no quantification could be used and the analysis aims to find out basic trends, types and periods. It is presumed that these results will be corrected or modified through systematic research, which will analyse newspapers and journals, etc. This is not only presumable, but also desirable. With few exceptions (cf. Hahnová 1997a) no such research exists in the Czech republic.

## What is Europe?

The general overview of the development of the meaning of Europe is based on data from three national Encyclopaedias, each of which being of representative importance to Czech national culture. The oldest one was published from the early 1860s, the second around the year 1900 and the third one at the end of 1920s. Naturally, we find in these texts an extensive geographical, biological, etc. description of Europe, but besides this are also some significant features of what is regarded as the proper meaning, the 'quality' of Europe. This meaning was different in the various Encyclopaedias and these differences are rather symptomatic.

The oldest Encyclopaedia stressed that 'Europe was exceeding all other continents through its power and the level of education' and was somehow 'predestined' by its geographical position to become the centre of trade and civilization of all the world. This modernizing understanding of Europe was accompanied by the opinion that Europe was developing towards a civil society, equality of citizens and peasant liberation – all these progressive changes were regarded as resulting from the French revolution ('Evropa', in: *Riegrův slovník naučný, II*, 1862: 528). This article expressed the opinion of the editor, František L. Rieger, who soon became the leading personality among the Czech liberals.

The Otto-Encyclopaedia shared the opinion that Europe exceeded all other continents and that it was moving toward civic freedoms, but it put the origins of the idea of freedom in the Middle Ages, when Europe was fighting against the 'barbarians' from the East – Huns, Mongolians and Turks. Besides this, we find a further specification: Europe as 'some sort of federation of nations' whose further improvement depended on the opportunity given to each of these nations to contribute to European development. In this process of improvement and growth, an important role would fall upon 'young nations' and their ability to be more efficient than 'older' ones, who could sometimes be in decline. ('Evropa' in: *Ottův slovník naučný, VIII*, 1997 [1894]: 854–5). This Encyclopaedia expressed the concepts of the new generation of the Czech positivist scholars.

The Masaryk Encyclopaedia again included the meaning of Europe as being the most prosperous among all the continents (with a short reference to North America), and as being a continent of many nations and nation states. The central characteristic was nevertheless regarded as European cultural specificity based on Christian tradition and on highly developed historicism. In this respect it mentioned the discussion on whether Russia belonged to Europe – or was outside of it ('Evropa', in *Masarykův slovník naučný, II*, 1926). This Encyclopaedia claimed to represent the official (political) concepts of the newly formed Czechoslovakia, but it did not necessarily express the opinions of scholars.

The development of the meaning of Europe roughly corresponds to the development of the priorities in Czech national discourse: from the successful struggle for civil rights through the successful struggle for national emancipation to the efforts at Europeanization of cultural life in the newly founded nation state. Naturally, this is only a hypothetical generalization and it will be the aim of following reflections to assess if the shift of emphases observed in the three Encyclopaedias really corresponded to the general trend of Czech discourse on Europe.

Besides the analysis of the change in time, it is preferable to break up the analysis according to the three basic meanings of 'Europeanness':

- Europe as a normative context and moral engagement
- Europe as a value to be protected
- being proud of belonging to Europe.

Nevertheless, we cannot neglect the fact that there were also alternatives to European identity, which are presented below.

*The Czech Discourse on Europe, 1848–1948*

## Europe as a Normative Context and Moral Engagement

The conservative Czech historian, W.W. Tomek, included in his memoirs an ironically written episode from the 1848 Revolution in Prague. In an almost empty street, a young man started to built a barricade. Some anxious women tried to persuade him to stop doing it, but he answered with a high voice: 'Let me to do it, all Europe is watching us' (Tomek 1904: 286–7). Tomek did not know that these words could be heard rather often in Vienna and other cities at that time. Nevertheless, he preserved important evidence that among the Czech population also, some people spontaneously regarded Europe – the revolutionary Europe, not the feudal one – as a normative model. This included both political identification with Europe and the concept of European identity as a moral imperative of their behaviour.

There is no spontaneity without previous communication. The founder of the modern Czech political programme, journalist Karel Havlíček-Borovský, in his articles in 1848–49 presented Europe as a protagonist of progress on the way 'from absolutism towards liberty'. (Havlíček-Borovský 1956: 409). Further, both Czechs and other Slavic nations had to join this progressive path. František Palacký, the then most prominent historian and unofficial leader of the Czech national movement, expressed a similar view in the manifesto of the Slavic Congress, which opened in Prague in June 1848. According to this proclamation, Slavic nations sought to participate in the 'new history of Europe' because they were definitely not enemies of freedom (Palacký 1977: 183–4).

Dreaming about establishing a Czech democratic republic, the radical democrat Emanuel Arnold related his dream to Europe: this republic would adopt 'European ideas' and spread its light through Europe (Arnold 1848: 162). Some years before 1848, a small group of Czech democrats had already considered the necessity to 'concentrate themselves around the European family as their centre of action', following the example of the Poles (Záček 1948: 202).

With some exaggeration, we can say that Europe entered Bohemia for the first time through the revolutionary process and the struggle for constitutional rights. Therefore, it is understandable that very soon some patriots tried to take credit for the fact that in earlier times, Czechs were pioneers of the European way towards freedom: the Czech nation was the first one in Europe which started (in the Hussite movement) the struggle for freedom against absolutism. It was a struggle not only for their own freedom, but also for the liberation of 'all nations' (Sojka 1953: 6).

Europe was a normative context for the Czechs not only as the model of civic virtues, but also as the focal point of education. According to F.L. Rieger, who later became the national leader after Palacký, all European nations were moving toward higher education and civilization – some nations started earlier, while others like the Slavs would have to follow them as soon as possible: 'The time for Slavic enlightenment is coming'. In the past, Czechs had occupied an important position among educated nations, and this would have to be the case again (Rieger 1923: 89, 94).

In the 1840s, some intellectuals expected relevant advantages for the speed of Czech cultural improvement due to Bohemia's position in the middle of Europe, 'at the crossroad of almost all cultures of our continent'. This advantage of geographical position is related to values: the position in the middle of Europe, in its 'heart', could be interpreted as a position in the centre of European virtues (Nebeský 1953: 35).

This was nevertheless not a Czech exception: several decades earlier similar ideas were developed by early German patriots for their own nation (Jahn 1817, 11). The Czech specificity could consist – so Palacký asserted – of transmitting and unifying different cultural elements, such as Germanic, Roman and Slavic ones. The myth of the middle as a positive value survived until the twentieth century and inspired the later ideology of 'Central Europe' developed by Czech dissidents in the 1980s. In this concept, belonging to Central Europe is – as a specific form of being European – a matter of national pride (see below).

To understand this opinion, we have to notice that besides being aware of the struggle for freedom as a normative context of Europe, Czech politicians felt inspired also by another trend which they voluntarily accepted as a 'European norm': the process of nation-formation. Czech national leaders could declare their movement as a natural component of the generally accepted 'principle of nationality'. 'A strong feeling of national revival is moving all Europe', wrote Nebeský in the 1860s (Nebeský 1953 [1845]: 15). As a nation, Czechs became compatible with all other Europeans. 'Europe knows us and appreciates our honest efforts in the name of the true humanity', declared Rieger in 1873, and three years later he stressed that Czechs knew that they had played an important role for Europe and that they still signified something for it (Rieger 1923: 185, 199).

The idea of belonging to the general European national movement was further developed by T.G. Masaryk in the 1890s. He regarded the Czech national movement as a natural part of that movement which in Europe started with the French revolution. In this perspective, national movement and the struggle for freedom formed one unit: 'Since the end of the eighteenth century, a progressive and liberal minded movement emerged both in Bohemia and in all Europe' (Masaryk 1990 [1894]: 17). Symptomatically, in this book Masaryk regarded Czech nation-building as strongly influenced by the moral and cultural traditions of the Reformation which had given a new sense to European society and its history. It was not by chance that Masaryk developed this concept at the same time as the Otto-Encyclopaedia regarded nation-formation as one of the European specificities.

This operation included a symptomatic syllogism: if we understand the normative European values as both civic and national ones, then all our political activities (including the national ones) that follow this path can be regarded as being in favour of Europe. To accept European values obliged or legitimated the Czechs to continue and to strengthen their national movement.

This syllogism was implicitly integrated by the Czech national movement at least at the beginning of the twentieth century, if not earlier. It was then explicitly used as a political argument in the Czech anti-Habsburg struggle during the First World War. Masaryk presented this struggle as being in the name of old European values. 'The real federation of nations will only appear, if all nations will be free and join each other. This is the trend of European development.' Supporting this goal were the entente powers fighting the war. Only if Europe accepted the democratic ideas of the entente powers would the federation of nations become easier (Masaryk 1994 [1918]: 102–3).

Under conditions of war, Masaryk formulated his concept of the post-war European values in his pamphlet *New Europe* (1994 [1918]) which was addressed above all to European politicians. The central position was democracy: europeanization meant democratization. Nevertheless, the basic and inevitable condition for this democratization was moral re-education of nations according to the principles of rationality, humanity and Christian spirituality. Symptomatically Masaryk ended his pamphlet with a rather pathetic sentence: 'Jesus, not Caesar – this is the slogan of the democratic Europe' (Masaryk 1994 [1918]: 192).

Even though the existence of the Czech nation after the achievement of independence was still not self-evident, the Czech understanding of European specificity moved from the picture of the continent of nations toward the concept of a Europe whose nations were joined by a common cultural atmosphere and heritage. Principles of rationality and spirituality seemed to be more important, because they were less self-evident than principles of national self-determination or those of liberalism. To be European within this concept meant to share a common culture.

This concept of Europe was explicitly analysed by František Krejčí, a philosophy professor in Prague. His book was a singular attempt to analyse systematically the relationship between the Czech and European identities (Krejčí 1931). Krejčí defined Europe as a continent with the highest quality of arts and with the most extensive spread of arts and other cultural artefacts among the population.

This Europe gradually became a cultural community, a community of spirit, which was formed from ancient times through the Christian Middle Ages to the Early Modern time, where the borders of cultural community corresponded to the geographical unit 'Europe' – i.e., they included also Russia. Hence, deduced Krejčí, the criterion of being European: it was the level of participation of a given community (nation) in the consumption of European cultural production, above all literature and music, measured through the quantity of translations, concerts, reviews. In this sense, the point of departure of Czech Europeanness was represented by two important Czech poets in the last third of the nineteenth century. One of them, Jaroslav Vrchlický, systematically translated the most important works of various European literatures into the Czech language; the other, Julius Zeyer, used in his poems and novels motifs from the history of almost all European cultures from Ireland to Russia (Krejčí 1931: 197).

It was, however, not only consumption of European culture but also the active contribution to the improvement of this culture that, according to Krejčí, marked the level of being European. In the case of the Czech nation, he regarded their achievements in the field of music as the most important contribution to European culture. Nevertheless, he argued, Czech Europeanness reached its height in the work of Masaryk, who was able to demonstrate the transition from cultural to political Europeanness. Krejčí, who regarded the cultural unity of Europe as the main precondition for political unity, regarded Masaryk as a pioneer of this trend (Krejčí 1931: 203).

Some years later, F.X. Šalda, who became one of the most influential intellectuals of his time, gave a less optimistic evaluation of the relation between Czechs and Europe. To him, Europe was defined by a common culture, above all by the cultural heritage of Western universalist Christianity. He regarded this culture as a normative context also for Czech cultural development. It was the moral imperative for Czech national culture to contribute to the European one. Hence his critical call for applying the highest artistic criteria in the national context: to become really European, Czech culture had to relinquish its 'petty-bourgeois' mentality and its 'fainthearted taste' in favour of heroism and originality of progressive ideas. Nationalism was – as an outdated heritage from the past – not compatible with this concept of European culture (Šalda 1934–1935: 226).

## Europe as a Value, to be Protected

The argument in favour of European defence against external danger is a topic traditional to almost all reflections on Europe. It is also present in the Czech discourse, nevertheless not without some paradoxical features. In April 1848, the German Vorparlament, preparing for German unification, invited Palacký, as the representative of Czechs, to participate in the elections for the Parliament in Frankfurt. Palacký refused this invitation in a famous letter where he not only stressed the difference between the German and Czech nations, but also warned against destroying the Habsburg monarchy by realizing the Great-Germany concept of unification. He described the Habsburg monarchy as the 'most Eastern' European great power, saying it had 'by the call of nature and of history, the mission to be a protector and guard of Europe against all kinds of Asian elements'. These elements, under given conditions, were represented by both the Ottoman and the Russian Empires. Russia was dangerous not because it was Slavic but because it was an absolutist system suppressing all liberties. He continued: 'If the state of Austria would not exist, we would have in the interest of Europe' to try to construct it (Palacký 1977: 161). Implicitly, this warning included a denunciation of the Great-Germany concept as one that indirectly endangered Europe, because it opened the door to Eastern invasion.

It would be an erroneous simplification to say that Palacký's warning was confirmed in 1849, when Russian troops invaded Hungary and suppressed the national revolution there: this intervention was invited from Vienna just to protect Austrian absolutism. Another 'European' observation of Palacký's falls into an ironical context: shortly before the Russian intervention, Palacký declared the internal stability of Austria to be of importance for all Europe (Palacký 1977: 222).

The Czech vision of the European enemy switched very radically twenty years later, when Czech politicians, deeply disappointed by Austro-Hungarian dualism which totally neglected Czech claims, made a demonstrative journey to Russia in 1867. It was Rieger, above all, who included the topic of European defence in his speeches. He stressed the positive role of the Russians who had saved Europe from Mongols and Turks and made a parallel between the two protectors of Europe, i.e. Russians standing against the danger from the East, and Czechs doing likewise for 'the civilization of all Europe' in their struggle against the Germans. Naturally, this concept was more or less a rhetorical exercise (Rieger 1923: 81).

Nevertheless, we cannot say that it left no stains. The positive appreciation of the role of Russians as protectors of Europe against the danger from the East can be found in the Otto-Encyclopaedia. Russians, it notes, took over from the Roman Empire the role of defending Europe against barbarians, the Ural-Altaic tribes and Mongolians. On the other side, the encyclopaedia stressed expansion as the historical 'mission' of Europe, with the mission fulfilled above all by two powers: Great Britain in the West and Russia in the East (*Ottův slovník naučný VIII* 1997 [1894]: 905).

The efforts to stress Czech participation in the defence of Europe also included some historical arguments. Perhaps the most popular of these was the peace project elaborated by the Czech king, George of Podiebrad, who in 1464 (ten years after the fall of Constantinople) sent a delegation to the French king, proposing a coalition of Christian rulers against the common enemy – the invading Ottomans. Naturally, this project enjoyed no success and was soon forgotten, but under conditions of the nineteenth-century discourse of Europe, this political initiative could be interpreted as an expression of a long-standing Czech devotion to the defence of European interests and values. Significantly, this interpretation was restored to life by the reformist communist ideologists in the 1960s.

At the threshold of the First World War, Masaryk accepted the entente powers' axiom that it was a war protecting European democracy. He modified this in his book 'New Europe' to the concrete sense that it was a struggle against anti-democratic Pan-Germanism and against the degenerated dynastic principle of Habsburg rule. He claimed that if the liberation of citizens and nations belonged to the aims of this war, then it could not be fulfilled without the liberation of Czechs and the constitution of their nation state. (Masaryk 1994: 160). In other words, if Europe was defined by the plurality of fully-fledged democratic nations, then the construction of Czechoslovakia would help to protect 'European principles' of democracy against alien, anti-democratic (and hence anti-European) Pan-Germanism.

The success of the Bolshevik revolution in Russia opened a new level of European defence-discourse. In Western Europe of that time, the idea of defending democracy and capitalism coincided strongly with the idea of defending European values. This was also partially the case in Czechoslovakia. Nevertheless, it seems to me that the 'main-stream' of Czechoslovak politics and culture did not exclude Russia from the European context.

Relevant authors, such as Beneš and Peroutka, often stressed that Russia remained a part of the European continent, peculiar above all through its backwardness in comparison with other parts of Europe and because it had never experienced capitalism and civil society (Krejčí 1931:170–1). On the other hand, Krejčí, who strongly defended the Europeanness of pre-Revolutionary Russia, put this adherence into question. The reason for him was that Soviet Russia refused to participate in European culture – and cultural community was to Krejčí the basic criterion of being European. (Bugge in Hahnová 1997a, 104).

## Belonging to Europe as a Matter of National Pride

It would be one-sided to conclude that the Czech national movement tried to strengthen its self-consciousness only by emphasizing its European merits. For the decisive part of Czech intellectuals, journalists and politicians, the European horizon of Czech national existence was a commonplace, which did not need to be argued using European 'merits'. Describing his experiences in Russia, Havlíček compared – as early as the 1840s – life in Russian towns with life 'in other European cities', such as London, Paris or Vienna. At the very same time, he described his hierarchy of identities: 'I am Czech, in addition also Slav, European, human being' (Havlíček 1924: 67, 200). Symptomatically, a half-century later, Masaryk explicitly appreciated and shared this statement (Masaryk 1990 [1894]: 344–5).

During the 1848 Czech Revolution, Europe was mentioned not only as a classificatory scheme, as mentioned above, but also as an expression of a proud self-consciousness: Czechs were participating in a European revolution through their own will and decision. In a speech to his comrades, the student leader J.V. Frič said in June 1848: 'Europe is waiting for you – you have to become the starting point of the European revolution!' (Frič 1889: 121). According to the opinion of a young lecturer in modern history, Anton Heinrich Springer, it was the mission of Slavs (implicitly of Czechs) to create a social state (Pfaff 1997: 189, 191–2). Also during the following decades, Europe was a self-evident part of Czech politics and cultural consciousness. In this sense, Czech politicians argued with Vienna, Czech culture tried to find a way out from provincialism. At the turn of the century, the young Šalda included Czech literature within the European context. With the same self-evidence, the European context included, according to him, both Western Europe and Russia: he had no difficulty in analysing the work of Duhamel and Čechov in one and the same review. The *Manifesto* of the 'Czech Moderne' from 1894, in which Šalda also participated, self-consciously criticized the 'European bourgeoisie' for having forgotten the achievements of revolutions and for neglecting the people. The *Manifesto* explicitly refused nationalist limitations and professed its allegiance to European Modernism (Šalda 1950: 361–2).

Thirty years later, in his essay on 'Czechs and Europe', Šalda regarded the position in the middle of Europe as an extraordinary favourable precondition for a 'European engagement' of Czech culture: 'I believe in the mission in the middle of Europe' (Šalda 1934–5: 228). In this connection, Šalda was only one of many authors who included their discourse on Europe in the discourse on Central Europe. The Czech consciousness of belonging to Central Europe could be interpreted as a distinct national value.

This somewhat spontaneous understanding of becoming European through being Central European reached a new level in the 1980s. Milan Kundera and other authors afforded good ideological grounds for it: their concept of Central Europe was totally compatible with modern Europeanness. Three out of four elementary central-European features were also fully related to Europe as a whole: first, the shared elitarian culture second, the shared system of values; and third, the diversity of cultures which enriched each other. Only the fourth characteristic was, according to Kundera, a specifically central-European one: the repeated experience of having been defeated and held captive. In connection to this fourth peculiarity some authors stressed that under conditions of oppression, intellectuals such as scientists, writers and scholars were able to keep their influence: also this phenomenon was regarded as exclusively European. Nevertheless, almost all this discussion proceeded outside of the Czech territory and never became a part of the internal Czech national discourse: it was and continued to be an international discourse among cosmopolitan intellectuals, such as Kundera, Konrad, Milosz and Havel. As a consequence of it, the concept of Central Europe in the Czech discourse of Europe played a less relevant role than was the case in Western Europe (Kundera 1984; Havel 1994; Lord 1999).

## Alternative European and Anti-European Visions

The Czech discourse on Europe also included another – negative version – represented above all by the myth of Czech historical exceptionality and by the Slavic myth. In the first case the 'collective memory', the historical consciousness, played a decisive role, but in the second case only a supplementary one. The Hussite myth followed from the fact that during the Hussite revolution 1419–34 Czech adherents of the reformer Jan Hus successfully defeated several crusades from Germany and other European countries. This fact could be instrumentalized in the course of the national movement as a tool of anti-German and anti-Catholic agitation. Nevertheless, it could scarcely be used as a tool of European identity. On the contrary: the national pride of the 'anti-European' resistance could be fed.

'You never trembled by fear face to face to Europe', proclaimed the poet Rudolf Mayer of his fatherland in the 1860s. 'All Europe was in fear of the Czech material power', which was fighting for its truth, wrote at the same time the biographer of Czech patriots, Sojka (Macura 1997: 10). The novel *Against Everybody* (*All*), written by A. Jirásek, glorified the Hussite wars against feudal Europe and became something of a bestseller. On the place of the first glorious Hussite victory, on the hill Vítkov (nowadays in a suburb of Prague) a commemorial tablet was placed in 1910 with an inscription saying: 'At that time, there existed two parties: Europe and we. And Europe was bloodless and pale' (Macura 1997:10). Using these examples, V. Macura constructed a 'dichotomy' of pro- and anti-European feelings in Czech public opinion. This construction seems, nevertheless, not to be very convincing. In this relation, the value of Czechs was based on their (positively connotated) difference from the (feudal) European context. At the same time, these texts admit their fascination with the rich, well-equipped Europe. The victories of the poor Czechs gained greater importance, because they were achieved against such a strong enemy.

While the Hussite struggle against 'all' was situated in the fifteenth century and could be interpreted as a path-breaking attempt to open the way toward freedom (i.e., one compatible with the general trend to European modernization), another anti-European criticism was a genuine nineteenth-century phenomenon. This attitude toward Europe emanated from the conviction that Czech identity was above all compatible with Slavic, not European, identity. Even though this was originally a rather marginal phenomenon, it has to be represented by one example in this context. The poet Svatopluk Čech, very popular in his time, published a long poem in 1878 telling a story about a proud vessel called 'Europe'. As a result of a revolt, outlaws from its steerage took over rule of the ship, but then quarrelled with each other and were unable to find a consensus. Eventually, the ship with a red flag on the mast (an allegory of the Commune of Paris) capsized and sank. Six years later, Čech published another allegory – a poem 'Slavia', presenting a ship sailing for a happy future, as a 'morning star of new worlds', even though the crew was poor and rejected by the rich. The poverty, nevertheless, was accompanied by spiritual virtues that are higher than traditional (i.e. Western) virtues (Čech 1884, 1886). This alternative vision was naturally inspired by Russian Slavophilism, but had its specific anti-German background. The Slavic alternative was used in the context of a defence against the concept of Germanic and Roman Europe that was propagated by German nationalists in order to exclude Slavs from Europe. This concept seemed to offer to the Czechs two alternatives: either to remain European becoming Germans, or to remain Slavic Czechs and exclude themselves from Europe.

Russian discourse played the central role in this discussion about the size of Europe. It was in this context that Masaryk decided to write an ambitious interdisciplinary monograph on 'Russia and Europe' (Masaryk 1995–96 [1913]). Masaryk did not exclude Russia from Europe but regarded it as a specific part of it: 'Europe is not essentially foreign to Russia, but Russia still did not master it totally'. Russia represents in his view 'the childhood of Europe': Russia is what Europe was (ibid.: 15). For this reason, the relationship between Russia and Europe is a matter of comparison of two parts of Europe standing on different levels of development. Russia was behind Europe, behind the European Enlightenment and constitutionalism, but its educated elites do not regard this time-lag (belatedness) as relevant, since they were convinced they were spiritually superior to Europe. Russia was, according to Masaryk, decadent and theocratic. On the other side, Europe was weakened through its internal struggles for democracy and social justice, while Russia, should it cure its sickness, could become the most powerful state in Europe (ibid.: 370).

A new variant of anti-European alternatives emerged in inter-war Czechoslovakia. Some radical left intellectuals saw an alternative in the new social system of the young Soviet Union. Former anarchist and later communist Stanislav Kostka Neumann, a poet, wrote: 'Europe, you are not more, what you were' – you are not any more the spiritual Europe but Europe of murdering weapons (Hahnová 1997a: 29). The new world, the new culture was born in the East.

This anti-Europeanism received political support after 1948, but even from 1945 young Czech writers attacked Europe as 'rotten', as a satellite of American imperialism, as a traitor of its own ideals, as a system that tolerated fascism in Spain and Portugal, etc. Later on, Europe changed in the eyes of some communist poets into 'casemates', or 'pyramids of nuclear shelters', inhabited by 'fossils of men and wrecks of women'.

The late Zdenek Nejedlý (1950: 69) gave a theoretical background: the true Europe moved to the territory of the USSR. Even though the rhetoric and the vocabulary changed, the basic concept remained: the 'socialist countries' were a part of Europe, they accepted its best traditions and offered to all Europe a progressive alternative. There were two important features which both parts of Europe had in common: common history and shared cultural tradition.

## Conclusions

The concept of Europe never played a dominating, decisive role in Czech national discourse and not even in Czech political vocabulary. It never became a mobilizing slogan of politics, despite the fact that from the end of the nineteenth century the mostly spontaneously accepted European horizon strongly influenced the concept of Czech culture. The discourse on Europe cannot be neglected, above all due to the introduction of different connotations and interpretations into Czech national consciousness. These connotations survived, sometimes non-verbalized and 'unconsciously', until the present time.

The conceptualization of Europe in Czech discourse had three successive levels which were mutually compatible. These three levels roughly corresponded to the development of the Czech national movement and Czech society. Initially, it was above all a continent, which introduced liberal and democratic changes in its revolutionary way toward civil society. Later on, at the second level, Europe was understood also as a community of free nations and as a protector of unfree nations. In the third level, which grew to dominance during the inter-war period, the concept of Europe was based on the community of high culture.

The Czech understanding of Europe until the Second World War was complicated by its position in the middle – between East and West Europe. This position was sometimes interpreted also as a position between Germans and Slavs (or Russians) and contributed to a dichotomy in the understanding of Europe. This East-West dichotomy played a different role according to the changing political circumstances in the Habsburg monarchy and in Central Europe.

Under conditions of German domination, the Slavic component was rather strongly represented, and after the defeat of Germany, under conditions of Russian-Soviet domination, the Western component became dominant and the Slavic component was almost totally forgotten. Despite all of these contextual changes, the concept of Europe was verbalized as a positive value. We do not have enough data, however, to allow us to generalize our observations. It seems still not to be a given fact that the integration of Europe influenced not only journalists but also the broad Czech public as a mobilizing, constitutive factor for civic engagement.

## References

Arnold, E. (1848), *Děje husitů* [History of the Hussites], Prague, reprinted in: '*Čeští revoluční demokraté*', Prague.
Frič, J.V. (1889), *Pameti IV.*, Prague.
Hahnová, E. (ed.) (1997a), *Evropa očima Čechů* [Europe through Czech eyes], Prague.
—— (1997b), 'Češi a imaginární hranice mezi západem a východem Evropy' [The Czechs and the imaginary border between the West and East of Europe] in E. Hahnová (ed.), *Evropa očima Čechů* [Europe through Czech eyes], Prague.
Havel, V. (1994), *Toward a Civil Society: Selected speeches and writings 1990–1994*, Prague.
Havlíček-Borovský, K. (1924), Vybrané spisy [Selected Works] II, Prague.
—— (1956), *Politik a novinář* [The politician and journalist], Prague.
Jahn, F.L. (1817), *Das deutsche Volkstum*, Leipzig.
Krejčí, F.V. (1931), 'Češství a Evropanství'. 'Úvahy o naší kulturní orientaci' [The title is difficult to translate: 'Czech national feeling and European identity'], Prague.
Kundera, M. (1984), 'The tragedy of Central Europe', in *New York Review of Books*.
Lord, C. (ed.) (1999), *Central Europe: Core or Periphery?*, Copenhagen.
Macura, V. (1997), 'Semiotika Evropy', in: Hahnová (ed.), *Evropa očima Čechů*, Prague.
Masaryk, T.G. (1990 [1894]), *Česká otázka: Naše nynější krize* [The Czech question: Our contemporary crisis], Prague.
—— (1994 [1918]) *Nová Evropa* [New Europe], Prague.
—— (1995–96 [1913]), *Rusko a Evropa* I–III, Prague.
*Masarykův slovník naučný, II* (1926), Prague.
Nebeský, V.B. (1953 [1845]), 'O potřebě oslavit dějiny národa [On the need of the glorification of Czech history], in Ibid., *O literature* [On literature], Prague.
Nejedlý, Z. (1950), 'O Evrope', in *Var 3*, Prague.
*Ottův slovník naučný, VIII* (1997 [1894]), Prague.

Palacký, F. (1977), *Úvahy a projevy* [Reflections and speeches], Prague.

Pfaff, I (1997), 'Češi mezi západem a východem Evropy v 19.století [The Czechs between the West and the East of Europe], in E. Hahnová (ed.), Evropa očima Čechů, Prague.

Rieger, F.L. (1923), *Řeči dra Františka Ladislava Riegra* [F.L. Rieger's speeches], I, 1868–78, Prague.

*Riegrův slovník naučný* (1862), *II*, Prague.

Šalda, F.X. (1934–1935), Češství a Evropa [The Czechness and Europe], in: *Šaldův Zápisník*, Prague.

___ (1950), *Kritické projevy* [Critical writings] 2, Prague.

Sojka, J.E. (1953 [1862]), Naši mužové [Our men], Prague.

Svatopluk Č. (1884), týž, 'Slavie', Prague.

—— (1886), *Evropa*, Prague.

Tomek, W.W. (1904), *Paměti z mého života* [Memory of my life], Prague.

Žáček, V. (1948), *Češi a Poláci v revoluci 1848, I* [Czechs and Poles in the Revolution of 1848], Prague.

# -11-

# A.E.I.O.U. – Austria Europae Imago, Onus, Unio?

## Gilbert Weiss

A.E.I.O.U. is the famous signature which the emperor, Frederic III (1415–1493), allowed be imprinted on many buildings and personal things. As far as we know, it first appeared in 1437. What it really meant is not so clear. There are controversial interpretations; an Austrian historian once presented as many as eighty-six different meanings including, for instance, the hegemonic claims: *Austria est imperio optime unita, Austria erit in orbe ultima, Austria est imperare orbi universo*, or *Alles Erdreich ist Österreich unteran, Aller Ehren ist Österreich voll* (v = u), etc. (cf. Kleindel 1995: 87).

The historian and sociologist Eugen Rosenstock-Huessy (1888–1973), in his epochal work *Die Europäischen Revolutionen und der Charakter der Nationen* (1951), provides another reading of the famous signature: *Austria Europae Imago, Onus, Unio* – Austria as the very picture of Europe, as its burden as well as its constraint for unification (Rosenstock-Huessy 1987 [1951]: 432). This interpretation fits very well with the 'mirror' metaphor – Austria as mirror of Europe – often to be found in official Austrian documents as well as literary works. In the semi-official *Österreichbuch* from 1948, for instance, we read the following lines which are framed by the memory of the 'glorious' Austrian victory against the Osmanic empire in 1683: '[Austria as] . . . shining mirror of the Occident, of Europe. Unifying Europe's contradictions into a many-voiced, polyphonic concert. This is the miracle of that victory' (*Glänzender Spiegel des Abendlandes, Europas. Heimholung seiner Gegensätze [der Gegensätze Europas] in ein vielstimmiges, vieltöniges Konzert. Das ist das Wunder jenes Sieges . . .* ) (Marboe 1948: 78 quoted in Breuss et al. 1995: 128). The year 1683, the Turks' siege of Vienna and the victory by the Habsburg forces under Duke Karl V of Lothringen and King Johann III Sobieski of Poland, is indeed a constitutive experience out of which Austria's self-interpretation as *the* representative of Occidental-European culture has grown. From this point on, the weal of the country became the weal of the whole of Christianity, as Duke Ferdinand proclaims in Franz Grillparzer's late drama *Bruderzwist in Habsburg* (Grillparzer 1998: 35). The Occidental 'Kulturmission' (Hugo Ball) had become the organizing idea, the *dispositif idéel* (M. Godelier) of the *Casa de Austria*. Still in 1917, facing the final decline of the monarchy, the poet Hugo von Hofmannsthal states, not without nostalgia, in his notes on the *Idee Europa*: 'Saying "Austria" is saying: millennial struggle for Europe, millennial mission by Europe, millenial belief in Europe' (*Wer sagt 'Österreich', der sagt ja: tausendjähriges Ringen um Europa, tausendjährige Sendung durch Europa, tausendjähriger Glaube an Europa*) (Hofmannsthal 1979: 54).

In 1922, Ernst Karl Winter, a strong advocate of Austria's Catholic mission, arguing for a political union of the 'Catholic states of Europe – from France over Bavaria, Austria, Hungary to Poland', identified Europe's 'redemption and renewal' with that of Austria (Winter 1922: 74). His essay, by the way, is entitled: *Austria Erit In Orbe Ultima* (!).

Jumping to the end of the twentieth century, we find that the *Austria Europae Imago* still seems to be the guiding principle: in 1994, the major slogan of the federal government's campaign for the plebiscite on joining the European Union was: 'We are Europe' (*Wir sind Europa*) (Breuss et al. 1995: 126). Austria as the mirror of Europe, as the true Europe, so to speak – the construction of Austria's Europeanness which at the same time means an 'Austriazation' (*Verösterreicherung*) of Europe is an important feature in the 'ideal discourse of the nation' but it is of course not the end of the story, nor its beginning. Unsurprisingly, the matter is much more complicated. In order to get further into the substance of the problem, we have to investigate the sentiments, conflicts and traumata out of which these discourses emerge. We have to ask for the 'mental map' behind the actual discourses.

## From the Subject of Occidental *'Kulturmission'* to the Object of European *'Zivilisationsmission'*

From the sixteenth through the eighteenth centuries, Habsburg Austria was able to cover and maintain a gigantic territory including, apart from the homeland (*Stammhaus*), numerous hereditary possessions (*Erblande*) – from parts of today's Netherlands and Belgium down to Spain and Sicily, etc. The Habsburgs became the most powerful dynasty of the continent. As commonly known, the success of this expansion was based on a policy of strategic intermarriage. Contradicting Machiavelli's *Principe*, the Habsburgs followed the famous motto: *Bella gerant alii, tu felix Austria nube* ('Let others wage war; thou, happy Austria, shalt marry'). The two formative poles constituting and legitimating this empire were the *Kaisertum* and the Roman papacy. Habsburg Austria represented the Holy Roman Empire – that is, it represented the institutions of the Occident.

This is not the place to describe the development of the empire – the internal problems, the territorial fragmentation, confessional division, and the problems of succession (*Erbfolge*) which reached a high point under Maria Theresa (1717–80) when the Holy Roman Empire was transformed into a secular Austrian Empire because, as a woman, she could not become Roman emperor. For the first time, Habsburg-Austria lost its universal idea, its character of representing something absolute; 'it was nothing but a natural agglomeration secularized through the accident of feminine succession, not a living body politic with a definite role in the European concert' (Rosenstock-Huessy 1993: 618). The Roman *monarchia universalis* turned into a mere Danube-monarchy – one that became more and more shaken by conflicts between the different nationalities.

Joseph II, Maria Theresa's son and successor, became known as the great reformer in the history of Habsburg-Austria. Under his regency (1780–90) the Holy Roman Empire and the House of Austria were brought together again. Joseph II himself was a deeply ambivalent personality: on the one hand, he truly wanted to be Roman emperor in the old universal sense, but on the other hand, he saw his mission as bringing enlightenment and institutional reform to the state. His *Aufklärung von oben* (enlightenment from above) was doomed to failure because the resistance of the aristocracy and the Austrian, Lombardic and Hungarian estates against the reform projects was too strong, so that Leopold II, his brother and successor, had to revoke almost all of them.

This is a crucial point in the history of modern Austria for two reasons: first, the process of enlightenment was slowed down, and did not (re)gain political significance for many years; Austria's history of the last two centuries is therefore characterized by a *Verzögerte Aufklärung* (delayed enlightenment) (Benedikt and Knoll 1995); second, enlightenment became identified per se with enlightenment from above; the possibility of an enlightenment from below, so to speak, did not enter Austrian sentiment. Up to the end of the twentieth century, it has only been conceivable with great difficulty; this has certain consequences for the formation of a civil society and a modern state – and not least for the perspective on a modern 'Europe', as we will show in a moment.

Finally, in 1806 the Holy Roman Empire came to an official end. On 6 August Francis II, son and successor of Leopold, abdicated from the position of Roman-German imperial status. After more than one thousand years the Latin-Western *Kaisertum* (empire) ended (Matz 1999: 265). Why did Francis abdicate? What had happened? The answer is rather simple, two things had happened: 1789 and Napoleon Bonaparte. The universal revolution replaced universal Christianity. For centuries, the *raison d'être* of the Habsburg empire had been its role as 'bulwark of Christianity', as defender of European culture against the East ('Turkish danger'). This was the only principle that gave the Habsburg empire, this 'patch-work in the middle of the European map' (H. Schulze 1999: 86), some form of logical existence character. Even in 1782 Joseph II considered Rome as the true capital and the real centre of the empire (Schulze 1999: 128). Since 1789, however, European culture no longer came from Rome but from Paris (Ball 1984: 173). Its universal ideal was not Latin-Roman any more, but French. Habsburg's European *Kulturmission* became an imaginative construction that no longer fitted the historical reality.

In order to understand the ensuing Austrian development, the meanings of both *Europe* and *Occident* (Abendland) have to be further elaborated because they form a crucial bi-polarity in the Austrian perspective – one that mostly remains unarticulated, though. Their meanings closely depend on each other. This, of course, is true not only for the Austrian case, but it is particularly true here. Occident is a concept directed to the past, a projection into the past; it construes an origin; it refers to roots; it forms a *Kulturmission*. Europe, in contrast, is a concept directed to the future, a projection into the future; it is a project – it constitutes a *Zivilisationsmission*. With reference to the meta-historical categories developed by Reinhart Koselleck (1989: 354), one could say that Occident construes a universal *Erfahrungsraum* (area of experience), whereas Europe construes a universal *Erwartungshorizont* (horizon of expectations).

Europe as a political concept – i.e., new *Erwartungshorizont* – replacing the idea of the Christian *Abendland* – i.e., the old *Erfahrungsraum* – became effective with the French Revolution. The French revolution created modern Europe. This creation was based on three elements: Democracy, Liberalism and Nationhood (nation in the sense of a political community of will, a matter of free decision, in the words of Ernest Renan: *un plébiscite de tous les jours*); and the essence of all three elements was and is contained in the French word *civilisation* (cf. Rosenstock-Huessy 1993: 145; Schulze 1999: 169). Europe was the project of the French *civilisation* carried across the continent by Napoleon's soldiers. 'In the mouth of the Frenchman "Europe" means a field of action for the

philosopher, the artist, the thinker, the democrat, the republican, the soldier'
(Rosenstock-Huessy 1993: 145). The emphasis must be put on *field of
action*. Not contemplation but the *evocation* of a new political '*cosmion*'
(E. Voegelin) is at stake here. Since 1789 being a 'good European', as
Nietzsche put it, means being a *citoyen*, i.e., a citizen of the liberal
civilization introduced by the French Revolution. As *citoyen*, one is no
longer caught in the tradition but rather directed to the future, that is, to
an ideal project to be realized in the future. Time – potentially – gives
the answer to all questions. The revolutionaries think in terms of becoming,
not in terms of being (E.M. Cioran 1990: 38f). *L'Europe* in this sense was
the most extreme contrast to Austria's interpretation of Europe as *Abendland*. And indeed, for Austria, the speed of the events after 1789 was
breathtaking. In summer 1791 with the peace of Sistowa in Bulgaria,
Austria finished her last war with the Turks; in spring 1792 revolutionary
France declared war against Austria (and Prussia). In other words, within
less than one year Austria had to dramatically change its role and position:
from the subject of Occidental *Kulturmission* to the object of European
*Zivilisationsmission*. Not only did Austria no longer represent Europe
(*Abendland*), she was also now threatened by Europe (*l'Europe*) – threatened in an existential sense because the very existence of the Habsburg
empire contradicted the 'new' Europe and vice versa. Note that in official
French textbooks of geography, before the First World War, Austria was
called a '*contresens dans l'Europe moderne*' (cf. Rosenstock-Huessy
1993: 612). Only from the French – i.e. 'new' – European perspective was
this verdict true. The guideline of the universal revolution was: *Il faut
liquider le passé*. The imaginative construction of the Austrian world, by
way of contrast, followed the guideline of *Il faut liquider l'avenir*.
Defending the Occident, in this sense, meant defending history as cultural
tradition against history as civilizational progress. The difference between
the two 'Europes' could not be greater. In 1809, however, Napoleon
marched triumphantly into Vienna. The universal revolution was stronger
than the universal empire, *l'Europe* was stronger than the *Abendland*.

## Franz Grillparzer and the Resistance Against '*l'Europe*' – from 1809 to 1955

In the Austrian perspective of the early nineteenth century, Europe
became identified with France's mission of universal civilization, and the
latter became identified with Napoleon Bonaparte, i.e. a '*habsüchtiger
Eroberer*' (Archduke John, quoted from Schulze 1999: 195) – a tyrannical

conqueror, almost the Antichrist. Accordingly, the new French *esprit*, for Austria, had assumed two 'dangerous' forms inseparable from each other: (a) the collective form of a *volonté générale* of the nation, and (b) the individual form of the Machiavellian *virtù*, i.e. the enormous political will and energy of a *Principe*-like leader. An intoxicated people guided by an intoxicated leader – this could only be the end of the traditional world as Austria represented it – or rather, wanted to represent it (if there was one thing that the Habsburgs did not have, it was *virtù* in Machiavelli's sense).

This sentiment found its representative expression in the work of Franz Grillparzer (1791–1872), *the* national poet. It is particularly two dramas that are of relevance here: *König Ottokars Glück und Ende* (1825) and *Bruderzwist in Habsburg* (1872). The first one, *König Ottokar*, is based on the traumatic experience of Napoleon's triumphant march through Vienna in 1809. Grillparzer conceived Napoleon, alias Ottokar, as the prototypical personification of the subjectivistic hubris of modernity. For him, Napoleon is not so much the hero of a new civilization as the grave-digger of the old cultural cosmos (tradition); he is not, as for Hegel, the *Weltgeist* on horseback, but a parvenu dreaming an apocalyptic dream. Both Napoleon and revolutionary France represented the 'fever of a sick era' (cf. Magris 1999: 79). Ottokar's/Napoleon's end is the triumph of historical necessity over psychological contingencies such as will for power or megalomania. The certainty of the past, one more time, defeats the uncertainty of the revolutionary, i.e. European, future. That this picture no longer fitted all too well into the reality of the years after 1806 was not so important; it served as the basis of the Habsburg myth and its twin brother, the *Mitteleuropa* myth, both constituting the co-ordinate system of Austrian self-interpretation until the end of the twentieth century and beyond. After 1806 Austria replaced history with historiz-ation. History is seen as tradition, not as progress, as a closed entity, not as an ongoing process. It is a field of retrospection and contemplation, not a field of action and evocation. From the early nineteenth century on, political actions in the true sense do not take place anymore, they are replaced through '*Parallelaktionen*' in Robert Musil's sense (Musil 1970), that is, through theatrical gestures. The monarchy has indeed become '*Kakania*'.

The Austrian refusal of modernity and French 'Europeanism' – embedded in a general pessimism identifying historical process per se with decline – was further strengthened in Grillparzer's late drama *Bruderzwist in Habsburg*. There the revolutionary situation of 1848 is reflected, as in *König Ottokar*, through the transference of the plot back to another historical period, this time to the time of Rudolf II who, in the years before the Thirty Years War, had been attempting to sustain a balance between the religions, estates and nations in the empire. To act or not to act – this is the crucial question of the 'fraternal feud'. Rudolf II was a tragical figure because he refused to act in a time when everybody, particularly his brothers, expected him to act in the sense of making history – i.e., rationally/strategically forming the future. Rudolf is the great vacillator, he suffers from the new confused times and is most sceptical about deeds in general; he puts contemplation instead of evocation. Grillparzer celebrates Rudolf as the prototype of the 'grandiose Habsburg stasis' which is based on a fantastic asubjectivity in the modern sense, a strong 'reluctance to act, the defensive posture of those who do not aim to win but to survive, who dislike wars because, like Francis Joseph, they know that wars are always lost' (Magris 1999: 135).

For Carl Schmitt, the problem as well as the greatness of Grillparzer's drama is that Rudolf is no active hero, but an *'Aufhalter, Verzögerer, ein "Katechon"'* [delayer, a 'Katechon'] (Schmitt 1981: 80) who indeed succeeded at least in holding back and delaying the Thirty Years' War. Schmitt called the corresponding sentiment 'neutro-passive' (1981: 82) which not only fits very well with the Austrian mentality just described but also links to Austria's status of neutrality after the Second World War and thus helps to explain the continuity in the history of modern Austria. I will come back to the particular problem of neutrality in a moment.

There is one major dualism framing Grillparzer's entire work which finds expression *par excellence* in the *Bruderzwist*, and that is the dualism between being and becoming, eternity and temporality, order and disorder, objective nature and subjective dead, etc. (cf. Bachmaier 1998: 102). This is also and foremost the dualism between history understood as cultural *tradition* on the one hand and as civilizational *progress* on the other; in other words, it is the dualism between restoration and revolution, between *Abendland* and *l'Europe*. In characters such as Ottokar and, moreover, Don Caesar in *Bruderzwist* (the illegitimate son of Emperor Rudolph II, an impetuous, revolutionary character who – like a Dostoevskian figure – ends in insanity), Grillparzer seems to revoke enlightenment and revolution, insofar as the 'free' subject after negating the traditional metaphysical obligations gets caught in a self-destructive nihilism (Bachmaier 1998: 103). Nevertheless, the author keeps the ethos of enlightenment (Rudolph several times promotes clemency and tolerance), but – and this is the decisive point – he grounds the latter not in the acting subject but in the ahistorical order of a dynasty connected to the *'Geist des All'* (Spirit of the Universe) and deliberately delaying progress. Here we find a fundamental difference between Grillparzer and Hegel, between Austria and Prussia: for Hegel, Napoleon the revolutionary subject represented the *Weltgeist* in the sense of the historical synthesis of reality and rationality, for Grillparzer, in contrast, it was not a subject but a dynasty that represented the ahistoric *Geist des All* – two different forms of universality. In Grillparzer's case, history (becoming, movement, progress) and subjectivity (autonomy, reason, action) are called back into the eternal order of being, so to speak. In this perspective, historical progress, just as modern subjectivity, is only an illusion. Accordingly, nineteenth-century Austria refused more and more to act politically, and stopped moving – became indeed a *'contresens dans l'Europe moderne'*.

The resistance against the civilizational project of the French Revolution, Europeanism and modernity as expressed in Grillparzer's dramas, one might argue, is part of nineteenth-century sentiment, but the Austria of the twentieth century, i.e. the modern post-war Austria, looks naturally different. But does it? When in 1955, the year of the Austrian state treaty and of regained independence, the Vienna *Burgtheater* was ceremoniously reopened for the first time since the war, its first production was Grillparzer's *König Ottokar*! In other words, *the* intellectual foundation act of the Second Republic (we shall not forget that the Burgtheater is and always was the major intellectual institution of the country) celebrated Austria's non-Europeanness, Austria's resistance against the civilizational project of *l'Europe*; it celebrated the past of the *Abendland* and the Habsburg dynasty: Austria is Habsburg is Abendland. The play ends with the general crowd claiming: *'Hoch Österreich! Habsburg für immer!'* (Long live Austria! Habsburg forever!). Needless to say, this was only two years before the Roman Treaties were signed.

## Mitteleuropa as Medium-level Europe

In the course of the nineteenth century, the Austrian monarchy had more and more become a *'Theaterwelt'* (Musil 1970), a world of illusions and *Parallelaktionen*. The state decided to withdraw from history but was, nevertheless, again and again painfully called back into historical reality – mainly through military and political defeats. It was also the disasters of Austrian politics in relation to Prussia and the respective loss of Habsburg's guiding role in Germany (further dramatized in 1871 by the foundation of the German *Reich*), which created the *Mitteleuropa* idea as an ersatz ideology, i.e. an ideology replacing the idea of German unity under the leadership of Habsburg. Since Austria had been unable to realize this German unity which was then driven forward by Prussia, the Habsburg monarchy was looking for a new mission and identity for this supranational empire – a melting pot of fourteen different peoples and cultures. The old idea of the Roman-Universal *Kulturmission* was dead – buried by the French revolution and Napoleon's soldiers, i.e. by *l'Europe*. In this situation, the concept of Mitteleuropa had several advantages: it emphasized the cultural variety and the added value, so to speak, of this variety; what the unifying principle really was, was not so clear; in this sense, Mitteleuropa was like Europe and unlike Occident a notion emphasizing variety and 'concealing' unity. But even if hidden or concealed there must have been some form of unifying common ground. What was it? Now, it was precisely the '*Mittel*' in *Mitteleuropa*, that was a medium level of being European, i.e. being civilized in the French sense. The mental map producing this idea functioned as follows: Western Europe was *l'Europe* in the French/modern/revolutionary sense. The east was uncivilized anyway: it was 'primitive' in terms of both Occidental *Kulturmission* and European *Zivilisationsmission*. Habsburg-*Mitteleuropa* positioned itself exactly inbetween – a sort of middle-range enlightenment entity, if you like. As with Grillparzer's Rudolph II, the ideas of the Enlightenment were accepted, even promoted – but only in a limited version. *Mitteleuropa* meant a little bit of *l'Europe* but not too much. *Mitteleuropa* wanted to be middle-range Europe and middle-range modernity. It meant enlightenment as a quality not embodied in the historically acting/revolutionary subject, but in the ahistorical order of a dynasty.

How should this construction work? How should the supranational state not explode sooner or later in nationalistic struggles? How should the vital spark of enlightenment and emancipation from traditional obligations and institutions be kept at a medium level? Indeed, this was an impossible undertaking. The idea of Mitteleuropa was just as illogical as the de facto existence of the Austrian monarchy which, in 1866, became an Austrian-Hungarian monarchy. This construction was 'a hopeless case of contradictory political principles' (Rosenstock-Huessy 1993: 619) – 'yet it existed, against all logic and reason' (ibid: 610). Unsurprisingly, this illogical character was noticed from a Parisian perspective in particular. The French historian, Émile de Laveleye, wrote in 1869: '*Le malheur en Autriche c'est que de divers côtés on veut à la fois obtenir les libertés modernes et conserver des institutions empruntées au moyen-âge*' [The problem in Austria is that, from various sides, one wants to obtain modern liberties and at the same time conserve the institutions of the Middle Ages] (de Laveleye 1869 quoted from Popovici 1906 : 139). The Danube monarchy wanted to proceed with the old institutions and at the same time inject them with some new spirit. Politics excluded all *either-or* options and followed exclusively the *this as well as that* principle which, as Robert Musil beautifully described it, often ended up in the ontological vaccuum of *neither-nor* (Musil 1970: 1230). The monarchy had become a pure *Erhalterstaat* built on an 'unparallelled staff of civil servants, the "Hofrat" being the outstanding type in this system of civil service' (Rosenstock-Huessy 1993: 612). The *Kaiser* had become the fiction of a universal *meta-norm* (in Hans Kelsen's sense) which – supported by a huge police and informer force – held the whole system together.

Geopolitically and intellectually the monarchy was sandwiched between West and East, which basically meant revolutionary France on one side and 'barbaric' Russia on the other: Europeanism on the one side and Panslavism on the other – not indeed an easy position. This sandwich-position led again to paradoxical results: on the one hand, Austria formed a 'Holy Alliance' together with Prussia and Russia (!) to maintain the traditional order in Europe which, of course, meant to keep down the revolutionary, i.e. French, spirit. On the other, Austria had to fight growing Panslavism. Austria's paranoia was directed to the East and to the West at the same time. Equally, Pan-Germanistic ideas got stronger and stronger. The *Deutsch-Österreicher* (German-Austrians) saw themselves in a traditional – i.e., hereditary – role of political leadership in this *Mitteleuropa* complex. After 1871 (at the latest), however, it was not any longer the Habsburg dynasty which represented the 'German nation', but the Hohenzollern one. Accordingly, so-called *Alldeutschen* such as Wolf and Schönerer devoted themselves to the motto: 'Down with Habsburg! Long live Hohenzollern!' (Ball 1984: 175). They were against Habsburg, *Mitteleuropa*, and Austria as a state separated from Germany.

Part of the *Mitteleuropa* conception was the conviction that, through the monarchy's supra-national sentiment, the middle-range enlightenment status, the intellectual as well as geopolitical sandwich position, Habsburg Austria had the 'binding' power to maintain the world's peace; as Hugo Ball put it, one allowed oneself the bad joke that the European peace problem was concentrated in the Austrian state problem (Ball 1984: 174). It is this bad joke which, almost one century later, was still to be found in the government's campaign of 'We are Europe' from 1994.

It is, important however, to see that *Mitteleuropa* was not only a more or less artificial political concept held together, in the words of Claudio Magris (1999: 160), 'by prudence, conservative scepticism, the art of compromise and also the art of living'; it really existed as a cultural form and sentiment. Mitteleuropa was the German–Hungarian–Slavic–Romance–Jewish ecumenic culture constituting itself along the line of the

Danube; it died with Auschwitz when one of its fundaments – the Jewish element – was exterminated. *Mitteleuropa* was an 'Intermarium' – between the Adrian and the Baltic Seas; its formative element was land; it lacked the open horizon of the ocean; it was a prison of time and repetition – Melancholia. To quote, Claudio Magris one more time:

> Central Europe is of the earth earthy, alpenstock and clothes of heavy green homespun, the meticulous of Exchequers and Chancelleries; it is a culture that has lost its familiarity with the liquid element, with the maternal amnion and the aboriginal waters, and finds it hard to strip off, because without boundaries, a jacket, a rank, a badge and a number in the registry, it feels exposed and ill at ease (Magris 1999: 155).

Austria-Hungary and the political concept of *Mitteleuropa* broke down in 1914. The monarchy, withdrawn from history, entered one more time into history, and – as a result – the latter put an end to this *contresens dans l'Europe moderne.*

## 'L'Autriche, c'est ce qui reste' (Clemenceau)

The House of Austria was transformed into the Republic of Austria, the monarchy became a small state – 'a state that nobody wanted' (Hellmut Andics quoted from Breuss et al 1995: 258). In 1918/19 all political camps pressed for an affiliation with Germany and were more or less convinced that this small entity of *Deutsch-Österreich* was neither capable of surviving nor worthy of it, as it were. And indeed, the so-called First Republic existed only for a short period of time, from 1918 to 1934. It was succeeded by four years of an authoritarian corporative regime until, in March 1938 the *Anschluß* with Hitler's Germany took place.

The history of the First Republic was not a success story. Unlike the other succession states, a nationalistic sentiment could not serve as an legitimizing principle for Austria because precisely from this point of view Austria had no legitimacy at all for it was only the 'second German state', and accordingly nationalism would have meant unification with Germany. In principle, this young state offered 'a curious problem', as Eric Voegelin wrote in 1937: 'While other countries are centres of unrest because they have got what they wanted and are trying to keep it against other claimants, or because they have not got what they wanted and are now trying to get it, Austria has been during the greater part of the last two decades a danger-spot of Europe because of its strong inclination towards non-existence' (Voegelin 1999 [1937]: 367). Finally, the resistance to history and the lack of subjective political will (and action), which already characterized the last hundred years of the monarchy, turned into an explicit will to non-existence. One is seduced to admire this logically consistent development. The old Austria, already an illogical construction, wanted to withdraw from history (as described above); the new Austria, not less illogical, sought a deeper level of ontological disappearance.

The core of the Austrian problem can be put in one paragraph:

Austria is a nationally uniform state without being a national state. The population of the present territory of Austria has never formed in history a political unit. Austria has a long and glorious history, but it is not the history of the present Austria as an independent body politic; it is the history of Austria as part of the medieval empire or as an integral and dominating part of the old Austrian monarchy. (The Germans of Austria have been during their history an empire-building and colonizing people; Vienna has been, up to the rise of the present Reich, the seat of the only German Great power. And, when in 1918 the break-up of the old Monarchy ensued, the population on the Austrian territory was 'left' as a 'residuum'. While the other succession states are products of an evolution towards national independence of the population on their territory, the Austrian population was never inspired by a will to independent national existence.) Austria, when it was created after the war, had a population, but it did not have a people in the political sense of the word. (ibid.: 367–8)

Accordingly, Austria was unable to form a nation in the French (i.e. modern) sense. There was no will to common and independent political existence – no *volonté générale*; there was only a history of collective traumas (running from 1806 to 1918). As a consequence, the population of the young state did not so much identify itself with the latter but with political parties. Party interests always ranked first, leaving only the second place for interests of common national importance – if the latter were understood at all. 'The written constitution was considered as a formal instrument being at the disposition of the parties for the attainment of their private purposes' (Voegelin 1999 [1937]: 370). The Austrian population was divided along party lines in a very rigid way. In the 1920s, the series of general elections proved that the party adherence of individuals would not be shaken. Austrian politics absolutely lacked the elasticity of Western democracies, which arises from the fact that a sufficient number of citizens are capable of changing the party of their choice, so that a change of the parties forming the government is possible (ibid.). The strong identification with parties, and the strict division of the country along party lines, to a certain degree is still true for today; the Austrian Social Democratic party, for example, now has more members in overall than its German sister party.

As Eric Voegelin put it, in 1918 a state was 'established' but not 'founded' by political decisions; this state had neither a *Staatsvolk* (*peuple*, i.e. people in the political sense) willing the existence of the state, nor any state leadership that could claim to be the author or creator of the state. The real powers were the parties. Against this background it is clear that the 'inclination towards non-existence', the will to make this state disappear from the map, also followed party lines. In the beginning all parties wanted to eliminate the state through unification with Germany; then further differenciations were to be observed; the Social Democrats kept the idea of the *Anschluß* with Germany until 1933, when Hitler came to power. Basically, however, the Social Democrats did not so much think in terms of nations or states as in terms of classes and class struggles. They devoted themselves to the universal revolution – not of course in the French sense, but in the Russian one. In other words, they represented the rare case of modern revolutionaries who skipped the French Revolution and jumped straight to the Russian one, so to speak. Accordingly, for the Social Democrats, *l'Europe* did not play any significant role as point of orientation, as political dimension or project.

Parts of the Christian Democrats still emphasized the *Mitteleuropa* idea and promoted an economic and political integration into a Danube confederation. Catholic camps aimed at something like a 'Catholic International' as contrast to the 'Socialist International'. Most prominent exponent of the Catholic internationalists was Ernst Karl Winter who called for a political union of the 'Catholic states of Europe' (Winter 1922). The *Deutschnationalen* camps became increasingly fascistic and anti-Semitic. Neither the Social Democrats nor the Christian Democrats used the notion of 'Europe' in any political sense, but only as a geographic notion. *L'Europe* was not present. Europe was not seen as a project for the future, the categories of *civilisation* did not exist in political discourse.

There was, however, one notable exemption, namely the foundation of the 'Pan-Europa' movement by Richard Coudenhove-Kalergie in 1923. In his journal *Pan-Europa* Coudenhove-Kalergie, a 28-years-old aristocrat, strongly promoted a 'United States of Europe'. Therewith, he did not mean *Mitteleuropa*, he meant a Europe with France and Germany as the heart; England and Russia were excluded. This was indeed a kind of anticipation of the later European Union; in fact, it represents the oldest European unification movement. Coudenhove-Kalergie realized that 'Europe as political concept does not exist' (1922: 23); in order to repoliticize the notion and to delimit the political Europe from a purely geographic Europe, he called it Pan-Europa. It should include 'all democratic states of continental Europe including Iceland' (1922: 36). The main goal of such a union was pacifistic, and was based on democratic and liberal ideas. In other words, with Coudenhove-Kalergie's Pan-Europa, the Europe of the French revolution – *l'Europe* and *civilisation* – found some articulation in Austria. Europeanism became a political concept; in his journal, for instance, Coudenhove-Kalergie distinguished between Europeans on the one hand and Chauvinists on the other – a distinction absolutely new in the Austrian discourse of the time. We must also not forget that Coudenhove-Kalergi founded Pan-Europa in Vienna roughly at the same time that, in Berlin, Oswald Spengler suggested that 'the notion of Europe should be deleted from history'; for Spengler, 'there is no "European" as historical type . . . Only Occident and Orient are concepts of true historical substance' (*es gibt keinen 'Europäer' als historischen Typus . . . Orient und Okzident sind Begriffe von echtem historischen Gehalt*). 'Europe is empty sound (*leerer Schall*)' (Spengler 1972: 22). Spengler wanted to undo *l'Europe* in the sense of the French revolution and its *Zivilisationsmission,* and to reformulate the Occidental *Kulturmission.* He saw the *Untergang des Abendlandes.* His book was very influential in Germany, and the distinction between *Kultur* and *Zivilisation* was shaping the discourse of the 1920s.

The Pan-Europa idea, which initially in 1922 was definitely a real revolutionary phenomenon in Austria, found quite a support among the public in Austria and other European countries. More and more, however, the movement became attached to Christian Democratic politicians (as, for instance, Chancellor Ignaz Seipel, who, for a certain period, even assumed the role of chairman of the Austrian committee). As a consequence, *l'Europe* again came to be replaced more and more by the *Abendland*; the European *Zivilisationsmission* could not win through against the Occidental *Kulturmission*, the past was stronger than the future. Today, Pan-Europa defines itself explicitly as an Occidental movement (cf. http./ /www.paneu.or.at) and implicitly sees Austria representing *Mitteleuropa* representing the old Monarchy as having a guiding if not missionary role in the enlargement of the European Union. Accordingly, it is not surprising that Otto von Habsburg had been president of the international Pan-Europa movement for almost twenty-five years.

The years of the First Republic, however, also brought an enormous process of critical Austrian self-reflection and self-observation; this process took place predominantly in literature but also in the arts, philosophy and sciences. From Karl Kraus to Robert Musil, from Sigmund Freud to

Ludwig Wittgenstein, from Otto Wagner to Arnold Schönberg, Vienna developed infinite resources of intellectual, artistic and scientific modernity. In the 1920s it was a European metropolis like Paris or Berlin. Here is not the place to describe in more detail the ambivalence of modern spirit, on the one hand, and political immobility, on the other (cf. Knoll and Kohlenberger 1994). Of course, writers such as Robert Musil, Hermann Broch or Heimito von Doderer – not to speak of Karl Kraus – had a clear idea of Europe in the sense of French civilization. Furthermore, they clearly saw the tensions between tradition and modernity, subjectivity and dynasty, contingency and history, etc. being typical for Austria (and the modern world in general). In their writings, they were critical of both the 'old' idea of *Kulturmission* and the 'new' idea of *Zivilisationsmission*. They formulated a notion of Europe transcending the dualism of *l'Europe* and *Abendland*. In his essay *'Das hilflose Europa*, for instance, Musil (1961) elaborated an idea of Europe that was very similar to what the philosopher Edmund Husserl had in mind in his famous lectures held in Vienna and Prague in 1935, *The Crisis of the European Sciences and Transcendental Phenomenology*. Here, Europe as a *Geistesform* (intellectual form) combines the strong confession to enlightenment and the modern idea of civilization with an equally strong criticism of the political, cultural and intellectual deformations produced by this modernity. The ambivalence between an enormous gain in knowledge (scientific/technological progress) on the one hand and a loss in life on the other, as Musil put it (1961: 15), came into view. Musil, as well as Husserl, clearly realized the (not least political) consequences of the fact that civilization had become predominantly industrial/technological in aspect. Their notion of Europe emphasized *modern* humanity, human dignity, truth and the idea of nurturing man to the good, and it was accompanied by a strong sense of crisis.

However, this critical self-reflection and the emerging intellectual notion of Europe could not become socially or politically effective in the inter-war period. On the contrary, the more critical the political situation in Austria became, the more the construction of an ersatz reality was driven forward. The former *Theaterwelt* of the monarchy became transformed into Hugo von Hofmannsthal's *'Großes Salzburger Welttheater'* (Great Salzburg World Theatre). Various kinds of second realities were replacing the first reality (cf. Doderer 1992). Reality denial became the programme. In 1919, Hofmannsthal, in his programmatic essay *Die Salzburger Festspiele*, wrote *'Das Salzburger Land ist das Herz vom Herzen Europas'* (Salzburg is the heart of the heart of Europe); and: *'Das mittlere Europa hat keinen schöneren Raum, und hier musste Mozart geboren werden'* (Central Europe has no place more beautiful; here Mozart had to be born) (1979: 261).

With regard to the general political inclination towards non-existence, the authoritarian regime from 1934 to 1938 constituted a change. This inclination was replaced by an Austrian 'mission' again. Since National Socialist ideology with its totalitarian claim, of course, proved to be incompatible with Catholic ideas of personality, society and humanity, Chancellor Dollfuss attached particular importance to the *authoritarian* quality of the new government as opposed to the totalitarian ideals. A movement made itself perceptible which endeavoured to clarify the particular qualities of the true Austrian (the 'Österreichische Mensch') as the bearer of the new Austrian mission founded in a century-old tradition. The Austrian German was discovered to belong to that region of Europe (*Mitteleuropa!*) which had developed under the influence of Mediterranean culture, while the Reich was said to be dominated by the German type which had not been imbued by the Latin spirit; Austria was said to be the representative of the German *Romanitas*. And, last but not least, the monarchist movement which had no real meaning during the period when the idea of Anschluß was dominating the scene, gained in force, because it offered a reasonable solution for the problem of an independent Austrian political organization and a safeguard against all projects of a 'union' (cf. Voegelin 1999 [1937]: 376).

One important element of the corporative organization of Austrian authoritarianism in the 1930s may be found in the idea that 'economic interests' should participate in the government of a nation and perhaps replace the 'political' representation. A representation of economic and other functional interests can, however, never be a political representation of a people. It is a system of private interests and not an organization of the *Res Publica* as political unit. So, this was precisely the problem: there was no 'people' in the political sense; accordingly, there was no nation, i.e. no representation of a political unit – the later was replaced by an economic disposition. This replacement of the political by the economic remained a crucial characteristic after 1945, in the so-called Second Republic. The Austrian post-war self-confidence (the identification with the Second Republic) was not a matter of *political* regeneration but of economic reconstruction. The economic recovery was what made the Austrians proud of their country. For the post-war generation, the major tool of identification with the Austrian state was not the (regained) stability of democratic institutions but economic success.

## 'Europe is our Economic Future'

It is also this economic element that introduces Europe as a *Projectum,* i.e. future notion, into the Austrian post-war political discourse. After 1945 Europe as a political-civilizational project was still only marginally present in Austria. And – we can add – this did not change until the year 2000. In the basic programme of the *Österreichische Volkspartei* (Austrian People's party) from 1958, it says: 'Europe will be our economic future' (Kleindel 1995: 413). Political categories did not play an important rule; what was crucial was economic success. To a certain degree this was still the case in 1994 when, in the referendum about joining the EU, an impressive two-thirds of the Austrian population voted for Austrian membership of the EU. The reason for such an overwhelming majority was simply that political questions of sovereignty, democracy, and republican representation, etc. did not play an important role; economic arguments dominated (being part of a common market or staying outside) – and from an economic point of view, the accession to the EU had naturally only advantages. In other words, we must not misinterpret the 66 per cent of the Austrian people voting for the EU as the manifestation of a nation's political will to join a supranational political unit; the vast majority of this 66 per cent did not vote for *l'Europe* in the political sense but for an 'economic future' – as it was said in the ÖVP programme from 1958. It was what Josef Dobretsberger once called a *'kalter Anschluß'* (cold affiliation). Against this background, it is no wonder that Austrians were quite surprised when in February 2000, after the formation of an ÖVP/FPÖ government, they were painfully reminded that the European Union is also a political-civilizational project.

The process of Austrian nation-building only slowly developed after 1945 – in the Second Republic. The common sense among Austrian political scientists can be summarized as follows: Austria has been – slowly but surely – becoming a normal modern and democratic state. Data from opinion polls show that this process works more slowly than surely. In 1964 only 47 per cent of the interviewees agreed to the statement: 'The Austrians are a nation' (*Die Österreicher sind eine Nation*); in 1994, the year of the EU referendum, it was at least 72 per cent – which is indeed much better than 47 per cent but still not convincing for a modern *demos*. On the other hand, when asked about their national pride, for instance in 1989, 53 per cent of the Austrians said that they were 'very proud' of being Austrian and 35 per cent 'rather proud'. Therewith, the Austrians' national pride is higher than the Swiss (31 per cent and 40 per cent, respectively, to the above questions), the German (21 per cent and 45 per cent, respectively) and also higher than that of the French. As reasons for this national pride it is mostly aspects such as beauty of landscape, political and social peace, neutrality, sports, music and literature that are named.

In 1955 Austria became independent and declared her status of neutrality. This neutrality became the central symbol of political self-interpretation and identification in the Second Republic, i.e. in the years after 1955. It allowed the maintenance of a form of *this-as-well-as-that* policy – or *neither-nor* policy – which had already been typical of the monarchy; Austria understood herself as being part neither of *l'Europe* nor of the 'east'. It was a prolongation of the *Mitteleuropa* idea in the sense of middle-range modernity; Austria did not fully enter *l'Europe*, but remained medium-level European. As the great mediator between east and west and as the charming host of international negotiations and conferences (Vienna as UNO-City), so to speak, Austria celebrated its 'neutro-passivity'.

Usually, political scientists argue that the concept of neutrality helped to create something like a normal Western national identity and self-confidence in Austria. This seems to be a myth, however. There are no indicators that allow such a conclusion. On the contrary, the concept of neutrality served as a counter-concept contradicting the idea of *l'Europe*, namely that civilization is not something that is simply there – like trad-ition – but something that has to be created, that needs active *citoyens*, political deeds, cosmopolitical strategies, etc. The Austrian neutrality was directed against all that: it was neutro-passivity in Carl Schmitt's sense (Schmitt 1981: 80). Unlike with the Hegelian form of neutrality estab-lished, for example, in Finland (see Henrik Meinander's Chapter 6 in this book), the Austrians performed a Grillparzer – i.e., non-active – neutrality. It led to the *Insel der Seligen* (Island of the blessed) mentality.

To be sure, neutrality was indeed something Austrians were proud of, as mentioned above. Nevertheless, national pride and a 'normal Western' national consciousness are two very different things. The first can refer to elements such as landscape, achievements in sport events, science and culture (as is prototypically the case in Austria), the second must refer – in one way or another – to democratic, republican and civilizational principles. The Austrian neutrality even contradicted these principles, or at least prevented their full internalization into the political culture. Summing up, the concept of neutrality – to be sure – gave the Austrian state some form of political meaning and sense but it definitely did not help to create a people in the political sense, i.e. a nation.

From the late 1980s, with Austria's petition to join the EU, the fall of the Iron Curtain and the end of the East–West conflict, the concept of neutrality lost (emotional) significance, and at the same time the notion of Europe in the sense of a positive goal gained importance in the political discourse. An analysis of presidential speeches on the National Holiday (26 October) – the day of the flag (comparable to the Independence day in the US) – from 1970 to 1996 shows the change in the use of 'Europe'. Until 1987, 'Europe' is predominantly used to denote a locality (Austria as 'Centre of Europe', in the 'Middle of Europe') and as some form of abstract noun – partly geographically, partly ideationally determined ('We are no longer the sick child of Europe', 1974; 'What was once the sick child of Europe is today a state which has to fulfil a task on and for this continent', 1983); after 1987 the geographic use almost disappears, Austria defining itself no longer through reference to a factual geographic position in Europe but through reference to Europe on an ideational level (cf. Benke 1999). Europe becomes a metaphor for certain principles, although nowhere in the presidential speeches is it clear what these principles are. They seem to be taken as a given – which is of course problematic in a country like Austria in which if anything at all is not simply given it is the European civilizational project. However, the accession to a 'bigger Europe' is described as 'a primarily intellectual task' – one that requires 'drastic inner changes' (Federal President Klestil in a speech from 1994).

The year 2000 showed that Austria apparently had not fulfilled this intellectual task, but had become again the sick child of Europe; but Austria does not understand the reaction of the mother because the latter thinks in different categories than does the child. Still the political and civilizational meaning of Europe as a project – *l'Europe* – is not understood. This becomes very clear when we read only the first paragraph of the preamble to the governmental programme of the coalition government between the ÖVP and the Haider-FPÖ from February 2000. This declaration, entitled 'Responsibility for Austria – A Future in the Heart of Europe', was demanded by the Federal President, Thomas Klestil, as a guarantee of the government's – and particularly the FPÖ's – 'European' character: that is, the conformity with the European *'Wertegemeinschaft'* (value community). The declaration begins with the following sentence:

> The Federal Government reaffirms its unswerving adherence to the spiritual and moral values which are the common heritage of the peoples of Europe and the true source of individual freedom, political liberty and the rule of law, principles which form the basis of all genuine democracy.

What is referred to here is not Europe as a project, Europe as a *dispositif idéel*, Europe as *l'Europe*, but 'the peoples of Europe'. As in the title 'Europe' is used as a purely geographic notion. One could say that as early as the very first (!) sentence of the declaration the authors miss the point. In other words, right at the beginning the government demonstrates that it has no idea of Europe as a civilizational project. The political meaning of Europe does not shine through. The problem is that it is not the 'spiritual and moral values of the peoples of Europe' that is requested by the other member states but the spiritual and moral values of *Europe*. This is the point that makes all the difference. The project character of Europe and its unity as well as singularity is lost behind the plurality of 'peoples'. Europe as *one* civilizational project is not present. Furthermore, the prominence of 'heritage' and 'peoples' in the sentence implicitly refers to tradition, cultural roots, and the past, and not to civilizational goals and the future. Europe is *Kultur*, not *Zivilisation*. In the words of Reinhart Koselleck (1989), the sentence construes a common *Erfahrungsraum* (area of experience), but no common *Erwartungshorizont* (horizon of expectation). Without the latter, however, the very basic idea of the European Union is lost. It is replaced by pre-1789 formulations.

## References

Bachmaier, H. (1998), 'Nachwort', in Franz Grillparzer, *Ein Bruderzwist in Habsburg*, Stuttgart, 101–4.

Ball, H. (1984), 'Österreichs Kulturmission', in *Der Künstler und die Zeitkrankheit*, Ausgewählte Schriften. Frankfurt: 172–6.

Benedikt, M. and Knoll, R. (1995), *Verdrängter Humanismus, Verzögerte Aufklärung. 3. Band. Bildung und Einbildung. Vom verfehlten Bürgerlichen zum Liberalismus*, Philosophie in Österreich (1820–1880). Klausen-Leopoldsdorf.

Benke, G. (1999), '"We are no longer the sick child of Europe": An investigation of the usage (and change) of the term "Neutrality" in the Presidential Speeches on the National Holiday (26 October) from 1974 to 1993', in R. Wodak and C. Ludwig (eds), *Challenges in a Changing World: Issues in Critical Discourse Analysis*, Vienna, 101–26.

Breuss, S., Liebhart, K. and Pribersky, A. (1995), *Inszenierungen: Stichwörter zu Österreich*, Vienna.

Cioran, E.M. (1990), *Über das reaktionäre Denken*, Frankfurt.

Coudenhove-Kalergi, R. (1922), *Pan-Europa*, Vienna/Leipzig.

Doderer, H. von (1992), *Die Dämonen*, Roman. Frankfurt.

Grillparzer, F. (1997 [1825]), *König Ottokars Glück und Ende: Trauerspiel in fünf Aufzügen*, Stuttgart.

—— (1998 [1872]), *Ein Bruderzwist in Habsburg: Trauerspiel in fünf Aufzügen*, Stuttgart.

Hofmannsthal, H. von (1979), *Gesammelte Werke. Reden und Aufsätze II. 1914–1924*, Frankfurt.

Kleindel, W. (1995), *Österreich: Daten zur Geschichte und Kultur*, Vienna.

Knoll, R. and Kohlenberger, H. (1994), *Gresellschaftstheorien: Ihre Entwicklungsgsgeschichte als Krisenmanagement in Österreich 1850–1938*, Vienna.

Koselleck, R. (1989), *Vergangene Zukunft: Zur Semantik geschichtlicher Zeiten*, Frankfurt.

Magris, C. (1999), *Danube: A Sentimental Journey from the Source to the Black Sea*, London.

Matz, K.-J. (1999), *Europa-Chronik: Daten Europäischer Geschichte von der Antike bis zur Gegenwart*, Münich.

Musil, R. (1961), *Das hilflose Europa*, Hamburg.

—— (1970), *Der Mann ohne Eigenschaften. Roman*, Frankfurt.

Popovici, A. (1906), *Die Vereinigten Staaten von Groß-Österreich*, Politische Studien. Leipzig.

Rosenstock-Huessy, E. (1987 [1951]), *Die Europäischen Revolutionen und der Charakter der Nationen*, Moers.

—— (1993), *Out of Revolution: An Autobiography of Western Man*, Providence/Oxford.

Schmitt, C. (1981), *Land und Meer*, Cologne.

Schulze, H. (1999), *Staat und Nation in der Europäischen Geschichte*, Münich.

Spengler, O. (1971), *Der Untergang des Abendlandes*, Frankfurt.

Voegelin, E. (1999 [1937]), *The Authoritarian State: An Essay on the Problem of the Austrian State*, Columbia/London.

Winter, E.K. (1922), *Austria Erit In Orbe Ultima*, Vienna.

# –12–

# Continuities and Changes of Europe in German National Identity
## *Willfried Spohn*

## Introduction

There is perhaps no other nation in Europe with a similarly oscillating and unsettled collective identity, and corresponding European orientations, as Germany (Nassehi 2000). Although the German nation gained certain contours within the framework of the Holy Roman Empire from the High Middle Ages, a modern German nation state – as compared to others in Western Europe – only developed relatively late and with enormous conflicts with the European inter-state order (Breuilly 1992; Dann 1993; Langewiesche 2000; Winkler 2000). With the onset of the European modern age, the German-speaking lands became confessionally divided, fell behind into economic backwardness and for centuries remained politically fragmented and militarily weak against the surrounding state powers. Only in the nineteenth century after the French revolution, with the Napoleonic dissolution of the Old Empire and supported by absolutist modernization, did national unification of the German-speaking territories become a possibility. But the first German unification in 1871 could only be reached after three wars against Denmark, Habsburg Austria and France, and at the price of a late-absolutist semi-democratic political order. This type of state formation laid the ground not only for the highly conflictive and oscillating process of nation-building and democratization, but also for the two world wars fought to defend and expand German hegemony in continental Europe in the first half of the twentieth century. The result was not only the 'German catastrophe', the Holocaust and the destruction of old Europe, but also the division and territorial limitation of Germany in the context of a divided Europe during the cold war. Only with the Western integration and democratization of West Germany, and after the collapse of Soviet communism, the inclusion of East Germany and the second unification of Germany in 1990, did a consolidated democratic nation state in an equilibrium with the surrounding European inter-state system and family of nations finally materialize (Schoch 1992, Spohn 1995).

Although in a political-institutional and geopolitical-European sense the second unification of Germany has solved the German question, German collective identity in its domestic currents and in its relations to other national identities in Europe is still haunted by the traumatic experiences and memories of the past (Giesen 2000; Jarausch 1997; Westle 1999). The basic insecurity of German national identity relates, on the one hand, to several internal features. At the core, there is the burden of two totalitarian dictatorships articulated in a soul-searching guilt feeling by the political and cultural elites, but at the same time challenged by an intensified xenophobic neo-nationalism. In addition, the growing together of two separate post-war trajectories has been accompanied by a sharpening opposition between a Western and an Eastern German identity. The Westerners perceive themselves as more liberal, cosmopolitan and European and consider the Easterners to be more traditional, socialist and nationalistic; whereas the Easterners see themselves as more collectivistic, German and patriotic, and take the Westerners to be rather un-German, Westernized and individualistic. As a result, a low national self-esteem combines with a weak confidence in German democratic culture. The basic insecurity of German national identity, on the other hand, shows also in some external characteristics. At the core, the regained national sovereignty and the renewed power position of Germany in the European centre has translated in a more self-conscious German foreign policy. At the same time, the tendency is to restrict German self-confidence by the moral scruples of the past and therefore cover German national interests under the roof of international alliances and particularly of the European Union (Markovits and Reich 1997). As a corollary, the West European, and particularly the old challengers of German central-European power aspirations, France and Great Britain, are suspicious of German hidden intentions to regain a hegemonic European power position. Also, the East Europeans and particularly the main victims of Nazi-German aggression, suspect that German reconciliation rhetoric and support of the Eastern enlargement of the EU primarily aims at the expansion of German hegemony in Eastern Europe (Katzenstein 1997a).

This chapter attempts to analyse this mostly neglected European dimension in the formation and present reconfiguration of German collective identity. Which meaning or meanings did and does 'Europe' have in German national discourse and attitudes? What meanings were and are connected with the different geopolitical directions from the European centre to Western and Eastern, Southern and Northern Europe? How did and do the different meanings of Europe within the different political, social and cultural layers of German society relate to each other? Which components in the meanings of Europe remained constant and which components changed over time? In order to give some answers to these overarching questions, I will outline a long-term historical-sociological perspective in three major phases. First, I will analyse the historical foundations of the meaning of Europe in the formation of German national identity in the transition from the old German Empire to the first formation of the German nation state. Second, I will characterize the oscillating and conflicting meanings of Europe in the development of German national identity between 1871 and 1945. Third, I will analyse the restructuring of the divided meanings of Europe in West and East Germany after 1945 and their recombination in the contemporary post-unification phase.

## Historical semantics of Europe from the Old Empire to the Foundation of the German Nation State

The meanings of Europe in late medieval and early modern Germany or the German-speaking regions within the Holy Roman Empire share some general features of an emerging common understanding of Europe. Appearing first in the Carolingian Empire, but used in a more consistent sense only in the late medieval and early modern ages, 'Europe' basically signified the cultural area of Western Roman Catholic Christianity in a certain contrast to Eastern Greek Orthodox Christianity and in a sharp opposition to the Islamic world (Davies 1996; Delanty 1995; Eisenstadt 1987; Heffernan 1998). This basic meaning crystallized more forcefully first with the division of Western Christianity between Catholicism and Protestantism and then with the dissemination of the Enlightenment, and pluralization and secularization of Western Christianity. Europe thus came to signify a secularized identity of the Western Christian civilization with an ambivalent inclusion of Eastern Christianity. The early German understanding of Europe shared these general features, but at the same time reflected the specific geopolitical location of the German nation within the Holy Roman Empire (Gollwitzer 1964). On the one side, an important element consisted of the continuing imperial claim to represent legitimately the old Roman Empire. With the political fragmentation and decline of the German-Roman Empire this imperial-universal claim became increasingly anachronistic, and similar imperial claims were also raised by the other rising European great powers such as France and, later,

Spain or Britain. Still, it remained a powerful legitimacy core for Habsburg as the centre of the German-Roman Empire since the Protestant Reformation, and served as a framework of Catholic Reform to reunify Europe under the aegis of Catholic universalism. On the other side, this universal claim of a Christian European civilization was also translated from Catholic Southern to Protestant Northern Europe. In confessionally divided Germany, in a parallel, the remaining Habsburg imperial and universal claim to represent the whole of Europe found a counterpart in an ascending Prussian Protestant and Germanic-centric understanding of Europe. Here, the Germanic civilization, through the conquest and transformation of the Roman Empire, was imagined as the true founder of Europe (Gollwitzer 1964).

The confessional division of Western Christianity destroyed a common religious foundation of a European identity, but on this basis the dissemination of the Enlightenment recreated a new common understanding of Europe in a secularized form. This secularization process did not dissolve the Western Christian cultural basis of Europe nor did it mean a breakdown of the adversarial universalistic-missionary claims of either Catholicism or Protestantism. Rather, it created an overarching trans-confessional bridge of a common European culture (Delanty 1995). With the Enlightenment, a stronger trans-confessional inclusion of Eastern Europe into the European civilization of Europe also became possible, particularly since the Habsburg Empire had pushed back the Ottoman sphere of influence from South-eastern Europe, and also since more or less simultaneously Tsarist Russia, with its expansion to East Central Europe, had become more involved in European affairs. But at the same time, the notion of an enlightened Europe created new divisions between the Western enlightened 'civilized' – that is, the developed and modern parts – and the Eastern non-enlightened 'barbarian' – that is, the backward and traditional parts of Europe (Wolff 1994). Within this European geocultural context, the German proto-nation in the framework of the German-Roman Empire was affected by the confessional division and enlightened transformation of Europe in two major directions. On the one hand, the Western European confessional division went right through Germany and divided the German-speaking lands into a southern and western German Catholic part, and a northern and eastern German Protestant one, with a considerable confessional overlap and fragmentation within the ascending territorial-absolutist states. In this direction, their European perspectives were divided between an orientation to the Habsburg universal monarchy to the south and an orientation to the rising Prussian absolutist state to the north (Gollwitzer 1964). On the other, the dissemination of the

Enlightenment embedded the German-speaking lands into a Western-Eastern gradient of progress and backwardness, of modernity and tradition, of light and darkness. Frederick's enlightened absolutism in Prussia saw itself, and was seen, as more progressive and modern than Joseph's Habsburg absolutism. Yet, both empires claimed their missionary task to bring Western progress to Eastern Europe as a legitimization for partitioning Poland and incorporating Hungary (Gollwitzer 1964).

At the same time, the German-speaking lands within the framework of the German-Roman Empire increasingly lost their former power position in the centre of Europe. The primary reason was the developmental shift toward Western Europe. The colonial conquest of the Americas by the Western European sea powers, the rise of the Atlantic economy and the early formation of centralizing nation states shifted the economic, political and military power balance to the West. The religious and dynastical wars of the Reformation and Counter-Reformation made this gravitational shift manifest, further weakening and devastating the imperial centre. The Westphalian peace order brought this process of implosion to a halt, enabled the formation of German territorial absolutist states and laid the foundation for an economic and political revival of the German-speaking regions. But for some time this did not reverse the Western-Eastern gradient of development and for two centuries the German regions remained dependent on the surrounding great powers. Under those international conditions, seen from the predominant German perspective, Europe came to take on the meaning of a European peace order as a political balance of European states and nations (Gollwitzer 1964). German legal scholars, political scientists and historians made a special contribution to international law and the history and sociology of the European state system. Of special significance, here, was the doctrine of power equilibrium between the different national states in Europe. German philosophers reflected upon a European peace order based on the moral-civilizational progress of Europe. At the one pole in a republican-cosmopolitan state orientation, Immanuel Kant's treatise on 'eternal peace' developed an international peace order of European states. On the other pole, in an ethnic-cultural orientation, Johann G. Herder developed a European idea of a solidary and equal family of peoples.

The French Revolution and its imperialistic export to continental Europe through Napoleonic warfare meant also a crucial break in German conceptions of Europe and a clearer crystallization of its major components. For many German observers, the French Revolution seemed to represent the incarnation of Enlightenment principles, the materialization of a modern nation state based on popular sovereignty and a democratic constitutional order, and was welcomed as a model for their own democratic-enlightened aspirations, either revolutionary or reformist. Despite the Caesarist anti-democratic elements of the Napoleonic imperial regime, French imperialistic warfare was also first greeted by major parts of the German intellectual and political elites as a means to modernize their own *anciens régimes* and to create a new Europe on the basis of French republican principles (Nipperdey 1987; Sheehan 1989). On this basis, the Holy Roman Empire of the German Nation was finally dissolved in 1803 in order to reorganize the politically completely fragmented German lands of more than 300 principalities into the form of more centralized German absolutist states. As well, modern legal orders modelled after the Napoleonic Code became institutionalized and liberal-constitutional reforms were introduced. The most far-reaching reforms were carried through in the French-occupied German territories west of the Rhine, whereas in the rest of the German regions, the Republican principles were limited to a liberalizing reform of territorial absolutism. Thus, the French revolution and Napoleonic European warfare triggered the crystallization of a German liberal nationalism in its Jacobin-Republican and reform-democratic varieties. At the same time, Napoleonic warfare imposed a European order based on French supremacy rather than on a pluralistic European order of sovereign nation states. As a consequence, only a few German admirers of Napoleon were able to follow him also in his European aspirations (Gollwitzer 1964). Some German Jacobinist republicans, such as Joseph von Görres, wanted to see in Napoleon an emerging republican universalist European order; others in a Protestant-enlightened tradition, such as Karl von Dalberg, saw in him the restitution of an enlightened Carolingian Empire. Others in a Catholic orientation, for example Johann Christoph von Aretin, could view in Napoleon the restitution of a Catholic cultural Europe and again others, such as Jean Paul, found in him the reconstruction of an Occidental European culture. But these German justifications of a Napoleonic universalist Europe were exceptions to its growing rejection by the emerging modern German nationalism and alternative German conceptions of Europe.

The core of German modern nationalism as it emerged in the resistance against Napoleon's European order consisted in a specific combination of ethnic-cultural and political components. On the one hand, it was based on a developing German high culture in literature, music, poetry, science and philosophy as the nucleus of a cultural communication community of the German-speaking regions (Dann 1993). The German *Kulturnation* centred around an enlightened humanistic idea of cultural education carried by the German-speaking cultural elites in the regional German states and urban civil societies, and was based on a developing common German language. On the other hand, German modern nationalism oscillated in its political-territorial orientations between the restoration of the old Reich, the political unification of all German-speaking lands and a marked regional patriotism embedded in the multiple ethnic-regional cultures and territorial dynastic states. The experience of the French revolution presented the model of a culturally homogenous, politically centralized and democratic-constitutional nation state, and the liberation struggle against Napoleon's armies intensified a sense of German national identity. However, the institutional framework bringing together the cultural nation and the political order remained contested. An imperial patriotism went along with a cultural universalism taking German culture as an ethical measure of other civilizations. The national patriotism imagined the unification of all German-speaking regions, but wavered in its political implications between a Catholic Habsburg, a Protestant Prussian or a more pluralistic German federation. And only regional patriotism found in the territorial dynasties a site for democratic-constitutional reforms. These coexisting layers of a crystallizing German identity found their expression in differing images of Europe (Gollwitzer 1964; Lützeler 1992). On the one pole, in a political pragmatic orientation, there was the *idée directrice* of a European power balance combined with a German federation. On the other pole, in a romantic mood, Europe was imagined as a renewed Christian Europe either by Novalis (Friedrich von Hardenberg) in a Germanic and a pietistic way, by Adam Müller in a Catholic cultural orientation, or in Friedrich Schlegel as a reconstitution of a Germanic-Romanic Occident. In between, early German nationalists such as Johann Gottlieb Fichte, Ernst Moritz Arndt or Friedrich Ludwig Jahn were dreaming of a strong unified Germany based on the superior German culture mediating between the more developed but rationalistic West and the backward and barbaric East.

These different initial layers of the meanings of Europe in German identity or identities unfolded in changing constellations during the course of the nineteenth century until the actual political unification of Germany in 1871. In the restoration period after the end of the Napoleonic wars, the predominant layer became the re-establishment of a European power balance as a *pentarchy* between the five great European powers: Great Britain, France, Habsburg, Prussia and Russia. Duke Metternich was the leading intellectual and political mind, but most German, Prussian and Austrian statesmen and reform politicians followed his lead (Gollwitzer 1964; Nipperdey 1987). In the context of this European power balance, such Catholic and conservative thinkers as Franz von Baader were attracted by the traditional power of Habsburg and the stabilization of its imperial role in Europe, whereas Protestant philosophers such as Georg Friedrich Hegel identified with Prussia as the more modern state and hoped for its greater European influence. Underneath this predominant idea of Europe as power equilibrium, on the one hand, the romantic idea of a reconstituted Christian Europe first played an important role (Lützeler 1992; Mosse 1988). It was particularly inspired by the foundation of the Holy Alliance between the great European powers including tsarist Russia and accompanied by an irenic reconciliation of the three main branches of Christian religion in Europe, but then lost its attractiveness due to its aristocratic-conservative outlook. On the other hand, a European counter-project of a brotherhood of democratic nations began to emerge. Inspired by the betrayed ideals of the French Revolution, the young European movement under the leadership of Giuseppe Mazzini became increasingly influential in an unfolding democratic movement in Germany. For a short while, the German revolution in 1848/49 brought this national-democratic and European pluralistic layer in German national identity to the surface.

The German democratic revolution from below failed, and with it the aims of a democratic national unification of Germany and an international order of democratic nation states in Europe. This failure was due not only to the resistance of the absolutist monarchies to accept democratic-constitutional control and their capacity to crush the revolutionary upheaval by military means, but also to the powerlessness and contradictions of the democratic movement itself (Nipperdey 1987; Wehler 1995). The Frankfurt Parliament aimed at a great-German national unification that neither the Habsburg Empire nor Prussia could accept. But also the offer of the imperial crown to the Prussian king and the creation of a small-German constitutional monarchy failed, because of the traditional-divine authority conception of Prussian monarchical rule. In addition, the Frankfurt Parliament was weakened by its inability to reconcile its German unification aims with the emerging claims to national independence by the small nations within the borders of the Habsburg and Prussian empires. Moreover, the national-democratic movement showed a split between the liberal-democratic reform majority oriented to the existing German and European state order and a socialist-revolutionary minority personified in Karl Marx and Wilhelm Weitling hoping for a European world war and a unified socialist Europe. As a result of the failing democratic revolution, the visionaries of a pluralist-democratic or socialist Europe went underground or emigrated. Instead, the absolutist monarchies were restored and with them the international power balance of the European state order. Yet, the democratic aims of the revolutionary movement became partially institutionalized in a limited liberalization and constitutionalization of the late-absolutist regimes. The national aims of German unification were overtaken and tamed by Prussia as the rising economic and military power in Germany against its Habsburg rival which was embedded in a weakening multinational Empire. The military defeat of Habsburg and France by Prussia cleared the way for the first German unification under Prussian hegemony, which brought a semi-democratic authoritarian nation state and at the same time changed the European power balance. As a consequence, German national identity or identities in their internal composition and embedded meanings of Europe also changed considerably.

## The German Reich 1871–1945 between a European Nation State and a Germanic Europe

Only to a certain extent was Imperial Germany both in its Bismarckian and its Wilhelminian phases a modern nation state in a Western sense of congruent state formation and nation-building with parallel processes of constitutional democratization. First, in ethnic-territorial terms, the small-German form of national unification, despite its name, contained some great-German elements including large non-German populations in terms of language and national identification (Nipperdey 1991). With the annexation of Alsace-Lorraine, a German- and a French-speaking population, both nationally oriented primarily to the French nation state, were included into Imperial Germany. With Prussia, in addition, a large Polish-speaking and Polish-feeling population in the Prussian Eastern provinces became part of Imperial Germany. And further, there was a considerable Danish minority in northern Schleswig. On the other hand, Imperial Germany excluded also a considerable number of German-speaking populations who, as a part of the German *Kulturnation,* felt German and therefore felt excluded from the German nation state. To some extent this was true for the German/Austrian speaking populations of the Habsburg Empire, particularly at the borders to Imperial Germany. To some extent, this was also true for German-speaking groups outside Imperial Germany and Habsburg Austria. Thus, on the basis of the geographical extension of the German-speaking population in Central Europe, the small-German solution of a German nation state was not small enough to avoid internal ethno-national conflict and, at the same time, it was not large enough to avoid the potential development of irridentism outside its borders. These internal and external ethnic-national tensions turned into growing conflicts with the evolving Germanization policy of ethnic minorities in Imperial Germany and, vice versa, with the rise of separatist nationalism in East Central Europe and the Russification policy in tsarist Russia against German minorities.

Second, with the unification of Germany under Prussian hegemony, a semi-democratic authoritarian nation state containing decisive obstacles to nation-building and national integration came into being (Lepsius 1991; Mommsen 1990). To begin with, the predominant role of Prussia in Imperial Germany imposed a centralized state structure, contributing to an institutional imbalance with the decentralized structure of the German federation or German federalism. Then, Prussian hegemony implied also a shift from a traditional numerical balance between Protestantism and Catholicism to a Protestant predominance over and simultaneously, with the emerging *Kulturkampf*, also discriminating against the Catholic minority. For a long time, the resulting ghetto-like situation of German Catholics impeded their national integration, only allowing for a sort of negative integration. The same was true for the working classes who in the framework of the semi-democratic authoritarian regime were largely excluded from political representation and decision-making. As a consequence, the social conflicts in Imperial Germany considerably sharpened, and a large part of the working classes organized in Marxist Social Democracy, strengthening the feeling of a separate working-class nation and again only allowing for a negative national integration. In addition, the developing authoritarian form of assimilation or enforced Germanization also impeded any national accommodation of the ethnic minorities and, last but not least, growing German anti-Semitism also undermined the integration of the German Jews. The only social strata identifying more or less positively with Imperial Germany were the educated middle classes; however, here also there were certain tensions with the semi-democratic authoritarian structure of the Imperial regime. Thus, the unification of Germany as a united nation state was followed, due to the lack of political democratization, by only partial and conflictual processes of nation-building, severely limiting a positive and unambiguous national identification (Dann 1993).

Third, the foundation of the German Empire in the centre of Europe decisively changed the international power balance between the European states. For the first time in the modern era, the weak European centre was replaced by a strong centre endangering the traditional European power balance. This geopolitical change was the result not simply of the existence of a new centralized nation state in the middle of Europe, but of its particular societal dynamics (Spohn 1995). First and foremost, the dynamics of German industrialization turned a conglomerate of moderately backward and only loosely economically integrated German regions into a fast-growing national economy that overtook the hitherto leading first industrial nation in Europe, Great Britain, at the turn of the century. To this, the German-Habsburg tariff-protected market after the economic crisis of the 1870s and modelled after the German *Zollverein*, particularly contributed. In addition, the German population, already enlarged by the annexation of Alsace-Lorraine, grew much faster than in the Western European countries and made Imperial Germany the most populated western- and central-European country. These socio-economic dynamics formed the social bases for the growing political and military power potential of Imperial Germany in the middle of Europe and altered substantially the European power balance. Under the rule of Bismarck and of Wilhelm I, German politics still tried to balance out the growing tensions between Imperial Germany and the surrounding European great powers. Bismarck's foreign-policy aim was to secure the newly established German nation state and to avoid any further international conflicts. Under Wilhelm II, however, Imperial Germany started openly to compete with the imperialistic policy of the other European powers, antagonizing France, Britain and Russia, and to rely more, and solely, on its special relationship with the declining and crisis-ridden Habsburg Empire. With this *Weltpolitik*, Imperial Germany headed towards a world war against all the other allied European great powers, thus endangering what it had just achieved: the unified German nation state (Mommsen 1990; Wehler 1995).

In these crucially changed domestic and geopolitical conditions, as a consequence of the foundation of the German Empire in the centre of Europe, German collective identity, its constitutive currents and European orientations, gained different meanings and played a crucial role in the rising domestic and international conflicts. Bismarck as the main architect of German unification under Prussian hegemony returned in a sense to Metternich's European equilibrium policy. His primary identification was with Prussia, and German unification was primarily pursued from the perspective of Prussian dynastical rather than German national interests. Accordingly, his annexation of Alsace-Lorraine was based on dynastical-military considerations rather than German nationalistic sentiments (Nipperdey 1991). But despite his power game to achieve German unification, he basically followed a conception of *Realpolitik* that tried to balance out the new German Empire with the other European powers and to contain its nationalistic forces. At the same time, Bismarck as a part of the Prussian court elite, had to accommodate the German national movement as the main pillar of German unification. In a continuation of the main currents of German nationalism throughout the nineteenth century, the German national movement was national-liberal, combining the wish for a strong German nation state, the conviction of the special value of German Protestant and humanistic culture, and a democratic-constitutional orientation. From the perspective of national liberalism, the foundation of the German Empire materialized first and foremost its national aspirations and deepened, even though not sufficiently, the constitutionalization and democratization of the German political regime. As a consequence, liberal nationalism articulating mainly the national sentiments of the German educated middle classes turned into a positive and affirmative identification with Imperial Germany (Dann 1993).

However, this Borussian national-liberal core layer of German national identity was unable, due to the imperial ambiguities of the German nation and the lack of democratic inclusion by the political system, to penetrate the whole of German society. As a consequence, with the rising national-istic and imperialistic tensions in the Wilhelmian period and the perceived threat of the German nation from inside and outside, the democratic liberal components in mainstream liberal nationalism weakened and the cultural components oriented towards a cultural integration of the German nation strengthened. At the same time, alternative currents in German national identity continued to play an important role and gained even more salience during the conflictive course of the German Empire. On the one pole, there were the imperial loyalties on the basis of an all-embracing German *Kulturnation* that resented the Bismarckian Empire as an uncompleted reconstruction of the German Old Reich. This great-German orientation had a Prussian cultural Protestant wing, including such as Helmut Treitschke who demanded a pan-German Empire on a Protestant basis. In the Wilhelminian period, this oppositional imperial nationalistic orientation became organized particularly in the anti-Semitic right-radical pan-German League (Dann 1993). The great-German orient-ation also had a Habsburg Catholic wing still hoping for an alternative ultramontane Habsburgian unification of Germany. With the stronger integration of political Catholicism in Imperial Germany, this imperial-ultramontane orientation receded in Germany, but it became, with the growing ethno-national tensions, more influential in Habsburg-Austria. This great-German orientation was also present in the Social-Democratic working-class movement that had a common German and Austrian con-nection and envisioned, though more implicit than explicit, a pan-German democratic and socialist future state. These various imperial-cum-national cultural orientations and sentiments were reflected in the social *Kaisertum* and foreign policy of Wilhelm II turning away from Bismarck´s European *Realpolitik* to a missionary-imperialistic *Weltpolitik*.

Under the new geopolitical conditions of Imperial Germany and related to the different layers of German national identity, the German meanings of Europe were also shaped in new directions. Although Bismarck conceptualized his foreign policy basically in the framework of a European equilibrium of the great powers, it was by no means a European peace policy, but rather a German power policy within Europe. In addition, by establishing a special link between the German state and the Habsburg Empire, Bismarck created de facto a German imperial hegemony over Central Europe. However, the specific colour of this German *Mitteleuropa* within Europe was dependent on the different national attitudes and political orientations, and developed a sharper profile in the Wilheminian period (Grunewald 1996; Nurdin 1980). In a Western orientation, the democratic and social wings of liberal nationalism were oriented to a strong but democratic German nation state in a European cooperation with the Western European great powers. Here, as in Max Weber's *Antrittsrede*, or in Friedrich Naumann´s *Mitteleuropa*, Germany was seen as a democratic-capitalist core in Central Europe in a European power balance. This national-liberal current was accompanied by a widespread mood of reconciliation with France and the wish for a European peace order. In this direction, Friedrich Nietzsche was the most outspoken philosopher, but Social Democracy also shared it in a heterodox version of a socialist and democratic European peace order. In a northern direction, the Protestant and cultural wings of national liberalism were moving towards a more authoritarian cultural nationalism, envisioning a strong Germanic Empire in Central Europe. Here, particularly in the face of rising international tensions and ethno-nationalist conflicts, the emphasis was on the defence against Western European capitalism and the missionary protection of German culture in Central and East Central Europe (Elias 1990, 1994). In a southern direction, political Catholicism hoped to strengthen a more Catholic Germany in cooperation with Habsburg and Rome. Here, German and Austrian social Catholicism imagined a stronger Catholic corporatist German Empire. And in a more eastern direction, the German Empire was envisioned as a future world power between America, the British Commonwealth and Tsarist Russia by protecting the Habsburg imperial hemisphere and expanding into the declining Ottoman Empire.

In the context of rising ethno-nationalist and imperialist tensions in the early twentieth century, an outspoken liberal, social-Catholic and Social Democratic European peace movement developed in Germany. It was increasingly outpaced, however, by a national sense of being encircled by a hostile Europe, of being denied a proper place in Europe and, in addition, of being internally weakened by ethnic, social and political divisions. On this basis, the outbreak of the First World War – triggered by the German military command, aristocratic court and political government – was supported by an overwhelming national feeling of the need to rally together in the hour of a deadly crisis of the German nation. This emerging integral nationalism was to some extent also shared by the Liberal Democratic and Social Democratic pacifistic camps' by accepting a *Burgfrieden* with the authoritarian regime. The warfare then intensified this integral nationalism but also – the more the hope for a decisive victory vanished – intensified the wish for peace. The end of the war brought general relief and the democratic revolution found widespread support but, at the same time, the defeat and the imposed Versailles peace treaty were overwhelmingly experienced as unjust and humiliating for the German nation. Under those circumstances, the Weimar Republic as the first fully developed democratic-constitutional regime in Germany was marked by a national stigma: it sealed the fate of a weak Germany imposed by a hostile Europe and, through the sharpening political-ideological conflicts, it renewed the internal division of the German nation (Winkler 2000). As a consequence, the Weimar democratic regime was not able to generate a positive national identification, but became increasingly divided between a weakening democratic camp and a growing integral nationalistic camp opposed to the Weimar political system. The world economic crisis of the late 1920s and early 1930s fundamentally weakened the Weimar democratic regime, decisively shifted the weight between the democratic-pluralistic and integral-nationalistic camps, and enabled the rise of the most extreme integral nationalism, eventually leading to the establishment of the Nazi dictatorship.

The experiences of warfare, defeat and the formation of Weimar Germany in the post-war order of Europe transformed not only the main currents of German national identity, but also the embedded meanings of Europe (Krüger 1995). The main political supporters of Weimar democracy – the Social Democrats, the leftist national liberals and the Catholic centre – continued their pre-war visions of a European peace order with a democratic Germany on equal terms with the other European nations. However reluctantly, they basically accepted the territorial reduction and ethnic-cultural homogenization of the Weimar state through the loss of Alsace-Lorraine in the west to France and Polish-speaking regions in the east to Poland. But also this democratic camp still followed a basically great-German conception of a German nation state by continuing the notion of a German Reich and resenting the Allies' denial of the opportunity for Austria to join it. This democratic camp hoped also for an economic reconstruction of a German *Mitteleuropa* in a close link between Germany and Austria, positive relationships with the new nation states in East Central Europe, and renewed partnerships with France and Great Britain. However, only a few political leaders in this camp, such as Gustav Stresemann, were also willing to act in this direction. And they met only a few leaders on the side of the Allies, such as Aristide Briand or Winston Churchill, who were pursuing a German-Western European reconciliation and, on its basis, a European unity. This European peace policy was thereby influenced particularly by Richard Coudenhove-Kalergi's Pan-European Union envisioning a multicultural politically united Western Europe (Bugge 1993; Heffernan 1998: 125–8).

In the context of the Allies' continuing policy of revenge and the strengthening of integral nationalism in Weimar Germany and in East Central Europe, however, this road to European unity was barred. Instead, the rising integral nationalistic camp in Weimar Germany came to disseminate quite another meaning of Europe. Michael Heffernan has called it the geopolitics of resentment (Heffernan 1998: 131). At its core was the wish and the will to restore a strong German Reich in the centre of Europe. The basic layer, here, was the German *Kulturnation*, with a corresponding imperial roof including Austria, and the defence of the now ex-territorial ethnic minorities in the newly formed East Central European nation states. In this German *Mitteleuropa*, however, the renewed German Reich was not embedded in a European pluralistic power balance, but envisioned as the only continental European power that could withstand and compete with Western Europe, under France and Britain, as well as with Eastern Europe under the hegemony of Soviet Russia. Again, several colours of such a renewed German Reich within Europe can be distinguished. In a cultural orientation, there was still the idea of a culturally unified great-German Reich able to mediate between Northern Protestantism and Southern Catholicism as well as between the capitalist West and the communist East. In such an orientation, Oskar Spengler could hope to renew declining Occidental Europe. In a political-institutional form, the renewed German Reich was seen as the dominating core of a continental European order. Such a vision guided Carl Schmitt in his conception of Europe as a *Grossraum*. And in ethnic-racial terms, the renewed German Reich was supposed to protect the space of German settlement from the German core regions far into the scattered German populations in East Central Europe (Heffernan 1998: 131–8). Here, many social and cultural geographers provided the material for an expanded

German Reich to the East. The National-Socialist orientation brought these different layers together and radicalized them in a totalitarian Darwinist vision of a racially purified and hierarchized German *Lebensraum*.

  With the seizure of power by Hitler, the German revolution and the formation of Nazi Germany, the most radical version of German integral nationalism became reality (Mosse 1981). The Third Reich did not only fulfil the idea of a restoration of the Old Reich and the notion of a culturally homogenous nation, but in addition attempted through totalitarian warfare and racial purification to materialize the vision of a Germanic Europe. The price was the exclusion of alternative political orientations and independent civic organizations, the exclusion and annihilation of German and European Jewry, the destruction of old Europe and finally the self-destruction of Germany itself. At the same time, the total collapse of Germany in its warfare against the European, Soviet and American alliance created the preconditions for the final demise of German imperial identities, feelings of cultural superiority, and militarist nationalistic orientations – and with them the visions of a Germanized Europe.

## The Divided Reconstruction and Europeanization of the German Nation State, 1945–2000

With defeat in the Second World War and the collapse of Nazi dictatorship, a fundamental break and redirection of German state-formation and nation-building and its geopolitical setting within Europe began. Under the rule of the victorious Allies, post-war Germany was divided into four military zones, its Eastern territories were lost to Poland and Russia, Prussia as the state unifier of Germany was dissolved and Austria as the great-German extension was separated onto its own path of state-formation and nation-building. In addition, with the emerging cold war division of Europe, Germany was also divided into a Western half, the West German Federal Republic under close supervision by the Western Allies, and an Eastern half, the East German Democratic Republic (GDR) under the direct military control of the Soviet Union (Klessmann 1986). For forty years, from 1949 to the collapse of the Soviet communist bloc and the GDR in 1989, both parts of Germany moved on distinctly different trajectories of political and socio-economic development. In West Germany, following the Weimar predecessor, a democratic-constitutional regime was established; and the state embarked on a thorough reconstruction. Dynamic development of a capitalist market economy complemented by an encompassing welfare system quickly occurred. In East Germany, following the alternative model of a socialist-communist class-nation, a Soviet-communist totalitarian system with a centralized state economy and socialist welfare system was institutionalized. As a consequence of these separate societal developments, also the West German and East German collective identities increasingly diverged, but they did not dissolve the common, historically formed German nation and national identity (Schweigler 1973; Weidenfeld 1981). When the Soviet communist regime collapsed, the overwhelming orientations re-emerging in East Germany were directed toward political democratization and national unification. In West Germany, the predominant sentiment was to include East Germany into the successful model of the Federal Republic. But the second German unification in 1990 only became possible because the Western Allies, the United States and the West European countries on the one side, as well as the Soviet Union and the post-communist Eastern European countries on the other, were basically convinced that a United Germany would not resume its authoritarian, nationalistic and imperialistic course (Merkl 1993).

As a matter of fact, the divided post-war reconstruction and reunification of Germany has resulted in a German nation state in which the historical ambivalences of the first German unification between a great-German Reich and a small-German nation state has come to an end (Spohn 1995). For the first time, there is strong congruence between the German state and the German nation. One important precondition for this was the limitation of German state borders to an ethnic-culturally homogenous territory. Germany lost about one-fourth of its former Eastern territories (in relation to its borders of 1937), primarily to a westward-shifted Poland. And at the same time, United Germany has also accepted this territorial reduction by recognizing the Odra-Neisse border between Germany and Poland. A second important precondition was the resettlement, primarily to West Germany, of German ethnic minorities from East Central Europe, particularly from Poland and Czechoslovakia. For a long time, the expellee organizations vocally resisted the legalization of their forced migration. Yet, in the end not only the majority of the population in United Germany, but increasingly also a large part of the expellees and their offspring themselves have come to accept the past. A third important precondition for the congruence between state and nation in United Germany was the national separation of post-war Austria from Germany. In contrast to the past when the majority of German Austrians aspired to an inclusion into the German Empire, post-war Austria went its own separate course of Austrian nation-building (Bruckmüller 1994). Although this national separation was at first quite contradictory, Austrian-German irridentism almost completely disappeared during the course of independent nation-building. Thus, as a result of the geographical disappearance of German lands and settlements in East Central Europe, the ethnic-territorial bases of a German Empire dissolved and enabled the development of an Empire-contracted form of a state-oriented and political-territorial national identity.

The divided reconstruction and reunification of the German nation state has also resulted in the formation of a constitutional and federal democratic regime in which the historical ambivalence of the authoritarian modernization path have, in the end, been overcome (Berghahn 1987; Graubard 1994). First, in West Germany, a liberal-democratic and federal order became institutionalized. It corrected some of the shortcomings of the Weimar constitution by minimizing the executive power of the president, upgrading the power of the Constitutional Court, introducing a 5 per cent clause for parliamentarian representation, and strengthening the federal decentralization and control of the political centre. But more important, the ideological commitments of integral nationalism and alternative communism weakened considerably, and this facilitated a more pluralistic democratic culture. In addition, the 1968 revolt marked the transition from a more paternalistic democracy to a more participatory democracy. In East Germany, under Soviet hegemony, an alternative communist regime was established. Though based on a strong anti-fascist identity, it reproduced certain elements of the German authoritarian past such as the strong political-administrative centralism, the paternalistic control of society, and an enforced privatized and apolitical culture. But with the collapse of the communist system, East Germany became part of the West German Federal Republic, partially assuming, and partially incorporated in, its liberal-democratic as well as federal structure. Certain legacies of the communist period, such as the post-communist Party of Social Democracy and a related East German identity, still play a role, but in contributing to, rather than restricting, the democratic and federal pluralism of a unifying German society.

The divided reconstruction and unification of the German nation state has further been accompanied by a fundamental geopolitical reconfiguration within Europe. On the one side, the reconstruction of West Germany's state and economy proceeded in close cooperation with the Western war allies, France, Great Britain and the United States. This included not only a general surveillance of the political development of the not yet fully sovereign West German state, the rearmament of the German *Bundeswehr* and its integration into NATO, but also the reconstruction of the West German economy in a primarily Western European market orientation.

The major vehicle to link Germany with Western Europe was thereby the formation of the European Community from the early Treaty of Rome and the Coal and Steel Union through the European Economic Community up to European Monetary Union and the Single Market. In this Western European framework, the West German economy quickly moved again to a core position of relative economic dominance (Spohn 1995). At the same time, the European integration of West Germany made a renewed power position of a German national economy neither possible nor desirable. On the other side, the reconstruction of East Germany's state and economy was much more restricted by the conditions of the Soviet economic frame, but compared to the other East Central and East European state economies the GDR economy also developed relatively well. In the background of these two powerful German economies, German unification again raised major concerns among the surrounding European states whether a United Germany would renew its former Central European hegemonic position within Europe. But this time, not only the Western great powers but also United Germany itself had an interest in avoiding the dangers of a nationalistic power course. Therefore, United Germany followed the same path of Western integration as West Germany previously had. In a sense, the formation of the European Union and the introduction a common European currency can be seen as major integrationist steps to counter the power potential of United Germany. As a consequence of the reopened Eastern European space and the geographical proximity to it, there still remains the possibility that United Germany would attempt to renew a more nationalistic course between Western and Eastern Europe. However, the pursuit of German national interests in East Central and Eastern Europe remains firmly anchored in the European integration framework. Instead of following a nationalistic course, United Germany has become one of the strongest supporters of the eastern enlargement of the European Union and the crucial mediator between the European Union and post-Soviet Russia (Spohn 2001).

Taken together, in many crucial aspects, the divided reconstruction and reunification of Germany resulted in a democratic and federal nation-state, geopolitically linked to Western Europe and the United States. But this structural break from and reconfiguration of the past authoritarian modernization model oscillating between a Central European Empire and a European nation state became possible only through a profound reconstruction of German national identity (Breuilly 1992; Dann 1993; Fulbrook 1998). The turning point for this structural break was the experience of the National-Socialist Third Reich as the perverse fulfilment of national unity and imperial greatness, and its destructive consequences for Germany and Europe. This experience was the moral foundation of the German resistance movement against Hitler, the implosion of German nationalism with the decline and collapse of Nazi Germany and the broad support of a democratic reconstruction of a territorially limited Germany. By contrast to the post-First World War period, no feelings of national humiliation and resentment against the victorious Allies emerged after the Second World War. There was not only general exhaustion after the horrors of the war and the struggle for everyday survival but also a widespread sense that the moral failures of Nazi Germany had found a morally justified punishment. The German catastrophe was more than a total military capitulation or liberation from a totalitarian regime, it was also a moral crisis and the opportunity for a moral catharsis. The core of this traumatic guilt feeling and hope for moral resurrection has gradually become the Holocaust and the coming to terms with the past. In a sense, this is one of the core elements of German civic religion (Dubiel 1999). The moral basis for it is again German culture, but this time from the critical perspective of why in the name of a humanistic-cosmopolitan culture one of the main carriers of this German culture, German Jewry, could have been annihilated. On this morally traumatized basis, the core of German cultural nationalism and the imagination of its superiority against the West and the East, have completely collapsed. Instead, German national identity has been first and foremost crystallized in a constitutional patriotism with regional layers of *Heimat*, Western and Eastern affiliations, with a spectrum of political orientations and renewed xenophobic currents. The imperialistic-nationalistic thrust of German cultural nationalism has been broken and the democratic and federal components have finally taken its place.

The reconstruction of German national identity or identities has also been accompanied by a thorough change in the meanings of Europe. The implosion of extreme and imperial German nationalism paved the way for the construction of Europe first and foremost as a peace and security zone of nation states without the atrocities of past ethno-nationalistic conflicts and warfare. Due to the division of Germany, however, this identification with a European security framework was divided in a Western and Eastern orientation. But, at the same time, the threat of an escalation of the cold war triggered a common West and East German sense of the need to overcome the West–East antagonism. Second, the successful reconstruction of the West German economy in the framework of the European Community shaped a strong sense of a common prosperity, democracy and welfare zone between Western Europe and Germany. And third, the widespread tourism to Western and Southern Europe supported the feeling of a common European multicultural space. Before unification, East Germans participated in a negative identification with this Western Europe, but afterwards they gradually developed a similar positive ident-ification. On these foundations, the German political elite from Konrad Adenauer, Theodor Heuss and Ludwig Erhard to Willli Brandt and Helmut Schmidt and, later still, to Helmut Kohl and Gerhard Schröder has been particularly oriented to develop the European integration process and to anchor first West Germany and then United Germany in this transnational framework (Katzenstein 1997b; Schwarz 1981). Accordingly, German and European interests seem to be largely identical. With the opening of the Eastern European space, the German elite, hand in hand with Western Europe, sees a special responsibility to bring Western European peace and security, as well as economic prosperity, political democracy and social welfare, to the East. The Balkan wars in Bosnia and Kosovo played a part-icular role, here, in overcoming the widespread pacifist orientation of the German population. Yet, the new German *Ostpolitik* was never carried through as a separate nationalistic course, but as a common West European mission to bring East Central Europe back to Europe.

Linked to this basic synchronization of Europe with German national identity – to be sure, more outspoken on the elite level than on the public opinion level – the former imperial and cultural layers in the meanings of Europe have also been transformed (Berghahn, Flinn and Lützeler 1997). On the one hand, an important political layer of contemporary German meanings of Europe is a quasi-imperial orientation which envis-ions the European Union as a renewed global player. In this vision, the EU fuses the power potentials of the European great powers as a counter-weight against America, Russia and the rising Asian global powers. This vision of a European continental global power has been shared by many German and French politicians. In addition, there is a German political conviction as articulated recently by Joschka Fischer that German federalism is the best model for the EU. This conviction is shared by a variety of European small states but opposed by France and Britain as a new form of German European hegemony. On the other hand, a crucial cultural layer in the current German meanings of Europe is the identific-ation with European culture rather than with German national culture. A standard notion of German politicians and intellectuals is the European value and culture community serving as an orientation for the boundaries of Europe and the European integration process. One more conservative-liberal variety, here, is the notion of a Christian Europe limiting Europe basically to the Western Christian part of Protestant and Catholic Europe, considering Orthodox Europe with ambivalence, and excluding Turkey.

Another more social-democratic and green variety is the notion of a secular multicultural Europe including Eastern Europe and Turkey, but there are difficulties defining realistic political boundaries. In addition, there are elements in the notion of European culture that continue the traditional value orientations of German humanistic culture. Here, European culture is basically seen as anti-materialist and anti-rationalist, and at the same time under siege by westernization and globalization. One negative variant, as articulated by Peter Schneider, is the classical cultural pessimism envisioning a continuous erosion of true European values by Brussels, another positive one, as represented by Peter Sloterdijk, is a more romantic optimism imagining their revitalization. Both versions share the classical sense of cultural superiority, but this time are fused with European rather than German culture. However, these imperial and cultural fusions of Germany and Europe do not mean a replay of the vision of a Germanized Europe. On the contrary, this option is kept in check not only by the European integration of Germany but also by German collective memory (Giesen 2000; Herf 1996; Markovits and Reich 1997). Its critical core remains the moral imperative that only reconciliation with Europe can overcome the past. Only on this moral fundament could Germany rebuild its relations with France, Britain and the other West European countries. And only on this moral fundament has the German *Ostpolitik* become possible, while now enabling support of the eastern enlargement of the European Union. The contemporary meaning of Europe in German identity and identities has decisively shifted from being that of a Germanic Europe to that of a Europeanized Germany.

# References

Balakrishnan, G. (ed.) (1996), *Mapping the Nation,* London: Verso.
Berghahn, V. (1987), *Modern Germany: Society, Economy and Politics in the Twentieth Century,* Cambridge, Mass.: Cambridge University Press.
—— Flinn, G. and Lützeler, P.M. (1997), 'Germany and Europe: Finding an International Role', in K. Jarausch (ed.), *After Unity: Reconfiguring German Identities,* Providence, RI: Berghahn.
Breuilly, J. (ed.) (1992), *The State of Germany: The National Idea of the Making, Unmaking And Remaking of a Modern Nation-State,* London: Longman.

Brubaker, R. (1992), *Citizenship and Nationhood in France and Germany*, Cambridge, Mass.: Harvard University Press.

—— (1999), 'The Manichean Myth: Rethinking the distinction between <civic> and <ethnic> nationalism', in H. Kriesi, (eds), *Nation and National Identiy: the European Experience in Perspective*, Zurich: Rüegger.

Bruckmüller, E. (1994), *Nation Österreich*, Vienna.

Bugge, P. (1993), 'The Nation Supreme: The Idea of Europe 1945–1945', in K. Wilson and J. van der Dussen (eds), *The History of the Idea of Europe*, London: 83–149.

Dahrendorf, R. (1965), *Gesellschaft und Freiheit in Deutschland*, Munich: Piper.

Dann, O. (1993), *Nation und Nationalismus in Deutschland 1770–1990*, Munich: Beck.

Davies, N. (1996), *A History of Europe*, Oxford: Oxford University Press.

Delanty, G. (1995), *Inventing Europe*, London.

Dubiel, H. (1998), *Niemand ist frei von der Geschichte*, Munich: Hanser.

Eisenstadt, S. (1987), *European Civilization in Comparative Perspective*, Oslo: Oslo UP.

—— and Giesen, B. (1995), 'The Construction of Collective Identity', in *European Journal of Sociology*, 36: 72–102.

Elias, N. (1990), *Über die Deutschen*, Frankfurt: Suhrkamp.

—— (1994), *The Civilizing Process: The History of Manners and State Formation and Civilization*, Oxford: Blackwell.

Fulbrook, M. (1998), *German National Identity*, Oxford: Blackwell.

Giesen, B. (1993), *Die Intellektuellen und die Nation. Eine deutsche Achsenzeit*, Frankfurt: Suhrkamp.

—— (1998), *Kollektive Identität: Die Intellektuellen und die Nation 2*, Frankfurt: Suhrkamp.

—— (2000), 'National Identity as Trauma', in B. Stråth (ed.), *Myths and Memories In the Construction of Community: Patterns in Europe and Beyond*, Brussels: 227–48.

Gollwitzer, H. (1964), *Europabild und Europagedanke: Beiträge zur Geistesgeschichte des 18. und 19. Jahrhunderts*, Munich: Beck.

Graubard, S. (ed.) (1994), 'Germany in Transition', *Daedalus*, 123(1).

Greenfeld, L. (1993), *Nationalism: Five Roads to Modernity*, Cambridge, Mass.: Harvard University Press.

Grunewald, M. (ed.)(1996), *Le discours européen dans les revues allemandes 1871–1914*, Brussels.

Habermas, J. (1991), *Staatsbürgerschaft und nationale Identität: Überlegungen zur Europäischen Zukunft*, St Gall: Erker.

Heffernan, M. (1998), *The Meaning of Europe: Geography and Geopolitics*, Oxford: Oxford University Press.

Herf, J. (1996), *Divided Memory: The Nazi Past in the Two Germanies*, Cambridge, Mass.: Cambridge University Press

Hutchinson, J. and Smith, A. (eds) (1996), *Nationalism*, Oxford: Oxford University Press.

Jarausch, K. (ed.) (1997), *After Unity: Reconfiguring German Identities*, Providence, RI: Berghahn.

Kaelble, H. and Kocka, J. (eds) (1994), *Sozialgeschichte der DDR*, Göttingen: Vandenhoek & Ruprecht.

Katzenstein, P. (1997a), *Mitteleuropa Between Germany and Europe*, Ithaca: Cornell University Press.

—— (1997b), *The Tamed Power*, Ithaca: Cornell University Press.

Klessmann, C. (1986), *Die doppelte Staatsgründung: Deutsche Geschichte 1845–1955*, Göttingen: Vandenhoek & Ruprecht.

Kocka, J. (1991), *Die Vereinigungskrise*, Göttingen: Vandenhoek & Ruprecht.

Kriesi, H. (eds) (1999), *Nation and National Identity: The European Experience in Perspective*, Zurich: Rüegger.

Krüger, P. (1995), 'Europabewusstsein in Deutschland in der ersten Hälfte des 20. Jhdts.', in R. Hüdemann, H. Kaelble and K. Schwab (eds), *Europa im Blick der Historiker*, Historische Zeitschrift, vol. 21, Munich: Oldenburg: 31–54.

Langewiesche, D. (2000), *Nation, Nationalismus, Nationalstaats in Deutschland und Europa*, Munich: Beck.

Lepsius, M.R. (1991), *Demokratie und Demokratisierung in Deutschland*, Göttingen: Vandenhoek & Ruprecht.

Lützeler, P.M. (1992), *Die Schriftsteller und Europa: Von der Romantik bis zur Gegenwart*, Munich.

Markovits, A. and Reich, S. (1997), *The German Predicament*, Ithaca: Cornell University Press.

Merkl, P. (1993), *Germany in Europe*, Durham: Duke University Press.

Mommsen, W. (1990), *Der Autoritäre Nationalstaat*, Reinbek: Rohwolt.

Mosse, G. (1981), *The Crisis of German Ideology: The Intellectual Origins of the Third Reich*, New York: Fertig.

—— (1988), *The Culture in Western Europe*, Boulder, CO: Westview Press.

Nassehi, A. (2000), 'Germany: The Ambiguous Nation', in L. Hagendoorn, (eds), *European Nations and Nationalism*, Aldershot: Ashgate.

Nipperdey, T. (1987, 1991), *Deutsche Geschichte 1800–1866 and 1866–1918*, Munich: Beck.

Nurdin, J. (1980), *L'idée d'Europe dans la pensée allemande à l'époque bismarckienne*, Bern.

Schoch, B. (ed.) (1992), *Deutsche Einheit und Europäische Zukunft*, Frankfurt: Suhrkamp.

Schwarz, H.-P. (1981), *Vom Reich zur Bundesrepublik Deutschland*, Stuttgart: Klett & Cotta.

Schweigler, G. (1973), *Nationalbewusstsein in der BRD und der DDR*, Düsseldorf.

Sheehan, J. (1989), *German History, 1770–1866*, Oxford: Clarendon Press.

Spohn, W. (1995), 'United Germany as the renewed Centre in Europe: Continuity and Change in the German Question', in S. Hanson and W. Spohn (eds), *Can Europe Work? Germany and Reconstruction of Postcommunist Societies*, Seattle: University of Washington Press.

—— (2001), 'Europeanization, the EU's Eastern Enlargement and Collective Identities: A Western and Eastern European Comparison', Working Paper EUI (forthcoming).

Wehler, H.-U. (1995), *Deutsche Gesellschaftsgeschichte 1948/49–1914*, Munich: Beck.

Weidenfeld, W. (ed.) (1981), *Die Identität der Deutschen*, Bonn.

Westle, B. (1999), *Kollektive Identität im Vereinigten Deutschland: Nation und Demokratie in der Wahrnehmungsweise der Deutschen*, Opladen: Leske & Budrich.

Winkler, H.A. (2000), *Der lange Weg nach Westen. Deutsche Geschichte 1700–1990*, 2 vols, Munich: Beck.

Wolff, L. (1994), *The Invention of Eastern Europe*, Stanford, CA: Stanford University Press.

# The Meanings of Europe in French National Discourse: A French Europe or an Europeanized France?

## *Robert Frank*

A national discourse on Europe is also a discourse on the Nation speaking about Europe. This assertion is especially true for France. A French discourse on Europe is always a discourse on France. And the French quest for the meaning of Europe may be identified with the French quest for the meaning of France. In French minds, for a long time, there was not much difference between Europe and the World. Europe was seen as the centre of the World, and France as the central country in Europe and in European civilization. So the French discourse on Europe was also a discourse on the meaning of the 'special relationship' between 'France' (that is, the self-representation of France by the French) and the World (that is, what is seen by the French as outside of France): after the Revolution of 1789, the 'Great Nation' was supposed to deliver messages to the rest of the universe and France's message was necessarily the best European message (that is, 'civilized message') delivered to the rest of the world. In brief, French discourse on Europe is mainly a discourse on French power or French influence in Europe and, beyond Europe, French influence in the World.

That does not mean that the French are not aware of their decline in the twentieth century, but precisely the quest for French centrality in Europe is supposed to be the best answer to French decline. And here is the huge difference with the British. France and Britain have in common their ancient status of being great powers, their old parliamentary traditions, their early entry into the industrial revolution, their colonial experience, their fear of decline – but they differ completely in their relations with Europe and the world. For many British (and many non-British), the question may be asked whether the United Kingdom is part of Europe or not. Even Winston Churchill, who advocated European unity in his

Zurich speech of 1946, perceived the unity of Europe without his own country. The question has no meaning for France because, undoubtedly, France belongs to Europe, with the latter as a continent, as a culture, as an idea, as a sphere for French influence, and as an integration process. Britain was a real world power and saw herself belonging much more to the world than to Europe. France saw itself belonging both to Europe and to the world. Another difference is that the French became aware sooner than the British of their decline and understood quickly what benefits could flow from taking the lead in European integration.

In this respect, Europe is the main horizon for France, and was so even when France had its colonial Empire. Europe was and still is ascribed as the future of France, whether it had a logic of great power or whether it converted its logic of power to a logic of simple influence. So the meaning of Europe for the French has to do with the future of France and Europe. It should be borne in mind that the French word for 'meaning' is *'sens'*. And 'sens' does not only mean 'meaning', but also 'direction', and precisely the direction gives the meaning. In which direction is Europe going, is France going, and are France and Europe going and, finally, is France going in Europe? Is the European direction a French one or is the French direction a European one? These are the explicit or implicit questions for the French. One may guess that, through the twentieth century, there was a big and difficult shift from one meaning to the other, from the perception of one future to the perception of the other one.

## The French Meaning of Europe (1789–1945): A Space for French Power, French Peace and French *rayonnement*

The French meaning of Europe was always ambivalent and still is a mixture of idealism and realism – an ideal cause written for a realistic aim, a European ideal imagined for a national goal. In the seventeenth and eighteenth centuries, Europe meant a European order where France could most develop its military power and its cultural influence. During the French Revolution and the era of the French Empire, Europe was the sphere of French expansion and conquest, through the exportation of freedom and by the means of military force.

In the romantic era, idealism seemed predominant. Victor Hugo in many speeches, the first time at the Peace Congress of 1849, militated in favour of the 'United States of Europe':

> All of us here, we say to France, to England, to Prussia, to Spain, to Italy, to Russia, we tell them: one day will come when weapons will fall from your

hands . . . One day will come when war will seem as absurd and as impossible between Paris and London, between St Petersburg and Berlin, between Vienna and Torino, as it would be impossible and would seem absurd today between Paris and Rouen or between Boston and Philadelphia. One day will come when you France, you Russia, you Italy, you England, you Germany, you all, nations of the continent, without losing your distinct qualities and your glorious individuality, you shall melt tightly in a superior unity and constitute the European brotherhood, just as Normandy, Brittany, Burgundy, Lorraine, Alsace, all our provinces did melt into France. One day will come when there will be no other battle-fields than markets, open to free trade,[1] and minds open to ideas. One day will come when shells and guns shall be replaced by votes, by universal franchise, by the venerable arbitration of a great sovereign Senate, which will be to Europe what Parliament is to England . . . and the *Assemblée législative* to France! One day will come when we will show a gun in a museum just as we show there today instruments of torture, asking ourselves how it could have existed! (Victor Hugo, opening speech to the Peace Congress, Paris, 21 August 1849)

Peace, free trade, freedom of ideas and opinions, democracy for the people, here are in Hugo's views the values of Europe, a continent with expansive limits, open to Russia. Of a future Europe, of course, because many things had to be done: the change of many political regimes (not only in Russia), the acknowledgement of all the nationalities and the historical unification of nations. European federation and nation states, 'Europeism' and patriotism were not inconsistent for Hugo or for Mazzini. Hugo cherished France as the model of revolution and freedom, and for the romantic poets and political thinkers, Italy and Germany had to be politically created, before Europe could exist.

This is why Hugo never forgot patriotic and maybe nationalistic aims. In his mind, Paris had naturally to be the capital of the future federation and France, the heart and the spirit of the great continent. During the war of 1870, in September after the defeat of Napoleon III and the proclamation of the Republic, Hugo came back from exile and, in his speeches, he showed himself ready for war against the Prussians and the Germans to save Paris and France: a present war for a future peace. He wrote an appeal 'To the Germans', where he explained that it was not the French people nor the French Republic that wanted war, but the Emperor. After the fall of the French Empire, Germans had to cease fire. If they wanted to take Paris, they would come back to the age of Attila.

---

1. Richard Cobden was attending the Peace Congress in Paris as organizer and as vice-president. (Victor Hugo was president.)

> Paris does not belong to us only. Paris is as much yours as it is ours. Berlin, Vienna, Dresden, Munich, Stuttgart are your capitals; Paris is your centre. It is in Paris that you feel that Europe lives. Paris is the city of the cities. Paris is the city of mankind. There was Athens, there was Rome, there is Paris . . . Germany would undo Europe if she mutilates France. Germany would undo Europe if she destroys Paris. Under your bombs and bullets, Paris will fight. And I, an old man, I shall be here, without weapons. I like the idea to be with the people who die, and I pity you to be with the kings who kill. (Hugo 1870)

After France's loss of Alsace and of a part of Lorraine, Victor Hugo did not attend any Peace Congress. He sent only letters to encourage the idea of Europe. But there were two ideas of Europe, two antagonistic principles, in the encounter between German Monarchy and United States of Europe, between Empire and Republic. Hugo still wanted peace, but considered war might be necessary. He refused the diminution of France and thought that the whole world should reject that situation. This Franco-centrist view of universality led to a French model of Europe, a European Republic. For the fourth anniversary of the Third Republic, on 4 September 1874, his letter to members of the Peace Congress in Geneva began: 'Dear fellow-citizens of the Republic of Europe', and finished in this way:

> When amputation is imposed on France, it is civilization which is bleeding. When France is diminished, it is the light which is reduced . . . Reparation will be the federation. The outcome, here it is: *United States of Europe.* (Hugo 1874)

Hugo felt uncomfortable with this new era of nationalisms after 1871. Nations and Europe were beginning to be contradictory, which was not the case during the Romantic period.

In 1870, Ernest Renan, like Vicor Hugo, refused the idea of the loss of Alsace and Lorraine: 'If France loses Alsace and Lorraine, it is the end of France. The building is so compact that the removal of two stones will make it collapse . . . The world without France would be as much mutilated as the world without Germany' (Renan 1970). He added that 'democracy does not want, does not understand war', and that the progress of democracy would be the progress of peace. Renan, who was in favour of the principle of nationalities, who was well known for his reflections about the principle of 'nation', and for his defence of the French meaning of nation against the German one, was the man who wrote in 1870 that he favoured the idea of European federation:

> The principle of independent nationalities . . . will not deliver mankind from the plague of war . . . I always feared that the principle of nationalities . . . may

degenerate . . . in racial exterminations . . . We will see the end of war when
we will join to the principle of nationalities the corrective principle of
European federation, superior to all nationalities. Let us add: when democratic
questions . . . will take again their importance (Renan 1870).

In his famous conference at the Sorbonne, on 11 March 1882, 'Qu'est-
ce qu'une nation?', he opposed the German meaning of nation (a race, a
language, a culture) with the French one, originated by the French Revolution: a nation is a consent, a common will, an 'everyday plebiscite'. This
debate was of course dominated by the Alsace-Lorraine problem: were
these provinces German (because of their German language and culture)
or French (because they wanted to be so)? On the European issue, Renan
slightly changed after 1870, and Europe was becoming a distant future:

> Nations are not something eternal. They had a beginning, they will have an
> end. The European confederation will probably replace them. But this is not
> the law for our century. For the present, the existence of nations is a good and
> even a necessary thing. Their existence is a pledge of freedom, which would
> be lost if the world had only one law and one lord. (Renan 1882)

The First World War did not put an end to nationalisms. And there was
certainly a French nationalism against Germany, in spite of the German
defeat and the return of Alsace and Lorraine to France. The occupation
of the Ruhr in 1923 to compel Germany to pay the 'reparations' is a good
example of nationalism in foreign policy. But, it is a defensive nationalism: France was afraid of German power and of the German capacity to
re-arm and to return to war. In fact, the real deep-rooted feeling in France,
after it had been bled by the massacre of 1914–18, was the fear of war
and a pacifism which was not inconsistent with defensive nationalism.
After 1924, pacifism was overwhelming in France, and helped initiate
'Europeism'. Europe was not only an idea for poets or a few political
thinkers. In the 1920s a real 'European consciousness' began, i.e. the
feeling, shared by large elites, of the vital necessity to build the unity of
Europe, in the sake of peace. The title of Gaston Riou's book written in
1929 is a good illustration of that new feeling: 'S'unir ou mourir'. The
European case was pressing and Europe could not any longer be a distant
future. Many French intellectuals, businessmen, politicians were part of
the numerous 'Europeist' associations, behind Coudenhove-Kalergi and
*Paneuropa*, and behind the Frenchman, Émile Borel and his *Coopération
européenne*. It is well known how the industrialist Emil Mayrisch, from
Luxemburg, managed to create the International Steel Pool in 1926 with

steelmakers from France, Germany, Belgium and Luxembourg, but also managed to bring together intellectuals from both sides of the Rhine and to try to work for Franco-German reconciliation. Intellectuals, such as Paul Valéry, Jules Romains, Julien Benda fought against nationalism or the aggressive forms of nationalism. Drieu la Rochelle wrote a book, with the title: *L'Europe contre les patries*. The recent thesis of Françoise Berger shows how in the inter-war period, French and German steelmakers created a real common culture of cooperation and integration (Berger 2000). The thesis of Laurence Badel analyses the domestic trade circles, the *grands magasins*: those *milieux*, around Jacques Lacour-Gayet, after the First World War were both liberal and 'Europeist' (Badel 1999). The European idea was not inconsistent with the colonial ambition: 'Eura-frique' was the possibility to conciliate the colonial idea and the European idea, two ambitions for French power in the world. The 1920s were a golden age for French 'Europeism' and it was the only period of the twentieth century when, in France, politicians, intellectuals and business-men fought together for the same cause – the European one.

All this movement leads to Aristide Briand's project of a 'European federation', to his 5 September 1929 speech on the necessity of 'a sort of federal link', and then to the memorandum of May 1930 on the organiz-ation of a regime of 'European Federal Union' (Fleury and Jilek 1998). The aim was to build a framework of 'union', and not of 'unity', flexible enough to ensure national independence and sovereignty. The Union had to be political first, and the economic union was subordinated to the political one, because it was induced by the question of security. But the goal of a 'common market' was written into the plan. This project failed for many reasons and suffered from the new context of economic depression after the Wall Street Crash.

In this great French European process of the 1920s may be found many national ambitions, and not only an idealistic discourse. For France, Europe was clearly or implicitly a matter of national interest, of national security and the right way to keep the status of a great power. A French Europe was the main goal. When Paul Valéry said that there was 'Europe' every time that there was the union of Greek, Roman and Christian culture, he obviously thought in terms of the superiority of the French humanities in his time, and considered France as the then best champion of European civilization: Victor Hugo was not far away from this.

In his *Discours à la nation européenne* (a paraphrase of Fichte's 'Speeches to the German nation'), Julien Benda tried to demonstrate that the unity of Europe would not come from economy or from common material interests, but from education and ethics: 'It's not the *Zollverein* which built Germany, but Fichte's *Speeches to the German nation* and the professors in ethics who came after him' (Benda 1933). Benda asked European intellectuals to become the moral instructors against nationalism and even against the old idea of nation. But the same Benda wanted one supranational language for Europe, a language placed above the national ones, and this language was, of course, French. Where Hugo wanted Paris as the European capital, Benda wanted French as the supranational language for Europe.

The Briand Plan was also very 'French'. In 1929, Aristide Briand was aware that the pact signed with Kellogg was a failure (he wanted a Franco-American treaty, good for French security, and he got a vague multilateral pact against war) and that Stresemann's claims for national minorities in Europe might make fragile the Locarno system (Bariéty 1998). The Locarno agreements themselves were, on the whole, good for French security, but French allies were worried because Germany acknowledged her Western borders, not her eastern ones. In short, in Briand's view, a European Union was the best way to enclose Germans firmly in a new framework, including all the French allies – Europe from the Atlantic to Poland, from Brest to Brest-Litovsk, including Britain, but probably without the USSR – a framework where it would be difficult to question the frontiers designed by the Peace treaties of 1919–20. Security weighed more than democracy, or was no longer linked with democratic values – some of the French allies were authoritarian regimes. Here was the beginning of a distancing from Victor Hugo's ideas and a return to the legacy of the *Realpolitik* of the end of the nineteenth century when the French Republic became the ally of tsarist Russia. As a matter of fact, in the 1920s, security was the French obsession, and European union was a good answer to French security matters. But was it a good response, in the same proportion, to other matters of national interest?

After 1933, the decline of the European movement is obvious. Many international or European projects failed, from the disarmament conference to the economic conference in London. Only the second International Steel Pool of 1932 was a success, all through the 1930s and in spite of the Nazi regime (Berger 2000). Nonetheless, interesting ideas emerged in France. Albert Demangeon, a geographer, thought of a more realistic Europe, that meant a Little Europe, limited to north-west Europe, i.e. to countries sharing the same type of industrial development. The economist Francis Delaisi had already said that there were two Europes, a rural Europe and an industrialized Europe: the draught-horse Europe and the horse-power Europe. It is important to note that more and more high civil servants were involved in European action. When war began in 1939, many of them convinced the Daladier Government (with Paul Reynaud as Minister of Finance) to integrate the Anglo-French war economies against Germany. Jean Monnet had his part in the move and co-ordinated Allied imports in the United States. The Anglo-French monetary and financial agreement of December 1939 was supposed to survive the war and to be a model for a monetary European union after victory.

After the defeat of France in 1940, some of the French 'Europeists', such as Gaston Riou, Francis Delaisi, Georges Suarez (friend and biographer of Aristide Briand), Drieu La Rochelle (although he became 'fascist' long before the war) drifted into 'collaborationism', thinking that Hitler could manage what democracies could not: the unity of Europe, the building of a 'New Europe', a Nazi Europe. Never was the gap between the idea of Europe and democratic values so great. But it was not so for long. Other 'Europeists', such as Émile Borel, joined the Resistance. And many Resistance members, and many antifascists, in France and in other countries of the continent, had their part in the European movement after the war. These included André Philip, a socialist, and Henri Frenay, chief of 'Combat', the greatest Resistance movement in the *zone libre* during the war, and future president of the French Federalist European Movement. Thanks to them, democracy came strongly and definitively back – the word had not appeared, for diplomatic reasons, in the Briand Plan of 1930 – into the political baggage of the European idea after 1945.

## The French Meaning of Europe (1945–69): An Answer to French Decline, a Space for French Influence

Thanks to the Resistance (the non-communist Resistance), the political base of European militancy was enlarged in France. In the inter-war period, 'Europeism' was mainly the matter of the radical party (socialists were then more internationalists than 'Europeists', even Léon Blum, though he was also a member of *Paneuropa*); after the Second World War, Christian democrats and socialists became the main political forces of European action in France. French socialists were involved in the movement, much more than German social democrats and the British Labour Party.

In spite of the Labour Party's reluctance, there was a hope that Europe would be built by the Anglo-French couple. The ideas of the 'phoney war' period of 1939–40 returned to the minds of the French side at least. The Marshall Plan and the Soviet threat offered a favourable context. Of course, because of the cold war, 'Europe' was no longer the whole continent, but became synonymous with Western Europe. The British and the French took the lead in the negotiation of the Brussels pact in March 1948, which was not initially merely a pact on security and military matters: there were also economic and cultural projects written into the text. Likewise, the two countries took the lead within the OEEC, the first real European organization.

But how far Britain and France diverged in many matters is well known. The differences could be found even beyond the governments. At the Hague Congress of May 1948, most of the French argued in favour of 'federalism', and the majority of the British in favour of 'unionism'. The economic policy of the two governments, their monetary attitudes, their ideas on planning, the way they used the counterpart of the Marshall Plan in national currency (against inflation in Britain, in favour of modernization in France) were also completely different. Discord was growing between the two inside the OEEC and during government negotiations for political organization proposed by the European Movement after the Hague Congress. The Council of Europe, born in 1949, did not satisfy the French. Even the name of the institution provoked harsh discussion. Robert Schuman proposed, forty years before its application, the label 'European Union', but the British view in support of a name which would not overly suggest the States prevailed. The unilateral devaluation of sterling in autumn 1949 was the final straw for the French and even for the Anglophile Jean Monnet. Europe had indeed to be built, but not with the old ally, rather with the ancient enemy: thus, the Schuman Plan of May 1950, inspired by Jean Monnet, was a sort of copernician revolution.

Is all this the story of a divorce between British realistic pragmatism and French conceptualism and idealism? No, not quite so simple! The real difference remained in the perceptions of identity and of national interests. It is difficult to say if the national interests were really different, but their perceptions were not the same. And it is difficult to say on which side of the Channel lay realism, because on the two sides one could find phantasms and questions on identity.

After 1945, the French were fortunate enough (so were the Italians and the Germans) to perceive easily the decline of their country, thanks to the defeat and the syndrome of 1940 (or of 1943 or 1945 for the two other nations). Britain had not had the 'luck' – if it can be put that way – to be defeated and she was able to take her place at the Yalta and Potsdam conferences with the two new Superpowers. Her decline was invisible. The victorious and heroic British still thought of themselves as a world power, overlooking especially a 'Little Europe', but also Europe as a whole, as too narrow a horizon for their greatness. They lingered to ask themselves questions about their belonging or not to a continent dominated by political and economic instability. The French took the opportunity and managed to build their leadership of European integration. They were helped by West Germany, a defeated nation too, but a 'guilty' one, who thus had not the same 'legitimacy' as France. A community of destiny arose, not between glorious and victorious allies, but between nations who had difficulty in dealing with their recent past, their memories of the Second World War. Building the little Europe of the Six was the best way for France to find a 'role' in international affairs, a cast in the play of the bi-polar world, the best way to rebuild a measure of French influence. It was also the best method to enforce economic modernization, the new French obsession forged by the syndrome of 1940. This was the main meaning of Europe in the national political discourse in France during the 1950s and 1960s, not only for General de Gaulle when he came back to power, but also for the preceding men of the Fourth Republic, supposed to be much more 'pro-European', such as Jean Monnet, Robert Schuman or Guy Mollet. In this respect, the absence of Britain presented a good opportunity for France. The European Coal and Steel Community (ECSC) came out of the Schuman Plan and was a success. But the French had their contradictions: they proposed the Pleven Plan which led to the European Defence Community (EDC) treaty and France, in the end, refused to accept it in 1954. This failure shows the difficulties for the French in dealing with the idea of the existence of German soldiers and with the concept of supranationality in military affairs. In the negotiations for the Common Market, the Guy Mollet government was divided in discussions over what was best in the national interest: the inclusion of overseas territories (the French dream of Eurafrica was not quite over in 1956–57) and of a 'saving clause' in case of economic difficulties caused by trade competition.

De Gaulle, who was opposed to ECSC and EDC, accepted the treaties of Rome, Euratom and the Common Market, because he knew how they were crucial for French modernization. In 1962, he played a decisive part in the definition and organization of the Common Agricultural Policy (CAP), so important for the interests of rural France and of the Gaullist electorate. He disagreed with the supranationality included in the treaty of 1957 and tried to bypass the Community's institutions: the Fouchet Plan, which failed, was an attempt to build a political unity based only on an intergovernmental process of decision-making. De Gaulle hated the idea of a future federation, or the principle of 'United States of Europe' and favoured the project of a 'Union of European States' which would keep their entire sovereignty. In this field, his ideas were close to the British ones. But he managed to make impossible the entry of Britain to the EEC, in both 1963 and 1967. More important than the institutions was the question of French influence, which was so easy to exert in a Europe without Britain, and in a 'European Europe' rather than in an 'Atlantic Europe'. De Gaulle was backed by Adenauer, and the Franco-German pairing allowed a good balance: Germany had the economic power and France the political and military influence (including, since 1960, the atomic bomb). After 1963, the dynamics of De Gaulle's European policy came to an end. There occurred a European crisis in 1965–66: France carried out her *'politique de la chaise vide'* in order to prevent the next step to supranationality, and the General was successful in maintaining in the Community the rule of unanimity in the decision-making process. But he understood, since he was no longer backed by the new Chancellor Erhard, that France could achieve no further concessions from Europe at that time. It is interesting to note that he then put an end to his European policy, and started after then a 'global' policy, a world policy, in the direction of Eastern Europe and of the Third World. For de Gaulle, if Europe had not a French meaning, Europe was meaningless.

In the European process after 1945 or 1950, politicians played the primary role. French intellectuals and businessmen who were so fond of the European idea during the 1920s were not as deeply involved at the time of actual European integration. Businessmen had many ideas on customs union (many were active in the *Ligue Européenne de Coopération Économique*) or on cooperation in the steel markets. Françoise Berger shows how French and German steelmakers were thinking of new agreements in 1948. When the Schuman Plan was proposed, their first attitude was positive. There were misgivings later about the anti-cartellist dimension of Jean Monnet's project. And in a third stage, they approved of the ECSC. French steelmakers were possibly more reluctant than the Germans, but they realized the advantage they might take of the ECSC's aid to modernization (especially for the financing of the new rolling-mills). During the negotiations for the EEC, the French *'patronat'* was concerned with the risks of German competition on the national market, and they insisted on a 'saving clause', although they did accept the Rome treaties. The European market was important to business circles until the 1960s, but thereafter they appeared narrow – in discourse, if not in reality– in comparison with world opportunities. In summary, then, French *businessmen* were not an obstacle to the European process, but their 'wait and see' strategy was no longer of great assistance.

The evolution of the *intellectuals* was much more negative. Following the *'Affaire Dreyfus'*, French intellectuals, on the pattern of the 1789

Revolution, sought to defend causes that referred back to the image of universality. They fought for the world to which they delivered definitive messages. After the European mass killing of 1914–18, peace was for the intellectuals a good universal cause to defend, and so was the cause of unity of Europe, the best guarantee for peace, the best message giving shape to their general pacifism. After 1945, things were different. The syndrome of Munich, and the syndrome of the defeat of 1940, put pacifism in a rapid decline among French intellectuals. Their *'philosophie de l'engagement'*, with the influence of Jean-Paul Sartre, praised action and fighting. Their typical need of universality found a more suitable issue in the East–West confrontation or the fight for decolonization and the defence of the Third World, South against North. Europe seemed to them a mean or petty case, a symbol of capitalism or colonialism. So the well-known intellectuals – here is the great difference with the inter-war period – did not contribute to the action in favour of European unity. Jean-Paul Sartre and Albert Camus were not Paul Valéry, Jules Romains or Julien Benda. They had contempt for the EEC, which they perceived as a bureaucratic organization. Raymond Aron had a different perception, but he too had a larger view: the whole Western horizon, and not only Little Europe. Christian intellectuals, such as Jean-Marie Domenach, militated for Europe between 1945 and 1949 and then, disappointed, fought for other causes, such as decolonization (Frank 1998).

At the end of the 1960s, French Europe or the French way to Europe was in crisis. The absence of the intellectuals – a social group so important in France – prevented the European Community from raising emotions or moving the collective imagination. Europe was accepted, but with a sort of apathy and indifference. The Monnet method was the best possible way to start the European process, but it did not make Europe popular. De Gaulle's style gave political roots to the EEC, but it enclosed the Community for a long time in an intergovernmental process, and this led to impotence. France wanted Europe to be a space, maybe not for French 'power' – that time was past – but for French 'influence', for French leadership. The problem was that in 1969 when de Gaulle resigned, the French were no longer sure of being able to maintain their influence.

## The French Meaning of Europe: A Space for a New French Identity (1969–2000)

It looks as if there were cycles in French European policy before 1969. Often, France initiated a process in order to be able to have the main influence on the continent. Then, as if afraid of the consequences of such initiative for the nation's sovereignty, France took a negative position which could isolate the nation in the Community: ECSC and then the EDC failure; the treaties of Rome, their acceptance by de Gaulle, and then the European crisis caused by de Gaulle.

We find the same sorts of cycle after 1969. The incoming French President, Georges Pompidou, understood that the French rejection of British entry to the EEC maintained France in a dangereous isolation. The achievement of the CAP process, so interesting for France, could be questioned by the five other partners. The principle of enlargement was accepted by Paris at the Hague conference of December 1969. The compensation obtained was an 'achievement' (the financing of CAP) and a 'deepening' policy before Britain joined, to be sure that the latter would not block the new path toward further integration: in particular, Pompidou proposed an economic and monetary Union. But then, in 1970, he refused the Werner Plan as too ambitious in his view and said it deprived the various States of economic and budgetary independence.

From 1974 to 1981, Valéry Giscard d'Estaing and Helmut Schmidt brought a new impulse: creation of the European Council, direct election of the Parliament, and creation of the European Monetary System. But, from 1981 to 1983, François Mitterrand's economic policy, a left-wing policy, came to contradict the other partners' policy in the EMS. A new cycle began in 1983–84, when France agreed to change her 'national' economic policy to a 'European' one: the new Franco-German twosome of François Mitterrand and Helmut Kohl, with the initiative of Jacques Delors, gave a new push to the integration process: a new enlargement, the Single European Act of 1986 and the Maastricht treaty. Then, after the referendum of 1992, France went through a period of Euro-scepticism.

Behind this continuity in these 'French cycles', there have been many changes since the 1970s. The entry of Britain modified the balance of influence within the Community, as did the rise of Germany as a political power – and not only an economic one. There was no more place for a French leadership, or even for an attempt of French leadership. One of the French obsessions was to fight against isolation. The Mitterrand archives show well how the advisers of the President were afraid of a coalition of Germany and Great Britain, or Thatcher and Schmidt. These two countries could take advantage of the specific French left-wing economic policy to contract a sort of alliance against Paris. Everything was done to avoid this 'catastrophe' (Frank 2001). After the about-turn of 1983, Mitterrand and his advisers, with the decisive help of Helmut Kohl, were very successful in weaving a real plot against Margaret Thatcher in order to isolate her.[2] They took advantage of the irritation inspired by the Prime Minister wanting her 'money back'. She had to accept the compromise proposed by Kohl-Mitterrand at the Fontainebleau conference of June 1984. France was no longer looking for 'leadership', and so accepted – having in fact no real choice – to share influence, and was looking for new meanings to give to Europe. All the events after 1984 show how the French were building a French (and they hoped a Franco-German) meaning of Europe as opposed to a British one: on one hand, Europe with political ambitions and, on the other, Europe supposed to be limited to an area of free trade.

Real or imaginary, this opposition helped French politicians to ask new questions and to manage a new shift. What were the French seeking in Europe? After the shift from 'power' to 'influence', came the shift from 'influence' or 'leadership' to 'identity'. 'What is it to be European today?' was also a way to ask 'What is it to be French today?' That means that national identity is capable of evolution and of new connections with European identity. The latter is a feeling of belonging not only to a culture or a civilization, but to a political community. The principle of 'national interest' does not vanish from French calculations. But, a distinction appears between 'national interest' and 'national sovereignty', even among Gaullist (the majority of whom were in favour of the Maastricht treaty and of the single currency): France might accept a loss of its national sovereignty for the sake of its national interest (more wealth, more influence).

There was in the 1970s the return to 'Europe' of some French intellectuals, such as Edgar Morin. A communist until 1951, then fighting for peace in Indochina and in Algeria, and fighting for the Third World, he was in the 1950s and 1960s in favour of a universal system of values and against European integration. With the oil crisis of 1973, he understood that 'Europe was a poor little dear thing. I became neo-European because I saw that Europe was ill' (Morin 1987).

As Morin points out, many intellectuals – with the decline of Marxism, of universalism and of general ideologies promising a future paradise on earth – came back to a more realistic cause, and a democratic one: Europe. Later, the events of 1989–1991 promote 'Europe' as a democratic horizon for the 'Other Europe', which was until then under communist rule. In the majority of French minds – and the intellectuals played a role

---

2. There is much evidence of that plot in the Mitterrand archives. I owe this information to Georges Saunier who is preparing a doctoral thesis on 'François Mitterrand and Europe (1981–1984)'.

in this change – the limits of Europe came back to their original geography. The appellation *'Europe de l'Est'*, synonymous with communist Europe, disappeared and was replaced by the old expression *'Europe centrale et orientale'*. Milan Kundera, the Czech novelist living in France, had already written an article in 1983 on the 'kidnapped Occident', this part of Europe – Central Europe – part of Western culture, but deprived of it by the USSR, representative of what is supposed to be the real East (Kundera 1983).

Since 1991, the meaning of Europe is also the difficult choice between enlargement of Europe to the East and the deepening of European integration. The French tradition of the long past – with many illusions – is to help and defend the people of Central and Eastern Europe. But this might mean the dissolution of Europe. 'Deepening' is more in the 'French way' of European building since 1950. Europe is also showed in France as a good intermediate space between the Nation and the World and the 'globalization' process: the European Union is large enough to solve problems nation states cannot solve, and has more human 'meaning' than the anonymous and huge world market forces. Zaki Laïdi (1998) speaks of *'espace de sens'*, a space which means something in the matter of identity, of hopes and dreams for the future. Again the choice is between Europe as a meaningful space or Europe as a useful but meaningless area. In many French views, Europe must be *'une Europe puissante'*, a powerful Europe, able to hold its own alongside its American ally.

If France gives up her ambition of leadership in Europe, does it mean the end of the *'exception française'*? Not quite. The shift exists from the political to the cultural field. Europe may be a good coalition of national cultural exceptions and a good counterpart to Americanization. In the French debate, the question is now how Europeans will manage to deal with the multiplicity of their collective identities: the national one, the European one, but also the provincial or regional one, and the Western one.

All these French changes have not been achieved. The past is heavy and maintains many habits and images. The EU conference in Nice in December 2000 opened a debate in the press about the French presidency and the *'arrogance française'* toward the 'small States'. The legacy of the old ambitions of French leadership has not entirely disappeared. However, the change is great enough to reverse the equation: since the 1970s and the 1980s, the idea of French centrality in Europe gave way gradually to the question of European centrality in France. Maybe the decline of the idea of a French Europe will lead to the reality of a European France: it certainly will be the great debate in the coming years.

# References

Badel, L. (1999), *Un milieu libéral et européen: Le grand commerce français, 1925–1948*, Paris, Comité pour l'histoire économique et financière de la France.

Bariéty, J. (1998), 'Aristide Briand: les raisons d'un oubli', in A. Fleury with L. Jilek (eds), *Le Plan Briand d'Union fédérale européenne*, Actes du colloque international tenu à Genève, 19–21 September 1991, Berne: Peter Lang. 1–13.

Benda, J. (1933), *Discours à la nation européenne*, Paris: Gallimard.

Berger, F. (2000), *La France, l'Allemagne et l'acier, 1932–1952*, doctoral thesis, December 2000, University of Paris I Panthéon-Sorbonne.

Frank, R. (1998), 'Les contretemps de l'aventure européenne', *Vingtième siècle. Revue d'histoire*, 60, Octobre-Décembre 1998, 82–101.

—— (2001) 'Les réactions internationales à l'élection de François Mitterrand et à l'action du nouveau Président de la République (1981–1982)', in S. Berstein and P. Milza (eds), *Changer la vie: Les années Mitterrand 1981–1984*, Paris, 2001.

Hugo, V. (1870), 'Aux Allemands', 9 September 1870.

—— (1874) 'Letter to the members of the Peace Congress in Geneva', 4 September 1874.

Kundera, M. (1983), 'Un Occident kidnappé ou la tragédie de l'Europe centrale', *Le Débat*, 27, November 1983.

Laïdi, Z. (ed.) (1998), *Géopolitique du sens*, Paris: Desclée de Brouwer.

Fleury A. with L. Jilek (eds) (1998), *Le Plan Briand d'Union fédérale européenne*, Actes du colloque international tenu à Genève, 19–21 September 1991, Berne: Peter Lang.

Morin, E. (1987), *Penser l'Europe*, Paris.

Renan, E. (1870) 'La guerre entre la France et l'Allemagne', *Revue des deux mondes*, 15 Septembre 1870.

—— (1882) 'Qu'est-ce qu'une nation?', conference at the Sorbonne, 11 March 1882.